'Say "Colonel Blashford-Snell, the fs
somehow not heard of him and they
creation from the age of children's
hunter, hand on hip, a glint in the e
Blashford-Snell is so much bigger, b........ ..., an
adventurer of fearsome courage, endurance and determination – but more
to the point an inspiration to generations of young people, a fighter for
habitats, conservation, scientific discovery and a greater understanding of
our extraordinary world. These fabulous stories, gathered from a lifetime
of intrepid journeys (I was a wide-eyed 14-year-old when he came to my
school to tell us about his legendary crossing of the infamous Darién Gap)
will thrill, educate and delight.'

Stephen Fry

"*I loved* From Utmost East to Utmost West. *It explodes in your face
with humour, true grit, and a never-ending living description of thrilling
adventures, lived by a true life 21st-century iconic hero.*"

Dr Dame Claire Bertschinger, DBE DL

"*This wonderful book will transport you to many remote regions of the world
alongside world-renowned explorer JBS. His fascinating stories of adventure
and service, always laced with humour, will leave you itching to join his next
expedition. One wild and precious life!*"

Catherine Lawrence

"*JBS is one of the great explorers of our age. His exploits have inspired
generations of new adventurers and his journeys continue to pioneer new
and exciting developments in the world of scientific discovery. This book is a
wonderful tribute to a lifetime of exploration.*"

Levison Wood

Colonel John Blashford-Snell (JBS), one of the world's most renowned and respected explorers, has organised and led over one hundred expeditions including an exploration and first navigation of the Ethiopian Blue Nile. In 1972, using the first Range Rovers and a Land Rover, he led the first vehicle crossing of the Darién Gap including the infamous Atrato Swamp. In 1971–72 this team was the first to complete the drive from Alaska to Cape Horn. In 1974 he navigated almost all 2,700 miles of the Zaire (Congo) River. Most of his expeditions have environmental, medical and scientific objectives.

In 1969, he and his colleagues formed the Scientific Exploration Society, which became the parent body for several worldwide ventures launched by HRH the Prince of Wales. JBS then raised funds and selected a team to run Operation Drake, involving 400 young explorers from twenty-seven countries on a two-year circumnavigation. Ultimately, a much larger global youth programme was organised and by 1992 Operation Raleigh, as it was then called, had enabled 10,000 young people from fifty countries to take part in challenges and expeditions around the world. As Raleigh, as it was then called, International, over 40,000 young men and women benefited from this unique programme. Many of them, like Major Tim Peake, have become explorers in their own right.

Retiring from the army and as Director-General of Operation Raleigh in 1991, his commitment to young people continued. In 1993, he became Chairman of a £2.5 million appeal to establish a centre to provide vocational training and guidance for the young of Merseyside. This centre, now known as 'The Door', has helped over 40,000 less privileged young people. Later he chaired The Liverpool Construction Craft Guild to promote the training of skilled craftsmen in Liverpool. JBS is also President of the water charity Just a Drop.

In 2000 he delivered a grand piano to the Wai Wai people of Guyana. A BBC film of this helped to raise US$2 million to conserve the tribal area. In 2017 he took an ambulance boat to a remote tribe on the Amazon.

The Colonel's work has been recognised by the award of the CBE, and in 1974 of the Segrave Trophy, the Livingstone Medal of the Royal Scottish Geographical Society (1975), the Patron's Medal of the Royal Geographical Society (1993) and the Gold Medal of the Institution of Royal Engineers (1994). He has also received medals from Bolivia, Colombia, Mongolia and the Explorers Club (USA).

His expeditions are acknowledged for developing inflatable boats for white-water rafting, paramotoring on scientific expeditions and other technical advances.

JBS has written sixteen books, broadcasts and lectures whilst leading expeditions worldwide with the Scientific Exploration Society of which he is Honorary President.

From Utmost East *to* Utmost West

My life of exploration and adventure

East
to
Utmost West

My life of exploration and adventure

John Blashford-Snell

Bradt GUIDES

First published in the UK in October 2022 by
Bradt Guides Ltd
31a High Street, Chesham, HP5 1BW, England
www.bradtguides.com

Print edition published in the USA by The Globe Pequot Press Inc,
PO Box 480, Guilford, Connecticut 06437-0480

Text copyright © 2022 John Blashford-Snell
Maps copyright © 2022 Bradt Guides Ltd; created with Mapchart (mapchart.net)
Photographs copyright © 2022 Individual photographers (see below)

Edited by Ross Dickinson
Cover design, layout and typesetting by Ian Spick, Bradt Guides
Production managed by Sue Cooper, Bradt Guides & Jellyfish Print Solutions

ISBN: 9781784778446

British Library Cataloguing in Publication Data
A catalogue record for this book is available from the British Library

Photographs
Front cover
Pushing the canoe upriver, Guyana © Yolima Cipagauta Rodríguez
Background image of aged map with compass © Andrev_Kuzmin/Shutterstock.com

Back cover
Portrait of John Blashford-Snell, Mongolia © Ian Robinson
John Blashford-Snell on horseback, Mongolia © Scientific Exploration Society

Colour section images All photographs © John Blashford-Snell or the Scientific Exploration
Society unless otherwise stated. Individual photographers credited alongside images.

Digital conversion by www.dataworks.co.in
Printed in the UK by Jellyfish Print Solutions

Dedicated to my dear friends, the late Ann Tweedy Savage,
Ruth Cartwright and Captain Jim Masters MBE, to whom
I owe much for their considerable help and encouragement
on many expeditions

CONTENTS

ASIA AND PACIFIC

FOREWORD

by
Sir Ranulph Fiennes, Bt OBE

In 1968, I read that John Blashford-Snell and his colleagues from the first navigation of the perilous Blue Nile were forming a charity to foster scientific exploration. Visiting John in the Ministry of Defence, I explained my growing interest in expeditioning and my desire to join this new organisation. Pushing aside a pile of files from his normal army job, he listened to me and, what was more, encouraged me to press on with a venture to ascend the Nile by hovercraft. At his home in Camberley, John had a huge caravan, which had become the office of the Scientific Exploration Society. There he agreed to work with Ginny, then my girlfriend, to support the expedition and thereafter has helped me on my expeditions whenever possible.

Without doubt JBS, as many know him, is one of the world's most eminent explorers who, by virtue of over a hundred expeditions, has inspired young people of many nations to carry out challenging and worthwhile projects. His organisation and leadership of the famous operations Drake and Raleigh, scientific challenges for young people worldwide under the patronage of HRH the Prince of Wales, changed the lives of up to 40,000 men and women who are now enthusing others.

This anthology records the highlights of his pioneering expeditions, carried out with a healthy contempt for human hostility, and respect of wild animals and other difficulties and dangers in dense jungle, deserts and high mountains.

Numerous remote communities, the environment, the fauna and flora have benefited, and today, at an age when most would retire quietly, JBS continues in the forefront of exploration. His motto seems to be 'Youth is a state of mind'!

PREFACE

Travel restrictions during the pandemic have provided me with the opportunity to recount the tales of many of my expeditions, often carried out with friends happy to endure the rough and tumble of life under extremes of climate and in testing terrain… many of whom have returned again and again!

In general, I have covered the ventures that took place after my autobiography *Something Lost Behind the Ranges* was first published in 1994, but as we have often returned to areas previously visited, I have included some updated stories from earlier projects.

Regrettably, space has not permitted the inclusion of the most enjoyable expedition helping the Mount Kenya Trust and working with Sophie and Murray Grant at their delightful El Karama Lodge at Laikipia, Kenya in 2018.

The account of following Dr David Livingtone's final steps in Zambia and our 2019 project in Bardiya, Nepal will also have to wait for a future book.

Working with my good friends, Mike Cable and the late Ann Tweedy Savage, the fascinating and worthwhile stories of the great youth endeavours, operations Drake and Raleigh (1978–90) have been covered elsewhere, although I have recalled some of the highlights of those earlier projects when returning to the old stamping grounds.

Having worked long and hard in the concrete jungles of inner cities as well as the green jungles of the tropics, I should have liked to include stories of efforts to help underprivileged youngsters in Britain's urban areas, but this will have to wait.

Over sixty years our expeditions have repeatedly taken us back to the same countries so, for the sake of simplicity, the chapters are not set out in chronological order, but have been divided into sections covering Africa, the Americas and Asia. Dates are included in the text to aid readers dipping in and out to find particular subjects of interest.

Without going into too much detail, I've included sketch maps and some relevant historical facts as well as describing the culture and recounting the legends of the people we encountered. Many of the photographs are from earlier colour transparencies, converted digitally, and I apologise for the quality of some.

John Blashford-Snell
Motcombe, Dorset
March 2022

EXPEDITIONS ON FILM At the end of several chapters in the book are links to films of some of the expeditions described. Simply scan the QR code with your smartphone or tablet to be taken directly to the relevant footage.

To see all videos on John Blashford-Snell's YouTube channel, visit
m.youtube.com/channel/UC1xx0IisGJB1ALBSV0Y5EmQ

AFRICA

CHAPTER 1

THE CHALLENGE OF THE

BLUE NILE

The good people of Maerdy, deep in Welsh Wales, are accustomed to groups of hairy, muscular kayakers and white-water rafters invading their village, threatening to drink the local Goat Inn dry. However, the arrival one wet weekend in 2005 of a mixed bunch of around forty assorted servicemen, scientists and explorers did raise a few eyebrows.

The purpose of the gathering at Maerdy's famous White Water Centre on the fast-flowing River Rhondda was to teach this group of enthusiastic adventurers how to handle their craft, read river conditions and survive on one of the world's most testing waterways, the Blue Nile.

As they sipped their drinks, I explained how the idea of navigating some of the most remote, inaccessible and previously unexplored stretches of the river had first begun in 1966 when, as Adventure Training Officer at Sandhurst, I had taken around sixty officer cadets on an expedition to Ethiopia. Having surveyed archaeological sites, collected

zoological specimens and generally enjoyed a pretty adventurous time, we were summoned to an audience with His Imperial Majesty Haile Selassie, King of Kings, Elect of God, Conquering Lion of the Tribe of Judah, Emperor of Ethiopia and also an honorary Field Marshal in the British Army.

On being welcomed into the presence of the Emperor, protocol demanded that one bowed three times – firstly when one entered the room, again halfway up the red carpet and, finally, when standing right before him. On leaving his presence one had to repeat the process in reverse. No problem, you might think, for well-drilled officer cadets. However, animal-lover Haile Selassie's pet lions roamed the throne room, and I could imagine the terrible incident that could possibly result if a cadet, walking backwards, should happen to fall over one of the royal beasts. So I consulted Tommy, an Ethiopian working in the British Embassy, who gave me the solution.

'You will notice,' he said, 'that we cast ourselves down very low when bowing to the Emperor, so low that we are almost pressing our foreheads upon the carpet.'

'Steady on,' I objected. 'Remember, we are British! A stiff little bow is all that is usually required.'

'I am not suggesting you be obsequious,' replied Tommy. 'The point is that if you cast yourself down really low, you can look between your legs and see exactly where the lions are lurking behind you.' By this means, sixty officer cadets and, surprisingly, two ladies in skirts successfully entered and left the presence of His Imperial Majesty.

'You must see my other pets,' insisted Haile Selassie, leading us into the palace gardens. The lions lolloped along and, outside, a regal cheetah sat upon a stone plinth looking very superior. Kay, our manager, went over to admire the magnificent creature; it was unfortunate that she was wearing a dress with a cheetah-skin pattern! The look on the animal's face said it all.

As we were finally taking our leave, the Emperor turned to me with a smile and said quietly: 'I hope you will return one day and explore my Great Abbai.'

I knew he was referring to the Blue Nile, but this was like asking an average hill walker to climb Everest. Trying diplomatically to avoid making a full commitment I replied: 'That would be quite a challenge, sir.'

The eyes of the nearest being to a living god I had ever met seemed to bore into mine. He said nothing more but simply nodded, put out his thin hand and shook mine with a noticeably firm grip.

Earlier I had visited Lake Tana, generally regarded as the source of the Blue Nile, or the Great Abbai as the Ethiopians call it. I'd also seen the famous Tissisat Falls over which the river dramatically cascades into a gorge that eventually becomes a mile deep and fifteen miles wide. From there the water cuts a gash, curving through the Ethiopian plateau for over 400 miles until it pours out into the sun-soaked plains of Sudan. Joining the White Nile at Khartoum it then becomes the Nile, flowing on for a further 1,750 miles to the Mediterranean, spreading the silt so vital for Egypt's survival.

Extraordinary as it might seem, in 1968 there was no accurate map of the entire length of the Ethiopian Blue Nile. Colonel R. E. Cheesman, the intrepid surveyor who had set out to chart its course in the 1930s, had been prevented from following it at water level by the terrain and, viewing it from the top of the gorge, had to guess at much of its route, which, from that vantage point, lay hidden beneath a blanket of low clouds. In 1936 he wrote: '(Charting) the course of the Blue Nile might be considered as offering the only bit of pioneering exploration left in Africa'.

It was a year after my meeting with Haile Selassie when my fiery new boss, Major General Napier Crookenden, Commandant of the Royal Military College of Science, sent for me. 'Emperor Haile Selassie has written to say he wants his Blue Nile explored,' he said, tapping a letter bearing a royal crest. 'I gather you have seen the river.'

Remembering the tumbling cascades at Tissisat Falls and the turbulent brown water flowing through the massive gorge, I reacted with hesitation. 'It's packed with rapids that have never been navigated and is the home to bandit gangs, huge crocodiles, herds of hippo and suffers from massive landslides. There are also rumours of radioactive gas.'

The general eased his chair back and snapped: 'You're being rather negative. And I don't like negative officers.'

'But I've only seen it briefly, in a couple of places,' I protested.

'Quite an adventure, good for morale, just what the army needs,' barked the general, brushing my reservations aside. 'And I'm told it's one of the last unexplored parts of Africa. So, of course we must do it. We'll need a committee. I'll be chairman and you can be secretary. I see no need for anyone else.' And so it was that Haile Selassie's challenge was accepted and I embarked on the expedition that would change my life.

Thirty-seven years later in 2005, I stood in a Welsh pub and, having described the geography, geology, history, fauna, flora and the numerous rapids of the Blue Nile, I briefed the team on some of the hazards of the region, including the *shifta*, the name given to the infamous bandits who inhabited the remote gorges. As I did so, it brought back vivid memories of my previous visit to the waterway, described at the time by the *Daily Telegraph* as the 'Everest of Rivers'.

It had started badly when our team manning the specially made Avon inflatable boats was descending the sheer-sided northern gorges, where the young river carves its way through the bands of hard igneous rock. With numerous lucky escapes, they had shot some fearsome rapids and had proved the Avons could withstand massive battering. Then they reached the spectacular falls of Tissisat, 'the smoke of fire', one of Ethiopia's most memorable natural features, where the river plunges over a basalt lip into a constricted canyon. Jungle-covered islands break up the falls, with the water plunging 150 feet into a boiling surge, sending up clouds of drifting spray that can be seen for miles. Here, for publicity purposes, we lowered one boat over the vertical cascades of foaming white water. Alas, instead of being carried clear by the ropes, the craft was sucked into the falls and disappeared. Mesmerised by the thunderous, tumbling downpour I had stood at the base of the falls, clutching the rope by which we sought to direct the falling craft. The spray, falling like soft rain, soaked me to the skin as the boiling water surged past, cannoning off the rock, while, in the midst of all this chaos, multicoloured birds could be seen diving under the rainbow that shimmered across the chasm. It was quite unreal. To our astonishment the boat bobbed up, undamaged, in a pool downriver. *Avon Inflatables will love that story*, I thought.

Back on the plunging river the three boats, appropriately named Faith, Hope and Charity, sped on, dodging boulders and being spun round in whirlpools. This was before we'd discovered how to make inflatables self-bailing and the hulls, being filled to the brim, were only kept afloat by the air in the tubes. Exhilarated, but mostly scared stiff, the crews continued to use all their strength to paddle and steer the boats downstream against the mighty current.

My air recce in our Beaver, sent with us by the Army Air Corps, had revealed a maelstrom of water churning over black rocks lining the riverbed between the near-vertical cliffs. The only way through this obstacle belt was to line the boats down on ropes, and so that's what we often did. However, in the process of moving around the blockage, the white-water team had to cross a tributary coming in from the west. The Abaya had its own canyon, through which a brown sinuous stream some forty feet wide raced over a series of cataracts and falls between ebony rocks. It was whilst crossing this that Ian MacLeod, a tough, popular SAS corporal, was swept away. Captain Roger Chapman, the team leader, bravely leapt in to save him but, alas, Ian was dragged from Roger's arms over a waterfall and disappeared forever.

'Ian's gone,' gasped Roger, who brought the awful news to my camp a mile or so ahead. Although a friendly US Army mapping unit operating nearby took me up for an aerial search in a small helicopter, there was no sign of Ian, only some very large crocs smugly sunbathing on the banks.

To make matters worse the locals, who were openly defying the government over taxes, then decided to take us as hostages until the rules were relaxed. Guarded by armed warriors, we tried to convince these people of the futility of their action, without success. 'Sir, why don't we try some 'earts and minds?' suggested Corporal Mike Henry, the joker of our team and cheerful as ever. He had taken over the responsibility as medical orderly following Ian's sad death. Unfortunately, Mike's knowledge of medicine was limited to West Country herbal cures.

However, setting up a makeshift clinic on the riverbank, he began to dispense remedies to the sick tribesmen. The queue of patients clad in their rather grubby, toga-like white *shammas* stretched fifty yards. They jostled for places and minor punch-ups took place between the warriors seeking to jump the queue. Our meagre medical resources were totally inadequate for anything more than first aid. Treating the tropical sores and eye disease as best he could, Henry gave out aspirins for tummy aches and his remedy for the numerous malingerers was a Horlicks tablet sellotaped over the allegedly painful area. In the case of one particularly unpleasant young tribesman, a couple of dozen high-strength cascara laxative tablets were administered with a glass of water. He then told the young warrior to run home as fast as possible, lie down and await results! I reckoned that dose would have moved a constipated elephant. We never saw him again!

Our escape from the income tax rebels was largely thanks to the intervention of the local police chief, who turned out to have been trained in Britain. Visiting us, courtesy of the US Army mapping unit's helicopter, he calmed the tribesmen and, as he was leaving, whispered to me in English: 'Get up very early tomorrow, go about your business as usual, then suddenly slip away in your boats, but keep your guns handy.' The ploy worked a treat and, taken by surprise, our guards were hardly awake when we took off at full speed.

Two old inflatable army recce boats fitted with small outboard engines, brought in by mule from our base camp, aided our flight until we were clear of our captors. Although exciting, the rapids were not as severe as those we had encountered upriver and by noon we were between banks of polished indigo basalt and vertical walls up to 200 feet high. 'No way to escape here,' commented Joe Rushton, the young Royal Navy sub lieutenant helming my boat.

Shaggy hamadryas baboons, stately Goliath heron, soaring fish eagles and startled herdboys watched us pass, paddling and bailing. Now less concerned, we dodged the circling whirlpools and half-submerged boulders, over which the café-au-lait-coloured flood hissed and swirled.

The current slowed to five to six knots and suddenly we found ourselves encased again between towering cliffs. 'Look,' cried Joe, pointing up the rock face. Thirty feet above us were the gaping mouths of two large caves, partly closed by walls of drystone. Seeing a convenient beach on the opposite side I yelled: 'Pull in.' Was this the entrance to the legendary subterranean city? And if so, how could we get in, I wondered.

A spot on the opposite side of the river to the caves provided a good campsite, with a stream of fresh, clean water running on to the small beach, loads of firewood and no inquisitive and possibly hostile locals. Mountaineer Chris Bonington was with us, photographing the expedition for our sponsors, the *Daily Telegraph*, and having studied the almost sheer rock face he told us: 'I think I could climb up from a boat.' So next day when Joe put the engine at full power and held his craft against the cliff face, Chris found a handhold and pulled himself up into the cave. Others joined him and radioed back that unfortunately it was not the entrance to a lost city, but simply a cavern with some old pottery and bones. 'Oh well, that will please the archaeologists,' said our historian, Richard Snailham, noting the discovery.

Meanwhile, I walked up the creek behind the camp to examine evidence of a copper deposit. As I fingered the greenish surface a loud crack echoed down the canyon and a bullet struck the rockface a few feet above me, sending down a shower of stone fragments. On the clifftop stood a man with a rifle. 'Watch out,' I yelled. 'You might have hit me!' As he opened the bolt to reload, I realised that was exactly what he was trying to do. Running back into the camp at top speed I shouted: 'Grab everything and get into the boats, fast.' Then, looking up, I saw that the clifftop across the river, only about sixty yards away, was lined with armed men.

To emphasise the urgency of the situation, a bullet ploughed into the sand a couple of feet away and a horn sounded, whereupon a fusillade of slingshot and bullets sent spurts rising from the shallows. At the same time a football-sized boulder crashed through the trees behind us and more warriors appeared above the creek. Clearly, we were surrounded. Raising my loudhailer I called out to our attackers. '*Tenyastalin, tenyastalin,*' I shouted ('Greetings, greetings'). 'We come in peace. Would you like a Mars bar?'

The booming electronic voice confused them for a moment, then one – the leader, I presumed – raised his rifle and put a bullet between my feet. By now our boats were moving off amidst a shower of missiles. To give us all a chance to escape, Joe Rushton had very courageously taken his boat upstream to try to draw the enemy's fire. Behind me a tribesman was reloading as he came down the cliff. He raised his old Italian carbine and, automatically, I fired a shot from my long-barrelled Smith & Wesson revolver. Whether I had actually hit him or not was unclear, but his weapon flew from his hand and he legged it back up the cliff.

'For God's sake, get in,' bellowed Joe, coming back downstream. Pausing only to grab a vital can of petrol, but sadly abandoning the artefacts, I ran out into the shallows and jumped aboard.

The skies seemed full of descending rocks, some of which bounced off the rubber tubes while one struck Chris Bonington, cracking a rib. Now the boats were under much more accurate fire and ahead were more warriors. I shouted to Colin Chapman, our young zoologist, and a pretty good shot, to return fire. We both pointed our revolvers towards the white-robed riflemen perched high above us and opened fire. Although the range was increasing, my third shot sent the leader staggering back out of sight. This had an immediate effect, and the gunfire was reduced to the odd shot as we raced out of the canyon.

The valley now opened up and, as we bandaged Chris, Joe put up the radio aerial. By good luck we managed to get through to expedition base with a brief report, urging that the incident be kept quiet. I did not want to risk the Emperor's fighter aircraft bombing the area until we were clear. As we cruised downriver the sort of yodelling cries often used by shepherds seemed to be following us. I did wonder whether the message that was being relayed was: 'Here come the tax collectors!'

On the banks of the river crocodiles basked lazily, apparently unconcerned by our presence, and peace returned. From a tall tree leaning over the river a majestic black and white fish eagle called and we began to relax. After twenty-five miles I reckoned we'd outstripped any pursuit, but from my air recce I knew a stretch of rapids lay ahead that should not be tackled late in the day. A low-lying island with a patch of trees and scrub appeared, a good place for defence, I thought, and we beached on the shingle shore. We quickly set up our 'bashers' – a covered sleeping arrangement – under the trees and erected a *zoriba*, a thorn fence, around the perimeter. As we sipped hot, sweet tea, three naked boys swam across and hesitantly approached our camp. Around their necks hung small silver Coptic crosses. None of us could understand their language, but they seemed friendly and simply curious. We passed out a few small gifts and the ubiquitous Mars bars for which they appeared grateful, but by now I didn't trust anyone and noticed they were paying particular attention to our weapons. Was it just boyish curiosity or something more sinister, I wondered, watching as they swam away. As dusk fell we held a short service from the army prayer book. Richard chose the hymn 'Now thank we all our God' which seemed appropriate. We worked out a defence plan with double sentries just in case, cleaned and made ready our guns and mini-flare launchers. Then I dressed my throbbing fingers, suppurating from rope burns suffered a few days before, swallowed a malaria pill and drifted into sleep. In my dreams a voice was crying: 'Stand to, stand to.'

It probably only took a couple of seconds for me to realise this was no dream. Roger, who'd been on guard, was shouting a warning. A horn was sounding. We were again under attack. Pulling out the loaded mini-flare launcher, a pen-size signalling device, I rolled from under the 'basher', pointed it skyward and fired. The rising flare lit up the island and illuminated the beach, alive with shining bodies racing towards the camp in hot pursuit of Roger. A tall man was trying to stab him as he struggled to cross the *zoriba*, when David Bromhead, the second sentry, bought up his .45. There was a crash and as the light of the flare died, we saw the attacker bowled over. Colin sent up another flare and, manning the perimeter, we all opened fire. The bandits, for that was what they must have been, fell back, dragging their casualties with them. But then, from the nearest bank, another group opened fire on us with rifles. Bullets zipped through the trees, so I fired a flare straight at them. It appeared to scare our attackers more than our bullets.

Being outnumbered and short of ammunition I realised we could not hold out for long. 'Joe,' I whispered, 'can you collect the radio and move down to the end of the island?'

'Aye aye,' came the instant reply from the young naval officer, who then, braving the incoming missiles, climbed the thorn tree above us to extract the aerial before loading the vital radio into his boat and slipping silently away between us and the enemy.

Garth Brocksopp, a tough young infantry officer, fired a volley from his shotgun to keep the bandits at bay while the rest of us, in pairs and bent double, moved as quietly as possible towards the downstream end of the island. Roger had already floated the rest of the inflatables here and we redistributed ammunition. Moving to each person in turn, I checked their arcs of fire. Richard, the historian, was crouched near me.

'You cover from that bush to—' I started to say.

'John,' he interrupted, 'I feel there is a small point I should raise.'

'What on earth is it?' I inquired tersely.

'I haven't got a gun,' he replied.

I found it difficult not to burst out laughing. Richard, as gentle as ever, was clutching his pipe. 'Would you like your pith helmet back now?' he said. Guarding it like an imperial eagle of Rome, he had carefully concealed it from view throughout the fight.

It was now 02:00 hours and I planned to hold out until just before dawn, then slip away when the light was sufficient for us to see our way through the cataract approximately a mile ahead.

Fortunately, the bandits' aim seemed to be as bad as their tactics and fieldcraft were good, so I doubted if they would be able to hit us as we moved downriver. I could probably discourage them from following too closely with covering fire from my rifle. But this plan meant holding them off for another three and a half hours at least. They were brave men and probably well-primed with alcohol. And I reckoned there were forty or fifty of them, against ten of us.

At 03:00 hours the horn sounded again and a flare showed some of the *shamma*-clad figures looting our camp, while others were advancing towards us. 'Man the boats,' I ordered, and fired at the approaching mass, which divided as they dived for cover. 'Go, go now,' I hissed, and with our boats already underway, we all clambered aboard. The recce craft was towing the Avons, but the forward compartment of Joe's boat was leaking badly.

Blindly, we crashed through branches projecting into the river. From the blackness ahead we heard the roar of the rapid. Grasping the pump, I rammed it into a valve and worked more air into the tubes… but it did little good. The next moment, unseen waves crashed over us and lifted the boat up like a piece of driftwood caught in a millstream. 'I'll try to beach,' yelled Joe, and he cast off the Avon. By some miracle he managed to take our sinking craft astern and with a crunch we struck a shingle bank. As Joe killed the engine I was hurled out and landed beside something long and black that slithered into the water. I'd narrowly missed a crocodile! To my relief the other recce boat and her Avon loomed up from the darkness, but where was the one that we had been towing? As if to answer my prayers a light winked downstream in Morse code: 'OK.' So all were safe.

However, we knew that as soon as it was light we would be sitting targets, so we prepared to move on. John Fletcher, our boats' engineer, worked on in the dark, repairing the damaged recce craft. 'How's it going?' I whispered.

'Slowly,' came the reply. 'And there is a problem. I've lost the nut that holds the propeller on to the shaft of Colin's engine.'

'Oh my God,' I gasped. 'What can you do about that?'

'Don't worry,' said our resourceful mechanic. 'I'll glue it on with Araldite, and given a few hours it will set hard.' However, we did not have a few hours – the eastern sky was already glowing. 'Right, then we'll encase it in a plastic bag and we'll just run on one engine until it sets,' he responded cheerily.

As dawn crept into the Blue Nile valley we pushed off, picked up our missing Avon and Joe set up the radio, optimistically hoping to make contact with our base. Clutching my heavy-calibre rifle, I scanned the shore for bandits, but a more immediate threat caught my eye. A leviathan of a crocodile was galloping, with its legs extended, down a sandbank towards us. The giant reptile plunged into the water and came speeding at the boat, its great head causing a bow wave. I simply yelled 'Crocodile attack!' into the microphone of the radio and raised the rifle. The huge twitching tail propelled it like a torpedo as I aimed the Mauser at a point midway between its evil yellow eyes.

'Don't shoot!' shouted Colin. 'He's only curious, he'll stop short.'

If you are wrong, my friend, I shall kick you off the cloud when we meet in Heaven, I thought. The ugly brute closed to within eight feet of the boat, when, without as much as a splash, it dived and passed beneath us, its scales rubbing the hull, only to surface on the far side. It then cruised alongside for about twenty-five yards, giving me a chance to estimate its size. It was certainly bigger than our boat. At a conservative guess I would have said fifteen feet in length! Suddenly, it disappeared beneath the muddy water, this time for good.

The signaller at base was trying to contact us on the radio. 'Sorry for that interruption,' I said, giving a brief outline of the battle.

'Don't get the authorities all worked up yet. Give me a chance to get well clear before jets come thundering in to deal with the bandits.'

'They've got troops standing by to be helicoptered in and get you out,' replied Nigel Sale, who was commanding the base. 'And John Wilsey is twelve miles south of the Bashilo junction.'

'Fine, but we urgently need ammunition and food in that order, so may we have a parachute drop when we meet John?' I went on. By now Garth was keeping the growing number of crocs away with well-aimed stones and, sadly, some of our precious geological samples.

We rounded a bend and there, to our delight, was an aluminium assault boat that John Wilsey, a tall, striking captain of the Devonshire and Dorset Regiment, had managed to bring upstream. John, a good man with boats, had driven his craft up the rapids, leaping like a salmon. 'The Beaver's coming,' he assured me, the single-engine plane appearing moments later, flying low over the water.

'No parachutes left,' radioed the pilot. 'It will have to be a free drop.' As he spoke, a sack tumbled from the open door and landed with a crunch on the mud. Luckily, the five-gallon plastic can of Scotch, being kept as a gift for the Ethiopian regional governor, still held a gallon of the precious liquid, but apart from that there were only a couple of packets of broken biscuits and a handful of ammunition. However, the effect of the whisky on our empty stomachs lightened the atmosphere. In the remaining few days we made do with biscuits and some crocodile tail that Colin procured with the rifle. But the welcome at Shafartak bridge made it all worthwhile.

As the Emperor was our patron, we felt we should take him a gift on our return to Addis Ababa. Consulting the Minister at Court, I learned that His Imperial Majesty's favourite pet was a male chihuahua named Lulu. Apparently, his driver had the same name, which could cause confusion at feeding times! However, it was suggested that we present the Emperor with a mate for his pet. So I phoned my wife Judith, who was enjoying some peace and quiet at home during my absence, and asked if she would find an attractive chihuahua bitch and dispatch it forthwith to Addis Ababa. For the princely sum of fifty pounds, a fortune in those days, she acquired Lulette.

At the start of the expedition, Colonel Philip Shepherd, our liaison officer in the capital, had suffered at the hands of an over-officious customs chief who refused to release our army composite rations, without which we would have starved. It was only after a considerable amount of hassle and, finally, the intervention of the Emperor himself, that the food was freed from the bonded warehouse.

Now, whilst we were battling through the rapids, Philip was landed with the task of arranging the passage of a chihuahua through customs. Unperturbed, he saw this as an opportunity to get his own back on the intransigent customs authorities. 'Are there any difficulties in importing a live dog into Ethiopia, and how long will it take?' he asked an official, who replied: 'There are several formalities to comply with, and these usually take from five to seven days.'

'Good God!' said Philip. 'As long as that? I need to get it through in one day!' The audience with His Imperial Majesty, at which the gift was to be made, was imminent.

'One day? That's completely out of the question,' insisted the official, adding: 'Anyway, who is this dog for?'

'Actually, it's for the Emperor,' said Philip. 'He's having the dog sent out from England, and he just wondered how long it would take. I can now inform him that it may take up to seven days. Thank you so much for your help.' And with that he put down the receiver.

He then walked into the adjoining office at the Embassy and told the warrant officer: 'If the telephone goes in the next two or three minutes and it happens to be someone from customs on the line, tell them I am not in.' He had barely finished explaining why when the telephone rang.

'Yes, British Embassy,' answered the warrant officer. And then, after a brief pause: 'No, I'm very sorry, Colonel Shepherd has just left.'

For the next twenty-four hours men from the customs department combed Addis Ababa in search of Philip, and eventually an extremely anxious-sounding high official was put through to him. 'Ah! Colonel Shepherd. About that dog,' he said. 'There'll be no delay at all; it'll be quite all right to bring it in straight away.'

And so it came about that a red carpet was rolled out as an Ethiopian Airlines plane halted at the terminal and a sergeant of the Imperial Bodyguard, his pith helmet bedecked with a lion's mane, carried a rather tired little dog into Ethiopia. We just had time to give her a shampoo before being driven to the Palace. Now came the march into the throne room. Although I had practised bowing low, it was quite a challenge to do so whilst balancing a chihuahua on a silk cushion. The King of King's eyes lit up as he reached forward to accept our gift. 'You could not have brought me anything nicer,' he said in perfect English. And having lovingly hugged the little lady, he put her down on the polished floor. Immediately, an excited Lulu appeared, rushing over, as dogs do, to inspect the new arrival and as a result Lulette, who could no longer restrain herself, delivered an enormous puddle. 'Never mind,' smiled the Emperor. 'It shows she is at home in my empire.' Whereupon Lulette went behind the throne and proceeded to deposit an even larger and more malodorous mess!

Last Great First, Ethiopia 1968

CHAPTER 2

INTO THE BREACH

ONCE AGAIN

The successful navigation of the tumultuous Blue Nile river at high water was certainly an event that none of us taking part would ever forget. But, as so often happens with a major groundbreaking exploratory expedition, the discoveries we made only led to more unresolved mysteries.

In 1969, the year after the Ethiopian expedition, the Scientific Exploration Society (SES) was formed as a charity aimed at bringing together servicemen and civilians on scientific projects. And it was especially interested in further investigating the Blue Nile region.

Was it true that the Bashilo, one of the largest tributaries of the Blue Nile, was a major breeding ground of the fearsome Nile crocodile, and what other fauna might there be in and around that mighty river? Furthermore, was it navigable at low water? Would the rapids be more difficult then, and would the Western Cataracts that we had cruised over at high water be passable? Or did the reduced stream simply descend into a cleft of black rock, impassable for even small white-water boats? Was it true that the wildlife of this remote region flocked to the rivers in the dry season? What evidence of man's early occupation might be found when the waters subsided? Was malaria, especially the deadly falciparum strain, found throughout the gorge? These questions and many more remained to be answered and they dictated what kind of experience and skills we would need to include in our new team in 2005.

Our plan was to aid the impoverished people of the region whilst navigating and gathering scientific information along the Bashilo and the Blue Nile, to a point near the Sudan border. A reconnaissance and support group (RSG) was to provide essential backing, especially important, as this time we did not have the luxury of an Army Air Corps aircraft to scout ahead and parachute supplies to us.

As far as boats were concerned, my old friend Ben Cartwright, formerly of the Royal Electrical and Mechanical Engineers and an experienced rafter, had designed a new type of white-water inflatable for the exploration of Bolivia's Rio Grande, another river in a gigantic canyon. These would indeed prove invaluable and, at the same time, Avon Inflatables, our long-standing supporters, kindly agreed to lend us four of their latest sixteen-foot Professional River Runners, the descendants of the boats we had used so successfully in 1968.

Robert Glen, chairman of E. P. Barrus Ltd, had provided outboard motors for the first expedition in 1968. He now produced two 15hp Mariners fitted with propeller guards that could be attached to one of the large Eurocraft inflatables, specially made for the 2004 Kota Mama expedition in Bolivia, thus giving us a tug to push the Avons on long, easy stretches or to ferry parties across the river.

A four-page list of stores and equipment, loaned by the SES and various sponsors, had to be airfreighted to Addis Ababa and cleared through customs by our advance party, which was led by Simon Hampel. Simon, a man of boundless energy and initiative, had been with me on several previous expeditions. Fortunately, we also had the support of Yusuf Abdullahi Sukar, the Tourism Commissioner, a most valuable ally. And economist Yolima Cipagauta, the SES representative for Latin America, known as Yoli, veteran of many expeditions, joined us from her home in Colombia.

Ethiopian Airlines had allowed us a generous baggage allowance of eighty-eight pounds each and on the evening of Wednesday 12th October 2005, Yoli efficiently handled our check-in at Heathrow with her usual Latin American charm.

The sun was rising as we crossed the golden Saharan sand dunes, bringing back memories of earlier expeditions in southern Libya. Around me the thirty or so boat crew members, medics, navigators and scientists were just awakening. 'Once more unto the breach,' murmured Ben Cartwright, stretching his long legs. I glanced out of the window and, 18,000 feet below us, I could see the sinuous Blue Nile glittering in the early sunlight as it wound out of the dissected green plateau into the scrubby plains of eastern Sudan. In a strange way it was like coming home.

'*Tenyastalin, tenyastalin,*' cried Solomon Berhe, our agent, throwing his muscular arms around me as I stepped out of the immigration booth. Simon was there too.

'The stores?' I asked.

'All through,' he replied, with a broad, reassuring smile.

'Thank God for that,' I muttered, congratulating him as we whisked off to the Extreme Hotel, selected as a rear base in Addis Ababa. A walled area in front of the hotel provided space for packing and unpacking equipment and there were secure rooms inside for the storage of any scientific specimens returned from the river. The accommodation was clean, reasonably spacious and the bedside tables contained Gideon Bibles and, rather incongruously, a supply of complimentary condoms! 'What more could one ask for?' commented Tim Harrison, our cartographer, who would not only be charting the river but, as a former lifeboatman, would also be helming one of the boats.

Having settled in, there now followed thirty-six hours of meetings, shopping for stores and equipment and repacking. Simon and his bright young assistant, Fiona Place, had worked miracles, greatly helped by the Ethiopian Tourist Organisation (ETO). Lieutenant Demelash Temesgen, a slim and serious-minded Ethiopian army liaison officer, arrived looking rather sheepish about his role and confessed that his only weapon was a small Russian pistol, which I doubted would stop a determined Nile crocodile or well-armed bandit. However, as the local Ministry of Defence had declined our request to be allowed to carry guns for self-defence we would have to find a way to improvise. So Simon bought some firework rockets that we could launch bazooka-like from a short length of plastic drainpipe. At least we would be able to look as if we meant business!

There was little time to explore the city with its wide streets, imposing architecture, incongruous donkey trains and bustling markets full of the enticing aroma of coffee and incense. However, we did manage to visit the British Embassy, which, standing in its own grounds, has been in place for well over a hundred years. A gift to Britain from the Emperor Menelik, it occupies 86 acres, with a six-hole golf course, a club and a clinic. The legendary explorer Sir Wilfred Thesiger was born here when his father was consul general and plenipotentiary. I knew it well from previous visits when I'd stayed at the residence and was delighted to find that the old game book was still displayed in the hallway. Amongst many shooting anecdotes, it recorded that a British ambassador, a keen sportsman, was once disturbed during dinner by the butler, who informed His Excellency that a hyena was rummaging in the kitchen's rubbish bins. It had been a long day for the diplomat, spent dealing with tedious problems, but he nevertheless folded his napkin and called for his shotgun. Leaving his unfinished meal, the ambassador and his butler stalked through the darkened grounds of the compound and eventually found the offending beast sniffing around just outside the clubhouse, whereupon the fearless minister wasted no time in shooting it stone dead, much to the alarm of the expatriates playing bridge within. However, having recovered their composure they invited him in for a brandy and the evening ended well.

As the current ambassador was on leave, Deborah Fisher, the Deputy Head of Mission, greeted our motley crew and introduced her staff, including Defence Attaché David Charters, who became a most helpful ally. Michael Sinel, with whom I'd been to school, was also there. Now working for the World Bank, he was to be a great help to us later. A jolly evening, which gave me an opportunity to learn of the political uncertainties in the country, paved the way for our departure next day.

Leaving our forward recce team, under an enthusiastic Sapper captain, Sandy Reeve, to head westward and check resupply routes to the Nile, the expedition headed north-east in four-wheel drives and a bus on the good tarmac road. The rains had been plentiful and the plains were heavy with lush green crops. During a comfort stop, where we could view both the Blue Nile and Awash valleys, we were given sweet green peas by a young goatherd, and local children appeared from nowhere selling horsehair hats.

Tunnels constructed during the Italian occupation took the road down into the Rift Valley. It is said that even in the face of the advancing Allied forces the Italians could not bring themselves to destroy such fine examples of engineering. Emerging into dazzling sunlight, we were confronted by the abrupt appearance of the Great Rift stretching out below us. The land fell away for over 6,500 feet and, leaving the invigorating mountain air, we became aware of the declining altitude. With ears popping, we zigzagged down the escarpment into the desiccating heat below and on to the flat, where we encountered swaying strings of well-fed camels carrying stores to market. Padding along the verge, the great creatures gazed superciliously at our photographers.

Keeping in touch on our Motorola car radios, our convoy climbed out of the valley and at dusk we entered the extended hilltop city of Dessie, sprawling along the highway. Here, a bed and a supper of spaghetti bolognese awaited us at the Ghion Ambassador hotel, which Simon and our girl Friday, Fiona, had found. There was not much to see in this rather decrepit trading post and no time anyway to look around. Turning westward, I'd forgotten how spectacular this part of the roof of Africa can look, although I'd travelled through it before *en route* to Magdala, the site of General Sir Robert Napier's epic battle and rescue of the European hostages in 1868, of which more later.

'What on earth are those? 'cried Yoli, pointing at some strange creatures that looked rather like cavemen in their furry capes.

'Gelada baboons,' I replied. 'Stop the car, let's get some photos.' Several handsome chocolate-coloured males with golden manes and bright pink patches on their chests bared their teeth and scampered away down the rocks. They really did look almost human.

'We should press on,' urged Solomon. 'The well is just down the road.'

Indeed, in just under a mile we came to a village of thatch-roofed *tukul* huts and there, in its centre, was a shining new wellhead, built with funds provided by the water charity Just a Drop and the Rivers Foundation. This was one of the community aid projects Solomon had organised for us, so we paused whilst Graham Catchpole, an enthusiastic dentist and a keen Rotarian from Somerset, officially opened it, with sponsor banners flying. Providing this sort of aid was an important part of the expedition and the RSG, which Simon would now lead, would be responsible for carrying out the various projects. Clearly, the work was appreciated and several of the older villagers came over to shake hands, saying '*Egzier stilin*' and bowing in the traditional fashion.

We had dropped down from 11,500 feet above sea level to 5,380 feet by the time we reached a new bridge being constructed over the Bashilo River. 'From here upstream it is very shallow,' warned Simon. 'So I guess this is the best point to start the navigation.'

Ben checked and found the water was indeed only a couple of feet deep, but the boats would float, so we pitched camp on a sandbank and prayed there would not be a flood overnight. As our tents went up Tim Harrison started his hydrographic records and measured the current at two knots and the water temperature at 24.3°C. At once Kayhan Ostovar, our eager young American scientific director, along with an Ethiopian botanist and a biologist, went off like a trio of terriers in search of fauna and flora.

At dawn the RSG team laid on a wholesome breakfast and I had some practice with our homemade rocket-firing device. Although it was somewhat inaccurate the optimists felt it might possibly frighten a hungry croc. Then our deputy leader, former Royal Marine Major Ram Seegar, gave everyone a well-prepared brief on safety on the river. Immensely fit, Ram had served with the elite SBS and had won the Military Cross in the Borneo campaign and we had served together on the staff at Sandhurst. He had taken on the role as deputy leader and also the task of doing the river reconnaissance using the Eurocraft inflatable canoe that had served us so well on the Rio Grande in Bolivia. Should I have the misfortune to get eaten by a croc, there was no-one better to take over the leadership.

Having heard about our earlier experiences with crocs, Ram would have preferred to have a pistol, and when the Ethiopian authorities refused to let us carry any firearms he briefly considered a mini-crossbow as an alternative. However, after I assured him that the crocs were usually only curious he settled for a huge sheath knife. His original partner in *Fearnought*, as the canoe was named, had cried off at the last moment, shortly before we left London. Perhaps our tales of fearsome rapids, crocs and hippo previously encountered were too alarming. However, Stephen Crosby-Jones, a fit young man and former cadet in the Birmingham University Officers' Training Corps, was a climber with canoeing experience and valiantly agreed to join Ram at the last minute. Their role was crucial.

Champion rafter Megh Ale, who had previously captained my white-water boats in Nepal, sent a string of Nepali prayer flags. Displaying these between boat paddles and using the wartime prayer book of my late father, an army chaplain, I conducted a short ecumenical service on the beach, heads bowed as I asked for God's blessing. Everyone was a little apprehensive. I was reminded of my father's words: 'There are no atheists before a battle.'

As the sun rose the temperature soon reached 35°C and we drained our water bottles. The clear, shallow Bashilo soon revealed its contents. 'Bloody hell!' cried a forward paddler, pointing downwards. 'Crocodiles! Dozens of them!'

A quick glance over the side confirmed the sighting. My friend Sir Charles Blois was measuring depths with a handheld echo sounder and got a good view of the riverbed. It was littered with immobile greeny-brown reptiles. Then the radio crackled into life. 'Crocodiles,' called Ram from *Fearnought* less than a mile ahead. At almost the same moment Ben, skipper of our flagship, the Eurocraft *Kessock*, announced calmly: 'Twelve o'clock, and coming at us.'

Yoli saw the snub nose and hooded eyes as a seven-foot specimen, its tail twisting from side to side, came straight at the boat.

'Stones!' I shouted, grabbing a tennis-ball-sized rock from a pile laid out in readiness on the cargo net and hurling it with all my might at the beast. At the splash the head disappeared underwater and I caught a glimpse of the shadow passing beneath the boat. 'That was just a small one,' I warned the crew. 'The big fellows won't scare that easily.'

Our zoologists were actually surprised to see them so far up the river. But now our attention was diverted to the vertical cliffs towering above us. Chattering in anger, gelada and later hamadryas baboons were scampering along like a pack of feral children. On the bank a stately Goliath heron flapped its huge wings and pairs of Egyptian geese rose quacking in alarm as we passed. The rapids were so shallow that we were frequently over the side, stumbling on the stones and pushing to get the boats through. Luckily, the crocs seemed to prefer the quieter stretches of water.

Pausing for lunch, we were soon surrounded by curious tribesmen. One sported a colourful Ethiopian army senior officer's peaked hat, probably looted during the recent civil war. Holding out their hands, they clearly wanted something.

'They are asking for malaria pills,' explained Demelash – but, unfortunately, we had none to hand. The sun was disappearing behind the sandstone clifftops when we reached the beach where Emperor Theodore and later, General Sir Robert Napier's forces, had crossed the Bashilo barefoot on Good Friday 1868. Brahman bulls now browsed in the prickly scrub where the Indian elephants bearing Napier's artillery had waded over. One could imagine the great beasts' enjoyment of a brief bath. I could almost hear the short Hindi commands of the mahouts and the curses of the muleteers and camel men as the Anglo-Indian army, pausing only to fill their water bottles, picked its way through the boulders and then climbed the steep slope to Magdala, where they defeated the deranged Emperor and freed his sixty or so hostages.

By 16:30 we had managed twelve miles; not bad for the first day. As we camped beside a dry riverbed at 5,127 feet, I was able to get through to Simon on the satellite phone to learn that his community aid projects were progressing well and that Sandy was five hours' march from the Western Cataracts. As dusk descended, sand blown by the nightly katabatic winds funnelled down the valley, adding flavour to our supper, but we slept well. A lovely African dawn, with not a cloud in the sky and with only the yodelling call of a lone fish eagle breaking the silence, raised morale as we stretched our stiff limbs and tucked into a breakfast of baked beans. However, within minutes of us packing up and getting ready to leave, dozens of locals appeared like vultures to dig up the tin cans and waste we had so carefully buried. Not even the loo pit was spared! On the rocks the baboons were back to cheer us on as we cast off. As we headed on down the river the crocs grew larger and bolder, several around eight feet long sliding down the banks to inspect the boats as we passed. A bombardment of stones had little effect on them.

Scouting ahead, Ram reported that a small group of men carrying AK-47 assault rifles had stopped him and his recce team. When we arrived on the scene a few minutes later we got Demelash to show the men the letters of authority he carried, which seemed to satisfy them. They appeared to be some sort of local militia and, in spite of looking pretty evil in their tattered garments, they were friendly. However, a few miles on another group pelted us with stones. I suspected this was maybe because they had not seen boats before. Stopping at a farmer's maize field, we gave them some malaria pills, which we managed to dig out of our rucksacks, and, having had enough of paddling and pushing for the day, we decided to make camp and pitched our tents.

On 20th October our zoologists became convinced that the Bashilo was indeed the crocodile breeding ground. There were certainly a lot more of them about and villagers reported that four men had been attacked by one monster at a crossing place in the last month. They pleaded with us to kill it, but we soon had other problems.

Although Tim's measurements showed a drop of a couple of inches in water level each day, the rapids were growing more severe. Wide beaches and floodplains extended between the walls of the valley and tribesmen working the fields crowded down to watch our flotilla. We called out: '*Tenyastalin. Salaam nous.*' ('Greetings, we come in peace.') Most of them bowed to us and, although a few were armed, they showed no hostility. Demelash was not concerned and all seemed well until I heard Stephen Crosby-Jones's urgent radio call from *Fearnought*.

'Contact,' he cried. 'Wait out.' A moment later he added: 'We are under fire from men on south bank.' Rounding a bend we saw the problem before we could stop. *Fearnought* had beached above a shallow ford through which we would have to wade and push, and an agitated, armed crowd had gathered on both banks. Quickly, Demelash managed to convince those on the north side that we meant no harm and they dispersed. But the handful on the south bank looked a rather nasty bunch and it was they who had fired at *Fearnought*. I watched our liaison officer and our Ethiopian scientists cross the river to show these people our permits and try to convince them of our peaceful intentions. However, it soon became apparent that these were not ordinary villagers, but an armed gang of *shifta* brigands. They carried some old Italian World War II rifles plus an AK-47 and refused to let us proceed unless we paid the equivalent of £200. Clearly, this was a hold-up.

'If you pay them there will be more hold-ups,' cautioned Demelash. He had no need to worry on that score – I certainly had no intention of coughing up. The problem was that although we outnumbered them – twenty-seven of us to five of them – we were outgunned, armed only with Demelash's pistol, some fireworks and a few mini-flares. We could not retreat upstream and if we attempted to push on through the ford we'd be easy targets. Sensing that this was likely to be a rather long-drawn-out affair, I asked Ram and Sapper Captain James Tiernan to organise a camp and its defence whilst I guarded the boats and set up communications.

'You'd better call your colonel,' I told Demelash, passing him the small Thuraya satellite phone. 'But don't let the *shifta* see you using it!' The lieutenant crouched behind our boat while several members shielded him from the view of our captors. By good fortune the colonel was at his desk and I asked if he could inform the British Embassy of the situation.

'Yes, yes,' he replied. 'I'm very sorry about this, but I'll alert the police and hopefully you will soon be released.'

However, we were at least twenty-five miles from the nearest police post and I did not expect rapid action. I was not due to speak to Simon on the plateau until 20:00 hours so was slightly surprised when, as I was briefing everyone, he called me. 'A couple of armed police have just told me of your problem,' he said, adding: 'We are forming a strong party of police and will set out for your camp soonest.'

'That's a relief,' I replied. 'I wasn't expecting things to move quite so fast.'

At that moment Yoli tapped me on the shoulder. 'Careful,' she warned. 'The *shifta* are watching you.' Indeed, they were only about twenty yards away, eyeing us like vultures, but they seemed to be in a dilemma. How could they handle so many *ferenji* (foreigners)? Eventually, their leader came over to us, clutching his AK-47. I quickly changed the phone for a VHF radio we used to communicate between boats, hoping he would think we were just talking within the group. He both looked and smelt pretty unpleasant as he stood barefoot before me in his ragged khaki clothing; but he seemed fascinated by Yoli.

'I doubt he's ever met an Inca,' I muttered to her as she tried her Spanish on the villain. Somehow, she got him to give an evil grin as she showed him her Polaroid camera. Obviously, he wanted his picture taken and as Yoli obliged I also took a couple with my waterproof camera to give to the police as evidence, if necessary. Thinking of ways to solve the problem, I looked for an opportunity to get him away from his pals so that we could lay him out and grab the AK-47. If I could get the automatic weapon, I thought, we might be able to overcome the two with the old bolt-action rifles, but wherever he went his two chums came too.

The smell of cooking wafted over from the camp fifty yards away. The *shifta* looked hungry, but we made no offer to feed them, although I did wonder about using the laxative trick Corporal Henry had pulled back in 1968.

Simon then called again to say that he had the local police commander with him who would talk to the bandit leader. We called him over and they spoke. Afterwards Solomon interpreted and Simon briefed me. 'This man is an illegal,' he explained. 'He wants money, but he is only just out of prison for killing someone in a tribal dispute. The police know this *shifta* well. He is very dangerous and unpredictable, so be very careful and don't antagonise him.'

He continued: 'We'll set out as soon as possible and will aim to be with you by first light.' It was already dark by now and knowing he was forty-five miles away and that even in daylight the terrain was extremely difficult, I very much doubted whether they would be able to get to us that soon, especially as the only transport available was Solomon's old pick-up. However, Simon, the police inspector and his few men all piled into the ancient vehicle and set off as fast as possible, bouncing over the boulder-strewn track. Nearly shaken apart, the lights failed but Gabre, the driver, skilfully navigated by moonlight. On some occasions there was a 1,000-foot drop on one side. At each village the police collected more recruits for the posse, all of them somehow clinging on to the pick-up. And finally, when the track came to a dead end at a precipice, they simply took to their feet and ran. The Ethiopians, of course, are renowned for their long-distance running ability!

Back at our camp it was pitch-dark, apart from our torches and the campfire. Ivan Wood, a captain in the Royal Canadian Air Force and an experienced expeditioner, joined Yoli and me in the beached boats to help keep watch. The temperature had dropped and a few spots of rain fell as our captors sat nearby, wrapped in their dirty *shammas*, clutching their weapons and keeping a close eye on our every movement.

In case of need our team had quietly gathered its weapons, Ram produced his enormous sheath knife and Demelash had his Makarov pistol with sixteen rounds at the ready. Ivan had some mini-flares in his survival kit. Similar to those we had used in our fight with *shifta* in 1968, at close range these could inflict a terrible injury. Most people had sheath knives and Yoli had her razor-sharp kukri and looked quite prepared to use it.

As the moon rose Ivan used the compact night-vision device to watch the bandits and I placed the head torch with a flashing light on the bow so Simon's team would spot us as they descended into the gorge. At 03:00 hours he called, this time on the Motorola car radio.

'He must be close,' said Ivan.

'Just coming off the plateau, I'd guess,' I whispered back. 'But our radios are not powerful enough to reach him.'

Ram came down then to discuss emergency plans, cheerfully remarking: 'By the way, did you know – today is Trafalgar Day!'

'England expects…' I muttered.

Now we could only wait. No-one slept. Yoli found the Scotch and passed a mug around. 'Not supposed to drink on guard,' I grunted, but took a welcome slug. At 05:00 hours we saw a goatherd moving down to the water on the far bank, and the *shifta* called to him asking for food. Half an hour later three of the bandits got up and waded through the ford in search of sustenance. As the first daylight filtered into the valley I scanned the cliffs down which the police would have to come. It looked perilous. Then Simon came through on the radio.

'We can see your flashing light', he said. 'We are descending a little downriver from you and will rush the bandits at 06:15. The police say that from now on everyone must lie flat on the ground.'

Thanks to the night-vision device I was able to tell him that there was only one bandit guarding us at the camp, adding: 'The leader and three others are on your side of the river, looking for food.'

Yoli had her camcorder ready. 'I must video this,' she said. In the half-light we then saw six armed men in pale khaki uniform walking steadily towards the *shifta*. As they neared them the newcomers put out their hands in a friendly fashion. The bandits stood up looking confused. Then in a flurry of rifle butts, fists and boots our captors were disarmed. Two police set off to capture the one who had left the group as they arrived, while more officers rushed into our camp. The *shifta* guarding us was knocked flying and his weapon, which turned out to be an axe, wrested from him. In seconds he was handcuffed and we saw the other captives being brought across the river.

'How about some breakfast?' asked our other former Royal Marine, Pat Troy, also reminding us it was Trafalgar Day.

As the sun came over the cliffs we snapped photos of our rescuers, congratulating them on what even the seasoned soldiers amongst us admitted had been a professionally executed operation. Not a shot had been fired.

Inspector Tadesse, with his beret balanced loosely on his head, said how relieved he was to find us all safe. I thanked him profusely, remarking on how amazed we were that he had been able to come so quickly over such difficult ground. He bowed and smiled, saying that two of his men would remain with us from then on in case we met up with any more *shifta*. Beckoning two officers forward, he gave them a few short orders and, although they had nothing with them except the clothes they were wearing and their weapons, they climbed into the boats without any apparent concern. Later I discovered they couldn't swim!

Simon and the inspector's men waved farewell and set off to climb back up on to the plateau. I noticed that the police made the bruised and dejected *shiftas* carry their captured rifles – now unloaded – up the escarpment.

'All aboard,' shouted Ben as we cast off once again. 'We've a long way to go, so let's get moving.'

 ▶ **Bashilo Blue Nile Expedition, Ethiopia 2005**

CHAPTER 3
RAPIDS AND REVOLUTION

The temperatures soared as we paddled, pulled and pushed the boats through the shallows. Sweat poured from us. A steady paddling would not have created too many problems, but some of our team were beginning to feel the effect of the sun and the physical strain. Skin was blistering and muscles aching. Old injuries were hurting and I could see several would have to fall out when we next met up with Simon's reconnaissance and support group (RSG). However, Arawak, our Ethiopian fish expert, was in paradise and had no trouble catching many specimens, some of which went into the pot. At night he would dissect and examine his catches, looking like a child with new toys, only pausing for a few moments to scribble notes about them.

The evening call from Simon told us they had reached his base on the plateau and the prisoners were now in the cells, leaving him to continue his community aid at Adjibar. At the local school a photocopier had been installed by our nurse Sarah Royal, who was creating a two-way relationship between the children there and those in a school in Britain. There were also the two wells that would serve up to 2,000 people, pumping around 880 gallons of water a day. Before the installation of the wells the locals had been forced to walk for up to three hours to collect water from a stream, otherwise resorting at times to stagnant, disease-riddled pools.

Our young doctor, Alice Mavrogordato, was working in the impoverished town of Mekane Selam, a couple of days' journey from our first resupply spot on the Nile. Simon and his RSG team were also in the process of installing a much-needed generator at the clinic there. Until then procedures often had to be carried out by candlelight, and there were limited facilities for storing consumables and sterilising equipment.

Graham Catchpole, our Somerset dentist, was filling and pulling aching teeth with alacrity. At the same time he had set about finding a few goats to be looked after by the local children who inundated the local campsites. In exchange for eggs or wood or just general help, he eventually managed to procure five goats that he handed over to the youngsters, with strict instructions that they were not for supper, but must be kept to sustain the families with a supply of milk.

Later, when Graham was extracting a local barber's rotten molars, he discovered the man had no salon in which to work, so he bought him a donkey with which to earn some money to build a mud-walled hairdressing shop. The barber was understandably delighted and showed his appreciation by naming it Terry's Salon, after the president of Graham's Rotary club.

Ethiopia was, and sadly remains, in desperate need of aid. As one UN aid worker told me: 'There are simply too many people, insufficient food production and very limited education and health facilities. If the rains fail you will have a famine.' It was comforting to feel that our help, however small, was appreciated.

Down in the canyon we set up a temporary scientific camp at the junction of the Bashilo and Jeta Shet rivers. Having inspired some of the team to assist, Geteneh, our botanist, also had a productive day locating a wide selection of traditional medicine plants, including some used for snakebite and malaria.

Meanwhile, on a rocky bluff above the river, Robert Webber, our young archaeologist, along with some of the fittest members of our team, had scrambled up the steep cliffs to explore an interesting-looking cave, while the geologist was excited to find some clear chunks of crystal and others occupied themselves trapping various small mammals on behalf of the biologist. However, it was sometimes difficult to get people fully motivated in the intense heat. Knowing that we would be approaching the main river next day, Ram, rightly keen on making safety a priority, had boat crews practising capsize and rescue drills. But by midday the debilitating heat had driven most to doze in the shade.

When the baking sun at last began to descend Yoli set about making pancake bread for supper. I offered to help but, alas, only succeeded in burning one batch, which ended up more like King Alfred buns! They nevertheless went down well with a stew of tender young goat's meat, purchased from the local villagers. As dusk fell the biting insects, especially the sandflies, increased their activity, forcing us to shelter behind the nets in our tents. In my log I also noted swarms of black ladybirds, but thankfully they did not bite. I poured a measure of Scotch into my water-bottle mug, and listened to the chorus of croaking frogs and the gentle swish of the river, whilst trying to foresee the next problem that we might have to face.

We had only paddled a few miles downriver the next morning when a warning call of 'Shifta!' came from Ben, and up ahead I saw nine armed men awaiting us in the shallows. However, the accompanying policemen assigned to us by the inspector, following the last hold-up, who had already seen off a couple of troublesome locals, had their AK-47s at the ready. As the gap closed, I saw that the *shifta* leader wore a military-style uniform and the fact that we were now flying the Ethiopian flag from a paddle seemed to convince him we meant no harm. Our police escort explained that these were unofficial militia, rather like village guards, and therefore no problem. It seemed that almost everyone on the river was armed and frightened of intruders to their territory.

The crocs were growing more numerous again and there was a startled cry from Yoli when a small one actually tried to climb on to the boat beside her! 'Totally fearless,' remarked Ben casually as he steered us down the next rapid.

Baboons shrieked and fish eagles called as we sailed on. The villagers became more friendly and even brought out *injera*, the local unleavened bread, which greatly pleased the Ethiopians among us.

Botanist Geteneh had just pointed out that vegetation was changing, becoming denser with all sorts of new species, and everything seemed to be going very smoothly when Ram's voice suddenly crackled over the radio with the urgent one-word alert: 'Contact!'

For a moment I thought it must be *shifta* again. But then he went on: 'Crocodile attack. Damaged and beaching – wait out.'

'Slap paddles!' shouted Ben and we beat the water hard as we hastened to close up on the recce craft's position. Ram and Stephen were on the bank with their deflated yellow canoe and a line of tooth marks, on the port side astern, were clear to see. The croc's jaws had missed Ram's overhanging elbow by an inch.

'Came up from underneath us,' he said. 'I guess we must have surprised him. I don't think this one was just curious. The attack happened so quickly that I didn't even have time to get my knife out to defend myself.'

Ben got out the repair kit and the rest of the flotilla pulled in to watch as he stitched and patched the damaged hull. It took an hour for the adhesive to set before we could press on towards the junction with the Nile.

Spectacular towering cliffs appeared as we approached the end of the Bashilo and on a sandbank there were the prints of a particularly large crocodile that I very much hoped we would not encounter.

Ram had found us a good campsite on a stretch of flat sand from where, a few hundred yards ahead, we could see the milk-chocolate flow of the Blue Nile racing down at a rate of over four knots. After the relatively much slower Bashilo, this worried several of our team's less experienced members.

Simon contacted us on the satellite phone to alert us to the fact that a couple of dangerous brigands had reportedly been seen on the Nile not far from Shafartak bridge, where our first phase was due to finish.

'I'll bring in two new policemen to replace the local ones when I resupply you,' he promised.

From then on my binoculars were in constant use as I carefully scanned the banks and the occasional *tukul* standing in the maize fields, on watch for signs of anything untoward.

'To my knowledge, we are the first people ever to have navigated to the Bashilo,' I told the team at the evening briefing. 'That is quite an achievement. But be warned, the Nile is a much bigger and even more formidable river.' After that, the crews needed no further prompting from Ram to practise the capsize drills before we once again set out.

Early the next morning we swept into the fast-moving brown flood and immediately felt the swirling current pulling us downstream. The rapids at low water were no great problem and we beached safely at the Dankoro junction, where I'd met John Wilsey and his relief force after the firefight in 1968. From there on we found ourselves moving noticeably faster than anticipated and

I became slightly concerned that we might arrive far too early at the Dabber River junction, where we were due to rendezvous with Simon and his resupply team.

It turned out that I needn't have worried on that score because, to my pleasant surprise, they were already waiting for us when we got there. With nineteen fully laden donkeys, they had marched twenty-six miles over rugged terrain in just seven hours, descending 5,000 feet into the gorge, carrying rations that included several dozen bottles of beer, which raised morale no end.

Also welcome was the relatively clean, clear water of the Dabber River, as no-one had fancied drinking from the mud-stained Nile, even after routine purification treatment. Our quartermaster, former commando Sapper David Hilliard, quickly organised the canvas Millbank filter bags and we topped up our containers. David then tried to catch a small snake for Kayhan and got bitten for his pains. Luckily, it did not appear to be especially venomous, although his hand did swell up rather alarmingly. Naturally, we took mischievous delight in kidding him that the bite was probably lethal!

The two new police officers duly relieved Inspector Tadesse's men and New Zealander Daryl Bayly, a young but experienced raft guide, also arrived to join us. I felt he would be especially useful in the stretch known as the Black Gorge, immediately after Shafartak, and also in the Western Cataracts, where some tricky rapids were expected.

That night we enjoyed some of our warm beer whilst Sarah Royal, veteran of many of our expeditions, cooked no less than twenty-nine powdered-egg omelettes for supper. The masses having been fed, I was feeling like an early night when Kayhan came over with various moans about the scientific programme. It seemed the pre-planned resupply points did not suit his collecting programme and he also felt there were too many local people involved. He had a reasonable point. The problem was that he had not been present during the original planning stage in London and his efforts to get everything amended to suit his requirements were not appreciated. I'm afraid I was too tired to listen to all his complaints and probably dismissed him rather summarily. 'One can't please everyone all the time,' muttered Ben from his tent pitched next to mine, having overheard our conversation.

Next morning, moving along at around five knots we negotiated some Class III rapids, watching anxiously as two large crocs slithered into the rippling water nearby. However, they showed no sign of hurrying. Villagers tried to get us to stop, calling out that one of the creatures had just taken their cow whilst it was drinking in the river, and Ram then spotted the poor beast being dragged downstream, flailing in the jaws of a giant reptile. Suddenly, a massive dragon-like head rose up from the water a few yards away from our boat and I hurled a large stone at it, with little effect. These menacing monsters were far from timid.

In the afternoon the wind got up and one of the crews improvised a sail to increase speed. We managed twenty miles that day and, having found a clean stream beside which to camp for the night, Pat and Ram and I commemorated the anniversary of the founding of the Royal Marines by cracking open a bottle of excellent single malt!

The following day, the river was positively teeming with crocs, some around fourteen feet long, and at one point we did pause to help some villagers extract a struggling cow that had got stuck in the mud on the riverbank, where it would certainly have been caught, dragged into the depths and devoured.

Making camp that afternoon I could see that some of the team were extremely tired. The doctor was suffering from sunburn and insect bites, and others had old injuries playing up. It was also noticeable that every time we stopped the locals approached our camp cautiously, begging for malaria pills. I did not recall malaria being so prevalent in 1968 as it clearly was now.

Having lost some time, I was eager to sail on and in order to speed us up Ben fitted the 15hp Mariner outboard on *Kessock* and having rafted up the other boats we pushed them down what were now some more turgid stretches of the river. This worked well as long as we separated before hitting the occasional rapids.

The scientific collecting continued apace, although a croc snatched away Arawak's fishing net. Happily, Kayhan spotted a family of warthog and found a rare Brahminy blind snake, which cheered him up.

Simon was now back with his community aid projects at Mekane Selam and at the clinic the local administrator had agreed to join them for an inspection. Alice had been appalled by the lack of proper hygiene and wanted to spur the official into getting something done about it. Taking a break from his hydrography, Charles Blois was to film the inspection, and the presence of the camera and talk of critical reports to the authorities caught the administrator's attention just as much, if not more than, the disgusting state of the clinic. There were unwashed sheets on the beds, human body parts in open bins, needles scattered across the grounds and layers of grime and dust everywhere you looked. Overall, the whole place lacked the resources needed to run a clinic fit for the 10,000 people that relied upon it. Our doctor really went for the wretched man, leaving him in no doubt about the full extent of the clinic's shortcomings, which did have the effect of leading to some small improvements.

Alice and Graham then decided to set an example and were soon hard at work on bended knees, scrubbing floors and sinks, cleaning out rooms and encouraging local health workers to join in. Ivan, who had also come up from the river, connected the generator and, using old electric cables, brought light to buildings that had previously relied on kerosene lamps and candles. In a couple of days the RSG had made improvements and raised morale at the clinic, inspiring and creating a whole new attitude, which they prayed would continue.

Back in the Bashilo valley I had been sitting deep in thought about the problems of getting through the Black Gorge when, tuning into the BBC World News, I picked up a report of widespread rioting in Addis Ababa that was spreading throughout the country. Worse still, Ben, our 'Admiral', was suffering from an old but worsening throat complaint and I doubted if it were wise for him to carry on any further. Cautious as ever, the Embassy recommended that we should come off the river and head west by road in case a full-scale revolution developed, so that we could be evacuated, if necessary, from Sudan.

Sweeping into the beach at Shafartak we unexpectedly found ourselves in the middle of a building site where a Japanese contractor was in the process of constructing a new bridge. Demelash gave orders that no photos were to be taken of the existing bridge. Quite why, no-one knew, but the local guards were nervous and the atmosphere was growing tense. Hotfoot from Addis, Simon arrived to tell us that in the present situation there was no hope of getting the aircraft from which we had planned to do an essential air recce of the Black Gorge. Furthermore, his group would be unable to provide back-up support for us if we went through this canyon.

'The roads are closed and there are police checkpoints everywhere,' he confided. According to a BBC report, the army had opened fire on rioters in the capital and many were dead.

Meanwhile, despite the noise and debris resulting from the bridge construction, the valley was beautiful. We could see the rocky bank rising steeply to the first boulder-strewn terrace and, at dusk, the basalt reflected a violet hue that contrasted beautifully with the emerald green of the trees and bushes. The Black Gorge seemed to beckon us on.

Ram, Yoli, Ben, Simon and I sat on the noisy beach and weighed matters up. Finally, after much thought, I told the others: 'I know it will be a great disappointment for some of us, but I feel we must skip the Gorge and go by bus and truck to Bure, where there is another bridge over the Nile. There, if the current situation cools down, we can relaunch the boats and complete the survey and scientific work westward, including the Western Cataracts.' All agreed that this was the best plan, with Simon taking out the sick and those who had always planned to leave at the end of phase one. So we took the team to supper in a small hotel at Dejen, on the rim of the vast canyon, where I could brief them in comfort.

My decision to abandon the Gorge was endorsed by a phone call from Holly Tett at the Embassy to say that tanks and the feared red beret soldiers were out on the streets in Addis and that both the American and the British embassies were surrounded by people seeking asylum. Furthermore, the riots were spreading into the main towns across the country.

A pretty Ethiopian girl with a highly decorative coiffure produced plates of steaming *wat* and trays of flat *injera*. Members of the team with more sensitive palates went for the pasta, but I'd acquired a taste for the one great truly traditional Ethiopian speciality. Well-to-do Ethiopians eat it every day, either hot or cold. It has to be said that it doesn't look particularly appetising. In his book *The Blue Nile Revealed*, my pal Richard Snailham – the Nilographer on our 1968 expedition – describes it thus: 'The *injera* is a flaccid, grey substance, looking like some sort of synthetic foam rubber, which comes in large sheets, or folded like a heavy napkin. Made from *teff*, or *Eragrostis abyssinica*, a kind of millet, it is laid before him on a special, circular, basketwork table. Then bowls of hot, spiced meats in a highly-seasoned sauce are spread upon it. This is the *wat*. One has to pluck pieces from the *injera*, as one might tear up a disintegrating old bath mat, and seize chunks of *wat* in the fingers with it. The *wat* can be made from chicken, mutton or beef, but in whatever way the Ethiopian gastronome might enliven it with clots of sour cream, or follow it up with slices of raw beef, the basic *injera* and *wat* is as unvarying as the afternoon thunderstorms in August.' Whether it was pasta or *injera* and *wat*, we ate hungrily, washing it down with beer and *osu*. Tensions and disappointments began to ease.

Some of the crews generally looked relieved by the change of plan, although several 'diehards' were clearly disappointed at missing out on what had promised to be one of the real highlights of the expedition. However, just as scenes of the rioting were screened on television in the hotel, a heavy storm hit the town outside. It was a sobering time. On returning to camp we found our tents drenched and flooded by the torrential rain, while Simon's had been blown into the Nile!

To make matters worse, an ill-mannered individual in charge of the Japanese construction crew announced that he was closing the road leading down to our camp. Feeling my temper rising at this arrogant behaviour, I wisely left it to Solomon and Simon to resolve the matter. I might have been tempted to throw the fellow in the river!

On 4th November a bus and truck arrived and we bade farewell to the outgoing group, which sadly included Ben, whose throat condition had deteriorated. At Debre Markos, the old capital of Gojjam province and the site of my 1968 HQ, police guarded us while Sandy and Solomon changed our money at a local bank. It was a prolonged process as the serial number of each US dollar note had to be recorded!

'You must get out of the town quickly,' urged Solomon. 'The police say there is about to be trouble with a lot of students.'

However, as we drove west the people were predominantly government supporters and the tension eased. Only pausing for a plate of spicy spaghetti bolognese, still favoured in Ethiopia ever since the Italian occupation of the late 1930s, we found an inn in the ramshackle old town of Bure. The rooms were filthy and the loo appalling, the town's electricity had been cut off and there was no water, but somehow the manager produced a meal and some warm beer. Outside the rain fell in rods. Demelash looked dejected as he crouched beside a radio set. 'What's the news?' I asked.

'More riots, and the Eritrean border conflict looks likely to restart,' he replied gloomily, adding: 'The UN have urged restraint.'

In the courtyard Yoli set up the satellite phone and I managed to get hold of Simon, who, thankfully, had reached Addis safely. 'It's quieter now, although the situation is still serious,' he told me.

'However, international flights are still operating and those people due to depart tomorrow should be able to get out OK.'

South of Bure, Sandy had found a superb campsite on open grassland beside a waterfall created by the Fetem River cascading over a cliff, creating a spectacular view as it tumbled for several hundred feet. At dawn he went ahead to clear boulders that blocked the cart track leading in that we would need to follow.

Luckily, word had reached the local municipality and we were expected. Yohanuis, a tall, English-speaking police sergeant, along with a handful of armed militia wearing tattered old uniforms and armed with World War II British rifles, arrived to guard us. However, we seemed to have left all the conflict behind and, as the sun climbed, dozens of excited children turned up to gape at the *ferenji* and in no time Yoli was in her element, entertaining them with balloons.

News from Addis was better too. And even the scientists were happy for once! A large python had been found, many birds and monkeys sighted and Ram had stumbled on a lesser kudu in the bush. Meanwhile, Alice went to work in the clinic at a nearby village and found a malaria testing kit, which was to prove very useful. That night being 5th November, we fired off some of our rockets and had a few beers before the chill of nightfall set in.

As the days passed and the political situation improved, I decided that we would relaunch the boats at the Bure bridge and as the temperature reached 38°C preparations for the move began. However, diarrhoea and vomiting broke out, caused, I suspected, by the poor hygiene in the town. And I also noticed that Yoli was not her usual irrepressible self and was looking an awful pale yellow. Using the village clinic's malaria testing kit, Alice diagnosed the poor girl with both vivax and falciparum malaria. Having myself suffered from both strains, I knew that this was serious and life-threatening. We laid her down in the shade of a bush, with a quinine drip in her arm, whilst Sarah nursed her. There was no question – we would have to get her to hospital in Addis as soon as it was safe for her to travel.

Alice came over to my tent looking grave. 'I'm sorry to say Demelash has malaria too,' she confided. 'Looks like falciparum, but he seems to be responding to my treatment.' She had already spoken on the satellite phone to a specialist in England and, as a young doctor without that much experience of dealing first-hand with malaria, she was happy to hear that the drugs she was prescribing were the best she could do. Meanwhile, Ben's throat infection had got even worse, and the political upheavals continued, with *shifta* firing on police in a nearby town. Sensing morale was low, I gave out recce tasks to everyone except those whose stomachs were still in turmoil, partly as a distraction.

Sitting beside the waterfall, I finalised the plan for the next phase. Previous expeditions had been attacked on the stretch of river downstream. Two Swiss canoeists had been killed in an ambush in 1962 and, more recently, an American group had come under fire.

It took a generous offer to persuade Sergeant Yohannis to send an armed policeman with us as an escort. This was all the protection we could muster, although I did not feel entirely confident that one pistol and an AK-47 would be much of a defence against a determined attack. As if to endorse my concern, my old friend and expeditionary colleague Jim Masters came on the satellite phone from my Dorset base to say that a British expedition, to which SES had given some advice, had been ambushed by rebels on the

White Nile in Uganda. 'One dead, two wounded,' reported Jim. Although we were nowhere near the White Nile this news clearly and understandably made some of our less experienced members rather nervous.

On 10th November, just as the first rays of sunrise crept across the dew, I went over to Yoli's tent. Sarah, who had nursed her all night, said: 'I think she's a little better, but far from well.'

'I'm afraid you'll have to go to Addis,' I told the stalwart and indomitable Colombian lady, as Sarah went round the rest of the sick. Yoli gave a slight smile, as if to say: 'I do understand.' We'd been together on so many expeditions and I recalled her nursing me when I was ill in Paraguay. I could ill afford to lose her now.

As the day progressed our attention was deflected by the arrival of a local mother, red-eyed and weeping in distress, clutching her small son with an ugly, bulging hernia, obviously in need of urgent hospital attention. 'If we can arrange to send him to Addis on the next transport, I'll pay for his treatment,' volunteered Ken Clarke, one of our older team members. In the midst of our own troubles, this was a generous offer.

Old traditions die hard, so at 11am on 11th November even the Ethiopians stood with us to observe the two-minute silence, just as everybody at the Cenotaph in London and around war memorials throughout the UK and elsewhere in Europe would be doing. We also remembered the British and Commonwealth troops who had died liberating this distant land during World War II.

I then had to make preparations for the loss of our excellent recce team, Stephen Crosby-Jones and Ram, whose time with the expedition had finished. Thankfully, the tough, laid-back and very capable Kiwi Daryl felt happy to do the job in one of the Avons.

Before he finally departed, Ram had done a short recce on foot downriver and had found no serious rapids or potentially hostile locals, which was comforting.

We were further cheered by the arrival of Simon, rolling in with reinforcements. I was especially glad to see ex-soldier Alasdair Goulden, who told me later that all of us in the camp looked like a bunch of POWs! Indeed, morale was not high at that time.

Birgitta Hartberger, our new German doctor, was also among the reinforcements. Apart from her medical skills she is an expert on Old Testament manuscripts, but she had joined us specifically to help with the community aid programme. But now I needed her to get the sick safely back to Addis. As slim as a beanpole, Birgitta hardly ate anything and she had no previous experience of expeditionary-style camping, but this didn't seem to worry her and she very quickly settled, becoming an invaluable member of our small medical team.

Simon also bought in Holly Tett, the bright-eyed young lady on the British Embassy staff who'd already done so much to help us behind the scenes and fully deserved to see something of the front-end operation. Another plus was that Sandy was willing and able to take charge of the resupply program, which meant that I could keep Simon as well. Now that we had some more paddlers I felt much happier, even if, in some cases, their experience was limited. Feeling a bit like a juggler, I had reorganised the expedition and only hoped that I wasn't going to drop the ball. However, I also planned to reduce the flotilla by sending one boat and the canoe back to Addis Ababa with the vehicles.

Soon everyone was busy packing up and as we prepared to break up our original team it seemed a good time to hold a traditional Burns Night supper, even if the date was wrong! The special demands of camp cooking often prompt innovative ideas, and special folding, self-standing cooking grids had been designed by Simon and produced in Addis. They were perfect for use with wood fires. James Tiernan made a field oven from roofing tin in which Sandy and Sarah cooked tasty scones and bread rolls. Quality food manufacturer Ken Stahly always supplies our SES expeditions with tinned Royal Haggis in Drambuie from Scotland. And so it was that by the light of the campfire Sandy read the Selkirk Grace and Andrew Holt, our Scots photographer, who had just arrived, read the ode to the wee beastie. Porridge and a few drams of Scotch, as well as the haggis, went down well, but there was not much energy for reeling. However, in general the team was in better spirits by the end of the evening. Now it needed some decisive action and positive results to give morale a real boost.

Next day, Ram and Sandy took out the party returning to Addis Ababa. Under Birgitta's expert care, but nevertheless looking very sad, Yoli reluctantly left us, as did Ben, his throat still giving trouble. Watching them go, I thanked the Lord that we had not been in the Black Gorge when all this sickness broke out, as would have been the case had we not had to make that last-minute change to our original plan. The very thought of trying to evacuate casualties out of that canyon appalled me. In retrospect, it seemed that maybe fate had been on our side, after all.

As we prepared to set off on the next stage, I was further heartened by the arrival of our new escort. A slightly built, smartly uniformed constable, Astmamow had a clean AK-47, loads of ammunition – and he promised he could swim!

CHAPTER 4
ON TO SIRBA

The Bure bridge had not been there in 1968 and judging by the many bullet pockmarks it had clearly been fiercely fought over during the civil war. It was a hundred feet from the parapet to the rocky shore of the gorge below and Ben Adeline, the new 'Admiral', together with Daryl, supervised the lowering of the boats and stores on long ropes from the parapet. A handful of rather bored policemen guarding the bridge watched the operation with looks of slight bemusement, but once Astmamow had explained what was going on they did not bother us.

It took time to inflate and load the rafts and it was almost 15:00 hours when we finally cast off. 'We're still actually in the Black Gorge,' commented Tim, who was now helming a boat as well as making his chart. Indeed we were, but after an hour the valley opened out and within a few miles the cliffs of the great canyon began to recede and the vegetation on the banks gave way to cultivation and the occasional *tukul* from which woodsmoke rose gently into the hot air. Near-naked farmers appeared on the riverbanks to gape as we passed, and a few even waved.

We also spotted antelope and baboons, while the ubiquitous Nile crocodiles were still very much in evidence on the muddy banks, their presence discouraging any idea of carrying out capsize drills! There was now a fresh, more confident spirit among the crews, the memory of dragging the boats down the Bashilo soon forgotten as the flotilla, using paddles and sometimes the motor, covered some impressive distances, averaging close to twenty-five miles per day.

Despite this rapid progress, the next few days were not without incident. The high drama of the earlier *shifta* confrontations was revisited at one campsite, where the team were subjected to abuse from a group of people on the other side of the river. However, it later transpired that they were simply villagers who were annoyed because we had stopped on the opposite bank, rather than on their side, and were trading with their competitors!

The very dark-skinned people here were almost naked. 'Shanqella?' I asked Demelash.

'They now call themselves Gumuz,' he replied. 'But they are basically Nilotic.'

Although busy tending their crops, a few waved and called out to us in what sounded like Arabic, so I responded with: '*Salaam alaikum, hum do lila*,' but this seemed to fall on deaf ears. Eyeing their bows, spears and a few old rifles, Demelash, as ever cautious, urged us not to stop.

It was much hotter down here in the valley than it had been up on the plateau and as temperatures soared and the boats' inflatable tubes became too hot to touch we prayed for a breeze while splashing ourselves with river water.

On 15th November we reached the junction with the Azir or Matin river, which, back in 1968, I had recorded as the start of the Western Cataracts. I remembered this stretch of water as being a series of especially tricky rapids, but now, at low water, they rated at no more than a relatively easy Class III.

Daryl led us through and after a good run of thirty-nine miles we pulled into a beach backed by jungle. Immediately, a group of people appeared on the opposite bank a hundred yards away, shouting and waving, apparently urging us to move on. I counted two AK-47s and an old Italian rifle, but it was too late in the day to go further downstream. 'They are illegals from Sudan,' said Demelash.

At that moment a few bare-chested villagers approached on our side of the river. They seemed friendly enough and, although they could not read Amharic, our permits impressed them. However, I did recall that it was near here that the Norwegian explorer B. H. Jessen had been attacked a century before and his Sudanese servant murdered, so as we set up camp we made a defensive plan, and Alasdair posted a guard. As darkness fell we put out all lights. The boats were packed and ready for instant launching and a quick getaway, and we used a night-vision device to keep watch on the 'illegals'. Simon and Ben Adeline also prepared batteries of firework rockets at either end of the beach. Demelash had his pistol to hand and Constable Astmamow stood ready with his rifle.

Apart from those on guard we all dozed fully clothed, which probably helped to protect us from the mosquitoes. It was a long night and at 04:00 hours a mist settled on the river as we strained our eyes in an effort to see what was going on. A satellite phone call to Addis Ababa meanwhile brought the good news that Yoli was safely installed in the clinic at the British Embassy and was improving, the doctor saying that Alice's early diagnosis had saved her life. We also heard that Ben had been evacuated to England. I said a silent prayer of thanks.

At dawn the more friendly locals were back. Topless girls, their hair anointed with greasy brown ochre and adorned with beads, necklaces and earrings, came asking for malaria medicine and cures for stomach ache. I dished out a few Rennie antacid tablets from my medical pack, which a wizened old man immediately claimed gave him relief. An impromptu competition followed, throwing their seven-foot spears, whilst Alice treated various other patients. They were very keen on our empty tin cans and we also handed out sewing kits, combs and pens. With the help of a rough drawing, I enquired if there were hippos in the area, but they shook their heads.

After only three days paddling through the broad valley we reached the resupply point near Korka and started the next science camp. This proved an excellent spot with an easy landing point for the boats, a firm sand beach for the camp and a clean freshwater stream. Strangely, this pleasant site was unpopulated and I guessed the people had moved to higher ground to avoid the malarial mosquitoes.

Despite the temptation to spend the days relaxing, the science camp was a tremendous success. One highlight was the fishing and in his log for 19th November Alasdair recorded an important discovery. 'Such excitement this morning! Ben, James, Daryl and I went out on the boat to the rock to bring in the lines we had left in place overnight. As James caught hold of the wire trace he got a hell of an electric shock – we had just landed a famous Nile Electric fish, weighing four pounds! We measured the charge, which was 370 volts, enough to give a hefty shock. We then went to look at the other line and there was a monster catfish on the end, weighing in at 16½ pounds. Ben started winding in the line and in his excitement dropped it over the edge of the rock. There were the two of us jumping up and down screaming at the others to paddle round and try to get hold of the line before it disappeared down the rapids. They just managed it, to the accompaniment of much hooting and braying and cheers from the shore. A really good team effort which is why we all claimed credit for catching this monster! Since we had by this stage run out of fresh rations this was a welcome addition to the food store.' James deserved special praise for capturing the electric fish, which was considered so rare that Kayhan wanted to get it back to the American Museum of Natural History in New York.

Rations were indeed now getting short and we keenly anticipated the next resupply, hoping that RSG had managed to fill our rather eclectic list of requests. Our supply team was now reduced to two men and a couple of 4x4s and was having a hectic few days. Ken Clarke's mercy mission to Addis had been quickly followed by Sandy Reeve bringing in more casualties before then rushing back to resupply us on the river. Ken volunteered to stay with Yoli, whilst Sandy headed back west with a Land Cruiser packed to the roof with supplies to meet us at Korka. On 18th November, donkeys were hired and next day we were pleased to see supplies arriving on the far side of the river. However, we were unable to communicate with them as Sandy, being slightly surprised by the prompt arrival of the donkeys before dawn, had left his radio behind. Some frantic semaphore solved this problem and we soon had an efficient ferry system in operation.

Once the supplies were safely across, Rob Webber, now our masterchef, ruthlessly identified the exact requirements for the final leg, whilst everyone else tried to pick out the goodies. Favourites were the Gouda cheese, which went into a tasty Welsh rarebit, and the wine, which was much appreciated. The prize for initiative went to Simon who, on realising that there was some extra beer that could not be taken on the river due to the combination of glass bottles and rubber boats, requisitioned one of the precious water cans to carry the excess!

After the resupply Sandy and his donkeys headed back out of the valley and marched to the remote town of Galessa, winning some hearts and minds by distributing spectacles and powdered milk to the clinic, as well as pens, pencils and a rugby ball for the school. This led to an inaugural game of rugger, which the schoolchildren took to immediately.

That evening Demelash presented me with another problem. 'Astmamow wants to go home,' he announced. 'He is missing his family.' With the notorious 'ambush alley' looming up, the last thing I needed was a homesick policeman. Most importantly, I didn't want to lose his authority and his weapon. It took a very expensive satellite phone call between the constable and his boss in Bahir Dar to keep him with us. Meanwhile, Kayhan had accidentally hooked a five-foot crocodile and broken my rod. So, not a good day! But in the capital Yoli continued to improve, although it would take six months for her liver to recover.

By noon the beach was oven hot, so I retired to the stream to do some planning. As the sun disappeared below the western hills, I heard a distinct, booming snort downriver. 'Did you hear that?' I called out to Alasdair. He hadn't. 'Listen again,' I said, and it came again, a double snort. 'Hippo,' I told him. And, in anticipation of a possible encounter with Africa's most dangerous animal – responsible for more than 3,000 deaths a year – I went over to my tent to unpack the secret weapon I had brought with me for just such an eventuality: a loudhailer!

'What possible use is that going to be?' exclaimed Alasdair incredulously.

'You'd be surprised.' I grinned, adding mysteriously: 'Let's just hope we don't find ourselves in a situation where I have to demonstrate.'

Setting off again the next morning, the few mild rapids we came upon were quite fun to run, and at one point a beautiful female kudu watched us sail past. We then tried to relocate the important archaeological site recorded during the 1968 expedition where, at the base of an eighteen-foot bank of black alluvium, our lean and serious archaeologist, Mansel Spratling, had uncovered fragments of pottery and artefacts. Dolerite axe heads and tools made of translucent chalcedony, one bearing what appeared to be sun symbols, had sent Mansel into a state of professional ecstasy. Later he had discovered almost all the pieces of a large vessel, many of them profusely ornamented, that had been protected from the current by some massive boulders. The finds indicated that the practice of agriculture and pottery making had been introduced from Sudan, further up the Blue Nile, in around 3000bc or earlier. At that time the site seemed to be the earliest in Ethiopia at which pottery was made and used. Although I had taken photographs, it had been during high water, and the river now looked totally different. As a result, we were unfortunately unable to locate Mansel's site, which had later provided Wilbur Smith with the inspiration for his novel *The Seventh Scroll*, the plot of which was partly and loosely based on our original Blue Nile expedition.

The river was now a couple of hundred yards wide and we were moving steadily in line ahead, admiring the view, when I spotted a movement some fifty yards from our bow. 'Look out! Hippo!' I cried, pulling the small electric loudhailer, which also featured an aptly named bullhorn siren feature, from its waterproof bag. The great shining black head was moving closer as I pressed the siren button, activating an ear-splitting, amplified screech. With hardly a splash the beast sank out of sight, while on the bank a younger one scrambled to safety.

Everyone thought this was very funny and had a good laugh, but I knew from previous first-hand experience gained during an expedition on the Congo in 1974 just what a threat hippo could pose. Venturing along Africa's second-longest river, one of our inflatables had already been bitten in half by one of these fearsome monsters when my own forty-foot flagship was threatened by another after we inadvertently blocked its path across the river at night. The local soldiers who were with us had been about to open fire, which could have been even more dangerous in the circumstances, so I had seized the loudhailer and blasted the intruder with the siren at full volume. The hippo immediately turned tail and fled and I thus discovered that loud, high-pitched noise can very effectively deter angry mammals. On another occasion I was to use a referee's whistle to scare off an ill-tempered elephant. Now, as we continued watchfully, more hippo began to appear. 'Be aware that they will sometimes duck down, walk along the bottom and approach underwater,' I warned the crews. 'And they can remain submerged for long periods, taking you by surprise.'

Amid all this excitement I'd almost forgotten about the crocs until I saw a particularly large one heading straight for us. Hurling rocks from our emergency stockpile and beating the water with paddles made it swerve away at the last moment with its malevolent yellow eyes still fixed on us. He must have been all of fourteen feet and the loudhailer did not affect him. Memories came back of being attacked by one of these brutes on an Ethiopian lake when I ended up with my rifle shoved into its gaping jaws.

Ahead of us, Alasdair's boat was weaving its way through a gentle rapid when I saw a ten-footer coming up behind them like a torpedo. 'Watch out, croc astern,' I yelled into the walkie-talkie.

Alasdair, on the helm, turned, saw it and went pale. Later he wrote on his blog: 'I looked around and there, about 30 feet from the boat, was this enormous – well it seemed pretty large – crocodile chasing after us as we moved into the rapid. I have this vision of snapping jaws a la Capt Hook chasing after us. As I was helming and so was the first to be the croc's supper I was quite keen to keep out of his reach so with a great deal of noise and cries of "for God's sake deep deeper!" we managed to get out of his way. Amazing how fast one can go in a 16-foot inflatable when one needs to!'

Handling the boats while at the same time dodging the wildlife often proves challenging and later Alasdair recorded another experience: 'We came to a pool at the head of which we saw four hippo. They spotted us, snorted and made their presence felt as we headed for the rapid as quickly as we could. Nearly came a cropper as the river split and we were supposed to go down the left-hand side but the current caught the boat and because I hadn't positioned it right we were being dragged towards the right-hand side which would have taken us 500 yards past our campsites for the night. We bounced off the rocks and managed to pull ourselves out of the current by some pretty powerful paddling. Thankfully the water wasn't too powerful otherwise we would have been in trouble. I'd learnt a lesson though!'

With the aid of the outboard engine, we pushed on, linked together, at around five knots. Charles Blois used his handheld echo sounder to record depths as Tim charted the river. I reckoned the high-water mark was sixteen feet above the current level and was surprised to find the depth was eighty-two feet. 'This must be a great cleft,' remarked Charles.

The areas we were passing through seemed uninhabited – there were many days when we saw no other human beings – but at the same time we noticed many more animals on the riverbanks. Scientists Kayhan, Arawak and Geteneh were delighted to record sightings of baboons, vervet monkeys and monitor lizards as well as hippo and crocodiles. And at one campsite we spotted a female kudu being pursued by African wild dogs. Wild dogs were not normally found in this area so this was a significant sighting. That same night a violent storm, with strong winds and heavy rain, came rolling up the river from the west, somehow reminding us of the remoteness of this place. I guess no more than seventy-five people, including us and those on the 1968 expedition, had actually sailed through here. That is fewer than have stood on the summit of Mount Everest.

The chart we had made of the river at high water in 1968 was a useful guide to the geography of the Western Cataracts, although the conditions now were totally different. Nevertheless, I was concerned that we were approaching a black basalt canyon that I'd seen on my first 1968 air recce in the dry weather. As we had also found on the upper reaches, the river sinks into a narrow channel during the dry season and could not be navigated. In 1968 we had shot over the top of this chasm at high water, but now we were to face the obstacle with the river at low level. Would we find ourselves squeezed into a cleft?

Meanwhile, although no-one had taken an involuntary dip, Daryl was keen for everybody to practise climbing back aboard, just in case. So, one by one the crew members held their breath, crossed their fingers and plunged backwards into the murky waters, never quite sure what was lurking below. As other members scoured the surface of the water for the telltale ripples of a croc on the move, we all agreed that one brief practice was quite enough!

The rainstorm had cleared the air and next day we awoke early to the booming calls of hippos, swallowed our porridge and prepared to meet Rapid C13, named in 1968. At one point in this section the Nile passed a narrow eighteen-foot gap between two massive blocks of dark rock. This would certainly be a dangerous rapid in the rainy season. However, another narrow gap came in sight and to give time for a recce we pulled in and made camp. A reef of blue-black rock had been cut through by the river creating a fifty-yard gap rather like a gate in a harbour wall. We named it Sandford Gates after Brigadier Daniel Sandford, who had brought Emperor Haile Selassie back to Ethiopia when the Italians were defeated in 1941.

This campsite enabled the scientists to get on with some serious fishing whilst I scouted ahead and Simon exercised the crews, stretching cramped muscles with some party games. Others washed their well-worn clothes in a clear spring. That night I sipped a tiny bottle of sloe gin that my daughter had given me for my birthday, watching the moon rising as a distant hippo gave its deep, booming snorts. In reply a Pel's fishing owl hooted melodiously all night long, much to the annoyance of those trying to sleep. In spite of our problems there was something magical about the river at moments like this.

As the sun rose we left Sandford Gates and floated down between the black boulders, listening intently for the roar of a cataract, but the air was still and silent. Not even the hippo grunted. 'The current is slowing,' reported Tim examining his GPS. 'We've done six miles, so I reckon we must be near your C13 cataract.' Suddenly, we rounded a bend and through my binoculars I saw forbidding low black cliffs that almost blocked the river. 'Beach on the right, before we are sucked into the gorge,' I radioed. But as it turned out there was no problem.

Running south, the river was divided by a 500-yard-long rocky island. The eastern channel was shallow, but in the main one, only some six yards wide, Charles recorded a depth of one hundred feet. Indeed, it was an incredible cleft, or was it a fault line? Whatever, the Blue Nile was flowing gently through it. 'But it would certainly be a different cup of tea at high water,' called Daryl, who had climbed a pinnacle of rock to view the full extent of the feature. So, this was C13, where we had almost lost a boat thirty-seven years before. We now named it the Avon Narrows in honour of the makers of our boats. The high watermarks on the banks indicated the river would be 200 yards wide in flood.

Scrambling over the burning hot rocks, the scientists found the sloughed skin of a large python before we pressed on along the waterway, at one point 151 feet deep and reduced to only five yards in width. We named this, the narrowest gap, after Barrus, our outboard sponsors.

In spite of my misgivings, no massive cataract appeared and as the surrounding hills moderated and the sky opened up, I realised we were through the Western Cataracts. 'Well that's the answer, then,' I said to Charles. 'The time to run this river is at low water, at least from the Bashilo downstream.'

As we spoke a gap appeared in the jungle on the left bank. 'The Didessa!' shouted Tim, pointing at his GPS. Indeed, there was the mouth of the wide, shallow tributary flowing into the Blue Nile with the 330-foot-wide island on which we had made a base in 1968. Covered in thick undergrowth and tall trees it was a zoologist's delight, home to brightly coloured birds, the ubiquitous fish eagle and troops of vervet monkeys. Kayhan rubbed his hands with joy when I assured him that we could remain there for three days.

Pulling on to the beach, we pitched our tents on the golden sand and noted several large crocs watching us from the far bank. It was all much as I remembered it.

On 24th November Alasdair and Demelash took a patrol to see if the Shanqella village of Shawe Bokup, which we'd visited in 1968, still existed about a mile westward on the northern bank. Equipped with compass, GPS, radio and water, they set off in search of a footpath that might lead them to some habitation. After two and a half miles of jungle bashing, they finally reached the location but found nothing. The Shanqella move frequently and Alasdair guessed this village had long been abandoned and led the patrol back. By this time the temperature had reached 38°C and the fierce heat was getting to him. While still more than half a mile from our beach campsite he started to stagger and then collapsed completely. Daryl and doctor Birgitta immediately attended to him, fanning him with their hats and pouring water on to his parched lips.

Back in camp I picked up Daryl's radio message giving the patrol's location and within minutes Simon and Ben, two of our strongest and fittest men, had grabbed a plastic container of water and GPS, crossed the river and were racing to the scene. 'Fire your pistol to guide them in,' I radioed Demelash and moments later two shots echoed from the treeline. The rescuers soon found the party, but it was clear that Alasdair's condition was serious.

Birgitta was doing all she could to cool him down but radioed back to say he couldn't walk. Hearing this, we dispatched four more stalwarts, plus the emergency canvas stretcher and plenty of water. 'Sounds like heat exhaustion,' said Doctor Alice as she prepared to receive the casualty. As the stretcher-bearers soon discovered, Alasdair was a large man! His log, written later, records his rescue.

'While they were hacking through the jungle I was being given about three litres of water – it appears that I drank like a drought-ridden camel! Simon and Ben then went back to meet the rest of the team and it was only when Simon got back that I was conscious, although not lucid. When the team arrived they rigged the stretcher using poles cut from the jungle and proceeded to carry me out. It took all six guys to lift me, with them changing position every so often. I have it on good authority that my belly and backside are the heaviest parts of my body! The stars of the rescue were Simon, Ben, James, Rob, Tim and Giles, with Daryl chopping a path ahead. They had to carry me about 900 yards. We eventually made it back to the beach, by which time I was desperately clammy and desperately needed to relieve myself! At the beach I was finally allowed to have a pee. Because I was strapped in Simon asked that I hang on to the contents of my bladder for the last 20 minutes. I had to be held up to pee as I couldn't stand – so much for my suggestion that I was okay and could walk out with a bit of help! The boat came then across and picked us up. I couldn't even put on my lifejacket. JBS met me with a handshake and "Dr Livingstone, I presume!" Simon and Ben carried me to my tent where Alice looked after me over the next 24 hours. I have this vision of her sitting on my thermarest with the sun behind her and her head was surrounded with a halo of light – no doubt that my guardian angel was there!'

A new incident then brightened my day. Squatting on a rock, Robert our archaeologist was reading Wilbur Smith's book *The Seventh Scroll*, about the progression of Nilotic people upriver from Sudan. Nearby, James, who was moving some stones, suddenly called out: 'Hey, Robert, isn't this pottery?' Standing up in the bright sunlight he handed over a small ceramic shard that seemed to be part of an ancient pot. At once, people scrambled up from the shade and gathered around Robert, who was now busy studying the surrounding area of beach. Within minutes he had found several other pieces. 'We must excavate this area carefully before the flood washes it away,' he said excitedly.

From the 1968 archaeological report I knew the river would have been much lower 5,000 years ago, hence the cleft at the Avon Narrows. It seemed likely that since then silt had covered our island and the layers of soil in the bank seemed to indicate this. Indeed, Holly and James had found more artefacts stretching out three or four yards below the top of the bank. Helping to brush the sand away, I then came to what looked as if it might have been a fireplace, along with some charcoal and mollusc shells. Amongst the rocks there were flints and pottery, ornamented with designs very similar to those found on our previous expedition. There was also an interesting curved hand tool some eight inches long. 'I think these items are important, we'll have to wait and see what the experts in Addis Ababa think,' said Robert, carefully packing the finds away.

Apart from some good-size crocs and a herd of hippos downstream, the area was uninhabited by any dangerously threatening animals or humans and our stay at the Didessa junction was interrupted only by annoying sandflies and mosquitoes, plus the monkeys who hurled wild figs from the trees on to those using the loo. On our chart we named the island after Eric Hotung, a leading supporter of the SES. Sadly, I thought it unlikely that this eminent Hong Kong businessman would ever be able to visit his island!

The scientist had a real field day. Arawak's net produced a fish he had not seen before as well as some Nile perch for the pot. Having identified forty-nine species of acacia, Geteneh was delighted to find a 50th one that was of special interest as, when touched, it closed up its leaves to discourage foraging animals.

The Mariner outboard pushed us along for most of the final run, a distance of almost thirty miles, to the old mission station at Sirba. Fleecy cumulus clouds boiled up over the Sudan border as we left the last of the Blue Nile gorge behind and cruised between the basalt outcrops and past sleepy crocs warming their scaly bodies on beaches and shiny black hippos taking their morning baths. Monitor lizards scuttled along the banks, whilst Egyptian plovers danced and dived overhead. 'Forty-eight point six metres, the deepest yet!' exclaimed Charles, reading his echo sounder.

We had done seven and a half miles before the first people appeared, working in their fields near the riverbanks. During our lunchtime stop some scruffy militia arrived to inspect our permits. Clearly, news of the disturbances elsewhere made them nervous, but Demelash convinced them that, in spite of our appearance, we were not rebels. Near Sirba village we ended our 375-mile journey and, just as the previous expedition had done thirty-seven years before, hauled the boats and stores up the steep, muddy bank.

We were greeted by friendly villagers and excited children who'd come to help and to beg. The unexpected arrival of our flotilla would long be remembered. As we pitched our tents a dusty British Embassy Land Rover rolled in to collect Holly, who was needed back at work, and another well-armed bunch of ferocious-looking militia came to ensure our safety. I was glad they were on our side!

Sandy called on the satellite phone to say that he was driving hard and that as long as the bus didn't break down he'd be with us tomorrow. I poured the last of the J&B into my plastic water-bottle mug and walked down to the river. A village elder who claimed to remember our previous visit joined me and I asked about the two Royal Engineer assault boats we had left behind. 'One went to a village upstream,' he explained. 'And the other one was used as a ferry here until a few years ago.'

After dark Sandy arrived in a battered truck. 'The bus is at a village seven miles away,' he explained. 'Couldn't get it down the track.' The driver looked solemn and pointed to diesel dribbling from his dented fuel tank. He had already lost several gallons. 'Chewing gum,' cried someone, but I found a tube of steel adhesive I'd bought in South America. *Might come in useful one day*, I'd thought, and indeed it did.

The long haul to Addis Ababa took three days, with stops along the way at hostels and hotels of varying quality. Apart from a few colobus monkeys and Chinese road workers there was little to see. Nearing the capital we came up behind a police lorry laden with scowling students who had been detained during the riots and sent out of the city to cool off.

On arrival in Addis, Yoli was there to meet us at the Extreme Hotel. Thankfully, she had recovered from her double malaria. With his usual cheerful efficiency Simon had everything organised and that left me free for meetings with our supporters. Tilly Makonnen, the Ethiopian naval officer who had accompanied us on the first expedition, looked relatively unchanged in spite of many years in prison under the Derg. Hapte Selassie, once of the Ministry of Tourism, who, by a miracle, had survived the persecutions following the Emperor's murder, took me to lunch.

The ever-helpful Ethiopian Tourist Organisation and the British ambassador seemed relieved to see us back. There were many friends we had to thank, not least historian Professor Richard Pankhurst, who gave us coffee and cake as he examined the artefacts that we had found and that we later delivered to Dr Kassaye Begashaw, the head of archaeology at the university. Seeing the curved hand tool, his eyes lit up. 'I believe it is a Neolithic grindstone,' he stated. 'Probably dating from between 3000 and 2000BC, in which case it is the only one ever found in western Ethiopia. It is very rare to find a grinding stone and pottery together.'

Beaming with pride, Robert noted: 'The pottery and the grinding stone compare very closely with the Neolithic finds in the Khartoum area of the Sudan. The grinding stone is an important indicator of the introduction of the craft of pot-making up the Blue Nile valley by the earliest Neolithic peoples from the Sudan, implying a shift from reliance on the Blue Nile for their dietary needs to a diet based on arable farming. The connection between the Sudan and Ethiopia is very complex. The location along the Blue Nile of the pottery and the grinding stone suggests a push up from the Sudan during the Neolithic period bringing pottery and agriculture to Ethiopia once the Sahara began the process of desertification we know today.' So, a major discovery!

Our other scientists were equally pleased with their findings. Over 600 specimens of fauna and flora had been collected and the biological and botanical studies they had undertaken would be of real value to Ethiopia. Fish specialist Arawak wrote: 'I am very excited by all the specimens collected. It was amazing to see such a diversity of fish, as well as some changes in species composition. For me it was the most important to find some fish I have never seen before.' Botanist Geteneh was delighted to have found so many very interesting plants and plant communities, many previously unknown. Kayhan, the scientific director, was excited by the discovery of remnants of wilderness remaining in Ethiopia where signs of human presence or activity are few. Furthermore, he had documented species not previously recorded here and added much to the scientific knowledge of the distribution of Ethiopian fauna and flora.

It was frustrating that our exploration of the Black Gorge immediately west of Shafartak bridge had had to be missed out due to the outbreak of the violence. The study of the little-known Western Cataracts at low water had proved very worthwhile, with a limited hydrographic study producing some extraordinary depths for the river, in some places over 150 feet deep. I expect these cataracts may now disappear beneath the new Blue Nile dam.

Great credit was due to the RSG, who covered several thousand miles by vehicle, mule and on foot to fulfil our community tasks and support the river party. On our return to Addis we learned of the progress of the aid projects that had been affected by the internal problems. Solomon's team had been up to Adjibar and Mekane Selam, overseeing the clinic redevelopment and the water projects. Amazingly, the projects had gone to plan, with the result that four wells were now producing clean, fresh water, a generator was providing lighting and cold storage at the clinic, a second clinic had been built, and computers and a photocopier had been installed at the school.

All in all, I reckoned that, once again, it was 'Mission Accomplished'.

CHAPTER 5

ETHIOPIAN MISSIONS

There had been a point during our voyage down the Bashilo when we passed the shallow crossing where, in 1868, General Sir Robert Napier's Anglo-Indian army had waded over the river with their camels, mules and elephants on the way to closing in on the forces of Emperor Theodore of Abyssinia, now Ethiopia, and successfully liberating sixty European hostages, including the British consul, who were being held hostage by the Emperor in the fortress at Magdala.

Along with the Relief of Mafeking, this epic rescue operation became one of the most celebrated episodes in the annals of Victorian military history during the colonial era.

It was at the suggestion of the Ethiopian Tourist Organisation (ETO) that, in 1995, the Scientific Exploration Society (SES) undertook a survey of the historic battlefields of that campaign. Reading up on the subject in advance of my preparations for leading the expedition to what has become a familiar stamping ground for me over the years, I was immediately gripped by the sheer logistical scale and high drama of Napier's long trek through the remote, rugged and inhospitable terrain and his eventual assault on the seemingly impregnable citadel at Magdala.

The sequence of events leading up to what turned out to be a bloody but heroic conclusion had their origin in the Emperor's fanatical desire to lead a crusade against the Turks. As a committed Orthodox Christian, Theodore hoped to destroy the forces of Islam and liberate Jerusalem, and he sought military aid and support from Britain and other European nations. To this end he sent a cordial letter to Queen Victoria in 1862, proposing not only diplomatic relations but also, some said, marriage to the great lady, who had been widowed the previous year with the death of her beloved Prince Albert.

Alas, the Foreign Office did not take any of this seriously and simply filed the letter away without even bothering to reply. Infuriated by this rebuff, the Emperor imprisoned the British consul, Captain Charles Duncan Cameron, and other European diplomats, along with their dependants, holding them as bargaining counters in a further attempt to secure the weapons, artificers and instructors he was demanding. Long before any modern communications systems existed, negotiations were then long-drawn-out and it was another four fruitless years before the British government finally decided to dispatch a full-scale military expedition to sort out the matter.

Sir Robert Napier, commander-in-chief of the Bombay Army, duly assembled an Anglo-Indian army of over 12,000 British and Indian soldiers, with 35,000 pack animals, including 7,000 mules and 44 elephants, to carry the artillery. Equipped with the latest military equipment, such as the new deadly breech-loading Snider rifle and naval rocket batteries, they landed unopposed near Massawa, in what is now Eritrea.

Napier, being a Royal Engineer, believed in sound logistics. He had a railway built to bring stores from the beaches up to the mountains, through which, rather ironically, Theodore himself had already constructed a road in order to facilitate the transport of his own heavy artillery to Magdala. There, with the hostages languishing in chains in the dungeons of the mountain fastness, the Emperor had holed up with a 5,000-strong army and 50,000 camp followers, armed with a number of cannons and also a giant mortar named Sebastopol. Like Saddam Hussein more than a century later, Theodore placed great faith in this enormous weapon, said to be capable of firing a twenty-inch shell for a distance of two miles.

The opposing forces met on Good Friday, 1868, at the Aroje ravine, where the Abyssinians had taken up a defensive position across the only road leading to Magdala. The Anglo-Indian vanguard did not expect them to launch an attack and were caught somewhat by surprise when thirty cannons opened up from the heights above – although when Sebastopol was fired for the first and only time it exploded, killing the crew. At that point the courageous Abyssinian warriors and cavalry, some clad in medieval armour, rushed headlong down the mountain slope, led by Theodore's most trusted general, Fitzaurari Gabri. Awaiting them stood a thin red line of 300 of the King's Own Royal Regiment, the 10th Company Royal Engineers, some Madras Sappers and Miners and Bombay Native Infantry. The Abyssinian soldiers were used to facing slow-firing muskets and, in expectation of the usual interval after the first volley while the enemy reloaded, they charged in for the kill. However, they now faced the newly issued breech-loading rifle, which could deliver seven rounds a minute and was effective at a range of up to 500 yards. 'Why do they not reload?' wondered the bewildered Abyssinians as they were cut down in droves.

Meanwhile, the Naval Rocket Brigade, positioned near Napier, was sending its six- pound rockets streaming over the heads of the King's Own and into the mass of Abyssinian cavalry. Fitzaurari Gabri was among the first to fall. The Abyssinians, bravely wheeling about and shouting out their challenges to single combat, were shot down relentlessly. The carnage was terrible. Those who survived these initial onslaughts continued to fight from behind rocks and bushes as they retreated. A thunderstorm then broke out from low, threatening clouds and, as dusk fell, Napier called off his pursuing troops.

Some of the Abyssinians, hungry for loot, had veered off seeking Napier's baggage train. However, the mules were carrying not food and camp stores but mountain guns that were quickly set up and fired. Some Abyssinians got right through to the Punjabi pioneers, only to fall not so much to the Indians' old muzzle-loaders as to their bayonets. Survivors scrambled away and hid in the falling darkness.

In all, around 700 Abyssinians were killed, most of them still bravely clutching their weapons, and a further 1,500 were wounded, while the British had just twenty men injured, of whom two later died. As night came Napier's men lay on the field of battle and huddled under their greatcoats, wet, cold, and hungry. At the same time, many of the Abyssinian wounded were left crying out pitiably, some of their uninjured colleagues trying to move them to safety under cover of darkness before the hyenas could get to them. In the early morning light the British buried 560 Abyssinian dead, while a hundred of the wounded were brought to British field hospitals.

Gabri's impetuous charge down the mountain had been a costly mistake, ultimately fatal for Theodore, who should never have allowed it. A controlled and spirited defence of the mostly sheer-sided 'amba', the rocky, flat-topped plateau on the edge of which Magdala was perched – 9,000 feet above sea level and 1,000 feet above the valley below – might have saved the day for the Emperor, who refused to surrender after the battle but then committed suicide when Napier launched an attack on the fortress itself, which he still held, and he finally realised the hopelessness of his position. By that time he had already agreed to release the hostages, but it was later discovered that, in a fit of rage, he had ordered 300 Ethiopian prisoners to be cast over a cliff after they had first been mutilated and dismembered.

I arrived in Addis Ababa in late 1995 with a reconnaissance team of sixteen SES volunteers that included barristers, bankers, a retired US diplomat and a former cavalry Regimental Sergeant Major. Setting out from Addis for Magdala, we drove through the Great Rift Valley, passing herds of Afar camels and the burnt-out wrecks of disabled Soviet tanks left over from the recent civil war before winding our way up escarpment tracks, lined with giant lobelias and *Euphorbia candelabrum* cacti. Around 300 miles north of Addis, at the hilltop town of Tenta, we got our first good view of Magdala, fourteen miles away in the distance.

Mounted on sure-footed mules for the final and most challenging stage of our journey to the citadel, we made our way up the narrow, precipitous track leading up on to the plateau. 'Don't look down, just hold on tight and let the mule pick his way,' our Ethiopian guide advised as we edged along the cliff edge. Coming to a gap just three feet wide where the path had collapsed, I prepared to halt the beast, but before I could act he had nimbly hopped across. However, others wisely dismounted at this point.

Breasting the last rise, we were confronted, as far as the eye could see, by a vista of emerald-green mountains rising to meet a brilliant blue sky, while on the plateau immediately before us was a large, open space, fringed by clusters of round brown thatched *tukuls* and neatly hedged fields. And just fifty or so paces away a low stone wall formed a rectangular enclosure to which Shimelis, our guide, pointed. 'It is here,' he whispered.

Riding forward, I found myself looking straight down the barrel of Sebastapol, the colossal mortar that lay on the ground, one massive trunnion pointing skyward. Theodore had had great confidence in his giant gun until that fatal Good Friday in 1868 when it self-destructed in the act of firing its one and only shot. Like excited schoolboys, Ben Cartwright and I dismounted, reaching for the Polaroid camera and tape measure. 'It's bronze, must weigh about ten tons,' exclaimed my companion who, when not exploring, restores vintage aeroplanes. I half expected it to be broken in pieces, but apart from a crack in the barrel it was complete.

The sun was high in the sky and, lying on the soft turf awaiting the rest of our team, I was about to have a snooze when a voice called. 'John, I think I've got a problem,' said our lady zoologist, leaning over against a nearby stone wall. 'I seem to have a hernia.' The poor girl was obviously in considerable pain. John Davies, our doctor, had gone to examine a cave full of human bones and I had no idea what first aid might be required in the event of a hernia. An hour later John returned, excited by his discoveries, only to become immediately concerned when I told him we might have a medical emergency.

Having examined the patient he turned to me, looking grave. 'She's got a strangulated hernia and I can't get it back,' he told me in a whisper, so that others standing nearby would not overhear, adding ominously: 'This is life-threatening'.

This was, indeed, an extremely serious situation. We were stuck up a remote mountain 400 miles from the nearest well-equipped hospital, our walkie-talkie radios had only line-of-sight range – probably six miles at most – and clearly the lady was in no condition to ride or walk fourteen miles back to our vehicles in Tenta. We needed a helicopter, but the only one was in Addis Ababa with the Mission Aviation Fellowship (MAF). However, as dusk fell, former soldier Graham Kerridge and one of our Ethiopian police escorts set off at a run for Tenta town, whose clinic had a radio that might reach the capital. Using only a head torch, it was a challenging and risky journey. I was not optimistic.

By the light of the full moon, John did his utmost to relieve the patient's suffering, but her condition was deteriorating. 'If there is no helicopter by dawn then we will have to find some other way to get her off the mountain,' he warned. Sisay, our guide, appeared at sunrise and told us that the local villagers had an old iron bedstead that they used as a stretcher to evacuate people who were seriously ill to Tenta. Graham then radioed to say that the MAF helicopter would arrive at 14:00. 'We daren't wait that long,' insisted John. So, we had no option but to strap the poor woman on to the bedstead and six barefoot villagers carried her down the cliff path, with half the bed hanging over the precipice! Accompanying the patient, John then radioed to say that he urgently needed more IV fluid. So Graham again rushed down the rock-strewn track towards Tenta ahead of the stretcher party.

Then, as if to answer our prayers, a small blue-and-white four-seater helicopter suddenly appeared over the rim of the plateau. With it were two pilots and a nurse and Ben climbed aboard to guide them to a rendezvous point with the stretcher. Thus the patient reached the little hospital at the British Embassy in Addis and her life was saved. But it had been a close-run thing.

The following year I took a full-scale expedition to survey the Magdala site, to search for artefacts and to produce a guidebook for the ETO. At the same time we were to run a clinic for the locals, who had been so helpful. With us were two ladies directly descended from Napier as well as my old pal, the historian Richard Snailham, who would be writing the guidebook. This was to include detailed engravings made at the time of the battle and originally published by the *Illustrated London News*. Mapping the area, we paid particular attention to the remains of the Magdala fortress itself.

Napier was aware that during the withdrawal to Massawa he would be dependent on the goodwill of the Ethiopian tribes, some of whom had suffered at the hands of Theodore. On learning of the terrible massacre of the Ethiopian prisoners, he decided he could not leave without destroying the Emperor's power base, avenging the terrible butchery of which he had been guilty by razing his fortress to the ground. On Easter Monday 1868 the assault began with an artillery bombardment that lasted an hour.

At 4pm the gunfire stopped and the 10th Company Royal Engineers, thirty-two strong, and the Madras Sappers and Miners set off ahead of the 33rd Foot, moving up the steep, stony path to the Koket Bir, the first of two gates that protected the fortress. Heavy rain was falling, and this proved more troublesome than the desultory musket fire from the few remaining defenders manning the walls.

However, when the Sappers reached the closed and barred gates, an incredible error was discovered: they had somehow forgotten to bring their gunpowder, axes and scaling ladders with which to force their way in. While waiting for these to be brought up, the impatient infantry approached the gate and found it undamaged by the artillery bombardment and heavily barricaded by several tons of boulders stacked up on its inner side. Private Bergin, a very tall Irish soldier, was able to climb up a ten-foot-high section of wall and clear away the thorn bush above it with his bayonet. A very small soldier, Drummer Magner, then climbed on to Bergin's shoulders and was hoisted up on the end of a rifle butt to the top of the wall, from where he managed to reach down and haul Bergin up. The large Irishman then covered his comrades with his Snider as they clambered over and cleared the Koket Bir from the inside. Both were to be awarded the Victoria Cross.

The men of the 33rd scrambled up a U-bend to the second gate at the plateau's edge. It was undefended and as the first soldiers scaled it and walked on to the *amba* top they saw a solitary figure retire behind a wall and heard a shot. They found a body with a gaping hole in the back of its head. According to an inscription on the pistol by the man's side it had been 'a gift of Victoria, Queen of Great Britain and Ireland, to Theodorus, Emperor of Abyssinia'. Theodore, who had previously attempted suicide with this pistol, according to reports, had now clearly been more successful!

Along what remained of the fortress defences, our team used a metal detector to locate shrapnel and bullets whilst we mapped the ruined buildings, discovering another mortar. After the custom of the time back in 1868, troops were for a while allowed to hunt for loot: the Irish soldiers enjoyed the stores of *tej* wine, but the womenfolk were left unmolested and there were few other pickings. Weaponry they could keep, but other artefacts – books, manuscripts, vestments, carpets, toys, ecclesiastical regalia and so on – were confiscated and later sold at auction in the field. The British Museum representative acquired most of what was found, the rest went to regimental museums and officers' messes. The proceeds were divided among the men, but each gained only about 25 shillings. Some of these items have now been returned to Ethiopia.

Theodore's body was laid out to view in a hut for a while and then buried in a shallow grave, now marked by a large standing stone near the site of the Medhane Alem church. His young wife Terunesh, who was in poor health, and her seven-year-old son Alemayehu were, on Napier's orders, properly looked after.

Napier was keen to leave Abyssinia before the July rains. It had been a neat, swiftly executed liberation exercise and the General now wanted to extricate his forces and the freed hostages as soon as possible. There were never any thoughts of colonisation. What to do with Magdala? The two rival widows of the Emperor claimed it, but it would have required a judgement of Solomon to satisfy them both, and so Napier ordered everything to be destroyed. Thirty-seven guns and mortars, many made by the missionary prisoners and painfully dragged to Magdala, were rendered inoperable by double-charging them and splitting the barrels. Sebastopol, the father of them all, had split on firing the first shot and was too big to be destroyed, so it was left where we eventually found it. The three gates and all the ramparts, stone buildings and wooden huts were blown up. Even the church of Medhane Alem went up in flames.

American journalist Henry Morton Stanley, who later famously found Dr David Livingstone and who covered the Magdala campaign for the *New York Herald*, landed a scoop by getting his story out before the official report. Then Napier's soldiers withdrew and began the long march to Zula, accompanied by many thousands of Amhara refugees and their livestock along with the Emperor's wife and son. Theodore had told Terunesh that he wanted Alemayehu to be raised in Britain, but her sickness worsened on the way and, sadly, she died before they reached Zula. Captain Speedy, a flamboyant and immensely tall British officer, who habitually wore local dress, took care of Alemayehu on the march and later in Britain and India. Queen Victoria befriended the boy, who was afterwards sent, somewhat bemused, to Cheltenham College, Rugby School and, eventually, to Sandhurst. There, sadly, he too died prematurely, aged just nineteen. He is buried in St George's Chapel, Windsor.

Within seven weeks Napier had marched his tired and hungry men through the storm-wracked mountains to the hot, fly-ridden coastal plain. Many mules were sold or abandoned, or died, and five of the forty-four elephants had to be shot. However, it is believed that some escaped and bred with African elephants in what is now Eritrea. But most of the reusable items, even the railway track, were most efficiently removed, along with all the men, in a fleet of ships – all except for a stock of weapons given to the loyal Ras Kassa of Tigre, who had aided the British.

Sir Robert Napier became Lord Napier of Magdala with a pension of £2,000 per year and the Freedom of the City of London. The rescue operation, budgeted originally at £2 million, in the end cost £9 million, which put tuppence (two old pennies) on the standard rate of income tax!

Questioned about the cost by a select committee, Napier is said to have commented that his job was 'to win battles, not keep accounts'. He went on to become Governor of Gibraltar, married twice, fathered fifteen children and died in 1910 aged seventy-nine. Theodore was exhumed from his grave on Magdala and reburied near Lake Tana with his ancestors. The SES produced the guidebook and visitors can still trudge up to the mountain and see Sebastopol and the ruins.

Had I known more of Napier's heroic campaign when in Eritrea in 1969–70, I would have made the point of visiting the Gulf of Zula, where the British Forces had landed. However, at that time my mind was focused on a set of desert islands in the Red Sea off Massawa.

At the end of our audience following the 1968 Blue Nile expedition, Emperor Haile Selassie had turned and, fixing me with his keen, sparkling eyes, inquired: 'Now that you have made history, what about your next expedition?'

'What would your majesty wish us to do?' I responded.

'Have you heard of my Dahlak islands?' he said with a smile.

I was caught slightly on the hop and had to confess that although I had heard mention of them, I didn't know exactly where they were. At that moment one of the court officials intervened and, as the audience was drawing to a close, the Emperor turned back to me and suggested: 'Why not go there? I know Hapte Selassie is interested in promoting them for tourism.'

I promised that I would look into the matter immediately. Thus it was that I came to confer with Ethiopia's head of tourism, His Excellency Hapte Selassie, and also my old friend John Blower, a senior adviser to the wildlife department. I learned that set in the Red Sea off the Eritrean coast of Ethiopia was a group of low-lying coral islands, scattered in a haphazard pattern over an area about the size of Devon and Cornwall. Of approximately 130 islands, only four were said to be inhabited. Barren and almost waterless, they supported only a scanty population of fishing folk, most likely more Arab than African, who eked out a pretty miserable existence under the blazing sun. From maps and charts, such as existed, it appeared that there were no harbours, other than natural ones, although we were told that the people based what economy they had upon the sea.

Although lacking modern amenities, the archipelago, with its white beaches and turquoise waters, was thought to have potential as a possible tourist attraction. Hapte told me that the average winter temperature by day was about 32°C. In the summer no-one knew quite how high it would go, but clearly the tourist season would need to be limited to the winter months. He explained that the islands were said to have a great variety of wildlife, including birds and gazelle. There might even be other, larger creatures, as few people had visited the islands and no serious scientific exploration had ever been carried out.

After further investigations I came to the conclusion that although there would undoubtedly be quite a wide variety of interesting wildlife on land, the greatest wonders were likely to be found in the shallow seas and amongst the coral reefs and gardens which surrounded most of the islands. Here, I believed, there would be countless specimens of marine life occupying the warm waters. There was just a chance that we might even find that rare and gentle creature, the massive dugong, whose almost-human appearance had given rise to the legend of the mermaid. If we could examine the islands to see if they were suitable for tourism, Hapte promised to provide most of the financial backing necessary for the expedition. Already I felt my old love of exploring beneath the sea returning and thus, with the backing of our newly formed SES, we launched the Dahlak Quest.

As always, there were funds to raise, members to recruit, information to read up and equipment to procure. Fortunately, I was then at the Staff College in Camberley and, although my military work took up a fair amount of time, I was centrally placed to liaise with all our potential sponsors. The *Daily Telegraph Magazine* kindly offered to help support us again, sending the amusing and topical writer, Anthony Haden-Guest, and a fine photographer,

Stuart Heydinger, to cover the expedition. Other friends from the 1968 Blue Nile expedition – including Kay Thompson as general manager, Captain Nigel Sale as deputy leader and Richard Snailham to study the history and archaeology – joined the team. Captain Jim Masters came as chief engineer and Lieutenant Colonel Philip Shepard as surveyor, while Staff Sergeant Hank Mansley would seek water resources.

Following his filming success on the Nile, Johnny Johnson agreed to do the land-based ciné work and ornithology, with diver Slim MacDonald taking care of underwater filming. Zoologist Dr Malcolm Largen would lead a team of scientists who would study the botany, conchology and entomology. Architect Gerald Batt would examine the buildings and produce designs for the ETO. Not having much faith in the charts, I invited Captain John Cuthill, a keen army sailor, to be the navigator. Sue Fyson, a lively secretary, joined us from South Africa.

David Bromhead and Jim Masters did a recce in April, and in December the expedition happily left freezing Britain for Eritrea and the sun-soaked Dahlaks, where the British company Mitchell Cotts was supporting us. Trained at the Royal Naval College, Dartmouth, Haile Selassie's favourite grandson, Prince Iskinder Desta, was Commodore at the Imperial Ethiopian Navy and also kindly offered support, which was especially welcome as the Eritrean People's Liberation Front were already building up towards an insurrection. However, to be on the safe side we brought in our own modest collection of firearms.

Hapte Selassi provided a couple of *sambukhs,* local freighters, to transport us around the archipelago, and at the Massawa Naval Base we loaded on two Avon inflatables, outboard engines, rations, camping kit, explosives for well drilling, a couple of Lambretta motor scooters and bicycles.

Sheikh Siraj, ruler of the Dahlaks, joined us on board. A small, delicate man in a pale green turban and flowing robes, he spoke no English, and my Arabic and Italian were limited, but we just about managed to make ourselves understood. We set off at a steady five knots on a sea as flat as the proverbial millpond, our bow wave furrowing the glossy surface and sending flying fish skimming away on either side. Garth Brocksopp spotted a hammerhead shark in our wake, but I was more concerned by John Cuthill, who felt we were off course for our proposed base at Nocra island, site of the former Italian colonial prison.

The sky turned black and heavy waves rose to break over our bow. The boat rolled, and the engine made ominous rattling noises. Ali the skipper would rush down into the hold every now and again to scream hysterically at the engineer, a mystical figure living in the bilges whom we never met. Fearing we might flounder, I wanted to seek the sheikh's advice – after all, he would know these waters intimately – but I was told that unfortunately he was now at prayer in his cabin. I thought I'd check anyway and, sliding back the door, I was about to speak when I realised that the poor man was not communing with the Prophet, but being seasick into a bucket!

For no apparent reason we suddenly appeared to be making slow progress again, despite the fact the weather continued to be as bad as ever. It was when the light was fading, just before dusk, that I spotted the next hazard. Ahead, in the growing gloom, I could make out a line of breakers on what appeared to be a long, low reef. Undoubtedly, we would end up on this stretch of scissor-bladed coral unless Ali took us astern very promptly. Protesting loudly, I pointed the reef out to the deputy master, who had now taken over. Peering at me through his cataract-infested eye he nodded and gave me a toothless grin.

The breakers were only a few hundred yards away and beyond them rose the black outline of some jagged rocks. We were heading straight for destruction. I had reached a point where my patience and nerves could stand no more, and considered taking over the helm by force, when the door of the cabin opened and the sheikh stepped on to the bridge. I pointed over our pitching bow at the reef. Squinting into the driving spray, he said several quick words to the helmsman who altered course by barely a degree. Then turning to me, he said simply: 'Dahlak.'

'There's a channel, there's a channel,' shouted Richard from the bows. Sure enough, as darkness fell, we entered the narrow passage that led from the open sea to a lagoon. Minutes later we altered course to the north and saw the lights of the prison on Nocra. By the time our anchor was down and secure, the wind had risen to an even greater force.

On the shore, Jim and his advance party had rigged up lights to guide us and we began the difficult business of unloading people and possessions in a pitching sea. Fortunately, spirits were high, and the disembarkation was complete by midnight. The storm then ceased as abruptly as it had started and the moon rose to reveal the stark outline of our new home. The sheikh had disappeared, but in the distance we heard the beating of drums welcoming him home. We collapsed on to our camp beds in the old warders' quarters.

At dawn, I sounded reveille on my bugle and we breakfasted beneath the Ethiopian flag and the Union Jack, propping up the front door with a large Italian army fasces carved out of milky coffee-coloured coral.

To start the overland exploration, we crossed the sound from Nocra to the main island by inflatable and were sorting out our equipment when, to our horror, a crowd of apparently hostile islanders came running towards us, shrieking and screaming. I prepared to return hastily to the boats when something else caught my eye. In front of the horde was, believe it or not, a motor vehicle of some kind and, as it drew closer, I was able to make out Sheikh Siraj at the wheel. From his expression, he was having some difficulty in controlling the vehicle and it then became obvious that it had no brakes. However, he managed to stop by piloting it into a large pile of small rocks. Climbing out, with great dignity, he raised his hand and saluted me. '*Salaam alaikum,*' he said.

'*Wa alaikum salaam,*' I replied solemnly.

The archipelago's only motorised transport, the beaten-up jalopy he was trying to drive, was actually a 1935 Balilla truck of about a quarter-ton capacity, doubtless abandoned by the Italian Army. It now had no brakes, the minimum of instrumentation and tyres stuffed with straw. The engine only functioned on two cylinders and the steering was of doubtful efficiency. Nevertheless, it was the sheikh's pride and joy.

He had come to convey me to his village for a discussion on the expedition and the islands, he said. I clambered somewhat nervously into the back and, pushed by a number of people, we set out towards his village. The palace was an enclosure of low stone buildings and, sitting beneath an awning, we sipped tumblers of sweet tea and coffee. Communicating in a mixture of Arabic, Italian, English and Amharic, we learned that there were only two or three tracks suitable for his rather less than roadworthy mode of transport, whereas our Lambrettas could go almost anywhere. Otherwise, travel would have to be around the coast by boat. The sheikh went on to explain that the island people grew no crops, but did keep large numbers of goats, sheep, donkeys and camels, whose voracious appetite obviously helped to account for the sparseness of vegetation. He also mentioned that the dugong, locally known as the *aroussa*, could still be found in the waters around the shallow reefs.

We had already heard rumours of a tribe of people living on one of the islands to the north, all of whom were blind, but the sheikh then told us that blindness was common all over the archipelago. Unfortunately, not having a doctor with us, there was nothing we could do to try and diagnose what was causing such widespread sight deficiency.

Rummaging around for some small gifts for the sheikh's wives and children, I managed to come up with some costume jewellery and a few imitation pearls. The old man fingered the pearls thoughtfully, and then rubbed one against a tooth. He handed it back to me, and reaching into the folds of his robes produced a small leather bag of fat and very genuine pearls that his divers found around the islands!

Providing a plentiful supply of fresh drinking water was a priority for us and Jim and Hank had already begun blasting. At a depth of about seven feet the soil had started to become damp and fresh water had begun to trickle in. It seemed that rainwater, when it fell, soaked through the coral and then lay as a meniscus on top of the salt water already soaked into the sponge-like tissue of the island. Had we sufficiently powerful pumps with us we might have been able to prove this, but as it was we were still awaiting the stores from Britain.

Meanwhile, Johnny Johnson was in an ornithological paradise, finding reef herons, Caspian terns, tropicbirds and numerous osprey amongst the rocks of the arid landscape. On Shumma Island we found a few ruined buildings, once occupied by the Italian garrison who had manned a battery of guns, breeches now shattered by demolition charges. The low cliffs of dead coral guarding its coastline were deeply undercut, forming massive shelves cantilevered out over the incredible blue sea.

On the main island of Dahlak Kebir we saw around 150 dainty Soemmerring's gazelle and, accompanied by the sheikh, met fishermen who gathered to greet him and the *roumi* (strangers). Many were blind, and one man had lost an arm to a shark while diving for pearls. Another stepped forward and showed me a handful of huge worn molars. '*Aroussa*,' he grunted. These grinders were certainly the teeth of a large vegetarian. I accepted the useful addition to our collection and gave the man a shining cigarette lighter; thus encouraged, he rushed off and returned with a thick, yellowed hide and a six-inch tusk that he said also belonged to an *aroussa*. He explained that these gentle creatures sometimes became trapped in his nets and, being mammals, they drowned. He assured us that he did not hunt them – had not his ruler the sheikh specifically forbidden the hunting of the *aroussa* that fed on the weed banks at the water's edge?

As I had suspected might turn out to be the case, the sea was as rich in flora and, especially, fauna as the islands were barren. Here the muscular, rotund Slim, clad with the paraphernalia of an experienced underwater cameraman, plus an explosive-headed harpoon gun, and assisted by Sue, was very much in his element. Floating on the surface in a pellucid warmth, we watched Slim filming the manicured aquarium twenty feet below. Anthony Haden-Guest later cleverly described the scene: 'Luminous as an aqueous Disneyland but through a blue-green filter, and blurrier with motion... drifts of paper-white sand, and coral inhaling / exhaling, Constance Spry arrangements of sea-cucumbers, shiny-black urchins with foot-long spines, and giant clams – deckle edges opening on cobalt interiors – and anemones waggling their toupees and weeds. And the fish... fluorescent parrot fish, knobbly blueish Napoleons, and stripey fish, others flecked and mottled, angelfish, silky yellow-barred rhomboids, and a solitary scorpion fish, trailing plumes, elegantly venomous, a self propelling Ascot hat.'

Then the sharks appeared, circling Slim and Sue like sinister grey submarines, more inquisitive than hostile. Nevertheless, it was hard to dispel the uneasy feeling in the pit of my stomach as the predators swam effortlessly at the limits of visibility. Unconcerned, Slim continued to film as a seven-footer left the pack and came straight at the camera, swerving away at the last minute. Like a surgeon reaching for an instrument, Slim signalled to Sue who handed him the harpoon gun. The shark came again, faster this time. As it turned, Slim raised the gun. Propelled by compressed air the silver harpoon struck the beast in the gills, with a burst of bubbles the explosive warhead detonated. The pack scattered and we hauled the carcass into the inflatable. Even in death its eyes followed us as its mantrap jaws carried on working for a minute or two. Speeding back to our base across a lagoon alive with flying fish and dorsal fins, we had our next encounter. Suddenly, the mirror-like water heaved as the black carpet shape of a manta ray rose to the surface. Hurling itself into the air, it dropped back on to the sea with a crash like gunfire. Beneath us four more of these magnificent, harmless creatures passed by, with pectoral fins flapping gracefully as they fed on the abundant plankton.

'Their wingspan must be twelve feet,' shouted Slim as he plunged overboard with his camera to get some excellent film. In the still waters of the Lagoon of Hope, as we named the inlet on the main island, we found the wreck of SS *Urania,* an Italian cruise liner that the local people said had been scuttled following a fire in 1936. Capsized and tilted, her tiled swimming pool, wheelhouse and ballroom still windowed with Art Deco stained glass now served as a fish's playground. We also heard that a U-boat lay on the bottom nearby, but failed to find it.

On the shore Richard Snailham studied a vast necropolis by the ruined city of Dahlak Kebir. It contained numerous grave slabs of blue-grey stone, not found anywhere else on the islands and with highly decorative Kufic inscriptions. We also discovered underground cisterns tunnelled into the rock – a reminder of greater days in the island's history, when Dahlak Kebir was their capital. Now, only a handful of blind inhabitants eked out a living amongst the caved-in dwellings, ever watched by the vultures and black kites perched upon the ruinous mosques. Richard also identified evidence of prehistoric occupation.

The scientists were hard at work. Botanist Mike Gilbert found an example of the plant *Caralluma vittata,* the first recorded in Ethiopia. A wide range of flies, midges, ticks and scorpions were encountered and a few sluggish, mildly venomous snakes. The crown-of-thorns starfish (*Acanthaster planci)* that attacks coral was also seen, but did not appear to be multiplying. None of these constituted a serious hazard for tourists.

However, the problem of the widespread blindness amongst the people was of concern. Visiting one village with Sheikh Siraj, we found almost all had lost their sight. Jim was our first-aider, but we lacked a doctor to detect any reason for the widespread affliction. So Stuart took close-up photos to show to an ophthalmologist and I wondered if a future expedition could do something to help these islanders.

The entomological group spent a night in a mangrove swamp and were happy to report that it was not malarial. They also found 250,000 Rothmans cigarettes hidden in a smugglers cave. 'Pity it wasn't whisky,' commented non-smoker Garth Brocksopp drily.

As on most expeditions there were accidents. Having spent his time collecting spiky, venomous objects, Malcolm Largen contracted septicaemia, as did Woody Foster the entomologist. Sue was thought to have suffered an embolism, when air is forced into unsuitable parts of the body whilst diving. The Imperial Navy rushed two gunboats to her rescue and fortunately she made a rapid recovery.

Jim Masters had a lucky escape when, 150 yards offshore, he was thrown out of an inflatable by a heavy swell. In those days there was no kill switch fitted on our outboards and unmanned, with the engine still running, the boat circled. Swimming after it he spotted a black dorsal fin cutting the surface nearby. Jim swam frantically to get ahead of the runaway craft, but before he could grab a line the boat was on him, and he had to kick himself downward from the hull to avoid the thrashing propeller. Three times he tried and three times he was run down. At the last attempt a sharp pain in his leg told that the propeller had hit him. Blood attracts sharks and now he was too exhausted to make the shore. He just had to catch that boat.

His colleagues looked on anxiously from the shore, unable to help. There was no other boat to come to his aid. The craft came surging towards him yet again: this time Jim dodged the bow and hurled himself with all his strength at the trailing stern line. His fingers felt the rope and he seized it, immediately being pulled along in the wake. By the time he got one arm over the gunwale and turned the throttle down he was totally exhausted, without an ounce of energy left.

Thankfully, despite all these mishaps, we all got home safely and produced a full report and a film for Hapte Selassie and Gerald produced a splendid design to convert the Italian prison into a tourist hotel.

I suggested to the editor of the *Daily Telegraph Magazine* that we display the tusk of the great dugong, given to me by the fisherman on Dahlak Kebir and which I'd subsequently discovered was a noted aphrodisiac, in their Fleet Street window. 'To hell with the display,' he replied. 'Let's grind it up and keep it for ourselves!'

And there was one very rewarding postscript: keen to investigate the people's blindness, the family of the late Alec Gale, the blind founder of a Wiltshire honey firm, funded Freddie Roger, an eminent eye surgeon, to visit the Dahlaks with a small team to see if they could find out what was causing it. So in November 1971, The Alec Gale Memorial expedition carried out a study. Returning in triumph, Freddie declared that the blindness was largely caused by intense ultraviolet radiation and, what was more important, he believed that in many cases a cure might be possible. He suggested that we bring the Dahlak 'dresser'[1] Al Amin, Sheikh Siraj's young

---

1. The tribal term for a medic.

nephew, to Britain, and train him to treat the eyes of his people, and then send him back with another medical expedition to start work on those afflicted.

Al Amin duly underwent training as a State Enrolled Nurse at the Princess Margaret Hospital, Swindon. Alas, on completion of his course, communism had taken over in Ethiopia and the Dahlaks were said to have become a Russian submarine base. Whether or not that is the case, most of the islanders had fled to Jeddah in Saudi Arabia and it was here that Al Amin went to set up a clinic for them. Nevertheless, I felt with some satisfaction that we had perhaps helped these selfless people who, possessing few worldly goods, had shown us the sort of kindness and generosity of spirit that, sadly, you don't always expect to encounter in our own, so much more affluent, world.

 ▶ **Deserts in the Sea – the Dahlak Quest, Ethiopia 1970**

CHAPTER 6

WILDLIFE QUESTS

Ethiopia, more than anywhere else, shaped my future as an expedition leader. As a twenty-eight-year-old Adventure Training Officer at Sandhurst in 1964, my job was to dispatch officer cadets around the globe during their long summer vacation on adventurous and worthwhile projects 'for the benefit of building their characters with the least possible detriment to Britain's post-colonial foreign relations', as the Commandant put it to me. Scanning the world map, labelled 'Training Area', in my office, Ethiopia seemed an especially suitable and challenging wilderness into which to send a party of cadets on a zoological quest. But, first, we needed to get diplomatic clearance – and here I had an ace up my sleeve.

My godfather was Lord Forester, who served with distinction in World War I and later got to know Emperor Haile Selassie well, both before and during World War II, when the Emperor sought exile in Britain following the Italian occupation of Ethiopia and spent some of his time at Willey Park, Lord Forester's estate in Shropshire. My father was the vicar of the estate's parish, which was how Lord and Lady Forester came to be my godparents. I now enlisted His Lordship's help and a letter from him to Haile Selassie resulted in a formal invitation for the expedition, authorised personally by His Imperial Majesty.

To ensure that the sixty-strong party of officer cadets would be able to make a worthwhile contribution to science, they had to be trained to catch and preserve the various specimens they would be required to collect. So, under the direction of some of the Natural History Museum staff, we pursued adders and grass snakes around the army training areas and lured small rodents into humane box-traps. One overenthusiastic cadet, trying to anaesthetise a shrew held by a colleague, accidentally drove the hypodermic needle right through the animal and paralysed his friend's arm for several hours.

In order to get the team to Ethiopia we needed the kind help of the RAF to fly them as far as Aden, then under British rule. Some arrived early and the local brigade commander offered to send them upcountry to see some action against tribal rebels. At one small fort a group of dissidents opened fire from some distant hills. As the garrison took up its defensive positions, bullets pinged and ricocheted amongst the grey stone sangars. The range seemed to be at least 1,000 yards, but no-one could see the enemy. Suddenly, the machine gun on the watchtower opened up with uncanny accuracy, flushing the tribesmen from their position, sending them scampering away amongst the rocks.

'Fine shooting,' commented the commanding officer who happened to be visiting the fort. 'Who's on the gun?'

'One of the Sandhurst cadets,' replied the company commander.

'Well, I must congratulate him,' said the Colonel, climbing up the tower. Reaching the platform where the cadet lay behind the machine gun, he said: 'Don't mind me! I just wanted to say what good shooting that was; glad to see they're teaching you so well at Sandhurst.'

'Thank you, sir,' replied the cadet, turning about, his flashing teeth set in a broad grin.

Slightly taken aback, the commanding officer inquired: 'Which regiment will you be joining?'

'I shall be rejoining my regiment at home, sir,' said the young Kenyan.

Arriving in Aden a few days later, I was surprised to be greeted by a worried staff officer, who hastened to explain the potentially embarrassing oversight that had allowed a cadet from the armed forces of Kenya, a former British colony that at the time had only fairly recently gained independence, to be involved in action in the cause of what local propaganda would call 'British Imperialism'. I promised to talk to the cadet.

When I met him and explained the problem, he grinned and said: 'I really enjoyed the experience – and don't worry, sir, our President will never get to know,' before adding wistfully: 'I suppose I won't be getting the campaign medal now?' He went on to become a brigadier in the Kenyan army.

I recall many interesting encounters with wildlife during these expeditions. One particular quest was for a rare species of mongoose believed to exist in a remote and largely unexplored wilderness area. Reaching the end of the trail, we left our Land Rovers and proceeded on foot. Two regular army drivers were left in charge of the vehicles and I suspected that as soon as we disappeared they would indulge in an orgy of sunbathing and drinking. To keep them gainfully occupied, I handed out two large plastic tubs and indicated a nearby mosquito-ridden swamp.

'The Natural History Museum is in urgent need of small green frogs,' I told them. 'So by the time I return I expect these two tubs to be full.'

'Sir!' they replied in a tone verging on dumb insolence. Three days later, having successfully tracked down and captured a fine mongoose specimen, we marched back to where the drivers were camped next to the Land Rovers and, as expected, the two of them were dozing in the shade.

'Frogs?' I bellowed.

'In tub,' said one. To my astonishment, both containers were crammed with writhing green amphibians.

'How on earth did you do it?' I enquired, pleasantly surprised, not to say amazed.

'Oh, it was nuffing really, just a bit of hard work,' they replied with assumed modesty.

My opinion of these two seemingly plausible rogues immediately mellowed, to the extent that I even recommended them for promotion! It was only long after that particular expedition that I discovered the true nature of the method they had employed. They had gone to a nearby village armed with a copy of *Playboy*, and as soon as the local men had gathered round they had opened the centre pages and permitted just a momentary peep before snapping them closed again with the announcement: 'Three frogs, one look.' Thus encouraged, the tribesmen rushed off to collect frogs.

On another occasion, the governor at the town of Soddu, who had been educated in Britain, sought our help to eradicate a lion that was decimating the local cattle. So, that afternoon we set off in a Land Rover to the area in question, where we met up with a local guide. He was dressed somewhat incongruously in a blue sports jacket and loincloth, and in one ear was a large gold earring, indicating that he had killed a lion single-handed. Following him closely, we soon came on fresh spoor that led into dense bush. Marcos, the Ethiopian liaison officer, and I were ahead with the guide, while two cadets, David Bromhead and Andrew Penny, followed some ten yards behind. After a little time we came upon some thick bushes. From these came the sound of a cough or grunt and the guide gesticulated wildly and, pointing into the bushes, shouted excitedly: *'Oola, oola!'* I could see nothing, nor could Marcos. Turning, I gestured silently and quizzically to David to see if he had spotted anything. In answer he instantly raised and aimed his rifle and, at the very same moment, I was aware of a great yellow body leaping clear over me!

'What on earth…' I gasped.

'A bloody great lioness!' shouted David, whose knowledge and experience of Africa and its big game was much greater than mine. 'She was looking round one side of the bush, whilst you looked round the other!' The guide and Marcos were already in pursuit, but our quarry had disappeared and, after a fruitless search, we headed back towards the Land Rover.

As we rounded the final bend David suddenly froze and whispered urgently: 'Look up the track!' We all stood rooted to the spot. For there, by the vehicle, lay the lioness, stretched full length in the evening sun. A few feet away in the grass two cubs could be seen playing. *Cunning old thing*, I thought, *she's doubled back.* I raised my rifle, but the sight of this beautiful beast and her young was too much. We sat down, cursing that no-one had a camera. Even Marcos, an experienced hunter, agreed we should not kill her, so we decided to have a cigarette and then, if she had not moved, try to outflank her and reach the Land Rover.

But our plans were changed by the appearance of an Ethiopian shepherd boy strolling nonchalantly up the path towards us, completely oblivious of the great cat obscured from his view. Jumping up, Marcos yelled: *'Ambessa, ambessa!'* ('Lion, lion!')

The boy stopped with an expression of surprise. He saw nothing wrong and then, peering round the Land Rover, caught a glimpse of the hindquarters of the lioness. Like a Walt Disney character he leapt into a tree, scrambling to its highest and rather precarious branch. The lioness eyed him with mild interest. 'Keep together, safety catches off, and we'll walk towards her,' I said, trying to sound confident. We were twenty-five yards away, which is not far when one remembers a charging lion can cover a hundred yards in four seconds (that's twice as fast as world champion sprinter Usain Bolt!) before she moved. Then, with a yawn, she stood up and ambled to the roadside. The guide flung up his rifle, but luckily his shot was wild and in one bound the lioness and her cubs had gone.

'You people are extraordinary,' said the governor, shaking his head in sad bewilderment when we told him what had happened. 'In England, would you hesitate to kill a fox that had taken all your chickens and left you with nothing to eat for four months?' I felt like trying to explain that the attitude in Britain to foxes was, generally, a little different from our feelings about such a noble creature as a lion, but simply bit my tongue, apologised for our failure – and then went out to cull some boar that were destroying crops. Perhaps rather unreasonably, it never seems quite so bad to shoot an ugly beast!

The villagers formed a line of beaters and drove the boars towards us as we settled down to wait. Guessing it would take a while, I relaxed, sitting with my rifle resting against a tree, while my wife, Judith, who had joined on this particular expedition, was standing not far away with others in the team. Apart from the distant yelling of the beaters all was quiet for a time until a movement suddenly caught my eye and, to the accompaniment of much grunting and snapping, a large family of muddy brown bush pigs came trotting through the scrub, with a huge boar out in front. Breaking through the undergrowth no more than twenty feet away from me, he burst from cover, his sharp tusks flashing in the beams of sunlight filtering through the trees. I managed to grab my rifle a split second before he actually caught sight of me and, with head down, charged. Hardly having time to aim, I managed to squeeze off a snap shot. The beast squealed but staggered on as I worked the bolt and put in a second shot. Around 200 pounds of angry boar slid towards me, eventually dropping dead about six feet away. Meanwhile, the bush around us had erupted with panicky pigs running in every direction. Judith was pushed up a tree to safety in the nick of time by a handsome young Ethiopian cadet named Tek Negussie – a selfless act of quick-thinking protection that she vividly remembers to this day with the utmost gratitude, regarding all Ethiopians with the greatest respect and affection as a result.

An important task set for us this time by the Natural History Museum was to go in search of a rare black and white rodent known as Osgood's swamp rat. Only one had been collected and that was now in America. The museum needed one and provided us with a black-and-white drawing of the beast. Copies of the picture were circulated by runners to the tribespeople in the Lake Tana area in the hope that they might be able to help us locate one and, equipped with box-traps, we then set off to see if they'd had any luck. The rains had started, and we spent days trudging through marsh and scrub. Excited by the offer of a reward, the locals happily joined the search, bringing in a wide variety of black and white butterflies, birds and finally, to our horror, a full-grown colobus monkey. To capture the poor beast the hunters had felled an isolated tree in which it had taken refuge.

I was alone in the camp when it was brought in trussed to a pole. My Amharic was insufficient to explain that, although black and white, it was not a rat and so, handing a modest sum to the men, I awaited the return of Johnny Johnson, our zoologist. However, it was clear that the monkey would soon free itself and, opening the veterinary kit, I filled a syringe with anaesthetic and administered a low dose, which I hoped would put the animal to sleep long enough for me to untie it and house it in a large tea chest. I feared that, if released, the hunters would catch it again and this time would probably kill it. On return, Johnny's eyes lit up. He worked with Gerald Durrell at the Jersey Zoo dedicated to conservation and was sure the colobus would be most welcome there.

Back in Addis Ababa, we discovered that it would need a smallpox inoculation before being flown to Jersey and that this would take time. So having put all in hand at the Pasteur Institute, we flew home. Alas, this attractive primate did not survive the inoculation. Several years later, on return to Ethiopia, the institute said how sorry they were about the demise of the monkey and presented us with its skin!

However, on our return home at the end of the expedition the museum was delighted with our specimens. I apologised for our failure to find Osgood's swamp rat, but the mammalogist shook his head. 'No need to worry about that,' he told us. 'After you left we did some further research and having looked again at various reports decided that the rat Osgood found in Ethiopia is actually the same species as one already known in the Congo. It's not a rarity, after all, simply an unusual distribution.' How could I tell him about the many days spent searching the Ethiopian bogs in the pouring rain and the extreme disappointment on failing to discover the bloody rat? However, the museum encouraged us to continue our zoological quests on their behalf and was particularly keen for us to collect a complete Nile crocodile!

Returning to Ethiopia in 1966 we found that Lake Abaya in southern Ethiopia abounded with these reptiles, sunning themselves on the sandbanks and beaches. They would lie motionless, their great orange-yellow jaws agape, until one's boat was abreast, when they would suddenly come alive, rising on their short legs and waddling down to the shallows. Others would bask out in the lake, with only their protuberant eyes and nostrils showing above the surface, before then gliding away with scarcely a ripple or slowly and silently submerging.

Local people told of a Peace Corps volunteer taken by a croc nearby. And we saw for ourselves just how dangerous they could be while looking for a place to raft a Land Rover across the Kulfo River at the southern end of the lake. A hundred and fifty yards downstream, a large herd of native cattle had been brought down to the water to drink. Suddenly, there was a great commotion. The cattle started bellowing in alarm and scrambling frantically back up the bank from the river as their herdsmen rushed down, screaming and waving their spears. For a moment I was mystified by the uproar. What on earth was wrong? The centre of attention seemed to be a white Brahman bull, now standing with his long, heavy horns raised at the water's edge. His legs were deep in the mud, and he seemed to be struggling to draw something out of the river. Even at this distance I could see the muscles of his powerful body contorted in effort. 'He's got something in his mouth,' gasped a cadet. Through my binoculars I could now see that there was something, but it was not in the bull's mouth, it was around it! The poor creature's lower jaw was locked in those of a huge crocodile and very slowly, very remorselessly the fearsome reptile was dragging its heavy prey into the river. I had a high-powered rifle with me, but at that distance, with the demented herdsman dashing helplessly round the struggling beast, I dared not fire.

If we could have crossed the river, we might have been able to rescue the bull, but the sight of the massive croc did not encourage anyone to try a quick dip at that point. While we watched impotently, the reptile won the dreadful tug of war and, with its thick, squat legs working like pistons and its scaly tail thrashing the water into a foam, pulled its victim into the shallows. Suddenly, the bull was down, the froth turned red and, still kicking frantically, the stricken beast disappeared in the turbulent brown stream. The rest we could imagine. The croc would place the carcass in its underground lair until it had putrefied sufficiently for its liking.

A few days later, along with Negussie and an intrepid Sapper lieutenant named Bill Bullock, I set out to examine another rafting site on the shores of the lake. It was barely light and as we reached the water's edge we decided to walk out along a partly finished jetty to get a good view. I led the way, followed by Negussie and then Bill. We had our arms full of reconnaissance kit and made our way forward by hopping from the top of one timber pile to the next, never more than a couple of feet above the water. Almost at the end of the jetty I looked down and saw what I assumed was a large rubber tyre, with the tread just on the surface of the water.

'Is that a tyre or could it be a crocodile?' I asked Negussie. As if to answer he used a striped surveyor's pole he was carrying to press firmly down on the object. It sank without movement, and as he released the pole, bobbed up again. *Obviously a tyre*, we all thought and took another pace forward. At that moment, Negussie repeated the process but this time, with a great roar and a crash, a leviathan rose up from the depths. It was a large crocodile, and its tail came crashing round to strike the timbers just beneath my feet, sending splinters flying. At the same time it launched itself at Negussie, who fortunately, being extremely agile, leapt to the top of a convenient pile.

The monster then turned on me and, with its mouth wide open, displaying serried lines of yellowing teeth, tried to get my leg. In one hand I held a .303 sporting rifle and in the other I carried a valuable theodolite that I dared not let go of. Flicking the safety catch off with my thumb, I thrust the rifle down into the gaping mouth and pulled the trigger. The jaws closed about the barrel as the gun fired. Blood spurted out towards me, and at that moment Bill and Negussie discharged their weapons into it. With an awful gurgling sound, it slid back into the water and was still. 'Wait,' yelled Negussie, and before we could stop him, he had seized the thing, by now clearly dead, by the tail. It took the three of us nearly an hour to get the carcass ashore, after which we dragged it back to camp in triumph. It was a salutary lesson and one I'm not likely to forget. It brings out the old maxim that the crocodile will very often attack after you have stepped over him and not when you are about to. Frankly, it was as close as I ever want to get to one.

Although we had several dangerous meetings with wildlife, I always remained alert to the fact that in remote alien territory, where all strangers are understandably regarded with suspicion and hostility for various reasons, the greatest threat faced by explorers can come from fellow human beings. We made many journeys up and down the Great Rift Valley and found that, in general, the people we encountered along the way were friendly and hospitable. However, as already mentioned in previous chapters, there were several times over the years when we did find ourselves in tricky situations, even coming under armed attack from bandits and rebels.

Happily, there were occasions when our fears proved quite amusingly unfounded. Not long after the croc incidents on Lake Abaya we camped near a large village to the west of Lake Shamo. Supper had been served and the ration of whisky had been produced when suddenly the silence around us was broken by the sound of drums from the village. In a flash, Negussie was on his feet and disappeared into the surrounding bush. The drums got louder, but we carried on enjoying a wee dram and not really paying that much attention. But then Negussie returned and whispered to me: 'John, I am not happy about the villagers here. The last white men they saw were probably the Italians, who may well have mistreated them. I think we should take the initiative, go into the village, find out what is happening and, if necessary, make it clear that we are not a threat.' Respecting his greater local knowledge, I agreed that this sounded like a sensible plan. It was certainly an interesting experience for me to accompany a young fellow officer on a purposeful patrol, when only two years before I had been trying to teach him the art of patrolling on a Surrey common.

Picking up our rifles, we set off, the night noises drowned by the sound of the drums, which were now almost deafening. Clearly, the villagers were getting very worked up about something. Arriving at the stockade that encircled the village, Negussie went forward to the gate, leaving a police corporal and myself to cover him. Through the fence we could see a huge fire burning with half-naked figures leaping about and jumping through the flames. Around them the crowd ululated, and the drums beat faster and faster. Negussie paused, listening intently. He came from the north of the country and I doubted if he would understand the language these people spoke. Like most Ethiopian officers, he was smartly dressed and, even when working for long hours in the rain and the mud, Negussie always managed to look as if he had just come off the parade ground.

As we watched, he suddenly pushed open the gate and walked in. The drums and the ululating ceased instantly. He held up his hand; his pistol was still in its holster. I could understand a little of what he was trying to say. 'I am an officer of the Emperor, tonight the Emperor's friends are camping near here. What is all this noise about?'

A wizened old man dressed in a leopard's skin shambled forward to shake his hand, and in a whining, pleading voice talked to him for several minutes. Eventually, Negussie nodded, said something in Amharic and turned and strode out of the compound. At once the drums thundered louder than ever and the ululating began again. I must admit I thought it a pretty cool act, for had they been hostile he wouldn't have lasted long. 'It's all right.' He grinned. 'They are having a celebration for the return of their chief, who is expected back tonight.'

What I had witnessed only served to increase my respect for the Ethiopian as a courageous fighter, and not once in all our expeditions in that wild land did I ever have reason to doubt the bravery of these hardy people.

Meanwhile, we had yet to fulfil our obligation to procure a full-grown Nile crocodile for the Natural History Museum and, more challenging, get it back to England in reasonable condition. The museum had specified that it had to be female, no less than thirteen feet in length, and it had to be shot very precisely in order to avoid causing too much catastrophic damage to the specimen. The one that Bill Bullock, Negussie and I had shot after it had attacked us earlier at Lake Abaya would not do, partly because it was not quite big enough, but also because we had riddled the thing with bullets! So Bill, a marksman, was sent out on to the lake in a small inflatable, camouflaged with tree branches. His targets, as usual, were sunning themselves on a sandy beach as, aided by a gentle breeze, he slowly edged his boat towards them. At seventy-five yards he lined up a neck shot on a thirteen-footer that should break the reptile's vertebrae, killing it instantly before it could dive back into the lake. He did not miss, and radioed the zoological team who came rushing over, with scalpels and dissection equipment at the ready.

The day was hot and in no time the carcass began to rot, but undeterred by hordes of flies and the sun they carried on. Suddenly, the weather forecast became alarming. Early heavy rain was promised, and I knew there was at least one river that could flood and block our way home. 'We can't leave this precious specimen,' radioed the zoological director.

'Well, bring it as it is and you can finish the dissection in Addis Ababa,' I replied.

Placing the rather repellent load on the roof of the last three-ton army lorry in our convoy, we set out for the capital. By sheer luck we succeeded in crossing the rapidly rising rivers before they became impassable. We used the entire stock of formaldehyde from the Haile Selassie University to preserve the specimen that was skilfully boxed in a sealed tin coffin, sent overland to the coast with our army transport and carried by dhow to Aden. Flying ahead I found a helpful senior RAF officer who, without questioning us too closely, agreed to fly it to Britain on the first available freight plane.

Unfortunately, there were then delays and late one night back at Sandhurst I received a message from an irate RAF officer in Malta to say that a Hastings aircraft from Aden had been forced to land by the noxious fumes oozing from a leaking tin box that had been found to contain a very rotten crocodile. 'We are going to burn this bloody thing,' he cried down the phone.

Pointing out that the specimen was of national importance and that its transport back to the UK was a major priority that had the highest possible authority, I managed to persuade him to get the local Health and Hygiene section to re-preserve our croc, box it up and speed it home. On its arrival at RAF Lyneham, I received another call from yet another angry RAF officer. 'Get this health hazard out of here today or we shall destroy it!' he yelled.

So, setting off with a squad of guardsmen from the Sandhurst staff, we arrived at Lyneham to find the huge tin trunk sitting on a runway. The smell was indeed appalling but we'd provided some face cloths and aftershave for the men to use as they trucked the wretched specimen to South Kensington. It was lunchtime but the odour was so terrible that a zoologist was persuaded to meet us.

'Here is your Nile crocodile,' I gasped.

'Oh, thank you so much,' replied the scientist. 'Just pop it in the fumigator... and, by the way, this is the second one we've received this week!' It seemed that another expedition with the same request from the museum had got there before us. So we needn't really have gone to all that trouble!

It was years before I returned to southern Ethiopia and, thankfully, this time the only wildlife collection request was for some bats for the Harrison Zoological Museum. Nevertheless, we had our fair share of quite exciting encounters with the wildlife, including a twelve-foot python that slithered into the camp one night and ate a pen full of ducks.

There were quite a few other beasts around that needed to be treated with respect and sometimes took one by surprise. On one occasion, seeking a quiet spot in which to commune with nature, I found a clear path tunnelled through the reeds at the edge of Lake Abaya. Sitting quietly, with my trousers around my legs, trying to avoid the mosquitoes, I heard a great splash and suddenly found myself facing a four-ton hippo, in whose pathway I had inadvertently chosen to squat. I somehow managed to hurl myself out of the way as the great beast with gaping pink jaws and huge yellow fangs rushed at me, only to go lumbering past without taking much interest in the human being rolling around in a state of undress. Luckily, it seemed he was too eager to get to the grassland for his lunch to be bothered with me.

I am indebted to my scientific friend Malcolm Pearch for a colourful description of some of the highlights of the final part of the expedition, during which a collapsed bridge blocked our intended route south, forcing us to make a major diversion. He wrote:

'With the southern routes inaccessible, we headed north from Arba Minch, via Soddu and Shashatmene, to Dinsho and had several encounters with the rare Simien Fox and Mountain Nyala and, more frequently, the plethoric warthog. The village lies just outside the northern boundary of the Bale Mountains National Park and we were comfortably billeted for the next four days in a Swedish-built hunting lodge, which boasted its own sauna, the same being pressed into early service at the behest of the non-male members of the expedition, who comforted themselves with reciprocal preening and fussing at each day's end.

'Forays on both foot and horseback were instigated into the surrounding countryside, which harboured impressive volcanic peaks, deep wooded valleys, swiftly flowing rivulets and, it must be noted, a significant number of inevitably aqueous bogs. At dinner, those who were not preoccupied with the onset of trench-foot could be observed smiling bravely, while shifting gingerly on their chairs.

'After delivering books and stationery to the pupils of the local secondary school, the expedition mounted a motorised assault on the mighty Sanetti plateau, the route to which took us through the polychromatically painted town of Robe and the regional capital of Goba, the latter rather oddly and with no apparent necessity, availing itself of a dual carriageway.

'From Tullu Deemtu, Ethiopia's second highest peak at 14,365ft, we surveyed the lunar-like magnificence of the plateau's desolate landscape, which was punctuated at intervals by Giant Lobelia rising monolithically from the heather coated ground. The air was thin, and respiration required an increased effort, as did lighting a cigarette: smoking one took about a month.'

Returning to the capital we stopped at Wondo Genet and its eponymous hotel on the eastern escarpment of the Rift Valley. After the rigours of the expedition we were delighted to find the hotel's plumbing connected directly to a hot spring. Malcolm reported: 'The waters were diverted into manmade pools, in which we cavorted hedonistically, enjoying a degree of sensory pleasure. As we revelled in the pulchritude of our surroundings, a reflective silence descended, broken only by zoologist Paul Bates from the museum who enquired "Have you seen the monkeys?" adding: "Incredible blue testicles!"'

SES Ethiopian Wilderness Expedition 1997

CHAPTER 7
DESERT DISCOVERIES

As a Royal Engineer, an unexpected encounter with a small animal in the Libyan desert may well have saved my life. Checking a disused track for unexploded World War II mines, I decided to save time by sitting on the bonnet of my Land Rover, scanning the ground ahead intently while being driven forward at a snail's pace. 'If I shout, stop immediately,' I told my Sapper driver. For almost an hour I spotted nothing at all suspicious. Then my eye caught a slight movement right in front of the offside wheel. 'Stop!' I yelled, and the brakes were slammed on.

The baby tortoise retreated into his shell as I reached out to move him to safety, and it was only then that I noticed a set of three rusty prongs right beside the creature – and my heart missed a beat. 'Back off slowly and stay in your wheel tracks,' I ordered the mystified driver. I had instantly identified what was a German S-mine, designed to spring into the air before exploding and sending a deadly shower of ball bearings for a distance of up to a hundred feet. Slipping a safety pin into the mine's igniter to neutralise it, I popped the little tortoise into my pocket. Back at our base in Cyprus, I named him Churchill and planted a spinach patch for him and several others that we found.

I had another close shave at the end of a long-distance expedition deep into southern Libya. Eager to get back to the fleshpots of Benghazi, I asked my boss if I and two soldiers could go on ahead of the slow-moving main party in my Land Rover. We had radio contact and ample petrol and there was nothing much up ahead except the wide expanse of desert.

We were still 120 miles south of the coast when we suffered a puncture. As I jumped out and went to grab the jack and the spare wheel from the back of the Land Rover my driver gave me a dejected look and admitted very sheepishly: 'Sir, I lent my box spanner to Higgins back with the column last night and forgot to get it back.' Our desert vehicle's wheel had special hubs to which a rope could be fitted, for use as capstans, but a special box spanner was required to remove them. Try as we might, the wheel could not be changed without the spanner. Furthermore, the radio then refused to work. We were now truly stranded and in a bit of a fix. We only had four gallons of water between the three of us, the nearest well was a good seventy-five miles away and the convoy might easily miss us among the desert dunes and ridges. Walking out would not be an option.

Erecting a canvas awning to shelter us from the blistering sun, we lay there listening – first impatiently and then increasingly anxiously – for the sound of the convoy. Beads of sweat ran down our filthy skin and as the day wore on we became aware that we were giving off an odour that was far from fragrant. Night fell and there was still no sign of the convoy. Sleep was impossible, and a voice in my head kept saying: *There must be a way out.* Rather like shipwrecked sailors on a raft, I imagine, it's the waiting that is the worst.

I did eventually drift off, only to be awakened by a rattling metallic noise somewhere nearby. For a glorious moment I thought it must be the convoy, but when I jumped up and peered across the desert the noise ceased and I could see and hear nothing. *That's strange*, I thought. And then it started again, much nearer now. Drawing my Walther pistol I once again scanned the desert. At that point one of our discarded ration cans rolled into view, as if propelled by a strong wind, but the night was still. As I pondered this, it stopped and rolled back the way it had come. *I'm going mad*, I thought. Then it changed direction and came towards me. *My God, a haunted tin can.* When it was only a few paces away I raised my pistol and fired. The sharp crack rang out in the still air, waking up my companions, the bullet throwing up a spurt of sand an inch from the can, which instantly accelerated away. I fired again. The can stopped rolling and, to my amazement, a desert rat hopped out, clearly indignant at having his midnight feast disturbed.

At daylight the radio was still silent. However, just in case others might pick it up I sent out an SOS signal giving our position. By noon the temperature had again hit more than 38°C when we heard a distant rumble. 'That must be the convoy,' cried my driver, proceeding to fire a distress flare. As I had feared, the trucks were passing us on the other side of a ridge some distance away and for a moment I did think they might miss us until a Land Rover appeared out of the heat haze.

'Having a spot of bother, are we?' enquired our grinning rescuers. We had learned a lesson.

Years later, again in the far south of Libya, I had yet another lucky escape. Running the administration for an expedition, I quite regularly used to drive about 150 miles from our base to collect stores from Kufra oasis. It was an easy, fast run on a well-trodden trail and, equipped with a radio, I once again set out confidently in my Land Rover with a couple of colleagues.

As we sped along, we struck a few bumps, one of which caused our exhaust pipe to be deflected upwards so that it was pointing straight into our baggage panniers, soon setting alight a sleeping bag. 'Fire,' screamed my friend as, looking backwards, he saw smoke billowing from the pannier. The back of the car was packed with jerrycans full of petrol and it was a perilous moment. Driving into the wind I hoped to keep the flames away from the fuel, whilst my companions hurled the petrol cans into the desert.

We eventually stopped and managed to put out the fire, but the hour was late and it was already getting dark by then so we decided to camp in a nearby wadi while we recovered our senses. No-one felt hungry, but we munched on an army biscuit and some raspberry jam, washed down with a mug of coffee. The night was clear and before turning in I went out armed with a shovel to commune with nature. Squatting beneath the stars I could have sworn that I twice heard a voice calling me. The first time, I looked back towards the dull black outline of the Land Rover. The second time, I shouted, 'Just a minute', because I thought my friends had called out to me. Returning to the car, I asked: 'What's the matter?'

My two colleagues both looked up, puzzled, and replied: 'Nothing. Why?'

'Didn't you call?' I said.

'No,' they replied.

'Funny.' I shrugged, yawning. 'It must have been the wind.' Then, exhausted, I fell asleep.

I woke, just after dawn, with a shiver and a bursting bladder. Standing up, I shook off the sand, rubbed my eyes and stretched my stiff limbs in the half-light. I was still only partly awake when I caught sight of something odd that none of us had noticed in the darkness the night before. Sixty yards away was the wreckage of a truck. Around it were scattered items of equipment, weapon parts and ammunition. I recognised it as one of the legendary Long Range Desert Group (LRDG) Chevrolets from 1941. Similar wrecks lay nearby and, combing the area, we found two graves with wooden crosses. High amongst the rocks was a faded canvas British Army haversack, containing the rusty fragments of a Kodak folding camera and a toothbrush. Nearby was scattered a pile of empty .303 cartridge cases.

I then remembered reading that it was in this area that the LRDG's T Patrol had been destroyed by a force from its Italian opposite number, the Auto-Saharan Company, based at Kufra. History records that a running fight developed on 31st January 1941, when the Italians, with a heavily armed motorised patrol and three aircraft, caught T Patrol advancing on Kufra, in the valley of the Jebel Sherif.

Following the battle a New Zealander, Trooper R. J. Moore, and three colleagues remained undetected amongst the rocks of the arid hills. Almost everything they needed for survival had been destroyed along with their vehicle, three of them were wounded and, as all the wells within 200 miles were either in enemy hands or filled with rocks to prevent access, the situation seemed hopeless. However, they somehow managed to salvage a two-gallon tin of water and, scorning any idea of walking a few miles north-east to surrender to the Italians at Kufra, they buried the dead then turned and marched south towards their allies. The Free French Army's positions were known to be several hundred miles away across almost waterless desert.

The story of their remarkable and heroic escape over an astonishing distance is a worthy tribute to soldiers of one of the finest Special Forces units ever raised. Three of the men survived and, along with their leader, Trooper Moore, were found by the French 210 miles from Jebel Sherif, still walking steadily after ten days. Moore was awarded the Distinguished Conduct Medal for his leadership and courage.

We tidied up the graves, re-erected the crosses, stood silent for a moment and saluted, before then taking our leave and driving off towards Kufra. I reported the matter to the headquarters in Benghazi and a detachment from the Commonwealth War Graves Commission visited the site. And I was left to reflect on the origin of the mysterious voice that I firmly believed I'd heard calling out to me while I was squatting nearby in the sand that night.

Even before I read Wilbur Smith's novel *The Sunbird* I had always been fascinated by the Kalahari, that great arid wilderness in Botswana, the very name of which is so evocative. During Operation Raleigh in 1990 we organised an expedition for the over-twenty-fives, or 'the wrinklies' as the younger Operation Drake explorers called them. We recruited directors, managers and executives for a venture aimed at developing teamwork, decision-making, problem-solving and creative thinking, as well as promoting individual self-confidence in those taking part. Wilbur Smith was said to have been inspired to write his novel about the Phoenicians, their inland seas and ancient cities, following a visit to Kubu Island and the Makgadikgadi Pan. There were also stories of a lost city allegedly found by one

William Leonard Hunt in the 1880s, but never seen again. Talking with Mike Main, an acknowledged expert on the Kalahari, I learned that there could well be some undiscovered ruins. The expedition persuaded several leading Southern African archaeologists to join us, along with Philip Welch, an enthusiastic adventurer from

Johannesburg. Helpfully, Philip brought his microlight with him, while Mike Main hired a fleet of four-wheel drives.

Our first site was at Kuba, on the southern side of the Makgadikgadi Pan, once a great lake but now a flat, featureless area of hard, salt-saturated clay. Kuba, a plateau like a rocky island that rose about fifty feet above the pan, was dotted with huge, grotesque, stunted baobab trees. A large semicircular stone-walled enclosure, built sometime between 1,000 and 1,700 years ago by the kings of Great Zimbabwe, was flanked by around 200 cairns, thought to be linked to boys' initiation rites. The site was well known but, conversing with local bushmen, Mike learned of other walls to the north-west, at a place they called Thitaba.

We knew that aircraft searching for evidence of archaeological sites, flying in the middle of the day when the sun was overhead, had seen nothing. 'If I'm airborne at dawn or dusk I may be able to see telltale shadows not visible when the sun is directly overhead,' suggested Phil. So, with archaeologist Alec Campbell hanging on to his back, Phil set off as the sun was rising over the glaring white pans. Shivering in the early morning air, we watched him winging westward. He was out of sight when I got a radio call from him, reporting excitedly: 'There's definitely another large walled area at the edge of the pan.'

We had loaded the cars and were ready to move before Phil returned and, pausing only to hear Alec's full report, we set off like a pack of hounds. After seventeen miles across the pan we reached Thitaba. And there, indeed, we found an enclosure, around sixteen acres in size, with walls of calcrete stone up to around five feet wide and four feet high, sloping down to the edge of the pan. Within the walls were sets of building foundations and, at the pan, platforms of stone looking to my inexpert eye like piers jutting out into a lake. Pottery shards, eggshell beads, late Stone Age tools and flakes littered the ground. Most importantly, we also found a cowrie shell. Often used as a currency, this would have come from the Indian Ocean. The archaeologists were overjoyed, and reckoned it to be part of the Great Zimbabwe state of the 17th century, although they did not think this was the legendary lost city.

After a little celebration we went game-viewing by canoe through the Okavango Delta's thick stands of papyrus and phoenix palms. To sustain us, one of our team, a manager with Guinness, had arranged a supply of six-packs. To keep them cool we sank some of them in a shallow pool to be collected and enjoyed on our way home. Alas, on return they had disappeared, but later in a bar at Maun we overheard two very happy Australians exclaiming to fellow drinkers: 'Unbelievable! We hadn't had a beer for days and suddenly, right there in the water beside the boat, was a pack of Guinness! Bloody amazing!'

CHAPTER 8
THE MIGHTY CONGO

Seeking to discover the source of the Nile, Henry Morton Stanley set out from Zanzibar in November 1874 with three Europeans and 356 Africans. After an incredible journey by land and river spanning 999 days following his famous meeting with Dr David Livingstone in 1871, Stanley had crossed Africa, coast to coast, finally emerging with only 115 survivors. The vast central African territory – originally known as the Congo after its indigenous Bantu tribesmen, the Kongo – became the Belgian Congo after Stanley was persuaded to claim it on behalf of King Leopold II of Belgium. Having gained independence from Belgium in 1960, it was renamed the Republic of the Congo after the mighty river that runs through. In 1971 President Mobutu renamed it the Republic of Zaire and in 1997 it became the Democratic Republic of the Congo following Mobutu's downfall. It was in 1970, at the suggestion of historian Richard Snailham, that the Scientific Exploration Society (SES) started work on a proposal to navigate the Zaire River, which, rather confusingly, has since been renamed the Congo River. The plan was to use this ferocious waterway as a route through the Congo Basin, so that scientific teams

could explore the still little-known interior and commemorate the centenary of Stanley's epic journey.

After intense preparation the team finally flew into Lubumbashi in President Mobutu's DC-10 in October 1974. There were 165 of us altogether, including fifty medics, scientists and administrators, and although the majority came from Britain there were also members from the United States, Canada, New Zealand, Australia, Denmark, France, Holland, Nepal and Fiji, as well as twenty soldiers and scientists from Zaire itself.

A key person in the team was my PA, Pam Baker[2], daughter of the British chargé d'affaires in Kinshasa. An intuitive and warm-hearted lady, she had been the personal nurse to President Mobutu and gained his valuable support.

Now fully supported by the Zaire government with the President himself as our patron, we were also backed by the British and US armies, the Explorers Club and over 300 sponsors, including the *Daily Telegraph* and Anglia Television. Although born in Wales, Henry Morton Stanley had become an American citizen by the time of his legendary expedition and we thus received the enthusiastic support of His Excellency Walter Annenberg, the US ambassador in London, keen to foster Anglo-American co-operation.

In pioneering white-water rafting on the first descent of the Blue Nile in 1968 we had used Avon boats and we again turned to the Llanelli-based company for the new venture. However, the design of the giant inflatable craft needed to navigate the enormous rapids found on the Zaire River was specially developed, modified and tested on the Colorado River by rafting experts Ron Smith and

2. Later Lady Coleridge

his brother, Marc. In England, Royal Engineers fitted two Mercury 40hp outboard engines to provide power for these bulbous thirty-seven-foot vessels, one mounted amidships to give forward thrust and another fitted astern for steering. Smaller Avon inflatables were used by our scientists to explore the upper reaches of the river, where they survived some challenging rapids, only to have one boat destroyed by an angry hippopotamus. We were also fortunate to have a British Army Air Corps Beaver aircraft for vital air recces and parachute resupply.

The giant inflatables were launched at Bukama, from where they faced a journey through a wide, treeless morass. Royal Engineers went ahead in small boats, using explosives to clear blockages formed by islands of weeds and marking the best passage. Our first real test came at rapids known as the Gates of Hell which, despite this forbidding name, proved to be relatively easy. Meanwhile, the scientific teams working on and around the river used the expedition fleet as an umbilical cord.

Fearing that we might be attacked by anti-government rebels along the way, the Zaire Army issued us with an impressive array of small arms. However, as most people were now friendly there was fortunately no call to use them. After 200 miles of relatively peaceful cruising we reached the Stanley Falls, a series of seven dangerous cataracts concentrated in a fifty-mile stretch of the river, where we almost lost several craft. Nevertheless, by early December we had made it, relatively unscathed, to Kisangani, second city of Zaire and the halfway mark for our expedition.

While the boat party was our spearhead, many members had the less glamorous but nevertheless challenging and vital task of supporting the fleet with fuel, food and supplies at prearranged points in the tropical forest. They moved by Land Rover and even, at one point, a hired train. These support groups also looked after the scientific teams that were variously studying the botany, biology, entomology, geology and zoology of the region. The botanists were particularly interested in the water hyacinths, an attractive little plant that unfortunately blocks up the waterways of Africa.

Elsewhere, right in the centre of this vast country, our nineteen-strong multi-national team of eye specialists was busy studying anomalies in the distribution of river blindness, a disease affecting some 20 million Africans, of whom 2 million had gone blind.

At the same time, also deep in the tropical rainforest, zoologists sought the elusive otter shrew and the scaly pangolin. One group, studying primates under the leadership of Jeremy Mallinson of Jersey Zoo, had a memorable encounter with mountain gorillas. A huge male charged within six feet of the group, but luckily it turned out that he was really only bluffing, putting on a bit of a show for appearances!

Working with the tiny Aka people in eastern Zaire, we came across the strange okapi, or forest giraffe, and also had close encounters with aggressive forest elephants. However, there was one creature that proved particularly elusive. This was the rare bonobo, known at that time as the pygmy chimpanzee, that our zoological team was especially keen to locate. Our zoologist and some stalwart Royal Marines were duly dispatched to find the creature. As they penetrated deeper and deeper into the forest, their radio messages grew fainter, mostly reporting difficulties in moving through the dense undergrowth, with no sign of the bonobo.

Our fleet of giant inflatable boats was moored at a riverside town whilst the scientific work was in progress, and I was approached by two local ladies, whose knowledge of the English language was apparently limited to the words 'Buckingham Palace', which they kept repeating, whilst simultaneously beaming and nodding. Through my able assistant, Pam Baker, who fortunately spoke Lingala, I learned that one of the ladies had been a lady-in-waiting to Madame Mobutu, wife of the President, and in that capacity, she had indeed been to Buckingham Palace on one occasion. And she was now inviting us to dinner.

Dressing as smartly as we could, three of us duly went along and were met by several ladies attired in dresses bearing the upside-down face of the President. The bungalow into which we were welcomed had clearly been abandoned by Belgian colonists and still housed a large jukebox, which rendered a series of ear-splitting tunes in various languages. Copious glasses of palm wine were dished out and eventually a dinner of roast bushmeat was served. There was no indication of the type of animal that had been cooked, but with the addition of some strong curry powder it was reasonably edible.

Conversation with the ladies was somewhat limited, but the palm wine, along with some whisky that we provided, enabled us to toast Queen Elizabeth and President Mobutu.

After the remains of a sticky cake dessert had been cleared away, the evening was drawing to a close when, to my surprise, I felt a hand on my leg. With rising alarm, I couldn't help noticing as I glanced around that all those sitting on either side of me and on the opposite side of the table had both hands in full view. Then, to make matters worse, the mysterious fingers began to move up inside my trousers. When they reached my knee I decided that they had gone far enough and, bending down, reached under the table and seized the offending hand, heaving out what was then revealed to be a small monkey. 'Oh! You have found Sophie,' cried our hostess.

'It looks to me like a young chimpanzee,' I said, as it sat contentedly on my lap.

'Oh no,' I was told. 'Sophie is very old.' To our amazement we had at last found a bonobo!

Returning the next day after their arduous and fruitless quest, our intrepid search party took a while to see the funny side of this rather extraordinary coincidence. We never found another bonobo.

On the fleet the pets multiplied. Ken Mason, the expedition's leading humourist and an ace photographer from the *Daily Telegraph*, had bought for Pam a small grey furry bushbaby named Tiddlypush. Being nocturnal it was a useless pet, for when, in daylight hours, we wished to play with it, the creature was sound asleep up a tree. At night when we were trying to rest, the wretched beast was bounding about and usually tried to get into one's sleeping bag and do something unspeakable. Thus, to remove Tiddlypush from harm's way, Pam kept it inside her shirt. One day when she was interpreting a rather truculent chieftain, to my amazement the man's eyes suddenly came out on organ stops! The reason was simple: Pam's bosom was heaving up and down in a most remarkable fashion and then, suddenly, the goggle-eyed creature emerged from her neckline. The chief fled and we had no more trouble.

From Kisangani the river is easily navigable for almost 1,000 miles and our flotilla motored along at a steady fifty miles a day, crossing the Equator twice, celebrated on each occasion with traditional ceremony. As expected there had been casualties, especially from a particularly virulent form of malaria, several of our team becoming seriously ill. One soldier fell eighty-five feet from a jungle tree while fixing insect traps for the entomologists, and miraculously only suffered a minor brain haemorrhage. And Blue Nile veteran Roger Chapman was struck down with a liver abscess, his life saved as a result of prompt on-the-spot emergency treatment by our medics. A freight plane evacuated him for further intensive care by Mobutu's American doctor, Bill Close, father of actress Glenn, in Kinshasa.

At Christmas we regrouped in the capital. The expedition was now spread out over 1,000 miles and radio communication was unreliable. Political difficulties were a constant worry and our Beaver pilot had spotted jungle camps of foreign soldiers. Interestingly, we often picked up Chinese radio transmissions! However, after generous entertainment by the British Embassy and the local expats we manned the boats in good spirits for the final stretch.

A large multi-national crowd gathered on the riverbank to watch our passage of Kinsuka, the first of thirty-two previously unnavigated cataracts of the Livingstone Falls that cover some 200 miles between Kinshasa and the Atlantic. Thanks to a request from the Duke of Edinburgh, New Zealander Sir William Hamilton had sent two of his 220hp waterjet boats to assist us and they arrived just in time as we faced this challenging stretch of water. Stanley had stated: 'There is no fear that any other explorer will attempt what we have done in the cataract region. It would be insanity in a successor.' I was now about to discover if he was right!

At 11:00 hours our flagship *La Vision* passed easily through the narrows, where the river had now been constricted from something like nine miles wide to just one mile across. Running down a smooth tongue of water, the giant inflatables skirted the line of tossing twenty-foot waves that rose and fell in the centre of the river. Acting as rescue boats, the waterjet craft lay in the lee of weed-covered boulders. Anglia TV's *Survival* team and their cameras had been positioned to get the best possible shot of the drama, which they did when the *David Gestetner* appeared with her white ensign fluttering.

As the boat crossed the first fall, her stern engine struck a submerged rock that hurled it upwards off its wooden transom. The whirring propeller sliced through the neoprene fabric of the stern compartment, which then immediately deflated. Aboard the rescue boat, we could see with mounting concern that the great raft was being swept out of control into the angry, towering waves that we knew must be avoided at all costs. In an instant, jetboat pilot Jon Hamilton opened the throttle and drove the eighteen-foot craft straight into the pounding mounds of coffee-coloured water.

My second-in-command, rugged Royal Marine Mike Gambier, was in the water, his white crash helmet and red life jacket showing clearly as he bobbed amongst the flying spray. Our sister jet, driven by American Ralph Brown, was already making for him with a scramble net ready to pull him in. The deafening roar of raging water and jet engines combined to drown out all commands: everyone was acting instinctively now. *David Gestetner's* skipper was trying to pass us a line, his face contorted as he yelled against the din.

Suddenly I heard *Telegraph* photographer Ken Mason yell: 'Watch out!' I glanced up and saw that an enormous wave had flung the crippled *Gestetner* forward and upward, straight towards us. For a moment she towered above us, surfing a tumbling wall of white water, before crashing down right across us. Above me, the whirling propeller smashed off our windscreen and radio aerials.

For a few seconds we were locked together in the tempest, but Jon opened the throttle and we managed to break free. Circling our quarry, we seized a line and towed her, like a stricken whale, towards a mid-river island for repairs; we were probably the first men ever to land here.

On reaching the notorious Isangila rapids, which had finally forced Stanley to abandon his boats and leave the river, I decided to portage the giant rafts a short distance and avoid a suicidal stretch. So while we hauled them overland the smaller boats continued down the calmer side of the river.

In the final rapid, '*La Vision*', our flagship, was momentarily trapped in a whirlpool, like a cork in a washtub, and was bent downwards, spinning around and around with motors screaming. Following us, Alun Davies's Avon recce boat was capsized by a fifteen-foot wave. The upturned craft, with its crew of three clinging to it for dear life, was swept towards a yawning whirlpool. The jetboats at this point had returned to Kinshasa and, 1,000 yards downriver, I couldn't see what had happened. However, Royal Marine Neil Rickards, helmsman of the following boat, saw the accident and took his craft through the mountains of tossing water, right into the whirlpool, circling around inside it, like a motorcyclist on the Wall of Death at a fairground. In the centre of this swirling mass he could see Alun's capsized Avon with its crew still clinging frantically to the lifeline. Eventually, by going the same way that the water was revolving, Neil got alongside the stricken boat and pulled the crew to safety. Then he circled up and out of the whirlpool. Emerging, they looked back to see the upturned craft disappear into the vortex. Downriver, I was surprised a few moments later when it bobbed up beside us. The engine had gone, the floorboards were wrecked and for an awful moment or two we feared that we must have lost at least some of the crew. But all had been saved thanks to Neil's courage and skill, for which he was later awarded the Queen's Gallantry Medal.

From there on it was plain sailing to the ocean and the Thanksgiving service. Back in Kinshasa we were received by President Mobutu and HM the Queen graciously sent her congratulations.

The result of the medical work we had been able to carry out had certainly aided the treatment of river blindness and the scientific research was a clear success. All this had been achieved by a combination of careful planning, good equipment and teamwork. On a large-scale scientific expedition it is never just a question of getting one man on top of a mountain; the whole team must get through and, amazingly, in this instance, it did. Our experience only served to further endorse my great respect for Stanley, who, without the benefits of 20th-century technology, had somehow managed to reach the ocean, proving that the Congo was much more than just a tributary of the Nile, as had been previously thought.

Thirty-two years later whilst leading a party for my son-in-law's, Julian Matthews, travel company I stood on the northern bank of the mighty river at Brazzaville, watching the towering waves roaring over the Kinsuka rapids. 'Madness,' I muttered, setting out to seek lowland gorilla and a smaller, round-eared subspecies of forest elephant. Our group of two Americans, two Austrians and two Britons were enthusiastic wildlife watchers, eager to get to Nouabalé-Ndoki National Park. By plane, 4WD vehicles and local canoes known as a pirogues we passed over and through dense equatorial forest, bisected by sinuous coffee-coloured rivers and a few rough tracks. At the village of Mbele we found a lodge of wooden huts on stilts and, feeling the heat and humidity, made camp.

The next morning, after marching for nearly an hour along a jungle trail, we reached a large swampy *bai*, or clearing, of about

37 acres, noted for its crop of aquatic plants, much loved by the species that we sought. As we climbed up on to an observation platform an extraordinary sight greeted us. Two hundred yards away the rounded back of a headless animal was moving slowly in a deep pool. 'The Loch Ness Monster!' I gasped. But then, with a splash, the forest elephant raised its head and trunk above the surface.

Then, like actors entering a stage, eleven gorillas, including both young and mature, emerged from the forest as the sun rose to feed and play. It was delightful to observe the almost human behaviour as a huge grandfather among the troupe was plagued by his grandchildren, brushing them gently aside when they became too obstreperous. But my best encounter came later, back in camp.

Taking an afternoon snooze on the veranda of my hut, I became aware of the sharp cracks of breaking branches and the swish of leaves that could only be made by a large animal on the move. As the telltale sounds came closer I froze, cursing the fact that my camera was out of easy reach a few feet away. Then the leaves moved, barely thirty feet away and, without a care in the world, a massive silverback gorilla moved slowly down a tree trunk, clutching a fistful of vegetation. By the calls they were making it seemed that his family was nearby. As I tried to reach my Nikon camera, he saw me and gave a couple of sharp barks. Our eyes met and he paused, facing me with his shiny black hairless face, broad flat nose and extended nostrils. His marble eyes did not blink. What was he thinking, I wondered. He seemed more curious than hostile; then, still gazing at me, he dropped lightly on to the ground and, turning away, strode off on all fours, past the huts as if to say: 'This is *my* domain, and you are only here as a guest.'

The Great Zaire River Expedition

AMERICAS

CHAPTER 9
DARIÉN CONQUEST

Back in 1970, meals in the Ministry of Defence canteen were no great gastronomic delight, so when I was invited out to lunch by a gentleman from Canning House, an Anglo-Hispanic organisation, I accepted gladly. Julian du Parc Braham, a retired colonel wearing a purple bowler hat and sporting a monocle, greeted me at the restaurant and once we were seated at our table, came straight to the point. 'What do you know of the Darién Gap?' he asked as he filled my wine glass.

'Nothing,' I admitted, whereupon he proceeded to describe the inhospitable and almost impenetrable area of dense jungle, hill and swamp that lay between Panama and Colombia, forming an obstruction that was blocking completion of the 17,000-mile Pan-American Highway between Alaska in the far north of America and Tierra del Fuego, on the southern tip of South America.

I learned that it was in Darién that Balboa, the Spanish conquistador, had stood on a peak and caught his first glimpse of the Pacific in 1513. My host then went on to explain: 'Until the Pan-American Highway crosses the Gap there will be no uninterrupted road connection between the continents of North and South America, and the Latin American nations are now stepping up their campaign to persuade the US government to fund the construction of this vital missing link.' He added that several costly expeditions had already failed to blaze a trail right across the Gap, which includes the vast Atrato Swamp, and that this had not helped the case.

Having outlined what sounded like *Mission Impossible*, the Colonel paused momentarily before revealing what all this was leading up to. 'You're a Sapper with a reputation for overcoming obstacles,' he said challengingly. 'Can you do it?'

Never having been to South America, I asked for time to consider and went off to consult the army's Engineer-in-Chief, Major General Griff Caldwell, formerly of the SAS. He was immediately enthusiastic about the idea. 'Of course we must do it,' he insisted. 'It will be jolly good for international relations and excellent experience for the troops.'

And so it was that, with backing promised by the British, Colombian, Panamanian and US armed forces, our team set about planning the assault on '*El Tapon*', or 'The Stopper', as the Darién Gap was known on account of its reputation for impenetrability. Clearly, it would not be a picnic! Apart from exploring a possible route through it, we were also required to conduct a scientific programme, with scientists from the four countries researching the botany, biology, geology, geography, entomology and zoology of the region. Medical and veterinary subjects as well as the protection of the local indigenous people were also to be studied.

Over the next six months we recruited fifty-nine men and five women from Britain and the USA, plus forty Panamanian Guardia

Nacional, along with thirty very tough Colombian servicemen. I was fortunate to find a skilful logistician, Major Kelvin Kent, to act as my deputy, as well as several experienced field engineers and other members of the 1968 Blue Nile expedition. Rosemary, or 'Rosh', Allhusen, a very able young lady and experienced horsewoman, became my PA.

Tim Nicholson, secretary of the newly established British Trans-Americas Expedition committee, and the team worked non-stop to gather sponsors for fuel, rations and equipment from a host of generous companies. The Royal Automobile Club, the *Daily Telegraph* and the Scientific Exploration Society gave their support and Zenith Watches produced some rugged automatic watches.

In spite of all the support there were still funds to be raised and, as always, we needed some robust 4WD vehicles. Rover had just produced a new model intended to be a world-beater and agreed to lend us a couple of them. Thus in December 1971 two brand new Range Rovers were flown to Alaska by the RAF, along with a crew from the 17th/21st Lancers, under the leadership of Gavin Thompson, who then started the long drive south. There was an early setback when a 200-yard skid on the frozen ALCAN Highway led to a collision with a huge truck but rapid repairs soon got everybody back on track. Driving down the length of the United States and then on through desert and rutted tracks in Central America, they had already covered 5,000 miles by the time they met up with our main force in Panama City in January 1972.

The wet season here usually ends in mid-December, leaving about three relatively dry months in which to cross the Gap before the heavy rains return. Unfortunately, rain was still falling steadily in mid-January and as a result we set out through a sea of mud. During an air reconnaissance flight in an Army Air Corps Beaver provided by the Ministry of Defence, I got my first view of Darién, one of the most difficult and dangerous wildernesses in the world.

The sun glistened on the thick brown coil of the Bayano River, making it look like a giant snake. The altimeter read 400 feet, and yet it seemed as if we were almost brushing the tops of the tallest trees as we flew on. I looked again at the green carpet around their base. What we were seeing was merely the treetops: the real problem lay below. The thick undergrowth, looking like shrubbery, was in fact the canopy of lesser trees. The river alone provided the only break in the green mass that stretched as far as the eye could see in any direction. Making a tight turn for a photographic run, I found myself clutching the Polaroid camera to avoid it being sucked out of the open window. Our eyes searched in vain for any sign of a track. There was nothing to be seen.

One of our first priorities was to discover the best place at which to cross the river, so we circled until our fuel was almost exhausted. Several points looked possible, but all would require rafting – and the current was strong. Then suddenly we spotted what appeared to be a narrow muddy trail leading to the river; this looked like being the best way in.

I could not imagine how Balboa, in his full suit of armour, had staggered through this green hell to stand upon a peak from which he became the first European to gaze upon what would come to be named the Pacific Ocean. At the same time, I could more easily understand how Sir Francis Drake's lightly clad raiders had managed to cross the jungle to attack the Spanish treasure-laden mule trains, enriching the coffers of a grateful Queen Elizabeth I.

On 17th January our ground reconnaissance team under former Blue Nile expeditioner, David Bromhead, moved into the Gap, with the Beaver directing them by radio from above. Meanwhile, in the sprawling town of Cañita, the main body began to assemble. In addition to our vehicles we had acquired twenty-eight packhorses to help carry stores and equipment. It was still raining when, two days later on 19th January, we loaded up the horses, getting drenched in the process, and prepared to set off. We couldn't afford to wait any longer as even three months was little enough time to cross this formidable terrain.

For the first three days we marched in terrible conditions, through the heat and mud of the open pastureland. At night we camped with our hammocks slung between the trees, cooking our meals on damp-wood fires.

The Bayano was no mean obstacle, 150 yards wide and flowing at over four knots, but in three hours our Royal Engineers, under the command of my old friends Jim Masters and Ernie Durey, had used a unique Avon inflatable raft, transported in the Range Rovers, to get our vehicles and equipment safely to the other side. Men and horses had to swim! Ahead lay the darkening jungle of the Bayano valley.

Each day we marched further into the forest, moving in a long, straggling column. The vehicles followed as best they could. Our prison – for that is what it seemed like – was illuminated by a dull green light, at times giving an almost translucent appearance to this eerie world. Trees rose like pillars reaching for the sun that beat down on the canopy 150 feet above. Lianas and vines hung in a tangled mass to catch projecting pack-loads and to trip the unwary. The ground was carpeted in a mat of leaves and from a layer of humus beneath it grew thick underbrush. Visibility was rarely more than one hundred feet and all the time the jungle resounded to the constant drip of humid condensation, punctuated by the occasional crash of some giant tree falling at the end of its life.

The rain, whenever it came, was torrential, quickly turning the track into a quagmire, while fast-flowing streams, patches of poisonous palms and stinging plants added further elements of difficulty and discomfort as we pushed on through the dense jungle, our progress slowed not only by the glutinous mud but also by regularly having to negotiate potentially hazardous ravines and gullies. The heat and humidity were oppressive and even the nights brought little relief. Our sweat-soaked clothes started to rot on us, leather equipment growing mould and even our US Army jungle boots beginning to fall apart.

On top of that, the mosquitoes, gnats and flies were a constant plague, along with inch-long black ants whose bite stung for hours, stinging caterpillars and, in the rivers, electric eels capable of delivering a 500-volt shock. Centipedes an inch wide and black scorpions also took their toll, while spiders the size of dinner plates were certainly fearsome to behold. In brushing against the foliage we constantly picked up ticks that, almost unnoticed, buried their teeth into our flesh with such tenacity that they often had to be removed by the medical officer. Clusters of aggressive and vindictive hornets nested in hollow trees and swarmed out to meet anyone who disturbed them. Rosh Allhusen collapsed following a severe allergic reaction to a hornet bite. Swift action by our vet, Keith Morgan-Jones, saved her, but she had to be evacuated to Colombia.

The larger animals we encountered were rarely dangerous, although early one morning I did come face to face with a beautiful black jaguar on a jungle track. He eyed me for a moment and then, much to my relief, simply strolled away. There were also other, smaller cats such as ocelot and margay and some surprisingly large deer. The white-lipped peccary, a small wild pig, was a different matter altogether. Unlike his timid cousin, the white-collared peccary, this aggressive hog is to be avoided whenever possible. At night, in the impenetrable darkness, only the clacking of their tusks warned of their approach. A machine gun would have had little effect on the concentrated rush of these ugly-tempered creatures, and on one occasion they completely wrecked a camp, scattering our terrified packhorses into the jungle. Our night sentry only escaped by hurling a small can of petrol on to the fire, causing an explosive distraction that effectively scared them off.

At one point, while wading ankle-deep in glutinous slime, I stumbled and fell. Flat on my face in the mud, I felt an intense but momentary pain as my packhorse, Cromwell, trod on top of me, pushing me deeper into the black paste. As I struggled to breathe and extract myself, a strong smell of whisky helped to revive me – Cromwell's hoof had come down on my backpack with such force that it had punctured the flask that was in one of the pockets. The great bay horse looked down at me and I'll swear he laughed.

As it happened, being run over by your own horse in this way was a not uncommon occurrence. The problem was that if your feet suddenly got stuck in the mud and you lost your footing while leading a packhorse across a ravine, the heavily laden beast behind you would be unable to stop and would have no option but to trample right over you. As I hauled myself to my feet, bruised and covered in mud, the last drops of my prized Johnnie Walker Black Label seeping out of my pack, I found myself beginning to hate the

Darién Gap with a loathing that one might have for a cruel enemy in wartime. At the same time, I couldn't help but respect it.

The horses suffered terribly from the vampire bats that attacked them at night, biting their necks and injecting an anticoagulant to make the blood easier to drink. Their whinnying screams often kept us awake and they grew weak through loss of blood. Then 'Scouse' Yeun, a Chinese-Liverpudlian lance corporal in the Royal Engineers, came up with a cunning plan. Cutting up a pink parachute, he made a protective nightshirt for one particularly badly bitten creature. Eye and nostril holes were cut and the horse hobbled for the night. 'Well done, Scouse,' we said, congratulating him as we settled down to enjoy what duly turned out to be an undisturbed night – only to discover at dawn the next morning that the horse had completely disappeared. Going in search of it further along the trail, we came upon some very excited Chocó people who explained that the previous night the women of their village had been performing traditional fertility rites when, at the height of the ceremony, with dancing girls whirling faster and faster, a pink apparition had suddenly appeared in their midst, ruining everything. The village elders had at first taken it to be a sign sent by their ancestors to rebuke them for evil and licentious living. They were not best pleased when it turned out to be just our horse in fancy dress, so by way of compensation I allowed them to keep it.

Initially, we moved as a complete body, spearheaded by the leading reconnaissance team working between five and ten miles ahead, followed a couple of miles behind by another small group whose job was to mark the trail. Next came the first engineer section under the tireless Ernie Durey, using machetes and power saws to cut a track ten feet wide. Ravines were bridged with special aluminium ladders, two of which were carried on each Range Rover. These could be linked and used for both bridging and rafting. The second engineer team pushed jacks, blocks and tackle and the capstans fitted to the Range Rovers to the absolute limit of their capacity in dragging the heavy vehicles up some of the steeper slopes.

The animal transport and expedition headquarters brought up the rear of the column, with rations, petrol, radios and medical supplies making up the bulk of the packhorse loads. Meanwhile, the scientists roamed about the periphery of the expedition area, occasionally rejoining the column before once again disappearing into the jungle to observe and gather specimens of the indigenous flora and fauna. At the same time, Robin Hanbury-Tenison, chairman of Survival International, visited small communities along the way to check on the welfare of the local Chocó and Kuna people.

As the rain eventually began to ease and the delayed dry season finally started, we found ourselves facing another unexpected setback when the Range Rovers, with their immense power, developed differential trouble. Some actually exploded, with fragments piercing the floor of the vehicles like shrapnel. A specialist Rover engineer, Geoff Miller, flew over from the UK with some specially made parts and was helicoptered into the jungle, working for weeks to get the cars rolling forward again.

In the meantime, in order to maintain momentum, we bought an old Land Rover in Panama City, stripped it down to the bare essentials and arranged for a US 'Jolly Green Giant' chopper to fly it into the jungle to carry our engineering stores forward. Named *The Pathfinder*, it soon proved its worth.

The climate and pace were gradually beginning to tell. During the expedition more than thirty sick members had to be evacuated at various times and so, finding ourselves short of manpower, we employed local people armed with machetes to open up a pilot track.

In exchange for six bottles of whisky, the Panamanian jailers at El Real handed over twelve convicted smugglers to us, on condition that we only released them when we got to Colombia, happy to be rid of them. One of them turned out to be a girl and one of the ladies in our horse team had to take her aside to convince her that we had other women with us and that she would not be molested. Further reinforcement arrived in the form of a friendly American hobo who, seeking to leave the USA where he had some tax problems, had wandered south. Hearing that the British were building a three-lane highway he had joined us! Fortunately, he spoke the local language and when starving was taken in by the Chocó people. Kindly villagers told him the 'Locos-Englis' had a direct link to their God and gathering around an altar would pray. Very soon a great bird would appear and drop firewater and food to them. A nice description of our making a radio call for a parachute supply drop.

Kelvin Kent, my energetic deputy, organised supplies to be brought in by boat, helicopter, parachute, pack ponies and porters, including ten tons of rations, 5,000 gallons of Ultramar petrol, 2,400 cans of beer and 80,000 cigarettes (smoking was much more prevalent then), plus sacks of horse fodder and mail.

To help the army pilots find us, flares and bright orange gas-filled balloons were launched on the end of a line and sent bobbing up above the tree canopy. Even so, searching for a small party deep in the jungle took much skill.

By this time there had already been several close encounters with various serpents. While I was holding our ornithologist on my shoulders so that he could feel inside a bird's nest, a venomous coral snake slid along his arm and into his shirt. Luckily, this was not tucked in and the reptile dropped out, past me, on to the ground. On another occasion a six-foot bushmaster sank its teeth into the rubber heel of David Bromhead's boot. Its fangs stuck fast and, as it writhed, David blew its head off with his Smith & Wesson. Later, nearer the frontier, Limbu, a Gurkha sergeant, was even more fortunate to escape unscathed when a huge bushmaster reared up behind him. It struck twice, but each time the Gurkha happened to take a pace forward for his next swing at the vegetation and the snake missed. Behind Limbu came Ruby, a Colombian prisoner. He spoke no English and no Gurkhali, and as Limbu spoke no Spanish his timely warning went unheeded. However, he raced up, pinning the reptile down with a forked branch, whereupon Limbu spun round and beheaded it with one swipe of his razor-sharp kukri.

Skilful night flying by an USAF helicopter, answering an SOS call from a remote Kuna village on the Colombian border, saved one young soldier's life. He had developed acute appendicitis, initially undetected because penicillin taken for an injury had masked the underlying illness.

One evening our radio picked up the tragic news that five Colombian Marines coming to assist us had drowned when their boat capsized in heavy seas off Turbo. By some miracle, our liaison officer, Jeremy Groves, who had been with them on the boat, managed to swim ashore and survived. It was a bitter blow but, undaunted, the Colombians sent in a new team to support us.

As time went on we all lost a great amount of weight, despite the fact that our mostly dehydrated army rations were nutritious, albeit rather unappetising. In the hot sticky climate, usually around 32°C, with 85% humidity, we longed for fresh, crisp salads. To vary and supplement our routine diet we occasionally sampled local foods, including jungle fruit, wild turkey, fish that we caught in the river and even, for the more adventurous, iguana, monkey and snake. Lack of fresh water also became a problem at times and we would have to resort to tapping vines, filtering the water from slimy pools or awaiting delivery by parachute.

The first rains of the new wet season came as we were crossing one of the most difficult areas, the hilly frontier region known as the Devil's Switchback. As the torrential downpour soaked me I asked a local if these were the expected heavy rains. 'No, sir,' he replied. 'D'is jus' hoomity.'

We then came up against a severe obstacle. I had led the column straight up what you might call the jungle equivalent of a one-way street, a narrow valley that came to a dead end in the form of an impassable hilly barrier. For ten days we floundered, struggling in vain to find a way through. In the end we took a gamble by driving the Range Rovers up the bed of the shallow Tuira River. On reaching deep pools or rapids, we ferried the vehicles to the next shallow on our raft, towed by a pirogue, a large thirty-foot dugout canoe with an outboard motor.

Things were going well until we were in the process of negotiating one section of rapids and, looking back from the canoe, I watched in horror as the rubber raft suddenly reared up like a stricken beast. At the same moment I heard the helmsman yelling: 'She's going, lads, get away, get away, we're going over!' The tow rope from my pirogue slackened as the raft and its swaying Range Rover spun out of control in the foaming water, outboards racing and men plummeting over the side. I could see that water was pouring in through a two-foot gash in the hull of one pontoon.

Like a whaler's longboat the canoe was now being dragged backwards by the floundering grey whale of a raft. One man was still aboard – the raft commander, Royal Engineers Sergeant Major 'Ticky' Wright, boat expert and formerly a helmsman on the Blue Nile expedition. Thankfully, Canito, the Panamanian boatman who was helming the pirogue, realised instantly what had to be done and sliced through the tow rope with a single stroke of his machete. Somehow the raft remained upright as it was then swept downstream, still spinning, and then, just when all seemed lost, a grim-faced 'Ticky' Wright somehow managed to wrestle back control and as we watched with mounting anxiety, powerless to help, he succeeded in driving the wreck ashore on to a shingle bank. Meanwhile, the members of his crew were struggling in the water, clearly visible by their bright red life jackets as they made desperately for the bank, where most of them ended up clinging on to the branches of overhanging trees and bushes, exhausted and without the strength to climb out. With great skill, Canito swung the long canoe around and manoeuvred it so that we were able to pick them all up, one by one. Some laughed nervously, others grinned in sheer relief, but all were badly shaken and, in spite of the heat, shivering. By a miracle every one of them was safe and unharmed.

The next day we again nearly lost one of the Range Rovers when it sank into a deep unseen pool while driving through the shallows. But after winching it out, our mechanics got it going again within thirty-six hours. Finally, we used Tirfor jacks to winch both of the Range Rovers up a sixty-five-degree slope, part of an old smugglers' trail.

At this point a Colombian muleteer appeared to lead us the rest of the way up to the frontier. This was our summit; from now on we would be going downhill. Shortly before reaching the plinth that marked the frontier we found a rusting red saloon car, a reminder of an ill-fated Chevrolet expedition of 1962. Trees were growing through the engine compartment, ants were nesting in the boot, a coral snake slithered from the remains of the back seat and a tarantula emerged from the dashboard. Apparently, the car had been dragged this far by a huge towing truck, which we found abandoned nearby.

Above us, raucous macaws, big-beaked toucans and brightly coloured parrots clucked and called with ear-splitting shrieks. The air was heavy with the scent of blooms that I had not noticed when moving on foot because of the need to keep my eyes fixed on the ground in front of me most of the time, picking a path with great care. From the safety of muleback I was able to relax more and observe the many brilliant flowers, beefsteak plants and thousands of tiny creatures that lived in the vast overgrown hothouse of the jungle. We reached Palo de Las Letras at 13:50 hours, ten minutes before we were due to be met there by the Colombian military detachment who were to escort us across the border, but apart from the broken-down concrete plinth in a small clearing, there was no-one around and nothing else to indicate that this was the frontier. While we waited, I walked forward to photograph our four-man headquarters with the Union Jack, which – unexpectedly – the American hobo we'd collected *en route* was clutching.

At 14:00 hours precisely, we suddenly became aware of slight movement in the jungle behind us and looked round to find ourselves confronted at the edge of the clearing by a platoon of swarthy, purposeful-looking Colombian soldiers in camouflage uniform, their weapons spotlessly clean, silently watching us. From their midst an officer stepped forward, and introduced himself.

'Captain Sierra of the Fourth Brigade Infantry,' he announced, clicking his heels with Prussian precision and saluting. 'Welcome to Colombia.' His sergeant major seized our Union Jack and for a moment I feared that we must have unknowingly committed some unpardonable breach of international law, but he put my mind at rest, telling me: 'It is your right to carry your flag into Colombia, according to the Treaty of 1821.' This was true, but I was surprised that our new friends were so well briefed. The sergeant major then asked if he might be allowed to carry the Union Jack into his country, as indeed the Duke of Wellington's veterans had done when they came to support the colonists in their bid for freedom 150 years before. Thus we marched downhill into the thickening jungle of the Atrato valley.

Kelvin and the *Pathfinder* group were already a day ahead of us and going well, and that night we reached the riverside camp of the Colombian commander, Major Alberto Patron. We ate a communal meal with our allies and enjoyed the first of many cups of superb local coffee. I learned of the campaign being waged against the communist guerrillas. 'I think that Atrato is too unhealthy a place – even for communists,' said the unusually fair-haired officer. 'But we must take precautions; seven soldiers were killed in an ambush near Barranquillita last week.' So far the Darién Gap had thrown everything at us except bandits, but I made a point of carefully checking my revolver that evening.

Standing on a peak in Darién, just as Balboa had done almost five centuries earlier, looking out over the steaming green morass of the Atrato, a swamp the size of Wales, I realised that our challenge was still very far from over. We were two weeks behind schedule, the promised heavy rains threatened and we still had to cross thirty-six miles of extremely difficult terrain that no motor vehicle had traversed before.

A Colombian Navy gunboat awaited us on the river to support our crossing of the next major obstacle. Already on board was our recce officer, who had gone on ahead and had discovered a possible route through the morass that now lay immediately before us, presenting the next challenge. Much of the area was wetland, covered with a thick coating of waterweed and alive with mosquitoes, snakes and the occasional caiman. Our raft frequently became bogged down in the matted vegetation. We tried cutting a way through this with machetes, while also hauling the raft along with the aid of grappling hooks, but eventually resorted to using necklaces of dynamite to blast a way through, which had the added bonus of producing some excellent fish for breakfasts!

In some places giant logs were tangled in with the weed, forming even greater obstacles, which we also cleared with explosive. Gradually, more and more trees began to appear, strange unearthly shapes, growing up from the swamp around us, populated only by huge black waterbirds, lizards and giant otters. Here was a truly primeval forest uninhabited by man.

Eventually, we were able to unload the Range Rovers from the raft on to a firmer but still slippery crust. Once the wet season really started this would soon become flooded, but for now it was passably dry and, being about three feet thick, would stand the weight of our vehicles with their extra-wide tyres. This whole area was like a giant sponge, the surface perforated with holes descending into liquid mud. It looked fairly solid from a distance, but this could be deceptive, as I discovered at one point when I was flown in and out in a Colombian Army helicopter fitted with floats. Climbing gingerly out of the chopper on to what appeared to be terra firma, I was disconcerted to find that the ground beneath my feet wobbled like a jelly!

On 23rd April, just as the sun began to set with its usual livid orange glow, we finally emerged from the swamp, a column of ragged, filthy, hollow-eyed men, women, and vehicles. We were covered in bites and bruises, and our feet were mostly rotten with 'immersion foot' as a result of being constantly wet. But we staggered on until we reached the northern end of the southern section of the Pan-American Highway. The first complete crossing of the Gap had taken ninety-nine days, and that very night the sky opened, marking the start of the wet season. We had beaten the heavy rains by just eight hours. It happened to be St George's Day!

In Bogotá a message from Her Majesty the Queen awaited and we were driven through the streets in a motorcade to lay a wreath in memory of the Colombians who had been drowned. The Darién Action Committee presented the team with a gold medal and each member received a gallon of local spirit from the Colombian Army. It was a great party!

Fifty years later it remains rather frustrating that all our efforts in successfully charting a way through the Darién Gap seem to have been in vain and the two ends of the Pan-American Highway have yet to be connected, the road down through the USA still reaching only as far as Yaviza in Panama. Politics and the technical problems of bridging the Atrato Swamp still block the route. However, we took care to preserve the forest, and our scientific studies helped the establishment of the Darién National Park and the protection of the indigenous people.

The Rover engineers, inspecting the Range Rovers in Bogotá, were astonished by their excellent condition and, fitted with road tyres, they set off along the South American section of the Highway. Crossing over the Andes and continuing on through Peru, Ecuador and the deserts of Chile, they sped on, covering one stretch of 800 miles in a single day, during which they enjoyed the luxury of cruising at 99mph on near-empty roads, a dramatic change to what they had had to contend with over much of the previous few months. As they neared Tierra del Fuego, their final destination, they then encountered conditions of snow and ice similar to those in which they had set off in Alaska all those months before. Many mountain passes were blocked and it took five days to break through, during which the trusty vehicles bypassed the blockages by once again taking to the water and crossing a lake on a raft that had been acquired locally.

On 9th June 1972 the drivers gazed out over Cape Horn and switched off their engines for the last time after seven months and a total of 17,000 miles. Captain Jeremy Groves signalled: 'Mission accomplished'. It had been an incredible adventure, involving teamwork, determination, flexibility and some great practical engineering. I recalled an inscription on the wall of the Chief US Army Engineer in the Canal Zone that read: 'Only those who attempt the ridiculous can achieve the impossible'.

 ▶ **The Darién Conquest, Panama, Colombia and the Americas, 1971–72**

CHAPTER 10
SCOTLAND'S LOST COLONY

Whilst forcing our way through the Darién Gap we heard intriguing tales of an ill-fated colony, set up on the Atlantic coast of Panama in the 17th century by a pioneering Scots businessman, William Paterson. Indeed, the map showed Caledonia Bay at the southern end of the San Blas chain of islands and there were even rumours of fair-skinned descendants of Scottish settlers still living in the area. On one of our reconnaissance flights for the Gap crossing we had passed over the site and photographed what appeared to be the outline of a fort.

This immediately sparked my interest and having then gone on to read John Prebble's outstanding book *The Darien Disaster* I became even more intrigued by the full story of a highly adventurous and daringly ambitious early colonial project that ended in catastrophe. On then meeting the renowned author, I was surprised to hear that he had never actually been to the bay and went away determined to investigate further.

Among other things, my research revealed that Sir Francis Drake had used this remote bay as a hideaway whilst raiding the Spanish Main and that the lost city of Acla had been established nearby by Núñez de Balboa, the conquistador with whose exploits I was already familiar. Finding archaeological evidence of the doomed Scottish colony could, I thought, be a suitably challenging task for Operation Drake, the two-year round-the-world expedition for adventurous young people aged seventeen to twenty-five, including many from underprivileged inner-city backgrounds, that the Prince of Wales had encouraged the SES to launch and which I was in the process of planning. With the sailing ship *Eye of the Wind* as an ocean-going HQ, the expedition was to follow in the wake of Drake's 1577–80 circumnavigation of the world, 400 years on, with teams made up of scientists, servicemen and doctors as well as the youngsters, stopping off at four main locations along the way to explore and carry out scientific research ranging from archaeology to zoology, while also getting involved in local community projects.

It was not too difficult to persuade some American and British friends to join me on an initial recce into the steaming heat of Darién. So, in 1976, three women and seven men from the Explorers Club in New York and the SES in London flew in to the San Blas Islands, where Andrew Mitchell, an eager zoologist from Jersey, was waiting for us, having flown out ahead to arrange canoes to take us to Caledonia Bay, or Punta Escocés as the local Kuna called it. Greeting us at the airstrip, the shock of tousled black hair that flowed beneath his jungle hat making him look a bit like a Cuban revolutionary, Andrew announced a problem. 'I brought a letter from the government for the Kuna chief – but it was addressed to the wrong chief,' he explained. Fortunately, Gricelio, our Panamanian archaeologist, happened to have a spare sheet of government-headed notepaper, so we borrowed a typewriter and prepared a new letter, with a convincingly forged signature that I handed to the correct chief, who then produced dugout canoes and boatman, at an inflated price!

'Look at these people,' cried our American doctor, Dan Osman, standing in the shadows of a lean-to building were three blonde-haired white men and, to our amazement, one was actually named Robinson! However, after a quick examination Dan shook his head.

'I'm afraid they are not descended from Scotsmen,' he announced. 'They're simply albinos.' Rather to our disappointment, it seemed that one myth might have been laid to rest.

Three canoes paddled by stocky Kuna girls in brilliant scarlet and yellow dresses and shawls appeared and we stepped aboard. With their golden nose rings and chest discs flashing in the sun, the young women worked in perfect unison, their strong arms powering us forward through the swell, while we were kept busy bailing out the water that came slopping over the bows. Occasionally, the light breeze would lift a shawl to reveal dark flashing eyes.

'Oh, this is beautiful!' exclaimed Barbara Martinelli from the Explorers Club of New York, her long corn-coloured locks blowing in the wind as the leaning palms and golden beaches, the coral gardens and running surf, the bright green hills and shadowy mangroves combined to make this one of the most bewitching natural harbours I'd ever seen. Those Scottish settlers must have been awestruck when they arrived here all those years ago.

Rigging our hammocks in an empty *pueblo* at the water's edge, we set about exploring the dense jungle. Ruth Mindel, from our London SES PR team, was delighted to find a tree laden with ripe avocados to supplement our rations, and that night we toasted the settlers with plastic mugs of warm Scotch.

Sunrise brought the heat and the sandflies, but, making use of the Scottish Darién Company maps, we soon identified the location of Fort Saint Andrews, now a coconut grove, and I then stumbled into a shallow ditch, which had clearly been a moat, cut from the coral. Walking around, drawing rough sketch maps, we found ourselves crunching on pottery shards that littered the ground, and

Vince Martinelli, Barbara's husband, found a small cannonball the size of a cricket ball. However, there was no sign of the cemetery said to contain the graves of four hundred Scots.

Mel Trafford, a muscular US Army sergeant, had a set of scuba tanks and examined a reef, where it was thought that a French privateer, carrying captured Spanish treasure, had floundered when visiting the colony. I watched from the surface as he checked the seabed. A movement then caught my eye and I held my breath as a blue-grey shark, its tail moving rhythmically, approached in slow motion. The denizen's beady, unblinking eyes looked me over as it swam effortlessly off into the misty limits of my visibility.

There were more archaeological sites on other islets lying off the isthmus and whilst returning across the bay after visiting one of them I asked our Kuna boatman, Ricardo, if he knew the story of Balboa's Acla. He shook his head, but pointed to a palm-fringed beach lying beyond a reef crested by breaking surf, with the one word '*Muros*' (walls). Acla was thought to lie between two rivers, but looking ashore we saw no sign of any estuary emerging into the sea and the pounding surf on the reef looked uninviting.

'Can you get a boat through the reef, Ricardo?'

'*Si*,' he replied. '*Es possible.*'

Approaching the reef, we could see exposed heads of jagged coral projecting from the swirling foam. For a moment it looked dangerous, especially so when our motor stopped momentarily. But then I spotted something that was only visible from very close inshore – that there was a gap in the reef, and that if you knew the way, you could slip safely into a sheltered cove beyond.

On the palm-fringed beaches dozens of Kuna dugouts were drawn up whilst the owners harvested coconut in the forest. And we could now see there did indeed appear to be two rivers. '*Señor,*' insisted Ricardo, 'there is a wall in the jungle. I see it as a boy.' Ricardo was at least sixty years old, so I was not too hopeful that he would actually be able to lead us to it from memory. Nevertheless, it was definitely worth a try so we decided to go and have a look and split up, with one party going to the banks of the Aglatomate, whilst the other searched the shore and the Rio Aglaseniqua, the northern river.

Ricardo, Vince and I cut deep into a bamboo thicket that showed signs of flooding, but found no wall and no other evidence at all of civilisation. Back on the beach we discovered why the rivers had been invisible from seaward; during the dry season a high sandbar extended right across their mouths. By now, however, it was late afternoon and I decided that it all looked like a wild goose chase. 'Es here somewhere, I know, *señor,*' grumbled Ricardo and as we walked along the beach, the old man kept darting back in amongst the trees trying to find his wall.

We were about 200 yards from the boats when I heard the excited chatter of monkeys overhead and paused to watch a troop of them leaping through the tall palms. Suddenly, a furry, black feline creature, about twice the size of a domestic cat, leapt out of a tree, hurtled across the path and shot up a palm.

'What the hell was that?' exclaimed a startled Vince.

'He eat ze mono,' Ricardo informed us.

'It's a jaguarundi,' cried an excited Andrew Mitchell, chasing after it with his camera. Ricardo, meanwhile, had lost interest. He'd met a small Kuna boy with a dog and was jabbering away at him excitedly. The boy nodded and pointed.

'He knows, *señor,*' grinned the sage triumphantly.

So we turned back into the forest, and after only a few dozen paces arrived in a freshly burnt clearing. The boy pointed his machete at a tumbledown pile of stones running across the clearing. Apparently, he had been burning the jungle to make space to plant coconuts and had found what looked very much like the remains of a wall. I felt a surge of excitement as I called out to the rest of the team.

With compass and measuring tape we did a quick survey. The eighty-yard wall was around ten feet wide and four feet high with a bastion projecting at right angles. Gricelio was already finding pottery and, most important, glass. Lines of stones appeared to mark the foundations of buildings.

'What do you think?' I asked our archaeologist.

'I think we have discovered Acla,' he said solemnly.

Casting around in the surrounding jungle, we found the answer to the problem of the river. In the intervening centuries it had changed course. An earlier bed alongside the wall was just visible. On the shore Dan had located a small quarry and a low rampart, but it would be dark in an hour, so we returned to our base.

Next day we uncovered more artefacts and made a sketch map of the area. However, violent squalls were now striking the bay daily and a towering waterspout had passed five miles to the north. It was 23rd April, St George's Day – the very same date on which we had completed the earlier Darién Quest – so I knew from experience that the rains were coming.

Giving our surplus rations to the Kuna girls in whose huts we had stayed, we boarded our canoe and headed for Mulatupo, where our chartered plane was expected. José, another albino, kindly let us sleep in his two-storey tin-roofed home and that evening we enjoyed a display of Kuna dancing by a group of young locals. Girls with pudding-basin haircuts and bright *mola* blouses shook their maracas as the boys leapt about with their pipes of pan.

Sipping a welcome cold beer, we talked to the village schoolmaster, who turned out to know all about the history of the ill-fated Scottish colony and showed us a rusty old cannon, with a seven-foot-long barrel.

'*Escocés,*' he said, going on to explain in broken English: 'White man bring long time ago, son of Dr Paterson.' A carving of a man with a top hat and a frock coat was then produced by some of his pupils. Clearly, it was all in their local folklore.

As darkness fell and the humidity closed in on us, little lamps with naked flames flickered in the tightly packed huts. From the assembly hall came an eerie chanting as women bent over their needlework, responding to the exhortations of a priest or perhaps a politician.

José produced proper beds and a white sheet but no nets. 'No mosquitoes, *señor,*' he assured me. As I slipped into unconscious oblivion, I felt something prick my toe. Assuming it was an insect, I kicked out, then fell asleep. The storm broke at 1.15am and the monsoon rain upon the tin roof would have woken the dead. Then I realised my bed was wet.

Oh, hell, I thought, *the rain's coming in.* As I rose to investigate I felt the call of nature and so, groping for my torch, I stumbled down the external staircase to the evil-smelling loo. The rain had eased by the time I ascended again, but my torch revealed something that made me freeze: the stairs were dripping with blood. In six bounds I was in my room and, supposing murder to have been committed, seized my harpoon gun. As I did so something brushed my hair, and, swinging my torch around, the beam revealed a large bat flitting around the room. Then, in the torchlight, I saw to my dismay that my bed was drenched in blood, which I now realised was dripping from my legs, forming bright red pools on the floor. Both legs were scarlet from the knees down.

'Ruth,' I hissed through the cubicle wall, to where my SES colleague was sleeping in the room next door.

'What is it?' came a half-awake reply.

'You'd better come and give me a hand, I think I've cut a vein or something,' I whispered.

Ruth padded in. 'Mind where you tread,' I cautioned.

She stood for a moment, looking at me in horror. 'What on earth have you done to yourself?' she cried.

Before I could reply, Dan arrived on the scene, awoken by the commotion. He too looked horrified, asking: 'Hell, John! What happened?'

I couldn't remember anything at all untoward happening, except the prick in my toe just before I'd fallen asleep. Having cleaned me up, Dan looked puzzled. 'I've never seen anyone bleed so much from such a tiny cut!' exclaimed the doctor. 'It's only about a quarter of an inch long on your toe.' He then asked if there was any history of blood disease in my family and, on being assured that there wasn't, inquired whether I had cut myself anywhere else recently?

'Yes,' I replied. 'Yesterday, as it happens, on my knuckle.' I showed him the perfect scab and, still looking nonplussed, he plastered the cut, dosed me up with antibiotics and left me to sleep.

At dawn the room looked like a slaughterhouse and, interestingly, the blood had still not congealed. 'I've made some inquiries,' said Dan at breakfast. 'I reckon that bat you saw was a vampire. Apparently, the Kuna are often bitten and because the creature injects you with an anticoagulant to make it easier for them to drink your blood, you will bleed profusely,' he explained. I remembered how our horses had suffered during the Darién crossing. 'There's only a four per cent chance of a bat carrying rabies,' Dan continued, 'but you must start the shots the moment we get back to Panama City.'

Thus in the months that followed I was to undergo no less than three different series of anti-rabies injections, a total of thirty-two jabs in my stomach and backside. In terms of pain and discomfort, the bite itself was nothing by comparison.

Meanwhile, news of our discoveries and Gricelio's account hit the headlines in Panama City, although the British press were more interested in my vampire bite.

However, I was now convinced that a full-scale follow-up expedition was needed and that this would indeed be a perfect project to be included as the opening phase in Operation Drake's worldwide itinerary, which was now well into the planning process.

With the backing of the Ministry of Defence, I had been seconded to become the director in overall charge of masterminding the project for which a total of 414 young people aged seventeen to twenty-five had been selected from twenty-six nations to seek challenges of war in peacetime, as its royal patron, HRH the Prince of Wales, put it.

In October 1978, Prince Charles started the voyage by sailing our flagship, the brigantine *Eye of the Wind*, out of Plymouth harbour. Aboard were the first batch of thirty-six Young Explorers, on their way to joining archaeologists, scientists and Panamanian youngsters at Caledonia Bay in trying to uncover all that remained of both the Scots' colony and the fabled city of Acla.

Pausing for a short study of La Soufrière, an active volcano on the Caribbean island of Saint Vincent, they found it more lively than expected and beat a hasty retreat. That was just as well, for on Good Friday 1979 it erupted for the first time in more than seventy years!

Meanwhile, an advance party had set up a tented camp in Caledonia Bay where they joined other youngsters. Directed by the eminent archaeologist, Dr Mark Horton, they braved the heat, mosquitoes, sandflies and scorpions, to clear the site of Fort Saint Andrews. The main danger, however, came from falling coconuts that could easily split a skull and so everyone was issued with hard hats as protection.

In no time at all they had unearthed a significant collection of pottery, cannonballs, lead shot and fragments of swords and muskets. Although our RAF diving team could find no evidence of the French privateer, they did locate the wreck of the Scottish supply ship, the *Olive Branch*, using proton magnetometers.

Records showed that her store of brandy had been accidentally ignited by a careless seaman, sinking the ship in four fathoms close to the shore. The *David Gestetner*, one of the giant inflatables from the Zaire River Expedition, had been shipped out from England to provide an ideal diving platform.

Descending into the murky depths, our divers felt their way around the timbers, directing a suction pump to suck up silt and debris. At one point, as a bucket containing artefacts was lifted to the surface, something snatched it away. Visibility underwater was down to a few inches and several times divers felt movement around them. So we set a long fishing net around the site and hauling it in next morning discovered that the catch included five sharks, among them a five-foot mako and a ten-foot hammerhead! The divers were rather hesitant to continue the work after that, but they did identify barrels of clay pipes, bones from salt beef and several cannons, all of which had been faithfully recorded on the ship's manifest, still held by the Royal Bank of Scotland.

Eager to discover more about Acla, we dug a trial trench through the wall found on the recce and uncovered the base of an 18th-century wine bottle. Archaeologist Mark Horton reckoned that this meant the wall was part of the Spanish fort San Fernando de Carolina (1785–93) and not Acla. However, he then discovered more conclusive evidence that showed the actual site of Acla to have been just a few hundred yards away and that the coral blocks used to build the 18th-century fort had probably been brought from the Acla site.

When the experts confirmed this major discovery a group of VIPs arrived to visit the site, including our chairman, the charismatic General Sir John Mogg, along with the President of Panama, the Archbishop and the director of Panama's Patrimonio Histórico, accompanied by journalists from Britain and Panama.

Our visitors stood perspiring in the shade of several towering palms while Mark, with great enthusiasm, excitedly pointed out the stonework, gesticulating wildly and talking non-stop. Nothing would distract him as we saw a moment later, when a long green snake slithered towards the General. My hand dropped to my holster, but before I could draw, a Guardia Nacional officer beat me to it and blasted it to oblivion with his sub-machine gun! Understandably, everyone jumped out of their socks and some actually dived for cover. As the shattering roar of gunfire echoed across the bay, Mark continued unabated: 'And furthermore…'

Some miles into the rainforest immediately behind Caledonia Bay, Andrew Mitchell and Mike Christy, a talented Sapper, built walkways of Dexion and nylon strapping 120 feet up in the jungle canopy, to permit our scientists to study this unexplored region – 'Where the great trees have their sex lives,' as Andrew put it. An ingenious system of ropes lifted one from the ground and, ignoring his arthritic hip, our gallant General, aged sixty-six, insisted on being hoisted up for a bird's-eye view of the site. The Panamanian Guardia were much impressed. This elevated walkway became the first of its kind, later used in the tropics worldwide.

An unannounced visit by General Omar Torrijos, Commander of the Guardia Nacional and virtually the dictator of Panama, caught me by surprise. Enjoying a break in Panama City with my family, a Guardia helicopter rushed all of us out to the bay. There I found General Torrijos being briefed by our voluble archaeologist whilst he rocked back and forth in a camp chair, sucking gently at a fat Havana. 'Do you have any questions, General?' asked Mark, but before he had time to answer a nerve-shattering bang suddenly split the air. The great man's bodyguards hurled themselves flat. He himself didn't move a muscle.

My younger daughter, Victoria, had been given a cap gun for Christmas, which was smoking in her hand. There was a moment's awkward silence and then the Panamanian leader began to laugh, quietly at first and then louder and louder until, finally, his muddy aides picked themselves up and started laughing too, albeit a little nervously.

'Little girl,' Torrijos smiled. 'All this must be very boring for you, yes?' Victoria nodded. 'Come,' he said, 'I'll get you a coconut.' So saying, he removed his hat, boots and gun belt and, with astonishing agility, shinned up a palm tree and picked a large coconut which he then sliced with a machete and handed to her, saying: 'Go on, drink – the coconut milk is good.' Everyone cheered and the general strolled off for lunch.

'Who is he?' hissed Victoria.

'Well, he's like the Queen of Panama,' I tried to explain.

'Doesn't look much like a queen,' she whispered in reply, wandering off with her coconut.

Torrijos was an impressive man and became a good friend of Operation Drake. His personal interest was enormously helpful and ensured the complete support of everyone in Panama.

On another visit to Caledonia Bay, Jack Davis, a leading sponsor of the expedition, flew down with me in a local single-engine Beaver aircraft. Jack, an experienced pilot, sat with me in the passenger seats, the two of us conversing via our headphones. The young Panamanian flying the plane looked a little nervous, but assured us that he was familiar with Beavers. A few miles short of the bay we were still over the uninterrupted jungle when it suddenly became easier to hear Jack's voice and I felt my ears popping. Jack yelled in Spanish, and I realised that the engine had cut. Whilst the pilot's hands ran around the controls, the treetops rushed closer as we fell like a stone. Jack was still swearing at the pilot and pointing at something. A stretch of coastline appeared and, hoping that we would be able to glide to the beach, I prayed hard as the plane continued to plummet earthwards. By a real miracle, at around 500 feet the engine spluttered into life again and we roared over the forest to land at our camp's airstrip. Ben Cartwright, an experienced Beaver fitter, greeted us, shaking his head. 'The silly bugger forgot to switch fuel tanks,' he sighed, nodding in the pilot's direction. 'I've never known a Beaver engine being restarted in flight. And they don't glide well!' Once again, I thanked my lucky stars.

The expedition ended appropriately with a Burns Night dinner. Haggis and copious quantities of Scotch were airlifted in and in the warm, moist night we toasted the immortal memory. Piper Little of the Scots Guards excelled himself as we danced and reeled beneath the stars. Our Panamanian guests were totally confused. Most had thought it was going to be a birthday party and came with presents. Towards midnight a Guardia gunboat sailed in and ran right on to a reef by our jetty. The crew, who it seemed had already dined well, was rescued safely and the party went on. Towards dawn one of our visitors, an ugly little major, rather the worse for wear, seized my spirited blonde assistant, Sara Everett, and dragged her towards the bushes. Hearing her yell, I grabbed the wretch by his lapels and propelled him towards the sea. However, his pals intervened and apologised. Later I discovered his name – Manuel Antonio Noriega! Had he drowned, future events in Panama might have been different!

As the crossroads of the world, this little country attracted a great number of interesting folk, some just passing through. At the end of our stay we laid on a special little event in a local hotel for Panamanian youngsters interested in learning more about what we had been doing. Maps and charts were spread over the floor as we discussed future plans. Suddenly, I became aware of a very elegant, petite woman in a large hat. With amazing grace, she stepped over the papers and stretched out her hand. 'Hello,' she smiled. 'I just wanted to thank you for having my niece on the expedition.' It was the ballerina Margot Fonteyn, who was married to the Panamanian politician Roberto Arias. Her friendship in the years to come was immensely warm and helpful.

It was Dame Margot who, seven years later, encouraged Operation Raleigh, successor to Operation Drake, to continue the archaeological work in Caledonia Bay. Bringing our 2,000-ton flagship *Sir Walter Raleigh* into the bay, we lifted three cannons from the *Olive Branch* for a Panama museum. As we chipped away at the coral encrustations, there was a loud hissing and the unmistakable stench of gunpowder. We backed away as, with a soft 'poop', a cannonball appeared at the end of the barrel. The release of pressure on the breach when the gun was raised from a depth of thirty feet had caused it to be forced forward.

At Acla we then discovered the foundations of a circular tower, believed to be the oldest European stone structure yet unearthed on the American mainland. I was preparing to sail the British ambassador, Terry Steggle, and some friends down to see this when an emergency message flashed through to the ops centre. Michael Williams, a British venturer, had been sliding down a grass slope on a Colombian island when he had pitched over a ledge and gone head first into a rock, sustaining terrible injuries. General Jack Galvin, the region's US Commander, was a good friend of General Mogg's and thankfully he had instructed his staff to give us every support, thus a USAF C-130 loaded with doctors was on its way within minutes. Meanwhile, Terry handled the diplomatic clearances required to fly a British casualty from a Colombian island to Panama in an American aircraft.

Initially, the first aid and the Colombian emergency services kept him alive, but as we stood around the flagship radio, our senior medical officer looked grim. 'I'm afraid he doesn't have much of a chance,' she confided, as our US Navy radio officer recorded the details of Michael's deteriorating condition. We needed a top brain surgeon if he were to survive. I remembered meeting one at a Kiwanis Club lunch and called my pal, Billy St Malo, in Panama

City. He raced out in his speedboat to collect the surgeon from a holiday island and got him to the airfield just as the C-130 touched down. It was this timely rescue and the skill of that Panamanian surgeon, still in his shorts, that saved Michael's life.

In 1994 I returned to Caledonia Bay with twenty-six students from an American college in London and Lake Ridge Academy of Cleveland, Ohio, plus some from Panama. *What better place to do historical and environmental studies*, I thought. So, aided by Yolima Cipagauta, the charming and energetic Colombian university lecturer, otherwise known as Yoli, and some friends, we prepared to give the youngsters a character-building exercise.

Some parents expressed concern about the safety of their children, so on arrival in Panama I asked the Ministry of Education, who were supporting the project, if they could provide some local security personnel. A couple of tough officers from the Guardia Nacional were made available. When interviewing them, I asked if they had any personal insurance and, if so, the name of the company. '*Ah, si*,' replied these hard-featured policeman with a thin smile. 'Smith and Wesson!'

Yoli chartered local planes to fly the team to the San Blas Islands and canoes to take them to the old Operation Raleigh campsite at Caledonia Bay. She also found a yacht that would bring all the camp stores and rations to the site. On an early trip in the rainforest, my perceptive friend Anne Leonard, who was used to working with youngsters, was horrified to discover that in spite of some pre-expedition training by the US Army, none of the students knew how to use a compass. 'What did you do on your preparation course?' she asked.

'We just bonded,' they replied.

Although the Kuna were generally friendly, we did have one unfortunate incident when someone climbed aboard our supply yacht to steal rations and an expensive army radio. However, the Guardia Nacional officers soon found a Kuna teenager they believed to be the culprit. 'He is definitely the one,' stated Corporal Rodriguez, but the lad refused to confess, so the officer decided to detain him and handcuffed him to a palm tree, saying: 'I'll leave him there for a while until his memory improves.' Later I noticed the boy looking very uncomfortable and asked that he be released. 'Perhaps his memory has returned,' stated the policeman and indeed the accused confessed and our radio was returned.

Handed back to the angry Kuna chief, the village women popped him in the communal toilet pit as a punishment. That night the students were somewhat upset by the way the matter had been handled, so I explained that we were guests in Panama and had to respect the local ways of solving crime. 'Indeed,' I added, 'if a burglary in London were to be solved so speedily I'd be pleasantly surprised, so I think we should be very appreciative of Corporal Rodriguez's action.'

Whereupon the officer jumped up, insisting with a grin: 'It is not me you must thank, but the ants at the foot of the tree!'

After twelve days we emerged from the jungle and Yoli's aircraft came to collect us, only for the door to come adrift on one of them just after take-off, but it still reached Panama City. As a result, remaining passengers had to stay overnight on the remote airstrip while they awaited another aircraft. As the moon rose, a large jungle cat approached and the policeman's gun jammed. However, despite these minor incidents the students all got safely home, a little wiser and more mature. And neither the insurance companies nor a Smith & Wesson were called upon!

 ▶ Operation Drake 1978–80

CHAPTER 11
CENTRAL AMERICAN
EXPLORATION

Best remembered as the original and, many would say, the definitive James Bond, the late actor Sir Sean Connery went on to win over a new generation of film fans with his role as Professor Henry Jones, equally adventurous father of whip-cracking, swashbuckling archaeological explorer Indiana Jones, played by Harrison Ford. What is perhaps less well known is that Sir Sean had a genuine, real-life interest in history and archaeological exploration. As a patriotic Scot he was particularly fascinated by the story of the Scottish colony at Caledonia Bay and as a supporter of the Scientific Exploration Society he helped to sponsor our return to Panama in 2003 with an expedition which, among other projects, aimed to try and locate the long-lost graveyard where many of the 2,000 colonists who died there were said to be buried.

We had earlier examined an area of dense jungle behind the site of the fort, thought to be the most likely place. However, no mounds nor tombstones had been found at that time.

The great star's contribution went beyond simply helping to raise money for the project by hosting a fundraising dinner in the Bahamas, among other things. His contacts in Panama included the President himself, a personal friend to whom he wrote, seeking official government support for the expedition.

There was talk at one point of Sean himself joining us briefly during the expedition around the time of our traditional Burns

Night celebrations, but once the local Kuna got to hear about that they started demanding large sums of money and upping the price of everything to explore in their territory and so that idea had to be dropped. And we never did go back to seek the graveyard.

There was, however, plenty of other interest. Panama, and Darién in particular, had proved to be a happy hunting ground for the SES over the years. One expedition often leads to another and during our crossing of the Darién Gap in 1972 and again later, when we returned with Operation Drake and Operation Raleigh, we heard many rumours and intriguing stories about the possible existence of undiscovered evidence of early civilisations going back to the Aztecs, Toltecs and Mayans. As Panama was the major transit route from North to South America, especially following the arrival of the Spanish conquistadors, it was a potential treasure trove of archaeological remains.

One area of particular interest was Bahia Piña on Darién's Pacific coast, where the Emberá people had told me of a strange 'lizard rock' on the Rio Sambú. So this was where our research team headed in 2003, led by Bruce Mann, a professional and extremely energetic Scottish archaeologist, George Kozikowski from the Isle of Skye and Jules Chenoweth from Cornwall.

Thanks to the kindness of Terri and Mike Andrews, owners of the Tropic Star Lodge at Bahia Piña, and the chief of the nearby Wounaan village community, we were offered accommodation and also the use of a single-storey wooden building. Famed for marlin fishing, the lodge attracts big-game fishermen, and has a good airstrip into which we flew. The Wounaan people were delighted by the medical and dental aid we provided and also by two wheelchairs, brought as a gift from the Canadian Embassy.

I had been warned in advance of the presence in the area of Fuerzas Armadas Revolucionarias de Colombia (FARC), the Colombian terrorist organisation in Darién, so I was not surprised to find an escort of ninety paramilitary Panamanian Frontier Police, with three powerful fifty-foot launches awaiting our arrival. They also had a Huey helicopter on call. Commanded by the efficient and friendly Major Callegas, these tough, experienced men accompanied us on our sorties into the forest.

Shortly after our arrival, two muscular Colombian women in sombreros and wellington boots strode purposefully through the village, clearly looking us over. 'FARC,' whispered Yoli, who being Colombian recognised them straight away. 'They send their women in to scout.' The Major took note, but in this free and easy border area the women had not broken any law. However, after several recent clashes with FARC in the jungle our escorts were nervous. Within a week we learned that a senior terrorist had been captured together with his family at a hacienda deep inside Darién and speedily dispatched to the USA.

Bruce Mann was soon busy unearthing various artefacts, including pre-Colombian pottery shards and a stone axe. Meanwhile, using the police launches, we sent a party and escort to the Rio Sambú. It proved to be a very rough trip, but landing at what was known as 'The Beach of the Dead', near the mouth of the river, they canoed and marched up this striking jungle waterway for two days. Then their Emberá guide pointed to a huge boulder coated in moss and lying in the shallow water of a tributary. Running forward excitedly, Jules yelled: 'This is amazing!' – and indeed it was. The rock was inscribed with extraordinary petroglyphs centred around a lizard or caiman-like image, measuring 4.75 feet by 16 inches.

Cleaning off the thick moss revealed some eighteen petroglyphs, many in square shapes, carved around the centrepiece, with a series of paw prints, possibly of a jaguar, circling the design.

As the light faded and the temperature cooled, the team set up scaffolding to photograph the carvings and make dimensional drawings of each petroglyph. They noted with interest that all the designs were confined to the one huge rock. Hazarding a guess as to its significance, Jules suggested that the site might have been linked to the earlier Olmec, Maya, Aztec and Ticuna cultures.

Back in Panama, Professor Carlos Fitzgerald, Director of the Patrimonio Histórico, thought it could be up to 5,000 years old. Anyway, there could be no doubt that this study and the rest of the archaeological work at Bahia Piña was of considerable importance and Carlos announced: 'You have changed the early history of Panama.'

Sweating profusely as they struggled up the steep forested hills above our camp, London surveyors Christopher Boardman and Christian Sweeting mapped and boundary-marked the Bahia Piña estate. Working in temperatures of up to 45°C with humidity of 90% to 95%, this stalwart group also plotted the archaeological sites, and named a picturesque waterfall after the expedition patron, Sir Sean Connery. The healthcare aid provided by doctors Tatiana de Adam and Katherine Jones and dentist Slany McKeon was much appreciated by the local people, who only had a nurse and a traditional healer to care for them. As our medical team was all-female, the Emberá and Wounaan women found this very comforting. Also welcomed by the villagers was animal welfare advice from Clive Woodham, our veterinary surgeon, whose main task was to compile a valuable wildlife report.

We completed the expedition with our usual Burns supper, held in the huge circular *tambo* house of the Emberá. Inviting the chief to join us, I explained the programme and the reeling that would follow dinner. 'My people love to dance; may I bring them?' he asked.

That night 200 Emberá arrived, together with their girls in traditional *saruma* skirts, their upper bodies bare but painted with a black dye from the jaguar tree, said to attract a mate. A trio of Scots lasses led by our QM Judith Barker piped in the haggis, kindly provided in tins delivered from Scotland by my friend Ken Stahly. Morsels of the 'timorous beastie' were passed round whilst the astonished local people listened attentively to the ode and poems. Then came the reeling, with which they happily joined in, and as 'The Gay Gordons' blared out from a tape player, various Emberá seized us as partners. I must confess that dancing with topless ladies is an interesting experience. 'It's not quite like this in Aberdeen,' commented one of the Scots in our party. I'm sure our patron, so sadly absent, would have enjoyed it!

Lying off the south-west coast is a densely forested island, 123,000 acres, named Coiba, home to rare fauna and flora that have largely disappeared from the mainland. Until very recently the island had served as a penal colony, housing up to 1,200 murderers, rapists and political prisoners. The most dangerous of these were kept behind bars in a run-down concrete cell block, but others were allowed to live in open camps on the island shores. Sharks proved a deterrent to would-be escapees, and yet many had tried to flee on homemade balsa rafts. When recaptured, their sentences would be lengthened or, it was rumoured, they were simply shot.

Manuel Noriega, the dictator of Panama, whom I'd met before at Caledonia Bay, was said to have used it to dispose of his opposition, sometimes by dropping luckless individuals out of helicopters. However, Professor Carlos heard that prisoners had occasionally dug up artefacts and other objects made of gold, possibly originating from the Guaymi-speaking people encountered in the 16th century, which was why he had suggested an expedition to investigate.

After the prison was closed down, some of the guards had remained to look after the island, which had been declared a National Park. So, with British expats James and Marilyn Cobbet, Yoli and I carried out a recce. The ghastly 'Devil's Island' prison block still bore signs of its former inmates and reeked of death and decay. The remaining prison staff led us on a tour of the surrounding area, pointing out a large crocodile named Tito, who lived on the shore. A mean-looking specimen, he had, like the sharks, discouraged any would-be absconders. There were also dreaded fer-de-lance pit vipers and highly poisonous coral snakes in the undergrowth. Feral horses and cows roamed in the jungle, while wild dogs were killing off some of the unique fauna, and the guards reported strange screams echoing through the forest at night. Understandably, they locked themselves in their quarters after dark. Exploring it further certainly sounded like an interesting challenge, so I started making plans, only for permission to be suddenly and unexpectedly withdrawn by the Panama government. 'I think they are concerned about what else we might discover,' said Yoli, who was usually well informed.

The same year we made another expedition on behalf of Professor Carlos. There were said to be forgotten Spanish forts in the Gulf of San Miguel that runs into Darién, built as a defence against rebellious tribes in the 18th century. The task was to locate and survey them, while at the same time seeking evidence of pre-Colombian settlements. There was also a story of a mysterious wreck to be investigated. A young Panamanian on Op Raleigh told me that, on Isla San Telmo, just off the entrance to the Gulf, he had seen what was possibly a Japanese submarine, used during World War II to attack shipping using the Panama Canal, although this had always been denied by the Japanese. The local authorities reckoned it was simply an old ship's boiler, but James Delgado of the Vancouver Maritime Museum believed it might actually be a much earlier submarine.

The rising sun was heating up as our cabin cruiser cut through a turquoise sea alive with dolphins. Searching the island's shore with my binoculars I spotted a small, round, dark object breaking the surface. 'I reckon that could be a conning tower,' said Roger Cooper, our diver and engineer, as he loaded scuba gear into a dinghy. As the tide receded a bulky elliptical-shaped object thirty-six feet long and ten feet wide was revealed, with what definitely looked like a small conning tower. The cast-iron hull bearing patches of rust and weed was holed in several places, but without doubt it was a submarine, beached in the shallows. James Delgado had been right and he went on to trace the extraordinary history of the vessel.

Julius Kroehl, a German, had immigrated to America in 1838, becoming an engineer specialising in underwater work. In 1861 he designed a submarine and offered it to the Union Navy to attack confederate shipping. However, the navy selected another design and built USS *Alligator* as their first submarine. Kroehl then went on to design a submarine fitted with a dive chamber that allowed divers to move in and out underwater and set charges or disarm enemy torpedoes. Meanwhile the confederate navy built one they named *H. L. Hunley*, which promptly sank the union battleship *Housatonic* off Charleston. Submarine warfare had begun.

By the time Kroehl's boat was ready and accepted by the navy, the Civil War was over. However, the Pacific Pearl Company wanted it and tests were set up in New York's East River to attract investors. In 1866 Kroehl took his sub down for ninety minutes, leaving observers on the dock fearing that he had perished. He eventually surfaced, climbing out of the hatch smoking a meerschaum pipe and triumphantly holding up a bucket of mud from the riverbed. Thereafter, the *Explorer*, as it was named, was taken to Panama, where it was used to gather pearls. Kroehl died after one dive, but his divers worked for three years, descending to a depth of one hundred feet for up to four hours at a time. However, after a period of intense work they all fell ill and died. Although it was thought at the time that malaria had killed them, it seems more likely they died of decompression sickness, which was only discovered years later by workers on the caissons of the Brooklyn Bridge. *Explorer*, meanwhile, ended up on Isla San Telmo in 1869.

Using his scuba, Roger entered the hull at high tide to study and photograph the interior and make detailed drawings of the fascinating mechanisms. We reckoned the sub could have had a crew of five and that it had been propelled by a hand-cranked shaft. It was like seeing a vessel from Jules Verne's *Twenty Thousand Leagues Under the Sea*. We passed our report to Professor Carlos and James Delgado, who was considering the idea of salvaging the 140-year-old historic wreck for preservation. The problem of lifting the brittle cast-iron hull might be overcome by removing much of the sand from around the keel and raising her on a high spring tide, using inflation tubes. Once afloat, she could then be lifted by a net on to a cradle aboard a freighter. Roger reckoned this could be achieved in ten days, weather and the Panama government permitting, but I believe *Explorer* is still there today.

Archaeology and history have always intrigued me, and not far from Panama I'd been invited on another quest. As a young Royal Engineer officer in Cyprus, I'd led a diving team encouraged to help the local Department of Archaeology at a time when few qualified researchers knew how to dive. This had led to fascinating discoveries of underwater ruins and wrecks. So when in 1981 the Florida-based Institute of Underwater Archaeology, headed by David Pincus, invited me to investigate allegedly manmade structures around Bimini in the Bahamas, thought possibly to be part of the legendary site of Plato's Atlantis, I accepted.

A few weeks later I flew out to the Bahamas with a team that included Mick Boxall, a swarthy Royal Signals corporal from Op Drake, photographer Alison Hines and American diver Les Savage, plus an underwater TV crew. Once there we boarded the forty-six-foot yacht and a fifty-eight-foot cruiser from which we were going to work. Located fifty miles from Florida, Bimini, once home to Ernest Hemingway, is a chain of flat, featureless islands warmed by the Gulf Stream. Coral reefs, sandy beaches and big-game fishing attract many holiday visitors, but our task was to examine some rock formations that looked as if they could be manmade. First using a light aircraft to take us on an overhead recce, we spotted a Dakota DC-3 lying upside down in the shallows. 'Drug runners,' commented our pilot.

We also noticed an area of deep pot-holes that seemed worthy of investigation. Using an underwater sledge and an Aqua scooter for speed, we criss-crossed the site, finding heavy metal fragments that led us to the conclusion that the holes were probably the result of wartime practice bombing. There was also an area littered with roof slates, marble slabs, blocks and lintels, but the presence of packing case timber under the material indicated that all this had been cargo from a freighter wrecked nearby.

Sections of fluted cylindrical columns up to a metre long looked at first as though they might be Grecian pillars, but upon close examination we deduced that they actually came from barrels of cement, also lost in a wreck, that had set in that rounded shape before the wooden barrels then rotted away. Hiding his disappointment, David Pincus then led us to a J-shaped underwater causeway lying parallel to the shore and just a few feet below the surface. Most of the boulders had a rounded cushion-like cross section and at first sight did look like a manmade causeway. The corners were set at right angles and many of the slabs had a distinctly square appearance. Close inspection showed that opposing blocks were of identical material. We had been provided with several sketch maps of the formation made up with the slabs and a first-class mosaic photograph. However, by slowly towing a diver with the video camera behind the boat, we obtained an excellent view of the causeway and saw that the slabs were not continuous as indicated in the sketch maps, although they did extend for at least 1,000 feet parallel with the shoreline. Nor were they as regular as had been supposed.

Using a jet pump, we excavated around and under some of the stones. However, contrary to popular rumour, no pedestals or supporting pillar rocks could be found. In fact, the slabs appeared to be lying on a bed of sand. Samples indicated that they were made of a limestone beachrock and appeared to consist of shellfish. The causeways were similar to others I'd seen in the Mediterranean and I was convinced that this was a completely natural formation, although I'll admit it did appear to be manmade. Following full analysis, this was later confirmed in a report in the scientific journal *Nature*.

There was one other mystery to investigate. According to popular legend, a spring of apparently fresh water located in the mangrove near Bone Fish Hole, North Bimini, was said to be the fabled 'Fountain of Youth' that the Spanish explorer Juan Ponce de León was seeking when he discovered Florida in 1513. Allegedly, bathing in the spring would ensure perpetual youth, thanks to certain natural chemicals contained in the water. I wondered if there might be a link between this legend and the story of Atlantis. So, we piled equipment into Les Savage's Zodiac and set off one thundery morning across the shallow lagoon that is at the centre of North Bimini. As we edged over the sandbars, our propeller grinding through the sand, large black shadows glided away; the place was alive with sharks.

To reach the spring we had to push the boat into a narrow channel that ran for 165 feet through the mangrove swamp. Thunder rumbled and rain began to fall in heavy drops as we approached the 'Fountain'. Wading ahead in the shallow water, I was equipped with the sterile specimen bottles in which to collect samples of the supposedly magical water. Suddenly, the channel opened out to reveal the spring, which had actually formed a deep pool, and before I could utter a word my feet first sank into quicksand and I then plunged into what was like a well, ten feet deep and some forty feet in diameter. Dark snake-like mangrove roots protruded from the sides, but the water was crystal clear and quite fresh to drink. However, the thought of several middle-aged conquistadors diving around in a supposed Fountain of Youth seemed faintly ridiculous.

Samples were duly taken for analysis, which confirmed that, as had been suspected, there were traces of lithium present. Lithium is used for treating various psychiatric disorders and may act as something of a tranquilliser, so perhaps this was the reason for the legend of eternal youth.

Sailing back to Miami, we found an abandoned launch carrying weapons, ammunition, explosive and camouflage uniforms. David speculated that, like the wrecked Dakota, this probably had something to do with drug runners. We took the launch in tow and handed it over to the US Coastguard. I wondered whether the Institute of Underwater Archaeology might be rewarded with a bounty of some sort from the authorities, which might have gone a little way towards making up for their disappointment at our failure to find Atlantis. For me, the bonus was that this unsuccessful quest led to a meeting with the legendary author Gavin Menzies, who had also explored Bimini.

A former Royal Navy submarine commander, Gavin had long believed that the largest fleet the world had ever seen set sail from China in 1421, exploring and setting up trading links with the Americas well before the arrival of Columbus in 1492. Writing four bestselling books based on his beliefs, Gavin had a worldwide following of admirers and a few critics. Studying early maps, he felt it likely that the Chinese had found a waterway to take them from the Atlantic to the Pacific, centuries before the Panama Canal existed.

After a delicious lunch at his home in North London, Gavin invited me to investigate his hypothesis and I learned that a canal across the isthmus had almost been built in Nicaragua rather than Panama. Some 400 miles north-west of the present canal lies Lake Nicaragua, an enormous expanse of water forty-five miles wide and over 100 miles long. One of the largest freshwater lakes in the Americas, its level can rise or fall several feet along its shores, depending on the wind. Together with its smaller neighbour, Lake

Managua, it drains eastward into the Caribbean via the San Juan River, which flows for almost 120 miles through jungle-covered banks along the border with Costa Rica, with access from the Caribbean to the Atlantic. At the same time, it is actually much closer to the Pacific, which at one point lies only twelve miles overland to the west. As a result, Nicaragua suffered centuries of conflict with colonial powers, mercenaries and pirates struggling to dominate this potentially profitable path between the oceans. The Spanish had colonised the land in 1523 and used the San Juan River as a trade route. Unfortunately for the people of the prosperous city of Granada on the western shore of the lake, the pirate Henry Morgan found that he could navigate the river and its rapids in large canoes all the way from the Caribbean. Thus in 1665 he crossed the lake to sack their city and then carried his loot back to Jamaica.

In the 17th century the Spanish built an impressive fortress to guard the river. However, in 1780 El Castillo was captured by a British expedition that included the young Captain Horatio Nelson, but the invaders, driven out by malaria, eventually abandoned the unhealthy site.

In the 18th century, and possibly even earlier, engineers realised that as the lake was only cut off from the Pacific by the narrow strip of land to the west, with access on the other side to the Caribbean and on to the Atlantic via a river navigable over much of its length, it might be possible to create an interoceanic shipping route.

Serious plans were soon being made to excavate a canal linking the lake to the Pacific while also widening and dredging the San Juan River. Meanwhile, however, despite the fact that numerous studies favoured Nicaragua as the best route, Ferdinand de Lesseps, famous for his success at Suez, had already started work in Panama.

Experienced engineers advised him against his plan for a sea-level canal, but he pressed on, regardless, with obsessive vigour. However, yellow fever and malaria killed many thousands of workers, there were insurmountable construction problems, and financial mismanagement finally forced his French company into bankruptcy in 1888.

The Nicaraguan alternative had influential support in the United States, but de Lesseps and his colleagues were eager to dispose of their landholdings in Panama and lobbied the US Congress to take on the unfinished job. Then in 1902 Mount Pelée erupted in Martinique. The death toll of 30,000 shook the Americas and an enterprising French lobbyist sent every member of Congress a Nicaraguan stamp bearing the picture of an erupting volcano in Lake Nicaragua. Thus reminded of the danger of a geological catastrophe, Congress voted for the canal in Panama and bought out the failed company.

Nicaraguans nevertheless still hope that they will one day have a waterway to rival that of their near neighbours in Panama, one able to carry the huge modern container ships that are too big to navigate the Panama Canal.

But was there actually a way through long before? The famous globe and wallchart made in 1507 by the foremost German cartographer of the day, Waldseemüller, shows a distinct gap between North and South America. The Pacific coast of America is strikingly drawn on his chart, which was published before Núñez de Balboa 'discovered' the Pacific in 1513, clearly suggesting that a navigator must have been there before him.

Maps and globes by astronomer and geographer Johannes Schöner published in 1515 and 1520, and maps by 18th-century British hydrographers, showed a channel that would enable boats to pass between the oceans. Furthermore, Chinese DNA and artefacts have been found in Central America and local history tells of a Chinese presence, while European explorers have recorded Chinese wrecks on the Pacific coast. We wondered whether the Chinese might have sent smaller craft up the river system, into the lake and down the San Juan River to the Caribbean.

With Gavin's support and the backing of the SES, I decided to set up a recce expedition to see if there was any further evidence of an earlier way through. Yoli, ever eager for a new challenge, joined me and recruited two Nicaraguan archaeologists, a car and driver. We were given considerable help by the Nicaraguans, including Granada's Mi Museo, historians and businesses keen to solve the mystery. So, equipped with GPS, altimeters and dowsing rods, we set off in January 2010. Moving by vehicle and on foot through the hills and the jungle-fringed riverbeds, we checked the possible routes for a previous link. Several areas were found where rivers flowing east to Lake Nicaragua and west to the Pacific rose within a few hundred yards of each other. One headwater site between two rivers that we dowsed indicated possible walls of an infilled canal. At another site in the almost dry riverbed of the upper reaches of the Rio Ochomogo, a strange artefact – twenty-four inches by thirty-five inches – carved from volcanic rock was discovered. Talking to people in lakeside towns and villages, we learned that Caribbean bull sharks swim the San Juan River, leaping like salmon up the rapids, apparently adapting to fresh water. Attacks on swimmers had been reported, but this did not seem to have affected the local tourist trade. Our altimeters showed the lake was 105 feet above sea level and the lowest point between the lake and the Pacific some 144–154 feet above sea level, so any canal would have required locks. But that might not have been impossible – the Chinese were, after all, brilliant engineers.

We had been given freedom to move around the country, but the recent civil war was still fresh in local memory. Well-armed security guards at several haciendas turned us away and in one village an old woman waving a long machete, accompanied by an angry mob, pursued Yoli and attacked our car. Apparently, they thought we were Americans seeking to seize her land. Fortunately, we had a Union Jack with which to calm the woman. Apart from a few dents to our Toyota there were no casualties.

Whilst mapping the dry watercourses and checking the altitude levels we met thirty-five-year-old Mariano Hernandez, a local man who turned out to be a mine of information. Between 2005 and 2009, he had made three journeys by water from the centre of the isthmus to Lake Nicaragua for fishing. He and his brother used a ten-foot homemade canoe and, on reaching the lake, they were badly frightened by a six-foot bull shark, but returned home safely with their catch. Later, Mariano canoed westward for much of the way to the Pacific. Showing us his route, he and villagers pointed out that this was possible during the May to October wet season when a large area of flat land is inundated, becoming a shallow lake joining up the rivers and streams. There was clear evidence of the flooding, and it seemed that at high water small craft could have crossed the narrow isthmus. We also learned that a local farmer had once shipped his cattle by bamboo raft down the Rio Brito into the Pacific and then along the coast to sell them for a good price in an ocean port.

There were numerous artefacts that had an oriental appearance in the Mi Museo and on our return my friend Cedric Bell, an engineer surveyor who has become an authority on ancient canals, found indications in our photographs of what may yet prove to be early locks and canalisation.

Much more exploration must be done to confirm this. However, I believe the cartographers of the 15th to 17th centuries, who showed a channel at around 12°N, were acting on information from indigenous people who told them of a way through in the wet season and so they put it on their maps. But who was there in the 15th century to talk to the local people? If Gavin Menzies is right, it could have been the Chinese. Perhaps it was not surprising that on our last day in Granada I was invited to address a party of Chinese entrepreneurs! Later we heard a Chinese-financed canal was planned.

CHAPTER 12

A VOYAGE ON BALES

OF STRAW

Having been taught, like almost everyone else, that Christopher Columbus discovered America, I was intrigued by a report of a new discovery in Greenland in 1965 that confirmed the existence of Viking settlements in the New World. Were Vikings the first Europeans to land on American shores? Archaeologists and anthropologists have long theorised that there may have been ancient transatlantic contact, pointing out unexplained similarities between supposedly isolated cultures around the world.

Indeed, in the early part of the last century, European anthropologists identified striking similarities between the cultures of ancient Egypt and those of the Incas, Aztecs and Mayans in South America, citing architectural, calendrical and mythological parallels in proposing Egypt as the original source of all high civilisations.

Encouraged by the distinguished Norwegian explorer Dr Thor Heyerdahl, I began to study the fascinating possibility that man had actually succeeded in crossing the great oceans thousands of years ago. Thor Heyerdahl's 5,000-mile voyage from Peru to Polynesia on a traditional balsa raft had brought him both fame and controversy, but in 1970 his 3,800-mile Atlantic crossing from Morocco to Barbados in a reed craft had proved beyond doubt that such early voyages were possible.

Interestingly, Phoenician coinage dating from 350–320BC depicted the Atlantic and apparently part of the American coast. Furthermore, Roman amphorae found in a Brazilian bay and sculptured Olmec heads looking decidedly like proud Africans found in Mexico had long mystified anthropologists.

Then, in 1992, came the startling news that a German toxicologist had identified traces of cocaine and nicotine in 3,000-year-old mummies of Egyptian priestesses. Both substances were then unknown in Egypt, but were plentiful in the New World. Was this more evidence of an ancient and previously unsuspected trade route?

Thor Heyerdahl, whom Yoli and I met in London, was convinced that there had been a thriving maritime culture in South America, but could it be that people of the central regions had carried trade goods across the Atlantic?

It was in an effort to answer some of these questions that the Scientific Exploration Society supported a series of expeditions aimed at proving that traditional reed boats could navigate the rivers from central South America to the Atlantic and much further afield, while also seeking evidence of ancient trading routes. Aymara boatbuilders on Bolivia's Lake Titicaca were commissioned to build a reed boat for us and it was they who named the project Kota Mama – 'Mother of the Lake'.

Having consulted Bolivian archaeologists, the first project was to be a voyage down the Rio Desaguadero. Running south through desert from Lake Titicaca, the world's highest navigable lake, to Lake Poopó, this river is believed to have been a waterway used 3,000 years ago by an advanced pre-Incan civilisation known as the Tiwanaku. In March 1998 a variation in the El Niño weather system had reduced the river to a sluggish stream, winding for 250 miles through reed beds and sandbanks in oxygen-thin air at an altitude 13,500 feet above sea level. But it was here that we chose to test three traditionally built craft while also searching for undiscovered archaeological sites. In addition to these tasks, the venture would involve ethnographic and hydrological studies, wildlife conservation and assistance to remote communities.

The extensive wilderness of the Altiplano and desert regions of Bolivia is a potential treasure trove of archaeology, with an estimated 30,000 sites still to be explored – a huge job for the country's eight underfunded archaeologists, which explained the enthusiasm of their national institute of archaeology and anthropology for the project.

After years of reconnaissance and planning, construction of the craft began in December 1997. Gathering totora reeds from Lake Titicaca, celebrated reed boatbuilders Maximo Catari and his twenty-four-year-old son, Erick, set to work. Although 13,500 feet above sea level, their yard was a hive of activity as the three robust corn-coloured vessels took shape. Each was built of two tightly bound bundles of dried reed filled with tiny air pockets. Extra bundles were added to increase buoyancy. A light mast carrying a gaff mainsail was stepped in and a figurehead attached. The twenty-five-foot flagship sported a fearsome puma's head, baring vicious wooden fangs. A local ginger kitten had taken up residence in the jaws and was named Tittypusspuss. The two other, slightly smaller boats were adorned with uninhabited condors' heads.

Our team consisted of thirty Bolivian, British, American and Colombian explorers. Several, like Yoli and Jim Masters, had considerable experience, others were new to the game, but all were selected because they had skills to offer. Although landlocked, Bolivia has an extensive river system and a 5,000-strong navy, but had lost its outlet to the ocean after a disastrous war with Chile in 1879. Their sailors have understandably long yearned to re-establish some sort of navigable access to the open sea and many regarded the pioneering Kota Mama expeditions as a step towards achieving this.

On 14th March 1998 the boats were trucked into the town of Desaguadero, which lies on the Peruvian border. The Bolivian naval officers organised the launching ceremony for the following day and our tired team sank into their cots at the local 'fleapit' hotel. No sooner were they asleep than the alarm was raised. Peruvian thieves from across the river had sneaked in and stolen vital rigging from the boats. However, a Bolivian lieutenant bravely went after them, pistol in hand, and managed to recover the items. Next morning, government ministers, admirals and the British ambassador stood in the bitter, cold Andean wind as the Bolivian national anthem was sung with pride to a taped accompaniment on the town's loudspeaker system, followed by a somewhat shorter 'God Save the Queen', intoned a little self-consciously by the British. Speeches and a blessing by the priest came next, and then wine was poured over the boats' bows.

It was just as well that the guests had departed by the time Jim gave the order to cast off, because a sudden gust of wind carried the boats into the reeds on the Peruvian bank. However, the crews soon learned how to handle the gaff sails and, led by an Avon inflatable, the fleet disappeared downstream beneath an ominously darkening sky.

The boats were still out in midstream when a violent storm broke. With thunder booming, lightning flashing and rain and hail lashing down, our support group ashore watched with extreme anxiety as their colleagues out on the water battled this tempest, seemingly in danger of being overwhelmed. Thankfully, the little boats all came in safely, although some of the crews were speechless with cold by then. The QM's hot soup saved the day, but it was a miserable night, not made any easier by local pigs deciding to seek shelter in our tents.

Next day the overcast sky promised little relief and as the craft neared the village of Iruhito, another storm swept over the Andes. It struck the fleet just as the boats had run aground in mid-river, a mile offshore. It was a tense moment, as those on the bank could do nothing to help and if the stranded crews tried to wade ashore, they would either have risked sinking in quicksand or being forced to swim across several deep, fast-flowing channels.

Jim Masters, 'Admiral' of our fleet, radioed the support party to alert us to the fact that hypothermia was setting in and that if people could not be got out of the cold quickly, there were likely to be casualties. As the thunder crashed overhead and lightning forked into the black water, the Mayor of Iruhito appeared and, realising the danger, poled his tiny skiff to guide the boats to a safe channel leading in to the village. With teeth chattering, the sailors downed piping-hot drinks from cups they could hardly hold in their numb fingers. Several were also suffering severe altitude headaches.

The morning dawned fine and with it came our first major discovery. A local woman who had been busy ploughing a small plot of land on a low mound outside the village told our historian

Richard Snailham that she kept striking a large stone. Taken to the exact spot, he prodded around with a stick and detected the outline of a three-foot-square slab. The archaeologists were soon digging like terriers and just a few inches below the surface they came to what was gradually revealed to be a three-foot-high pedestal, carved from volcanic rock, at the base of which were two statues depicting the god Chachapuma. Further discoveries confirmed that they had found a temple later identified as a Tiwanaku religious centre dating back twenty-seven centuries. Morale soared!

Sailing further south, our boats encountered more shallows as the river narrowed. Now actually finding themselves praying for more rain, the team poled, pushed and portaged their craft. It was back-breaking work. Herds of gingery long-necked vicuña, a species of wild llama, stared in surprise as we passed and, at villages, children ran out to greet us. On arrival at settlements, bands played, school choirs sang and local ladies in voluminous skirts and traditional bowler hats insisted on dancing with the slightly dumbfounded expeditioners. At Calacoto the welcome was very special and we linked children from the local school to students in England via satellite phone, all speaking in Spanish. 'Do you play football?' was the first question the Bolivians asked.

Nearby, we made more fascinating discoveries, including the remains of three ancient settlements of a people known as Pakajes, or Eaglemen, a tribe that lived on heavily fortified table mountains, or *mesetas,* around the year AD1200. Vertical rock faces and concentric drystone walls were penetrated by the narrowest of entrances, only wide enough for one person. These would have presented a challenge even to well-trained modern attackers. Within the walls were beehive-like stone tombs, or *chullpas,* their shapes strangely similar to stone structures found in Turkey and also in the ruins of Great Zimbabwe, a medieval site in the south-eastern hills of modern Zimbabwe, thought to have been the capital of a once-great kingdom. Could this be a link with Africa?

Many of these elaborate graves still contained mummified bodies held in a foetal position by sacks of woven grass. Animals and tomb robbers had obviously been there, scattering skulls and bones about, like evidence of some terrible slaughter. Most skulls had been deformed and elongated during the person's childhood to suit the fashion of the day. A similar custom is found in Egypt. Like the Tiwanaku, the Pakajes had practised matricide, where wives and concubines were killed and buried with chiefs and great men. Evidence of this was seen in several *chullpas* containing one male skull along with those of up to eight females. It is known that human sacrifices, often of captured enemies, were made at such burials. We found remains of many children and it may be that they were also sacrificed.

At first, these mountaintop settlements seemed to be cities dedicated solely to the dead, but careful examination also revealed sites of dwellings far less sophisticated than the tombs. Clearly, the Eaglemen venerated the deceased and built the best for them. Masses of broken pottery, stone corn grinders, unsmelted copper and hand tools fashioned from hard rock littered the ground. One fortress had a tunnel connecting it to the hillside. Was it an escape route?

Beneath the cliffs lay square tombs decorated with painted patterns that showed what might have been step pyramids, like those found in Mexico and early Egypt. There were also designs looking like crescent-shaped boats filled with people. Beneath these were shafts running back into the mountain, but blocked with debris. Subterranean sepulchres hewn from the rock contained the remains of up to ten skeletons, and teeth marks on the bones indicated the presence of carnivores, probably puma. Fearing ghosts, locals kept clear, but we mapped the site and the underground passages whilst Lee Smart, a talented artist, produced some excellent paintings.

Support-team vehicles faced many a challenge. River crossings were a serious hazard and two vehicles spent a night axle-deep before recovery. Fortunately, most of us had trained hard to get fit. Six of us were in our sixties, but we managed to climb the precipitous slopes rising to almost 14,000 feet. Apart from the beautiful vicuña and sightings of a bushy-tailed fox and puma, the wildlife we encountered consisted of hares, small fat mole rats and countless waterbirds. The fossilised remains of a glyptodont, a massive tortoise-like creature that had roamed the Altiplano 5 million years ago, were also discovered.

Further south, in a remote barren wasteland on the edge of extensive salt flats, we met the Chipaya speakers. Said to be the direct descendants of the Tiwanaku, these people had a unique culture and spoke a language thought by some anthropologists to have similarities with Arabic and Hebrew. During the heavy rains of 1996, a river and ancient irrigation canals had burst their banks, flooding their village. Finding them reduced to living in tents and under wretched conditions, we designed flood defences that the British Embassy later financed.

In the desert west of Lake Poopó the expedition examined a three-mile-long channel that Atlantan scholar, Jim Allen, suggested might be a canal described by Plato in his account of Atlantis. However, Toby Mariner, a Royal Engineers geologist, considered it to be a natural fault line. It might possibly have been an early irrigation system, and indeed we certainly found evidence of several small Tiwanaku settlements along its length, but the site of Atlantis remains a mystery.

Hearing of a cave said to contain ancient wall paintings, Yoli, Richard and I set off in one of our four-wheel drives to photograph the site. A local man offered to guide us across the featureless desert, but he was taking a ram to market balanced on his bicycle! We tied his bicycle on the roof rack and popped the owner and beast on the back seat where the ram relieved itself on Yoli. After a while the man decided to leave us and go in another direction, so with some difficulty we tied the ram back on to the bicycle and he departed. To our relief a motorcycle then appeared bearing two parents with four children, and offered to guide us to the cave. To speed up the journey we took the wife and three children in the car, where the baby proceeded to pee over Yoli. However, we found the cave and gave Yoli a well-earned whisky.

On 11th April we reached a point where the Rio Desaguadero disappeared into the sand at the edge of Lake Poopó. El Niño had dried up the lake and so our voyage and impressive discoveries came to an end. We could go no further. However, the Bolivian archaeologists still thought that reed boats could have reached the ocean, so it was decided that the next voyage would attempt to navigate from Bolivia to Buenos Aires, a distance of some 1,700 miles. This would need the consent of the Paraguayan authorities, so Yoli and I visited General Lino Oviedo, commander of the army, who appeared to run the country.

The taxi driver seemed uneasy when Yoli told him where we wanted to go, the general being much feared by certain sections of the community. At the gate of the barracks an officer climbed in and escorted us to a group of unpretentious married quarters where a Guarani maid opened the door and the general, clad in an English sports jacket and cords, met us with a broad grin and a firm handshake. He was a small man with bright eyes that darted from one face to another as he spoke in Spanish and German. After generations of training by the German Army, Paraguay had recently started to send officer cadets to Sandhurst and the general was clearly delighted to have a visit from a British colonel who had once been on the staff at this academy, and was eager to help. The meeting went well and it was obvious that General Oviedo was much interested in the development of the Chaco and keen to assist its indigenous population. Placing his hand on Yoli's knee he said: 'Just tell me what you need, señorita.'

A staff car was then produced to take us into one of South America's least-known areas, with virtually impenetrable thorn forests covering an area roughly the size of England and Wales. The Chaco War of 1932–35, fought over territory wrongly believed to contain oil, had cost the lives of 60,000 Bolivians and 30,000 Paraguayans and was still occupied by the Paraguayan Army. No less than three generals, including Guillermo Escobar, led us on a rapid tour.

At one settlement we watched a birth in the army hospital and then penetrated far into dense bush on narrow trails. In winter, temperatures could drop below freezing, while in the summer there could be blistering heat. It was obvious that wildlife was plentiful. As we drove along, we saw foxes, hares, armadillos, deer, peccary and dozens of snakes.

A night game drive then took us along what appeared to be a wide tarmac road in the middle of nowhere. When I remarked on the lights set into the kerbs, Guillermo explained that the road actually served as an airfield. Three miles long, it was completely deserted. As we passed the darkened control tower, he went on to explain to us that the Americans had built it for emergency space shuttle landings. Later we learned that it in fact played a significant part in the smuggling of Scotch whisky into Argentina and Brazil.

When the subject of archaeology came up, the general didn't have a lot to tell us, apart from mentioning that there were rumours of stone buildings with strange inscriptions in the depths of the thorn forest. The problem would be how to get through this green hell where the thorns were four inches long. 'It is like concentrated barbed wire,' warned Guillermo. 'Make friends with the Indians, they have secret paths.' Then he added , with a smile: 'And tell your men to keep clear of the local girls, Paraguayan men will kill for a cow or a woman!'

Further good advice came from the Mennonite Christian communities we met, farming the land around Filadelfia. Originating in Germany in the 18th century, this peace-loving, hard-working Protestant Christian sect knew the Chaco well. 'Beware of Los Ayoreos,' they cautioned, describing an 'uncontacted' indigenous tribe that resisted attempts to clear the forest for farming. 'Our cars have been attacked with spears and arrows and men have died,' they told us.

Driving back to Asunción we hit something with a loud bump and when we stopped to check were confronted by an angry ten-foot boa constrictor, apparently undamaged, that rose up and struck at us like a cobra. Clearly, our next Kota Mama expedition would face some challenging conditions!

Titicaca to Poopó on Reeds, *Kota Mama 1*, Bolivia 1998

CHAPTER 13

ON TO THE AMAZON

It was sixteen months later, in August 1999, that we returned to Bolivia for the next phase of the Kota Mama expedition. Having benefited hugely from our earlier experience, we came well prepared for what promised to be the even greater challenge of a planned 1,700-mile river voyage right across the continent from Bolivia on the north-west side to the Argentine capital Buenos Aires on the south-east coast, via Brazil and Paraguay. The Rio Paraguay and the Rio Paraná are major rivers, so for this voyage a much larger reed flagship and a smaller tender were required.

Kota Mama 2 was 44.3 feet long with a beam of 10.5 feet, and had two large sails, one gaff rigged and the other square, that would provide propulsion when the wind was right. However, on a twisting river we would depend largely on current. A pair of traditional steering oars were fitted and, as she had no keel, a leeboard was also incorporated. To conform to local regulations and to ensure that we did not collide with the giant iron-ore-carrying barges on the river, a 15hp Mariner outboard was attached. Designed to carry sixteen, she had a main cabin that housed the navigation table and a ration store, whilst the aft cabin provided storage and just three bunks, with most people sleeping on deck or ashore, as we would always be mooring up at night. There was no galley and, in view of the inflammable nature of the material out of which she was constructed, no smoking was allowed aboard.

A British tug company, J. P. Knight, kindly sponsored this unique craft. An Avon safety boat with a 25hp outboard was towed and often pushed the craft. The twenty-foot tender *Viracocha* was similar to those used previously on the Desaguadero. Her design finalised with our boatbuilders on Lake Titicaca, she was propelled by a single sail and carried a crew of three.

We had recruited a new team of fifty-nine servicemen and civilians, including scientists, to take part in the expedition. Once again, our main purpose was to prove that traditional reed boats would indeed have been perfectly capable of making the voyage, while at the same time seeking archaeological evidence of transcontinental trading having taken place long before the conquistadors arrived from Europe. In addition, we also set out with the intention of providing medical and other aid to local communities along the way.

Our patron, General Hugo Banzer, President of Bolivia, wished to commission the boats in front of his palace in La Paz's Plaza Murillo. Jim Masters was thus faced with the challenge of getting the precious craft there, mounted on low loaders, and transported over narrow bridges and under a myriad of electric cables. This tricky operation was complicated further when *Kota Mama 2* arrived and was found to be far larger than the original design – it turned out that the Cataris had lost our plan and done their best from memory! Seizing saws, Jim set to work on cutting her down by three feet, but our flagship, complete with its fearsomely impressive puma figurehead, was still too tall to clear the power lines. The police produced wooden poles with which to push up the cables as we passed beneath, but when, almost inevitably, two of the wires accidentally touched at one point there was a splintering crash and a shower of sparks and the electricity supply to an entire suburb was cut off.

We did eventually manage to get one boat to the Plaza. The President, who was suffering from laryngitis and had lost his voice, took me on to an iron balcony to pronounce his blessing. 'I'm always worried when standing here,' he whispered hoarsely.

'Is the structure not safe, then?' I asked somewhat anxiously.

'Oh, yes,' he replied. 'But a predecessor of mine was hanged from it!'

With an inch to spare the boats squeezed through the tunnels along the trans-Andean road. At Santa Cruz, Yoli then arranged for us to transfer them on to a flatbed wagon attached to a train on what was known locally as the 'Railway of Death' on account of the number of inebriated passengers who regularly fell off carriages. The boat overlapped the sides of the wagon by quite a bit, requiring the train to take bends slowly, and so we trundled through the bush to the Rio Paraguay at a snail's pace. I reckoned that ancient mariners could have hauled them there, but we did not have time to attempt this.

At Puerto Quijarro we met our Bolivian Navy support vessel, also named *Puerto Quijarro*. What was effectively no more than a 300-ton self-propelled barge, it was to accompany us to Buenos Aires, carrying our stores and equipment whilst our two reed boats sailed ahead. This cost $38,000, our biggest expense. On deck, Jim Masters built an operation room housing our communication equipment, the computers and also a simple galley. By now, our website was already attracting a wide following.

Aided by the Bolivian Navy, we were preparing to sail when Neil Burrell, our expedition doctor, asked me if I was feeling OK, having noticed that I had suddenly turned a bright shade of yellow! A quick test by a local doctor revealed that my body was seriously deficient in sugar and I was put on a diet of fruit, brown bread, jam and glucose. Warning me off eggs, fats, milk products, red meat and – worse still!

– alcohol, Neil also told me to stop taking the antimalarial drug Lariam that I'd been using for some years.

I have rarely been ill on expeditions, apart from a few bouts of malaria, the occasional upset stomach and, famously, the side effects resulting from treatment for the vampire bite, and at this stage it was a real blow. Fortunately, however, my favourite mate de coca tea was permitted and, although not feeling my best, I saluted as the navy band struck up an eccentric version of 'God Save the Queen', followed by the lengthy Bolivian anthem and our flotilla cast off.

On being launched, *Kota Mama 2* was found to have a slight list – it was, after all, the first time she had been floated – but this was soon corrected and with the flat-bottomed naval support vessel in attendance, we headed for the sea. At our first stop, cows attempted to eat the hull and snakes tried to climb aboard, but otherwise our main problem was the weather. As we passed through the endless, putrid, insect-ridden swamps of the Pantanal, the wind changed, bringing in bitter, cold air from Patagonia. For several days we battered short, sharp waves, using our steering motor to help keep us on course and on schedule. And then the temperature rose to 42°C. This is a land of extremes and one could well imagine the difficulties faced by the conquistadors as they tried to sail up this waterway.

Arriving on 14th August at Paraguay's first river port, Bahia Negra, Noel decided that I was actually sicker than I felt and that I must visit a hospital without delay. In one of South America's most remote regions this was a problem, but from the earlier recce Yoli recalled that the Mennonite Christian community had one at Filadelfia. So, handing command to my able adjutant Stuart Seymour, I set off with Yoli on a 280-mile drive in a 4WD driven by Fernando, a pistol-packing Paraguayan. Bouncing along on dirt tracks through the Chaco's almost impenetrable thorn forest, scanning the headlight beams for bandits and wildlife, we saw only several large boa constrictors warming themselves on the trail. At a shack along the way a kind woman made herbal tea, which she said was 'good for the livers' as I downed the awful concoction.

Driving quickly past the high gates of a remote, isolated hacienda our driver grunted: 'Aeroplane farms, that's all they grow,' hinting at the lucrative cocaine trade. Gripping my pistol, I watched out for the Ayoreo, the indigenous people of the Gran Chaco, who were known to attack passing vehicles with bows and arrows. At midnight we drove into the darkened streets of Filadelfia. The hospital was firmly closed and a night nurse refused to admit us, but Yoli found a hostel nearby and I managed to get a couple of hours' sleep. Next morning, Dr Edwin Hauf, warned of my visit by satellite phone, had got everything ready with typical Teutonic thoroughness. As well-equipped as a Harley Street specialist, he even had an ultrasonic scanner with which to inspect my internal organs. In two hours, the tests were complete and several doctors gathered to deliver the verdict.

'You have drug-induced hepatitis, probably a reaction to the Lariam you have been taking against malaria,' they announced.

A strict low-protein diet was prescribed, with masses of sugar and water, and I happily paid $100 for one of the most thorough medicals I'd ever experienced, carried out in the shortest possible time and in one of the more remote areas of South America. As I took my leave Dr Hauf added: 'And stop taking the Lariam – there is hardly any malaria here.'

A chatty English-speaking nurse from Winnipeg sold us a load of glucose. Altogether, the care and efficiency with which I was treated said a lot about Mennonite organisation.

After I head eaten a whole pot of strawberry jam, as per doctors' orders, we headed back to the expedition, pausing at Chaco National Park, where Jim's team was designing a biological conservation centre. As night fell, I was asleep in the front of the car when a screaming local, armed with a revolver and knife, attacked the vehicle, but before I could spring into action, driver Fernando had already knocked out the inebriated fellow.

In the late morning the President's lovely wife, Señora Susanna González Macchi, a former Miss Paraguay and now First Lady, or 'Primera Dama', flew in wearing a beautifully tailored trouser suit and high heels. Tossing her blonde hair, she came straight over to our team and talked to them all in English. By now a large crowd of Paraguayan and Bolivian government officials, members of the American Nature Conservancy and other conservationists had gathered. Before starting on the formalities, this charming and unassuming Primera Dama then made a point of going straight to the open cookers to speak to the cooks and waiters, a gesture that went down well. Speeches and the unveiling of a plaque were followed by a walk up a steep hillside to a viewpoint overlooking the vast park. Impressively, the First Lady managed the 600-foot climb in her high heels with no effort at all, followed by a retinue of puffing, panting officials. At the barbecue lunch afterwards we briefed her on our programme and plans, and were delighted when she asked if she could come aboard *Kota Mama 2* in Asunción.

As we continued along our route, scientific and community aid projects were carried out, archaeological sites were examined and a fortress dating back 2,500 years was found in the Andes foothills. Petroglyphs located in eastern Paraguay were thought by some to be of Scandinavian origin, but our archaeologist dismissed this.

However, the lives and culture of some extremely interesting tribes were recorded by the anthropological team.

Aboard *Kota Mama 2* we had two dentists, one appropriately from the Royal Navy, who extracted no less than 1,400 badly decayed teeth from impoverished people unable to afford local treatment, while our doctor gave medical assistance to hundreds.

The Paraguayan Navy were extremely supportive throughout and their Commander-in-Chief sailed with us for short distances. The First Lady also came aboard, but had to remove her high heels to avoid puncturing the boat's deck, which she did without demur, while the Admiral was dismayed when not allowed to smoke on board. A satellite phone link to a school in Devon was established and Señora Susanna answered questions.

'How do you become a Primera Dama?' asked one teenager.

'Marry the leader of the opposition party and wait!' she replied, with a radiant smile.

Pam Coleridge, my former PA and a nurse from the Congo expedition, and harpist Marigold Verity appeared on local TV. As the harp was Paraguay's national instrument this proved highly popular. On board our support vessel we had a new honorary crew member – a Paraguayan piglet presented to us by villagers in gratitude for Pam's nursing and given the name Rocket.

Thriving on leftover food chucked into a bucket labelled 'Rocket Fuel', he became a lively pet… especially at night. A bitterly cold wind was blowing when I was awoken in the early hours one night by the sound of deep breathing. Then to my horror someone began to lick my feet and as I disentangled myself from the blankets there was a shrill squeal and our piglet emerged from where he had sought refuge from the cold out on deck. Heaving the protesting porker out,

I tried to get back to sleep. Meanwhile, Rocket was gathered up by a member of the crew and popped into the bed of a fellow shipmate. Pandemonium then broke out when the occupant returned from an all-night party in the camp ashore.

Working late most nights, I would often fall asleep as I wrote my log, my pen trailing across the page; then the writing would start again. A reasonably legible account of something quite unconnected with the events of the day would occasionally be scribbled whilst I was apparently more than half asleep, but with both eyes open, or so I am told! It was as if my mind worked on two tracks.

Having reached the Rio Paraná, we were joined by a jolly pilot from the Prefectura Naval Argentina (Argentine river police), who helped with navigation. An endangered marsh deer (*Blastocerus dichotomus*) lives in the swamps of north-eastern Argentina and, whilst our hydrographers charted the river, I took a group to survey this rare creature for the wildlife department. Englishman Charles Pettit and Dolores, his charming wife, farmed a plantation on which they grew famously caffeine-rich yerba maté tea and they invited us to camp in their garden.

Spotting the deer from ground level amid the swampland's tall reeds proved almost impossible but, very conveniently, Charles and his friend Titi Bruni both owned microlights. Flying low at 60mph, with cameras at the ready, we soon came across a fine russet-coloured buck and a group of females. Skillfully, Titi brought the floatplane down on to the water, but as we hit the surface a large black caiman reared up like a dragon right in front and a squadron of peccary plunged through the shadows. 'Phew!' grunted Titi, brushing aside a cloud of mosquitoes as we taxied to a halt. My heart had missed a beat or two!

Above: Near Shafartak bridge on the Ethiopian Blue Nile at expedition's end, 1968 (page 16)

Below: Presenting Lulette to Emperor Haile Selassie in Addis Ababa, Ethiopia, 1968 (page 18)

Below: Shifta bandits in the Blue Nile Gorge, Ethiopia, 1968 (page 31)

Above: Electric fish caught by Captain James Tiernan, Royal Engineers on the Ethiopian Blue Nile, 2005 (page 57)

Above: Dentist Graham Catchpole with barber, to whom he presented a donkey, at Tenta, Ethiopia, 2005 (page 38)

Below: Flotilla on the Ethiopian Blue Nile, 2005

Above: Opening a new well near Tenta, Ethiopian Highlands, 2005

Below: Ethiopian Police rescue party with Simon Hampel (*3rd from right*) on the Bashilo River, 2005 (page 32)

Above: Ann Tweedy Savage inspects an abandoned Russian tank near Dessie, Ethiopia, during our Magdala expedition, 2005 (page 77)

Below: Blind Dahlak islanders (page 90)

Above: Dahlak Expedition team, 1970 (page 85)

Below: Local boy on 'Sebastopol' on Mount Magdala, Ethiopia, 1996 (page 77)

Above: Magdala children

Above: Sheikh Siraj, ruler of the Dahlaks, 1970 (page 87)

Below: Sheikh Siraj's car (page 89)

Above: A peep at *Playboy* in exchange for frogs, southern Ethiopia, 1966 (page 100)

Below: Sandhurst Ethiopian Expedition, 1966 (page 2)

Above: Demolished Long Range Desert Group Chevrolet, south of Kufra, Libya (page 119)

Below: Driving my army desert-equipped Land Rover in the Libyan Sahara, 1962 (page 116)

Above: Richard Snailham (*left of centre*) and I (*left*) meeting President Mobutu in Kinshasa, Congo, 1975 (page 132)

Below: The river blindness team – including Carolyn Oxton, in her replica Livingstone Consular hat – in the Congo, December 1974 (page 126)

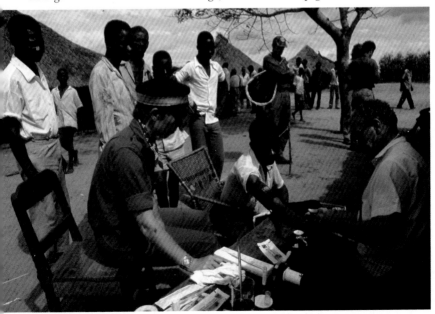

Above: The giant inflatable *David Gestetner* in the Kinsuka rapids, Kinshasa, Congo, 1975 (page 130)

Below: Special aluminium ladders were built by Royal Engineers to aid the Range Rover in Panama's Darién Gap, 1972 (page 143)

Below: A Panamanian Guardia Nacional soldier with his lunch in the Darién Gap, 1972 (page 164)

Above: Marching out of the Darién Gap into Colombia, St George's Day 1972 (page 152)

Below: Kuna women, Panama, 1972 (page 155)

Above: Cannon at Mulatupo, San Blas, Panama, 1979 (page 160)

Above: One of the RAF diving team, Mark Moody, with a hammerhead shark he bumped into on the wreck of the *Olive Branch* in Caledonia Bay during Operation Drake, Panama, 1979 (page 163)

Below: My friend Captain Vivian Rowe, Royal Marines (*left*) and archaeologists study the ruins of Acla, Panama, 1979 (page 168)

Above: Strange petroglyphs, possibly from 3000BC, Rio Sambú, Darién jungle (page 174)

Above: By Lake Nicaragua with Yolima Cipagauta and local archaeologists Oscar Paron and Luis Garcia, 2010 (page 186)

Below: Emberá people at Bahia Piña, Panama's Pacific coast, 2003 (page 173)

Above: The well-laden motorcycle in the Bolivian Altiplano which led me to caves near Challacollo (page 197)

Below: Yoli linking Bolivian children to a school in Devon by satellite phone, 1997 (page 207)

Above: Kota Mama 2 reed boat on the Rio Paraguay (page 201)

Below: The ancient Samaipata archaeological site, southern Bolivia (page 218)

Below: Moxos mound burial site on Rio Beni, Bolivia, with expedition members Jules Chenoweth (*left*) and Mike Brennan (*right*), 2002 (page 250)

Above: We met the Nichols family at their homestead on Rio Madidi, Bolivian Amazonas, 2007 (page 246)

Below: Flotilla leaving Rurrenabaque on *Kota Mama 6,* 2007 (page 249)

Below: Xingu the double-nosed Andean tiger hound (page 243)

Other wildlife included capybara and later, out on foot, I spotted a small herd of them at the water's edge of a lake. There was no cover, but clutching my Nikon I crawled stealthily down a long, open slope and after about half an hour was only twenty yards from them. Although they eyed me arrogantly, they were not alarmed, so I raised my lens and took some fine shots. The giant rats ignored me and even when I then stood up, covered in mud, they continued to feed quite happily, so it seemed that I needn't have endured that uncomfortable crawl, after all.

Walking forward I stood amongst the herd and their young, snapping close-ups. 'You were lucky,' said Charles when I told him about this. 'Yesterday they killed two big dogs belonging to one of my men.' It was indeed a doubly lucky day for me, because when I later called home on the satellite phone, I learned that my daughter Victoria had produced a son, who, in later years, was to join me on expeditions.

As we neared Buenos Aires a Force 6 wind blew up, and we were buffeted by six-foot white-crested waves, but the reed boat actually withstood the battering better than the metal-hulled support vessel. With flags flying proudly, we tied up in Tigre on the River Plate on 7th October 1999. The 1,690 miles had taken us two months, but *Kota Mama 2* and her tender were still in good shape, although now weighing over 21 tons due to the water absorbed. We estimated she would last six months, although some reeds were already starting to rot. We could only surmise as to how the early navigators had handled heavy sails, probably built of basketwork, or how the traders would have got back home. The southerly winds would certainly have helped. Maybe they just paddled hard, keeping to the banks. Reeds found growing *en route* could have been used for repairs, but a different craft would have been needed to cross the Atlantic.

The Prefectura Naval and the British ambassador gave us a great welcome, but to avoid causing any offence to post-Malvinas feelings, we mostly kept our celebrations to ourselves. However, the Argentinians we met could not have been more friendly. Alas, still yellow and suffering from the Lariam-induced hepatitis, I could not enjoy even a small celebratory glass of champagne.

Kota Mama 2 was shipped home on a cargo vessel and donated to a sailing craft museum near Lowestoft. Sadly, the museum later closed down and the great vessel was left to rot.

It now only remained to test our theory on the other river route to the ocean – via the Amazon. 'So, we've got to go down two thousand seven hundred miles of river and rapids on a bale of straw,' muttered Jim Masters when I told him of the new route. From the Andes to the mouth of the Amazon was certainly not going to be an easy voyage. Three cataracts would have to be negotiated on the Rio Beni in Bolivia, followed by 190 miles of rapids, some quite impassable, on the rivers between Bolivia and Brazil. Sandbanks, floating and submerged trees and a healthy population of mosquitoes all added to the challenge. Historically, it seemed that traders would have pulled their boats around the worst rapids, but we felt they must have had a craft that could negotiate at least some of the less severe ones.

A ceramic model of a reed trimaran found in a Peruvian tomb indicated that such craft were used around AD400–500. So with the help of the Titicaca boatbuilders and more support from J. P. Knight we designed *Kota Mama 3*. A central hull thirty feet in length was joined to twenty-three-foot side hulls, or outriggers, by rope ties. The hulls could rise and fall independently, so as to conform to the wave patterns found in a cataract. The giant flexible rubber rafts we used on the Zaire River expedition in 1974 had performed splendidly and we prayed that *Kota Mama 3* would do the same. For passage through narrows, the outrigger hulls could be detached, and we again fitted an outboard engine for steering. Some would argue that this was not authentic, but our main aim was to test the hull and the purpose of the engine was primarily to serve as a safety feature that would enable us to take evasive action should we find ourselves in danger of being run down by seagoing ships on the Amazon.

The sail arrangement on the new boat was the subject of much discussion. *Kota Mama 2*'s gaff and square sails had proved impractical, so this time we settled on a 'bird's wing' rig. In addition, fourteen of our crew of sixteen would be equipped with long-handled paddles. By various means of propulsion and with a current of 2 or 3mph we aimed to do thirty miles per day. The problem was that the trimaran could not be assembled and tested until we reached the river, at which point there would be no turning back!

A sixty-strong international team, including twenty-one serving and retired Sappers, volunteered for the expedition, with Jim again acting in the role of 'Admiral'. My friend Alasdair Crosby of the *Jersey Evening Post* came to cover the story. My HQ and support group would move by local craft until we reached the major cataracts at the Brazilian border. Thereafter HQ would transfer on to a double-decker Amazon ferry.

We also decided to test one of the traditional balsa rafts still used on these rivers. Eight very light and strong balsa logs, pinned with stakes of hard black palm, made up the thirty-foot craft. On the four-and-a-half-foot-wide deck a raised platform of plaited bamboo provided relatively dry storage for cargo. We calculated she would carry up to half a ton, including three paddlers.

Whilst the boats were under construction the expedition concentrated on another task for the Bolivian archaeological institute. It was believed that high in the mountains above our start point was the fabled lost city of Paititi. It became a formidable task to reach and survey the site. The jungle-covered slopes had the profile of a Toblerone chocolate bar, much of it covered in knee-deep mulch and alive with biting *tucandera* ants, hordes of vicious stinging sweat bees and small brown snakes. Entering the cloudforest, I was struck by the silence, although millions of eyes were probably watching our stumbling procession, drowning in perspiration but impelled onwards and upwards by the hope that we might find the legendary city.

An engineer section cut thirteen miles of track, made river crossings, and built a footbridge to get archaeologists and surveyors to the ruins. The journey to and from Paititi in the heat and rain remains one I shall never forget. Although the press declared 'Lost City of Patiti Found', it was not actually the legendary city of which we had gone in search, but an old Inca gold mine that had been located earlier by Hitler's photographer, one Hans Ertl.

However, on almost our last night at the site, Celso, the chief who had led us there, confided: 'If you are seeking an old city, I know a much better one. We call it Victor Pampa.' So we sent a small recce party with archaeologist Elizabeth Dix to investigate. To our amazement, they did indeed find a mass of what looked like very interesting stone constructions deep in the jungle, but further examination would have to wait for the next expedition.

Our investigations produced a backlash from neo-Nazis who, according to Bolivian Army intelligence, believed that so much

British military involvement indicated British government backing. It seemed they thought we were seeking 'Hitler's treasure', which it was thought Ertl might have hidden in this remote spot. As a result we encountered swastika-armbanded thugs in La Paz, were attacked in the press and falsely accused of dynamiting and firing the jungle with petrol. But that's another story.

Meanwhile Jim had convoyed *Kota Mama 3* in Bolivian Army trucks along the notorious 'Road of Death', over the Andes from Lake Titicaca to the riverside town of Guanay, where Ernie Durey, our QM, had established a base. Once again the national anthems rang out, this time from a school band arranged by Yoli, and on 14th June 2001 the flotilla set off on its voyage to the Atlantic.

An Antarctic cold front had us shivering as we shot the first set of cataracts, but the trimaran coped easily, and we began to see how the early traders could have transported gold and coca plants thousands of years before. Prehistoric rock carvings and partially eroded burial mounds provided more evidence of early navigation. Furthermore, we discovered axe heads of andesite, only found in the mountains, along the river.

The temperature was now decidedly tropical. Yawning caiman, turtles, colourful birds and leaping monkeys watched us sail by. At Esperanza we met the first big rapid and lowered *Kota Mama 3*'s masts to tackle the tossing, towering waves, the like of which no-one had previously navigated. To the cheers of locals, our reed flagship rode it magnificently, her hulls rising and falling just as intended. Thereafter, as we navigated down the river dividing Bolivia from Brazil, the rapids grew more severe and at Ribeirão we encountered a real monster.

An aerial recce had identified the route, but the powerful current swept the big boat away from a relatively smooth tongue that ran through the foaming breakers. To their horror, the crew saw a fifteen-foot-deep hole appear at the foot of a fall and beyond it a massive stopper wave. Racing down the slope the bows collided with the wall of creamy water. The rope ties on the starboard outrigger snapped, the central hull and the outrigger capsized and eleven crew were pitched into the torrent as the wrecked craft plummeted over another fall. As it did so, the central hull righted itself, bringing up those clinging to lifelines. But she was still afloat. The safety boats quickly picked up the survivors and as darkness fell *Kota Mama 3* drifted away downriver.

By a miracle no-one was seriously hurt. 'Looks like the end of the expedition,' some said, but Yoli, as always, had a friend and, through him, found a Bolivian pilot who flew us downriver next day. After thirteen miles there was the trimaran, neatly tied up to the shore. The Bolivian Navy had seen her drifting down the river during the night and thinking she was a drug runner had brought her in. 'God looks after little children and mad people,' commented Captain Ayala drily. Down from Lake Titicaca flew old boatbuilder Maximo Catari and within a day he had straightened the distorted hull, fitted new reeds and, having portaged some impassable rapids, we were again on our way to the Atlantic.

At Pôrto Velho in Brazil we hired the first of our double-decked ferries to act as the support vessel to accompany the rebuilt trimaran. Providing space for cooking, hammocks and stores, the good ship *Capitão Azevedo* would be with us as far as Santarém, where *Viageiro VI* would take over. When we were 375 miles from the ocean Jim abandoned the damaged and waterlogged outrigger and *Kota Mama 3* became a catamaran, actually going faster as a result!

In Brazil the expedition medical section co-operated with mission organisations working with remote communities, but in such a short time only basic assistance could be given and the team was frustrated to see many people it was unable to help. Pausing at a remote village we found an indigenous mother whose daughter had a double cleft lip and a severe cleft palate. 'Please make my daughter look like me,' she pleaded.

'In England, surgery could correct this,' said Sam Allen, our senior doctor 'But there's nothing we can do here'. However, back in Somerset, Jim Masters worked hard to raise $4,000 for the American charity Smile Train to perform an operation, if we could find Ronalda, as she was called, and get her to São Paulo. A year later Richard Drax, a BBC presenter (and now an MP) flew out and, following our directions, located the family and took them across Brazil for the operation. Today Ronalda is a beautiful young lady, married with her own family. Richard Drax's TV show and Viscount Gough, between them, went on to raise over £20,000 for SES to help other facially disfigured children.

Dentistry was again much in demand and Graham Catchpole established a record by extracting 1,125 teeth in 120 days!

On the Amazon the mosquitoes attacked in clouds, but we were more worried by the presence of pirates who had boarded a local ferry ahead of us. Having left our firearms in Bolivia we fashioned improvised bazookas with drainpipes and distress rockets. Our Brazilian Marine liaison officer, Marcelo Mendes, called in the navy and in the final stage a gunboat proceeded us. Less fortunate was the New Zealand yachtsman, Sir Peter Blake, who was murdered here a few weeks later.

Nearing Belém, I noticed half a ship protruding at an angle from the river a couple of hundred yards away. A quick glance at the chart alerted me to the danger. 'Sandbank dead ahead!' I yelled to the helmsman, who, not understanding a word of English, just smiled back. 'What the devil is Portuguese for sandbank?' I cried in frustration. 'Stop! Reverse!' I gesticulated at the captain, who had come up to see what the trouble was about.

Peering at the approaching channel, he shrugged. 'No problem, Colonel. Plenty water.' Then the good ship *Viagra* as we named her shuddered to a halt. '*Banco de areia*,' ('Sandbank') grunted the skipper. With the tide ebbing we soon developed a twenty-degree list, but it was a good time to hold a Burns Night supper. Ernie produced Stahly's haggis and Scotch. No-one really noticed the list thereafter!

At Belém we were greeted by another large crowd and a band, while the British Defence Attaché handed Yoli our mail. 'Do you know someone who lives at Balmoral Castle?' she asked me. Indeed, the letter was from Her Majesty the Queen, who, I was led to believe, had followed the progress of our voyage with some amusement!

Andean artefacts were found along the route. And we were told that from August to November the east wind blows sailing canoes upriver, so the traders could, indeed, have sailed home. The balsa raft we had built was still intact. *Kota Mama 3* was twelve inches lower in the water and had several species of plant and a small snake thriving among the rotting reeds, but she was still buoyant when presented to the Brazilian Navy. As Thor Heyerdahl predicted, it seems likely that the early people of South America could have reached the ocean. We thought that the drama was over as we headed home, but on the way most of the team had to change planes in New York and, sitting in the airport terminal, watched 9/11 as it happened. However, I was still awaiting the next flight to New York and was still in São Paulo when the awful news broke, but the ever-helpful American Airlines staff put me on to a BA flight direct to London. It was some days before our team managed to get home from New York. Unsurprisingly, there was not much media interest in *Kota Mama 3*'s incredible voyage.

 ▶️ Andes to Atlantic by Reed Boat, *Kota Mama 3*
Expedition, Bolivia to Brazil 2001

CHAPTER 14

RUINS AND CANYONS

The more we explored Bolivia, the greater the number of fascinating new challenges that presented themselves, inspiring us to return and mount further scientific exploration in this country so rich in archaeological history and biological diversity.

Encouraged by Jimmy Patiño, a senior member of a famous Bolivian family and supported by the Simón I. Patiño Foundation, the SES organised a series of ventures in July 2002. As before, our Latin American representative Yoli, making full use of her numerous contacts, skills and wide experience, played a leading part in planning and executing these next Kota Mama expeditions.

Co-operating with the Samaipata Museum, the *Kota Mama 4* expedition's first task was amongst the ruins of El Fuerte de Samaipata, a vast, carved rock hilltop structure dating back to 1500BC, located in the eastern foothills of the Bolivian Andes. Although called a fortress (*fuerte*), it was actually a religious and ceremonial centre with a settlement attached, believed to have been founded by the Chané, a pre-Inca Arawak people.

Some five miles from the hill town of Samaipata, this sacred place, along with the ruins of around 500 dwellings nearby, has now been declared a UNESCO World Heritage Site. The major feature is a complex system of channels, sculptures and raised reliefs of puma and serpents. A most intriguing pair of parallel channels runs downhill, giving rise to many theories, including a hypothesis by the author Eric von Däniken that they were an ancient spaceship launching pad!

Our main task was to investigate La Chincana, a mysterious deep shaft said to lead to a secret labyrinth of underground tunnels that could have been used to escape from the site if danger threatened. Previous exploration attempts had been abandoned because of floods, and also unexplained ghostly noises.

Our thirty-three-strong international team included Bruce Mann and other archaeologists, among them a couple of Bolivians and a Colombian. We found the shaft cut cleanly into solid sandstone, descending at an angle fifteen degrees off vertical for some twenty-six feet. Alfredo Jacobs, an enthusiastic Bolivian geologist, was especially keen to study La Chincana and insisted on being the first to be lowered down the shaft. As this was only three and a half feet in diameter and Alfredo was well built, I was a bit concerned as we roped him down. Although he could not find any inscriptions or side tunnels, he discovered rope marks on the wall and a small antechamber. Most importantly, he noted that the shaft intersected with a layer of conglomerate, which would have carried water from higher ground. Mystery solved! It was a cleverly made well.

Meanwhile, we dispatched a party under army pilot, Major John Greenacre, to study ruins in the Amboró area. Marching through dense forest and baked semi-desert for three weeks, they located intriguing caves filled with human bones, and masses of ceramic shards. Ruins of buildings and defensive walls revealed more pottery and stone tools, showing the area must have been heavily populated in ancient times. It was a notable archaeological success, thanks largely to John's leadership.

It was believed that the Inca in Samaipata had been protected by some outlying fortresses to the east, and the museum urged us to study ruins at a clifftop site named Parabanocito. So, accompanied by a Bolivian TV team, including an engaging Chilean presenter, we drove thirty miles to the edge of the mountain range. A logging track had been cut up to the site and although, sadly, it damaged some of the walls, it did give us vehicle access and we pitched camp there. We found that there were actually two large Inca forts with concentric defensive walls, still standing several metres high and facing eastward, where their traditional enemies lived.

Whilst surveyor Jerome Bradley and a team mapped the structures, Bruce and the Bolivian archaeologists examined the ruined Great Hall or *Kallanka* in the southern fort. At an elevation of 4,000 feet, our tented camp was frequently swept by gale force winds sweeping up the Chaco, making cooking on the open fires challenging. Powdered egg and local dried meat were supplemented with tinned food, vegetables from the village and a *jochi* (a large guinea pig) shot in the forest. Isabel Schaechterie, a German member of the team, proved to be a fine cook and made excellent bread, whilst Yoli also produced some tasty dishes. After dinner Fiona Leslie, a trained singer, would entertain us with an aria or two!

The presence of treasure hunters, known as *guaqueros*, had already been detected and the area was known to harbour a number of bandits. Following our earlier problems with the neo-Nazis, General Hurtado, Chief of Staff to the President, had assigned an experienced Special Forces Colonel to look after us. Although short in stature, Hugo Cornejo was a muscular figure with an easy, friendly attitude and considerable confidence. However, jaguars – which had attacked farmers – and a plentiful supply of venomous snakes proved to be more of a problem than the *guaqueros*.

To obtain some local game for the kitchen, I'd brought my .22 rifle and a shotgun, but also felt that they might prove useful if we were threatened. On several occasions I was woken at night by voices calling out from the jungle, but saw nothing, and wondered if this was an attempt to scare us off. Then on 8th August, about to fall asleep, I heard movement near our stores tent. Pulling out the shotgun and a torch, I eased myself from the tent. However, as I emerged I heard Hugo call out, '*Alto*,' followed by the sound of running feet and the roar of the Colonel's pistol. A white bundle lay on the track and for a moment I thought: *My God, he's actually shot someone.* But the bundle turned out to be nothing more than a sack of loo rolls the thief had dropped as he fled.

My one major concern was the attitude of the young Bolivian archaeologists. Being an experienced archaeologist, Bruce's skills were of the highest standards and although he was extremely tactful, the local archaeologists clearly resented him. Furthermore, they did not enjoy camping nor our rations. So, one way and another, Yoli and I had to spend a lot of time placating and encouraging them to help with the manual tasks. Rolando Marulanda, an unpredictable and talkative Colombian archaeologist with his own agenda, was another problem. He had been passed on to us by the museum, together with a French TV team whose chief mission was to promote him, but whose culinary skills were much appreciated by the rest of us. Despite these occasional personality clashes, we nevertheless made significant discoveries, including some fine Inca pottery in the Great Hall, strange rock carvings and a grave. It would have been exciting to excavate the grave but William Castellon, the senior Bolivian archaeologist, objected. And when he did eventually agree to go ahead the rain was falling and we had to abandon the plan.

The surveys and research were much appreciated by the museum and John Greenacre's team had produced excellent results from the Amboró area. Back in Samaipata, we were debriefed, enjoyed a farewell party at the museum and drove west to the charming, unspoiled colonial town of Vallegrande. On the high ground above the great valley of the Rio Grande, the town was famous for the demise of Che Guevara, but was now to be the starting point for a future Kota Mama expedition. A most helpful British expat, Alan Raven, had kindly arranged for a small Cessna, used by locally based missionaries, to fly Yoli and me on a recce of the river.

The two robust American pilots supposedly ran a flying doctor service, but their cropped hair and military style made me wonder if they were indeed true missionaries. The pocket on the back of the passenger seat held a .410 carbine loaded with slug rounds and a New Testament. 'Praise the Lord and keep your powder dry,' muttered one of the pilots.

Flying in a clear sky we soon reached the little-known Rio Grande. A distant tributary of the Amazon, it plunged through near-vertical-sided canyons of black rock. presenting a dark and forbidding view as it closed over foaming rapids. One gorge was ten miles long and, in another, house-size boulders had tumbled down, almost damming the flow.

To navigate and explore this formidable mile-deep cleft in the mountains would be a real challenge. Reminded of the Blue Nile, I was busy snapping photos when I noticed something out of the corner of my eye: two giant birds had suddenly appeared, dead ahead! Before I had time to say anything we tilted over and a black condor, huge wings beating, passed just beneath us. 'Christ, that was close,' exclaimed the pilot.

Most importantly, the recce had provided the information I needed to plan the future expedition. And I had also made some useful new friends in Vallegrande. We collected those who were continuing on the second phase of this venture, and drove west, pausing to enjoy lunch and dancing at Hugo Cornejo's home before reaching La Paz at 02:00 hours. Now, at 1,300 feet, it was bitterly cold.

The Bolivian archaeologists had arrived a day ahead and, as expected, had written a critical report on their time as our guests. The Director of the Archaeological Institute (UNAR) was unconcerned and, valuing British financial support, agreed to back our future plans. Somewhat embarrassed, he introduced us to the foreigner who had attacked us in the press during the *Kota Mama 3* expedition.

'Why?' I asked him.

'I hated your patron, the dictator General Banzer,' he replied nervously. It seemed the banning of neo-Nazi gatherings by Banzer upset this chap, but he was afraid to speak out whilst the General lived; an unpleasant business.

Now we had to investigate the Victor Pampa site discovered in 2001 and the burial grounds along the Beni River. Some of our team had changed and, working day and night, Yoli purchased new rations, sorted out the UNAR paperwork and collected schoolbooks for distribution. Then she interpreted as we presented medical equipment from Britain to the navy for their hospital boat.

Driving from La Paz at dawn, down the 'most dangerous road in the world', I glanced over the yawning precipices and prayed. Ominously, crucifixes and flowers marked the site of fatal accidents. The riverside town of Guanay, where we had launched *Kota Mama 3*, already proudly proclaimed Paititi Tourismo, in spite of our denials that the ruins we had found were the fabled lost city. Local outboard-powered boats carried us up the winding river to Mapiri, pausing only to help a three-year-old with a hernia and hugely enlarged scrotum. Old friends greeted us at the village and, hiring packhorses and porters from Celso, who had guided us previously, we set out on a three-day march uphill to our objective. The relentless sun, sweat bees and horseflies did not help. Water had to be carried between the few springs and pools on the way and a bushfire caused by our porters trying to clear out a nest of snakes almost cooked us alive! Eventually, we found a way to Victor Pampa and scrambled down a 1,000-foot jungle-covered slope to set up a camp amongst some overgrown ruins. Feeling a surge of excitement, we then set off to machete our way through the vegetation. As Elizabeth Dix told me in 2001: 'We found an extensive settlement with large, well-built stone buildings, a sophisticated water supply system, and roads for porters and pack animals running for several kilometres. The remains of a big house and a cemetery containing some large tombs were also discovered. Blocks of stone weighing many tons indicated that the early inhabitants were probably Inca, but Spanish colonists had built on top of the site. An enormous effort had been put into the construction, but the purpose was a mystery.'

A stone-floored plaza was quickly cleaned and revealed a metal chamber pot and a wine bottle. A few lime trees, coffee and tea plants were still evident. Irritated by insects and snakes, including the highly venomous coral species, the bite of which can lead to coma and death if not treated, we surveyed the site. Celso hoped it would attract tourists, although I doubted many would want to hike to this remote, unhealthy spot. Bruce reckoned it might have been a gold mine or a collection point for quinine or rubber. Once again, however, it was not Paititi, and later research indicated it might have been inhabited up to 1850.

On the way back to Mapiri two of our local helpers, moving ahead, bumped into a couple of armed thugs and were told to push off. Running back up the trail they told Hugo. Turning to me he said: 'You take another trail down.' And then, with his pistol swinging at his hip, he strode off saying: 'I'll investigate.' Meeting up with us again later he reported: 'They are just farmers, but they are not growing coffee. When you're gone, I'll return with some of my anti-narcotic forces.'

'How many?' I asked.

With a shrug and a sheepish grin, he replied: 'About two hundred.'

Celso and his people were rewarded with funds to buy a TV and a satellite dish 'for educating the children', but I suspect it was mostly used to watch football. We promised medical equipment for the local clinic, run by the dynamic Sister Rosario, and bidding farewell to our hosts at Mapiri we motored downriver in two large boats, passing semi-naked gold prospectors panning on the banks.

Camping at the smelly riverside town of Teoponte, people noisily celebrating its anniversary with a disco in the plaza, we replenished our stock of vegetables and found a shop selling Grant's whisky, which raised morale.

Jules Chenoweth, a former Royal Marine turned archaeologist, and Bruce photographed fascinating pre-Colombian petroglyphs inscribed on riverside rocks, before we reached the infamous Retama Rapids, which we had navigated previously. This time, however, the water level was low and we shot through without difficulty, seeing no sign of other humans, but many birds and giant otters.

As we came ashore at the Kaka River junction, a sleek black jaguarundi raced across the beach. On our previous expedition Bruce had identified an ancient burial mound, bisected by a creek at this point and, with permission from UNAR, this was to be our next excavation.

In Guanay we'd been joined by Francisca, a jolly Bolivian lady who had cooked for us previously. After a hot, humid night her tasty pancakes raised our spirits and, led by Hugo, we waded up the creek, beating off the midges and bees. At the site we found Bruce and Jules in ecstatic mood, as the dig had revealed funerary urns containing human bones. Maria Mason, our American osteoarchaeologist, and Paul Liddiard, a forensic dentist, were soon hard at work. As the temperature rose to 40°C at noon, they pieced together the bones and reckoned it was a female skeleton. Beads and shells that had formed a necklace seemed to confirm this. Thought to be a Mollo burial in a mound once forming the base of a dwelling circa AD1200, it was a splendid find.

By now most of us were covered in insect bites, and we had also been plagued by sudden storms with gale force winds and torrential rain. Cold fronts sweeping in from the south caused the temperature to plummet temporarily and, crossing a flooded creek, several of the team had to be rescued by Jules. Emerging from the gorges we reached Rurrenabaque – the 'Gateway to the Amazon' – a growing town somewhat isolated from the rest of Bolivia. The authorities remembered us from *Kota Mama 3* and, eager to encourage visitors, welcomed us back. Continuing on down the Beni River we located other mounds eroded to reveal Mollo pottery, and in one village saw the 1,000-year-old skeleton of a man who would have been around six-feet tall, a giant compared to the usual height of local people. Interestingly, local legends talked of a race of giant people. Paul said the teeth indicated remarkably good health. 'No Coca-Cola or sweets in those days,' he commented.

Our tasks completed, we headed back upriver, pausing to measure and photograph a strange ten-foot-high boulder that glowed in the dark. Back in England, geologist Dr Ken Reed said that this could be caused by thermoluminescence: 'During the day, heat from the sun is absorbed by the rock,' he explained. 'This energises the atoms of certain elements and the energy is returned as light over a period of time, not necessarily instantaneously, as the atoms return to their normal state after the original energising source has ceased to be active at night. A number of carbonate rocks are known to possess this property; the presence of lithium, as well as other elements in the carbonate, can give rise to the phenomenon. It might also be caused by bioluminescence, which is light emitted by certain organisms such as fireflies and glow worms. However, microbes, algae or fungi growing on the surface of the rock could conceivably be bioluminescent.' Whatever the cause, it was another interesting discovery to complete a highly successful expedition in some of the more remote parts of this wilderness.

In 2004 we returned to the Rio Grande that I'd seen on my air recce. Cutting a livid gash through southern Bolivia, it rises in the high Andes, plunges through enormous vertical-sided canyons and spills into a maze of channels and swamps, threading its way to the Amazon.

Sergeotecmin, Bolivia's Institute of Geology, was especially interested in finding minerals and oil; the navy wanted a hydrographic survey carried out; the *Alcalde* (the equivalent of a mayor) of Vallegrande needed the water supply sorted out; and the Tourism Ministry was keen to promote the area. Additionally, the archaeology of this unexplored cleft was virtually unknown. So, like our Blue Nile expedition, it was a multi-tasked project requiring some special craft to navigate a river that dropped from an altitude of 5,250 feet to 1,475 feet over a distance of almost 200 miles.

Having pioneered the use of white-water rafts, trialled the first GPS and tested numerous types of special equipment and clothing, the SES had a reputation as pioneering innovators. Ben Cartwright, a fine practical engineer who had accompanied us on many expeditions, worked together with Eurocraft Ltd, builders of special inflatables, and E. P. Barrus Ltd, who had provided us with robust, reliable outboards for thirty-six years, to produce a fleet of five unique crafts.

Sponsored by the Chatham tug company J. P. Knight, these included two sixteen-foot and two fourteen-foot self-baling inflatables with thwarts sealed with watertight zippers to store delicate equipment and an inflatable bladder. Built of extremely tough neoprene, their 15hp Mariner outboards could also charge batteries and were fitted with propeller guards. Although this reduced power rate by 35% it was essential for use in the shallows. The engines were mounted on a transom inside the craft and could be lowered through an opening in the hull when required. Otherwise, the boats were paddled by four-man and six-man crews.

A fourteen-foot inflatable two-man kayak named *Fearnought* – the same we used on the Blue Nile in 2005 – was also constructed to recce ahead of the flotilla. All the boats carried floating line, karabiners and pulleys for rescue purposes. Stores in waterproof bags were secured by cargo nets and each craft had a handheld Motorola radio in a waterproof case. Flying all this to Bolivia and coping with the usual customs problems was itself a daunting task.

After a training session with our boats in Wales, the thirty-eight-strong team, which was made up of doctors, dentists, engineers and scientists and included an Australian and several Bolivians and Colombians, assembled in Santa Cruz and then moved on to Vallegrande in May. I've always believed strongly that if we help the local people they will be more than happy to assist us. In this case the water supply was piped from two mountain streams sixteen miles away into holding tanks above the town. The simplicity of the system was that it was entirely gravity fed, requiring no pumps. The leaking thirty-five-year-old pipes urgently needed replacement and Just a Drop, the water charity, kindly contributed US$10,000 towards the total cost of US$20,000. Retired Sapper Colonel Mike Reynolds, a chartered engineer, took charge of the project, which went ahead at full speed. Meanwhile, Shirley Critchley, aria singer Fiona Leslie, Simon Hempel and our medical team carried out a host of other aid tasks while preparations for the assault on the river went ahead. Simon organised the reconnaissance and support group (RSG) that would meet the flotilla at prearranged points to deliver rations and supplies and take out any scientific specimens we'd collected.

Setting up a base at the house of a kindly townsman, Lalo Carrazco, we packed up our stores. On the 21st May, after driving down a hair-raisingly precipitous mountain track, we reached El Ajial, to be greeted by villagers in traditional costume. In return for our gifts of medical equipment, dentistry and reading glasses we were treated to a fine lunch of roast venison.

Next day, following a traditional Inca Pachamama ceremony to seek Mother Earth's blessing for our voyage, our deputy leader, ex Royal Marine SBS officer Colonel Malcolm Cavan, along with Hugo Cornejo, led the flotilla downriver in *Fearnought*.

The sun rose into the deep blue sky as we paddled on, scraping against rocks in the shallows. My log noted a descent from 5,000 feet in temperatures of up to 35°C. On 24th May, archaeologist Jules Chenoweth made his first discovery. Brimming with excitement, he showed us round a site on a bluff above the river. Pottery shards, mortars, hammer stones and axe heads indicated a 1,700-year-old settlement.

A few days later, Ken Reed, Mauricio Ordonez and geologist Oscar Almendras of Sergeotecmin were delighted to find evidence of smelting, including gold-bearing quartz and marine fossils estimated to be 430 million years old. The only setback of the day came when our doctor, Sean Biddulph, accidentally scalded his leg badly with hot porridge and would have to go out when we next met up with the RSG.

In these remote areas the almost total absence of humanity encouraged wildlife. Foxes were common and at night a puma came to drink beside our boats, while condors circled high overhead. For us, the only real discomfort was the constant, often violent wind that blew fine sand up the gorges.

The silt-laden, boulder-strewn river raced in torrents through nine grey-black rocky canyons, their barren walls rising for thousands of feet on each side. At the entrance to the western gorges we encountered a sheer-sided defile and, as we edged closer, I saw *Fearnought* swept up against the wall above a swirling eddy, hurling Malcolm and Hugo into the foam. The current held them and the kayak against the rock face until we were able to pull them out with lines. By taking a slightly different route the rest of the flotilla managed to enter the forty-foot-wide canyon and sail through. Above us, the abutments of a colonial bridge hung out. 'Probably built on an Inca site,' commented Jules.

At times our boats had to be lined through rapids that were deemed unnavigable and, facing a cleft in a massive rock wall that we named 'The Gates of Hell', a gale force wind and flying sand struck us bow on. Emerging from the water at this point was a series of rocks and, buffeted by the blast, one craft became wrapped around a boulder. Unable to free their boat, the crew scrambled on to the rock. It then took nearly two hours to pull the boat clear with ropes from the shore and to rescue the crew with throw-lines. Downriver, *Fearnought* picked up lost items and after giving the shivering men time to warm up we pressed on. By a miracle, our intrepid cameraman, Mike Laird, managed to preserve most of his precious camera equipment undamaged.

My own boat was twice forced against the sharp, stratified black shale of the protruding rocks, slicing open the tubes, but in most cases the boulders had been rounded by erosion and we simply bounced off. Some equipment was lost as a result of further capsizes but, generally, Ben's Eurocrafts were highly durable and performed excellently.

On reaching the road bridge south of Vallegrande we took a welcome break to visit the site of Che Guevara's last stand and held a Burns Night supper in the town before pressing on eastwards. The few villages we encountered were friendly and the dental treatment, in particular, was much appreciated. In gratitude for an extraction, one woman led us to caves, known only to the local people, filled with well-preserved wall paintings coloured red, black and white.

Other villages welcomed us with dancing, and in one, apparently run entirely by women, the ladies beseeched us jokingly not to lure their husbands away. 'We need them to work for us and keep us warm in bed!' they cried. At these settlements we were usually able to supplement our dried and canned rations with goat, sheep and vegetables. We also managed to shoot some jochi and catch fish.

One night I was woken by loud grunting. Assuming it to be a dangerous peccary, I went on to the beach with my gun to investigate. A local fisherman had set a net in the river from which the noise was emanating. There was no sign of any peccary, so I went back to bed, but at dawn we pulled in a sixty-pound *surubi* catfish, still grunting!

Heavy rain in the mountains filled the river with mud, making it difficult to obtain clean drinking water. To overcome this, we added a purifying product named PUR to a bucket of what looked like brown soup, but you had to be desperately thirsty to gulp down the resulting less-than-crystal-clear liquid. Occasional clear streams were prized for drinking and washing and a hot spring in the final few days provided a welcome, if somewhat sulphurous, bath.

The RSG used mules, horses, donkeys and an extraordinary cross-country go-kart named *Koyak* that Hugo had built to transport supplies to the flotilla. *En route* they made many archaeological discoveries, including a cave full of ancient skeletons, while also having to cope with rattlesnakes, midges and mosquitoes.

Howling gales produced sandstorms that reduced visibility to a few metres at one point, but when the wind was in the right direction the boats rigged up improvised sails. As the altitude dropped, the temperature rose and, entering Patiño Canyon on 13th July, we sailed smoothly through an extraordinary gallery of natural wind-polished rock sculptures, caves and crevices. A backdrop of sandstone, coloured yellow, red and white, reflected on water alive with jumping fish. 'Henry Moore must have been here,' muttered Ben.

The geologists had meanwhile located black shale, indicating oil; the navy hydrologist was a happy man; and the Tourism Ministry welcomed the archaeological and wildlife reports. Covering a few thousand miles, Simon's RSG, along with Shirley and the medical team, had done magnificent work with the local schools and hospital. Mike Reynolds's repairs to Vallegrande's water supply was much appreciated and Fiona, who had worked at the V&A Museum in London, set up a museum section in the town to commemorate Che Guevara.

Having dropped 3,840 feet in 200 miles and navigated over 400 rapids with no serious casualties, we could look back with satisfaction on a job well done. And to cap it all, Her Majesty the Queen sent the team her congratulations.

 YouTube Lost Civilisations, *Kota Mama 4* Expedition, Bolivia 2002

 YouTube Rafting the Rio Grande, *Kota Mama 5* Expedition, Bolivia 2004

CHAPTER 15
ON A WING AND A PRAYER

In 2006, Oscar Kempf, the Director of Sergeotecmin, Bolivia's Institute of Geology, congratulated us on the success of the Rio Grande project and with a wry smile announced: 'We have another little task that may interest you.'

Surrounded by fossils and various other specimens, he and geologist Eddie Baldellon produced a large-scale map of the Rio Beni area that they laid out on the table in front of us and, leaning forward, Oscar stabbed his finger on a blank space. 'Right here,' he said. And then, noting my look of slight puzzlement with a grin of quiet satisfaction, he reached across and pulled up a satellite image of a huge circular crater on a computer screen. Five miles in diameter, the Iturralde Crater, also known as the Araona Crater, lies 250 miles north-east of La Paz and is thought likely to have been caused by a meteorite, either an asteroid or a comet, colliding with Earth between 5,000 and 30,000 years ago. If so, it would have been one of the most recent of such events in our planet's history, the impact of a meteorite the size of a London bus producing an explosion equivalent to many megatons of dynamite that would have affected a large part of the Amazon Basin.

'The widespread after-effect would have been comparable with that of the eruption of Krakatoa in 1883,' commented Oscar Almendras, who had also joined us for the briefing. The long-term legacies of such impacts are important in the biological and geological history of our planet and, consequently, the crater was of considerable scientific interest. And if it was indeed one of the earth's youngest impact craters, its creation could well be indicated in the folklore of indigenous South American people.

'The fireball created by the meteorite as it hit the Earth's atmosphere at sixty thousand miles per second and started burning up could have been seventeen times brighter than the sun,' explained Dr Benny Peiser of Liverpool John Moores University, with whom I later discussed it, adding: 'They would certainly have seen it!'

The impact of a meteorite in what was a swampy area would almost certainly have thrown up a massive quantity of waterlogged matter, which could have fallen back into the crater. This might explain why it is only a few metres deep and why it therefore remained undiscovered until 1985, when satellite pictures from outer space revealed a telltale change in vegetation neatly contained within the circumference of its rim.

There remained many questions to be answered, several scientific expeditions having been defeated by the challenging terrain and adverse climatic conditions. All life within a fifty-mile radius would have been exterminated as a result of the explosion, but at the same time industrial diamonds and sapphires might have been created. 'No wonder they are so interested,' I remarked to Yoli as we strode off to the army's map depot. 'Clearly a recce is essential.' Hugo Cornejo was not able to come with us but through Admiral Marcos Antonio Justinano, whom we had met in Buenos Aires on *Kota Mama 2*, the navy offered to provide an officer from Riberalta.

Along with Yoli, Oscar Almendras and Eddie Baldellon, I prepared to fly to Riberalta in northern Bolivia. Smoke from bushfires had closed the airport, but clutching a Geiger counter, GPS, cameras and a copy of *Exploration Fawcett* – the book by early-20th-century explorer Lieutenant Colonel Percy Fawcett, who had mapped Bolivia's borders and sought lost cities in the South American rainforests – we managed to find a flight to smoke-free Guayaramerín and a decrepit minibus from there to Riberalta. Here, pistol-packing Sergeant 'Freddie' Roca and a sailor mechanic, Juan Carlos, joined us. Together, we set out for Ojaki, the nearest settlement to the crater. The absence of suitable planes and airstrips meant hiring a costly 4WD pick-up to drive some 200 miles to Cavinas, a lonely navy post on the Rio Beni, from where we were to go on by boat to Ojaki. Another problem then arose – was there a bridge of any kind across the Rio Yata, beyond which Cavinas village was isolated? No-one knew.

At this point Remberto – a sly, opportunist driver – turned up with his car. After the usual delays to get petrol, change oil, collect and eject relatives of the driver, we set off along the long, dusty red road. As the sun reached its zenith we lunched at the local Sheraton, not an outlying branch of the hotel chain, but a shack-like café, with billiard table and a jaguar skin on the wall.

After 160 miles, we arrived at a collection of thatched huts, strangely named 'Australia' on the map, where we turned on to a bush trail across a swampy plain, leading to the 165-foot-wide Rio Yata. There was no bridge, and a log-built ferry was lying half submerged under the front wheels of a large minibus, which had unwisely been driven on to it. The owners, two Germans from a Bolivia-based religious organisation, appreciated our help in retrieving their vehicle and we were then ferried over and rendezvoused with the helpful navy at Cavinas. After encountering several problems in trying to find a suitable boat, largely solved by the innovative Freddie, we eventually headed up the midge-infested Rio Madidi, and, cooked by the relentless sun, eventually reached Ojaki in a local *peke-peke* canoe. A village of 300 Tacana people, Ojaki boasted a school, a chapel and a radio linking it to the outside world.

At dusk the temperature dropped and the midges were replaced by mosquitoes. However, a hut was provided for us, albeit alive with rats, in which to sling hammocks. The *Corregidor*, official headman of the village, Don Renato Gonzalez, along with his family and workers, soon appeared on a well-worn tractor and trailer, returning from where they had been harvesting Brazil nuts. Surprisingly enthusiastic about exploring the crater, he agreed to let us use his tractor for a sortie the next day. Alas, its wheels broke through the deck of one of the rickety bridges we had to cross as we drove north into thick forest, but, unperturbed, Don Renato and some of his workers who were accompanying us managed to extract it. And further on along the way we all helped to pull a cow out of a creek in which it had got stuck. After seventeen miles we camped in a jungle clearing, where a blazing fire kept the mosquitoes at bay, whilst Don Renato described the local situation.

Conflicts over Brazil nuts with rival Brazilian growers had resulted in several deaths and the situation was still tense. Freddie tapped his pistol thoughtfully. Don Renato's brother had survived an attack by a jaguar, but had plastic surgery, which they claimed made him look younger. Rattlesnakes were common and, as we soon discovered, sweat bees could be a real nuisance. To my dismay, during the night the village hunter shot a 500-pound tapir, so our start at dawn was delayed by it being butchered, salted and hung high on a tree to dry.

Guided by GPS and Eddie's map, the march to the crater was no joy. Grassy knee-high hummocks and heat greeted us as we emerged into an open plain, and the noisy sweat bees began to drive us demented. These vile beasts swarmed all over us, sipping our salty sweat. On slipping off one's pack they crowded on to our damp shirts and bare skin was soon covered in supping bees. Wisely, Freddie took the acclimatised geologists forward whilst the rest of us dug a hole to provide a little water, finally taking shelter behind our mosquito nets, sweat pouring out of every pore. I noted that Don Renato had recommended tins of salt water and urine to deter the bees. After dark, peccary and a large armadillo visited our camp, but there was no sign of Freddie's party or any calls on the walkie-talkie that night, and at dawn I awoke shivering with fever. Yoli had a violent tummy upset too, but we pressed on, following the geologists' track in the pampa until thankfully we met them, totally exhausted and with Eddie feverish. Lack of water had prevented them reaching the crater and, feeling pretty groggy myself and having only a litre of water left per person, we were in no condition to go on much further.

By the time we reached the tractor, most of us flopped down, completely whacked, and Señora Gonzalez was praying. *And they live here!* I thought as we gulped down some sterilised swamp water and glucose tablets. I noted in my diary that it would take a robust team in good health with an ample supply of water to reach the crater.

At dawn, Yoli and I made pancakes to raise morale and then, having wrapped up the stinking tapir meat, we piled on to the tractor and, bucking and leaping as if we were riding an untamed bronco, set out for Ojaki. It was over 32°C and our pee became dangerously dark as our bodies cried out for water. Being hurled about in the trailer reminded me of a particularly violent fairground ride that I had hated as a child. Dust, sweat and decaying meat produced an aromatic challenge, whilst precious water was poured into the tractor's thirsty radiator.

At the village, children rushed to meet us as if we'd returned from the dead, and German the schoolmaster greeted us with large glasses of lemon and grapefruit juice. Keen on animals, he proudly produced his giant anteater, its long tongue flashing in and out as its fleas hopped on to us! But then a small, sad-looking and obviously pregnant grey dog caught my eye. It had strangely divided nostrils and I suddenly realised I was looking at a rare double-nosed Andean tiger hound, as first described by the legendary Colonel Percy Fawcett in 1913.

'We bought Bella in Riberalta,' explained German, adding: 'She has a good sense of smell and is a great hunter.' On his return to England Fawcett had been ridiculed for his tales of sixty-foot anacondas and dogs with what appeared to be two noses, but now I had confirmation that his tales of the tiger hound were true. Until then it had not been officially recognised as a breed, being regarded by many as a cryptozoological creature – a mythical beast rather like the Yeti or the Loch Ness Monster. It turned out that Bolivian hunters used these dogs to track jaguars, known locally as '*tigres*', hence their name. Back home, the *Daily Mail* was fascinated by stories about Colonel Fawcett, and I guessed this was something that would intrigue them.

The return journey was fraught with the usual difficulties. The unscrupulous Remberto incurred my wrath for attempting to smuggle turtles out in our car. Having released these endangered reptiles we endured the long, hot drive to Riberalta, during which the wretched driver kept falling asleep, compelling me to take over until the fan belt then broke. No spares of course, but Freddie improvised with a pair of Yoli's knickers! Back in La Paz, even though we had not reached the crater, Oscar Kempf was pleased and planning started for a further expedition.

In 2006 we made a second recce, driving over the Andes to Rurrenabaque and boating to Ojaki. Surprised but happy to see us back, Don Renato produced a list of requests. In return for the villagers' support they asked for medical and dental aid, a clean water system and an organ for their new chapel! I designed a water system, which I hoped Just a Drop might fund, and also agreed to seek an organ. Alas, Bella the dog had died, but fortunately one of her double-nosed pups, named Xingu, had survived fit and well. 'Guard him with your life,' I instructed German, as the *Daily Mail* had agreed to help finance the new expedition in return for the exclusive story about the tiger hound. 'We'll be back next year.'

All we needed now was a group of enthusiastic, stalwart people, including the usual collection of doctors, dentists, a few engineers, a geologist and an inexpensive means of air reconnaissance. Plus, of course, a pedal organ and an organist! SES secretary, Lucy Thompson, took the initiative here and managed to track down a redundant organ at St James's Church in Milton Abbas in Dorset.

A few days later, sitting in our garden at Motcombe, where the SES also has its expedition base, I was disturbed by what sounded like a motorcycle passing overhead! Over the apple trees there then appeared a flying bedstead attached to a parachute. The fearless aviators landed in a neighbouring field and turned out to be a young man and his teenage sister, who had told the staff at her nearby boarding school that she was going on a nature walk with her brother! They were leading a small squadron of other magnificent men in a variety of flying machines, including Gilo Cardoza, Motcombe village's resident inventor, and the intrepid Bear Grylls, whose parents I knew well. Strapped into their various powered paragliders, they took off again from an almost literal 'runway' of just a hundred feet and soared into the sky. Clearly, paramotors of this type were just what we needed for Bolivia.

We duly approached SkySchool Ltd, who sold us two paramotors, but Bear Grylls, who had been planning to join us on the expedition, then decided to paramotor over Mount Everest instead, so his place was taken by ace paramotorist, Dean Aldridge. Mark Williams, a well-built insurance underwriter, volunteered as the second pilot and went off to take lessons.

Colonel Patrick Brook, a friend from my days in Oman, agreed to lead a survey party to the crater, which included surveyor Tim Harrison and a Bolivian Army Geographical Institute team, equipped with a gravimeter to detect the meteorite. A Royal Engineers geologist, James Bryce, would join others from Sergeotecmin. Meanwhile, no fewer than four adventurous organists volunteered, plus two doctors and two dentists. Ben Cartwright could not resist another adventure and came as our mechanical genius. In total, thirty-six people from various nations set out in 2007.

Airlifting the team and gear to South America was no easy task, but American Airlines helpfully agreed to treat folded paramotors as sports equipment. Sent ahead, the pedal organ became stuck in customs at La Paz. 'It is not permitted to import organs,' insisted a stern customs officer, until Yoli explained that it was a musical instrument and not a human organ.

Several days were spent on meetings, shopping for equipment and stores and briefing three unenthusiastic Bolivian soldiers, sent by their general to look after our security. However, at dawn on 24th June we set out by unheated bus and lorry across the Andes, fortunately bypassing the worst of the 'Road of Death'. While one member suffered convulsions and a puncture was repaired, musician

Claire Roff gave us a tune on her violin. Bolivian ladies on the way to the market halted their donkeys and paused to listen, nodding their bowler hats in appreciation.

At Teoponte, on the Rio Beni, we boarded five twenty-six-foot mahogany boats, fitted with outboards that Yoli had hired. Sponsored by J. P. Knight Ltd, and flying Bolivian flags and Red Ensigns, they were named after the company's tugs. Rain and low cloud chilled us as we loaded the organ and stores and set off downstream. We passed smoothly through the dangerous Retama Rapids, enduring the usual arguments with the boatman over fuel and sailing after dark.

Finally, at 22:30 hours, the lights of Rurrenabaque appeared and we moved thankfully into the Hostal Balsero, while Yoli arranged for all of us to have a meal at Adelita Jordan's delightful Casa de Campo restaurant. Next day we liaised with the navy and purchased an old Toyota 4WD, hired a strange Chinese three-wheel tipper truck and reloaded our craft. Michael Cansdale, our 'Director of Music', pulled a muscle in his back and had to go home, but luckily we had three other organists!

On 29th June we sailed, passing through a tricky logjam to camp on a sandbank, where Francisca, our faithful cook from Guanay, served a tasty meal in the moonlight to Claire's musical accompaniment.

Pink flamingos, egrets and monkeys entertained us as we passed the mound on which we had found exposed ceramic pots in 2003. The sun was beating down on the yawning caiman and not a breath of breeze disturbed the overhanging branches of the jungle trees edging the muddy river, when a splintering crash echoed across the water. To my horror I saw the barge carrying our Land Cruiser and almost all our petrol listing dangerously, her superstructure a tangled mess. She had struck a partly submerged tree, which had ripped into the craft's deck, causing a heavy fuel drum to break loose, crashing into our water engineer, Julian Butter, and fracturing his femur. This was a major problem as we were a long way from help.

At the nearby village of Carmen del Emero we carried Julian to the health post. 'It's a hospital case,' pronounced Susan, our doctor. The indispensable Yoli immediately called a friendly colonel of the Bolivian Air Force on the satellite phone and, incredibly, two Huey helicopters appeared the next morning, having flown 500 miles, and airlifted the casualty to La Paz. What service!

Then, having repaired the barge, our flotilla of mahogany craft continued the 600-mile journey to '*El lugar donde nadie va*' – 'The place where no-one goes'. We had already passed through rapids and logjams, now we faced the shallows of the Rio Madidi. More submerged trees again nearly capsized the barge, but at last we saw the children of Ojaki waving excitedly from the high bank.

Hauling ashore the pedal organ, we were greeted by an excited Xingu, the double-nosed puppy, son of Bella. I'd now discovered that these canines were probably descended from a Spanish split-nosed pointer that may have accompanied the conquistadors. Reported to have an enhanced sense of smell, Chilean police were finding them very useful for detecting mines or narcotics, as well as jaguars.

In the village chapel we held a moving candlelit service, with the music provided by our organists, violinists and a flute player. Slightly to my surprise, the organ sounded fine, but now we had to train the Ojaki to play.

Then came the next problem. The bridge carrying a track through dense jungle towards the crater had been swept away by floods but the villagers felled some trees and rebuilt it in just a few hours.

More bridges had to be repaired along the way, but Patrick and the survey party eventually got the Toyota to within twelve miles of the crater. From here they had to scramble on foot over three-foot-high hummocks hidden amongst the tall grass of the savanna. To find a way through, the Ojaki fired the grass, creating a huge blaze that had the added benefit of clearing out the rattlesnakes.

Aggressive bees with red-hot-poker stings attacked in swarms, and they were also plagued by malaria-carrying mosquitoes and tiny sandflies. Water was scarce and one night was spent without any at all. 'God, this is an awful place,' radioed Patrick. Taking turns to carry the fifty-pound gravimeter on their backs, Bolivian soldiers, surveyor Tim Harrison and the geologists gathered soil samples and found huge metamorphic rocks of ferrous metal and pebbles that could be attracted by magnets, probably created by the crashing meteorite.

Taking off from the village football pitch, Dean and Mark, our paramotorists, soon proved invaluable for seeking water sources, taking photographs and helping to maintain radio links. They were a great asset, and the villagers were awestruck. 'They are talking to the angels,' a watching mother told her child as Dean and Mark winged their way over the jungle. It was like a scene in a James Bond movie.

Yoli was busy filming when I heard her cry: 'Oh no!' Looking up I saw Mark's paramotor diving towards the river, his engine having suddenly cut out. With fifty pounds of equipment on his back, landing in the water would not be a good idea. Thankfully, he somehow managed to glide to earth and landed with a thump and a stumble almost at our feet. The propeller frame was irreparably bent, but mercifully Mark was undamaged. From then on he became the cook for Patrick's team. Dean, meanwhile, continued to scout ahead for the surveyors.

A typically Bolivian problem was discovered shortly after we arrived at Ojaki. Fuel at Rurrenabaque had been donated by BP, but as no drums were available we had purchased new ones in La Paz. On route to Rurrenabaque these were dishonestly exchanged for old ones used to carry acid. As a result, 130 gallons of polluted petrol had to be jettisoned and the drums replaced – a costly business.

While the crater explorers were at work, our community aid team provided medical aid and extracted rotten teeth at settlements along the river, distributing much-needed schoolbooks and reading glasses. Funded by Just a Drop, we also built a thirty-five-foot reinforced-concrete water tower and installed a pipe system. I thought I'd given up trench digging when I retired from the army, but we all ended up wielding spades in order to encourage the locals.

Dentists David Daniels and John Holmes were hard at work pulling teeth, while at the same time John also made a study of a disease affecting the Brazil nut trees on which Ojaki's economy is based, discovering an invasion of yellow caterpillars that were sent off for analysis.

The weather, meanwhile, was extraordinary, rapidly changing from one extreme to another. One day we'd be sweating in tropical heat and on the next we'd have to pull on thermal underwear as bitterly cold fronts swept in from Patagonia, with temperatures ranging wildly from 9°C to 40°C.

Two Ojaki girls were successfully taught to play the organ and the village's religious services were further enhanced with performances by Claire of Bach's 'Toccata and Fugue'. Claire also entertained us during our campfire suppers of roast racoon (tasting like lamb) and piranha, playing everything from Mozart to Gershwin. And she presented a violin to a young girl she taught to play.

At the end of July our exhausted surveyors returned to base having established that the crater was almost certainly caused by a huge meteorite, which now lay buried about a mile underground. The date of its arrival has yet to be determined. However, in trenches dug for the water supply system we found ancient pottery pieces about 5,000 years old, but, alas, no diamonds nor sapphires. Maybe these artefacts belonged to a civilisation wiped out by the meteorite.

Visitors to our camp were rare, but one of those who did come was of special interest. Matthew – or Mateo – Nichols, in his forties, a former US soldier and a preacher, lived with his large family thirty-eight miles upstream from Ojaki. Arriving in a canoe, he sought advice on metallic pebbles found when sinking a well. A deeply religious man, Mateo and his German wife Tanya had produced ten children, whom we later met at their hand-built wooden homestead. On the 830-acre smallholding, Tom (fifteen), Shen (thirteen), Leah (twelve), Thelma (ten), Gabriel (eight), David (seven), Laura (five), Hainz (four), William (two) and Floya (seven months) were soon to be joined by yet another sibling. In many ways they were like a modern Swiss Family Robinson.

To educate their children, the couple had their American friend, Charlotte Krops, who also tended the prolific vegetable garden, supervised the milking of the cows and ran the family school. The garden produced cucumber, lettuce, cabbage, tomatoes, beans, herbs, peppers, mango, papaya, mangold (spinach), banana, pineapple, corn and watermelon. The domestic animals included cows, a prize bull, sheep, pigs, dogs, rabbits, horses and a tame peccary. Having no medical help, they relied heavily on herbal medicine. Catclaw was grown for the immune system and kidneys, whilst as a prophylaxis for malaria they took a herb named Chuchuguaza.

The surrounding area of savanna and swampy jungle abounded with wildlife, some of which they hunted. Tom, the eldest boy, had shot a puma that was attacking the cows, and they claimed a pampa wolf had taken sheep. There were also jaguar and other smaller wild cats. White-lipped peccary were a real hazard, these aggressive pigs having killed one of the dogs. They had seen herds up to 200-strong, but usually the groups were smaller. The white-lipped peccary should not be confused with the white-collared variety, which is usually harmless. In fact, there was a pet one in Ojaki that we nicknamed Gregory, who adored salt biscuits.

This 'Garden of Eden' in which the family lived had other hazards. Close to their canoe mooring, a fifteen-foot anaconda had stalked baby Floya, until her brother Shen drove it off with shots from a .22 rifle. They were also very aware of the rattlesnakes and coral snakes as well as some large caiman. In the past year there had been floods, with the river rising to within a metre of the bank top. This was the highest the locals had experienced since 1960. Being virtually self-sufficient they needed little and had no luxuries, not even a radio. However, they were fascinated by the paramotor and Dean did a demonstration flight around the homestead. As is often the case with people living in remote areas, the Nichols family were extremely kind and hospitable, serving us with plates of pork and fresh vegetables followed by the lengthy grace. We believed that the magnetic pebbles Mateo had found could be related to the meteorite.

The arrival of another cold *surazo* weather front from Patagonia had us all shivering for several days. Morale dropped and the Bolivian soldiers sent to guard us moaned incessantly until I got their colonel to speak to them on the satellite phone. Violin recitals by Claire and a local guitarist lifted our spirits and at our final service in the little church Ojaki girls played both the organ and the violin. Local hymns and 'Praise my Lord, the King of Heaven... praise him praise him' rang out in the humid night air.

On 29th July we embarked for the long haul to Rurrenabaque. Lines of immobile caiman basked in the sun as we dodged floating logs. Engine breakdowns, mosquitoes and midges plagued us, but Francisca's scrumptious meals and Claire's rendering of Mozart's *The Magic Flute* and 'Greensleeves' under the tropical moon were unforgettable. At Rurrenabaque, Adelita and Mark Williams set up a Burns Night supper with Ken Stahly's haggis and much laughter. However, the next day's drive over the Andes was interrupted by two incidents. A broken-down 20-tonner blocked the road for two and a half hours whilst the geologists' tools were used to dig around, but the second was more serious.

It was nearly midnight when, creeping along the 'Road of Death', the top of our hired bus struck an overhang, knocking out the driver and showering broken glass. '*Pare! Pare!*'[3] yelled Yoli. Ben and I tried to reach the stricken man as the vehicle continued to roll erratically down the slope, the headlights illuminating the five-hundred-foot precipice on our right and the sheer cliff on the left. Stretching across, the second driver managed to grab the wheel and, after careering for the most terrifyingly scary 500 yards I've ever experienced, we smashed into the cliff. Everyone was hurled forward, several people sustaining cuts and bruises. David Daniels had a nasty gash on the head and Yoli's face was black and blue, but thankfully we were all alive.

---

3. 'Stop' in Spanish.

Having two doctors aboard proved invaluable and we discovered that part of the problem was the driver's lemonade bottle stuck beneath the brake pedal. Fortunately, following buses gave us lifts into La Paz just as dawn broke. We had located the deeply buried meteorite and finally made it back to civilisation on little more than a wing and a prayer.

 ▶ **On a Wing and a Prayer,** *Kota Mama 6* **Expedition, Bolivia 2007**

CHAPTER 16

IN THE LAND OF THE MOXOS

For some 2,000 years in ancient times a race of 500,000 people known as the Moxos existed in the lowlands of central South America. The area is subject to annual floods when waters pour down from the Andes and, even today, this is still a major problem for the inhabitants of Bolivia's Beni region. However, the Moxos and other indigenous tribes managed to overcome these regular inundations by building their settlements on manmade mounds and cultivating crops on elevated fields, surrounded by an extensive system of irrigation canals, with causeways connecting the mounds.

Then, sometime around AD1100, the raised fields were abandoned and the people disappeared. Archaeologists and anthropologists are unsure why this happened. It could have been caused by climate change, the cultural impact of the arrival of the Spanish or, possibly, disease. Indeed, a so-called 'Bleeding Fever', thought to have been carried by rats, did break out in the region as recently as 1965. The fever was eventually eradicated, possibly helped by the introduction of hundreds of cats brought in to kill off the rodents. However, the disappearance of the early inhabitants remains a mystery, but some 40,000 Moxos still live in Bolivia.

Our good friends at Sergeotecmin believed that this civilisation might actually have been wiped out by the impact of another huge meteorite. A study of the configuration of Lake Rojo Aguado and nearby lakes and rivers had already suggested this might possibly be the case and, if so, there could be valuable minerals in the area as well as useful information relating to long-term climate change.

So in 2008 we planned a further expedition in conjunction with Sergeotecmin to investigate the theory and to study the geology and archaeology of the savanna, swamp and jungle around the lake, once again combining this with community aid projects on behalf of the local people.

After a briefing in La Paz, Yoli and I flew to Trinidad, Beni's tropical capital and the nerve centre of Bolivian Amazonia, to carry out a recce. On arrival in the city, founded in 1686 by Jesuit missionary Father Cipriano Barace – who, rather tragically, ended up being martyred by the indigenous tribe he was trying to convert – we stepped out of the aircraft to be enveloped in a wave of warm, moist heat. We were greeted at the airport by Señora Magaly Velis of the Department of Development, which had kindly agreed to sponsor our visit, and, along with her director, Miguel Chavez, and Nilo Teran, a loquacious geologist from Sergeotecmin, we made a rapid tour of a city awash with motorcycles.

The annual floodwaters were already encroaching on the suburbs and people, clutching as many of their belongings as they could carry, were evacuating low-lying homes. And in a special compound we found a handsome tapir and three lively anacondas rescued from the flood. A brief visit to a museum named after the celebrated American anthropologist Kenneth Lee gave us a vision of Moxos archaeology, while a collection of violins made by the Jesuits explained the interest in these instruments shown by the people at Ojaki. Despite all the problems they were facing, the authorities could not have been more helpful.

On Thursday 31st January we took a local flight north to Santa Ana, during which we got a dramatic bird's-eye view of the encircling waters lapping at the outer edges of the town. To my surprise, the aide to the town's *Alcalde* turned out to be an Englishman named John Legon, and he was to prove a useful ally. Indeed, the *Alcalde* and all the other local officials seemed eager to help. Meetings were held in the Hamburger Bar where a raucous resident macaw made conversation difficult.

We decided to set up a base at Coquinal, a remote village of around fifty families on the shores of Lake Rojo Aguado, a conveniently central point in the area to be explored that also had the added advantage of a short airstrip. John Legon found us a small Cessna that, for US$200 an hour, would enable us to undertake a quick aerial recce of the surrounding landscape. Meanwhile, Nilo was surprised to hear of uranium-bearing rock being found in the locality. And there were also enticing tales of lost cities!

Glancing down from the aircraft we saw the vast plain, dotted with the Moxos's mounds, more or less circular and up to 1,300 feet in diameter, covered with lush green trees and connected by straight canals and raised paths. The regular geometrical outlines of the long-abandoned fields and irrigation ditches stretched below us, and it was quite clear that many centuries ago a well-organised, knowledgeable and innovative people had come up with ways to hold the floodwaters at bay and to produce food to sustain themselves. Today it has reverted to virtually barren, uncultivated cattle country. Bouncing down on the earth strip at Coquinal we met the tubby, smiling *Corregidor* who led us around the village, accompanied by a little girl with two baby peccary and a trio of inebriated locals playing pipes and drums.

There were twelve separate communities living around the shores of the lake, mainly desperately poor indigenous people badly in need of medical and dental help, support for their schools and clean drinking water. Also, an ambulance boat would enable their sick to be brought to the small health post at Coquinal. I wrote out a 'shopping list' of requirements that we might be able to help with, but made no promises.

Getting back to Santa Ana just ahead of a torrential rainstorm, we made straight for the Hamburger Bar, where we worked on our plans for the expedition, while a small brown snake wriggled down the gutter and the macaw screeched louder than ever. The day then ended with a colourful and very noisy carnival procession led by the six beautiful finalists competing for the title 'Queen of Santa Ana', after which we dined on a rather leathery steak and a bottle of Kohlberg red.

Despite all her skills, Yoli could not get us on the scheduled flight back to Trinidad, so we hired the Cessna 182 once again. We were just preparing to climb aboard when three ladies and a baby arrived, having apparently arranged with the pilot to cadge a lift with us, despite the fact that there were not enough seats for all of us. Undeterred, the pilot then produced a school bench that he pushed in behind the seats right at the back of the aircraft. Luckily, we didn't have much baggage so there was room for it there. The ladies duly clambered aboard and, feeling unusually gallant, I offered one of them my seat, but she politely declined, saying: 'We prefer the bench – it's easier to get out in an emergency!'

As we neared Trinidad, the pilot pointed down into a swamp where a Boeing 727 had crash-landed in the shallow water. It was the very plane we should have been on! 'He ran out of gasoline,' explained our pilot, adding: 'Everybody got out OK. Only a dog was drowned.' Fate had intervened and saved us from a potentially fatal accident.

In July 2009 Yoli and I visited Sergeotecmin's head office in La Paz to confirm arrangements for the expedition. On arrival we were concerned to find that some of the senior staff had been 'retired' by the new government, including the people we had been dealing with, but thankfully our overall plan was nevertheless agreed.

Pressing on in an unheated taxi, we crossed the Andes at 13,000 feet and after a seven-hour journey finally reached the lighthouse-shaped home of Hugo Cornejo, the Bolivian Special Forces colonel who had been assigned to us on the Kota Mama expeditions. Hugo had kindly agreed to sell us his Koyak, the homemade go-kart type vehicle and trailer that had proved so useful for transporting equipment on the Rio Grande expedition. At the nearby Patiño children's hospital we were pleased to see that some of the medical equipment we had sent out earlier was fully in use and promised more of the ex-NHS gear that is available for charities. We also met Jackie Huertas, a lively local doctor who had joined the expedition to improve her English.

On 12th July, after a jolly evening with Hugo and his wife Nadir, we set out for Santa Cruz, Yoli and I in a taxi, with Hugo and a moody Bolivian soldier named Remi following behind with the Koyak, which soon broke down. Despite the fact that our taxi driver enjoyed overtaking on blind bends on the hair-raising mountain road, we somehow managed to survive intact and eventually, to our immense relief, the lights of Santa Cruz appeared.

So far, so good – but not for very much longer! Firstly, Sergeotecmin's new director suddenly announced without any warning that the institute could not proceed with the project, after all. At the same time, earlier-than-expected heavy rains turned the roads north of Trinidad into a quagmire and the river ferries connecting

Coquinal were out of action. As a result, the next ten chaotic days were spent sorting out various political and logistical problems.

Meanwhile, the expedition team was already on its way. Dashing about by plane and taxi, with Yoli glued to her telephone, we worked around the clock. Major Roca of the Bolivian Air Force Search and Rescue Group and other local people sympathised with our situation and gave invaluable help. The Director of Health, Dr Ernesto Moses, welcomed our medical and dental help and, especially, the provision of wells at Coquinal. A charming man, he was of Arab descent and explained that some 80% of the Beni population were of Palestinian origin due to immigration in the 1930s.

By the time our twenty-two-strong team assembled at Santa Cruz on 22nd July, we had put together a new plan. Our multi-national group included Bolivians, Brits, a Canadian, an Australian and a Colombian, between them offering a wide-ranging mixture of talents and expertise. We had a geologist, an archaeologist, a biologist, an economist, an ornithologist, a cartographer, a dentist, doctors, engineers, some equestrians and an IT expert in charge of signals.

The journey to Coquinal was to prove a real challenge. As our convoy of six vehicles finally set off it was still raining heavily, on top of which Yoli warned us that a *surazo*, a bitterly cold polar wind, was on its way, sweeping up from Patagonia. Only one road to Santa Ana was considered usable, so we'd taken the precaution of hiring a giant ex-US Army ten-ton truck named the *Yellow God* to carry stores. Thanks to the generosity of one of our team, Elodie Sandford, we'd also purchased a twenty-foot ambulance boat, plus 25hp outboard, to be donated to the Coquinal community. This was towed behind the leading 4WD, with our hired bus followed by the 'all-terrain'

Koyak and trailer, which was continuing to prove unreliable. Its crew, twenty-year-old Dominic Middleton-Frith and a grumbling Remi, were soon caked in mud as it frequently got bogged down and had to be pulled out by the lumbering *Yellow God*, which ploughed slowly forward, pausing to extract several other local vehicles from the morass.

One of the Koyak's chassis members then fractured and its trailer collapsed, but fortunately we managed to find a village welder who fixed it for a modest fee. Approaching Santa Ana, we had to negotiate a series of four pontoon ferry crossings, crude but effective. Thereafter the road did gradually improve, only for the Koyak's lights to fail as darkness fell, a problem overcome by means of Dominic holding a spotlight whilst Remi drove. It was 02:00 when we finally arrived in the sleeping town and, after dishing out emergency rations, we sought refuge in a welcoming hotel. Meanwhile, the *Yellow God* had fallen far behind, having been delayed by stopping to give first aid treatment to a ferryman who'd lost a fingertip in his winch as he ferried them across. It wasn't until several hours later that the mud-caked vehicle and its exhausted crew eventually trundled into Santa Ana.

Seeking information about conditions on the way ahead, we found people more interested in the parade of scantily dressed girls hoping to win the town's latest beauty competition, but it transpired that floods had blocked the route. The Koyak chassis had broken again, so we handed it to John Legon to sell in aid of the community. It was now becoming clear that only a plane could get us to Coquinal. A Swiss gentleman with an empty tourist hotel took pity on us and there we reorganised stores and relaxed in the pool. The local radio provided entertainment in the afternoons, as inebriated young men were hurled about by long-horned Brahman bulls as part of a rodeo at the town's festival.

Leaving our vehicles to join us as soon as the flood subsided, we flew to Coquinal the next day, a Cessna 206 taking us in a series of seven shuttle flights. As we were leaving, Remi arrived in a state of some distress. It seemed that the Koyak still belonged to the army, and that we might therefore have been sold it illegally! How this happened I had no idea, but at this point I was more concerned with events in Coquinal, where Andy Gray, our deputy leader, had set up camp.

In place of our vehicles left behind in Santa Ana, the *Corregidor* arranged horses and a wooden *carretón* (carriage) pulled by four massive oxen as alternative transport. Army dentist and equestrian Major Alex Jess duly set about forming a horse group to carry out studies north-west of the village. Other team members with little riding experience were also required to mount up or march to their objectives, some ending up to their armpits in swamps. Local *peke-peke* boats were also used, and it was from these that the legendary Amazon river dolphins, some of the pink variety, were first sighted. Some were indeed pink, others jet-black. Up to a dozen would often follow the boats, surfing along in the wake. Our biologist Kathryn Hutchison, who was making a study of these friendly creatures, was delighted by such close encounters, while the entomologists were particularly interested by the discovery of a large stick insect. Agouti, caiman, capybara, deer and tapir were also encountered, and a villager's cow was taken by a jaguar! The birdlife was prolific throughout these vast wetlands and enthusiastic ornithologist John Mackenzie-Grieve was able to compile an impressively long list of sightings.

As word spread, patients poured into Coquinal to be seen by our medical team. The doctors and dentists were especially welcomed in outlying villages and estancias. Army dentist Lorika Strickland handed out woolly dolls to comfort children needing extractions and one little girl without any dental problems asked if she could have a tooth removed just so that she could get a doll! Alas, the effects of eating sugarcane were reflected in the generally bad state of dental health.

Doctors Roy D'Silva and Jackie Huerta Ramos did splendid work with the villagers and treated me when I suffered an infected foot. However, the local shaman insisted on massaging the limb with a large frog, which eventually turned pink. Spotting the pink frog outside my hut, our biologist thought it might be a new species! A boatman suffered a snakebite and when his condition deteriorated Roy had him evacuated by air with the dead viper in a plastic bottle for identification purposes. Happily, he made a full recovery.

Midwife Grace Martin found the local mothers very self-sufficient, needing little help in giving birth. The provision of reading glasses was especially appreciated by the older ladies, who needed them to continue sewing, and who tested them by threading a needle. Chiggers that burrowed into one's feet were a problem. This wretched fly has plagued jungle travellers forever. When the larvae hatch, the wounds turn septic, creating an ulcer that is devilishly difficult to cure. However, in spite of the hordes of mosquitoes no-one caught malaria or dengue fever. Given my previous unpleasant experience, I was slightly wary of the family of vampire bats living in the roof of my hut!

At the village of Carmen, a horrific fight between the *Corregidor's* dogs and a very fierce racoon resulted in three dogs being severely injured before the predator was shot. Dentist Alex Jess, Dr Hazel Dobinson and Sarah Royal, our honorary vet, treated the hideous injuries and probably saved the lives of two that were bleeding to death. Delighted, the village chief showed his gratitude by taking us to see an extraordinary archaeological site. Simon Reames, our archaeologist, examined an area of several acres surrounded by a ditch and covered in broken ceramics probably dating back to somewhere between 200BC and AD400. Stone tools, possibly originating in the Andes, were also found.

Despite much searching, Dan Vockins, the British geologist, could find no evidence of meteorite impact, but without Sergeotecmin's instruments his work was limited. Meanwhile, our surveyor Tim Harrison was able to produce some excellent maps.

It looked at first as if it would be impossible to dig the four wells that we had promised without the vehicles to transport the drills and other equipment that the charity Just a Drop and the Bolivian Fundación Sumaj Huasi (FSH) had funded. However, the weather eventually started to warm up, hot winds began to dry the pampa and by 12th August the track to Santa Ana was passible and the level of the Rio Iruyanez was dropping. Three of the 4WDs and a high-clearance Unimog truck carrying the water project's stores braved the flood, towing the new ambulance boat. The drivers sealed up electric parts and waterproofed the engines as much as possible before a local tractor pulled them through the waist-deep water.

Work on the wells began with villagers, schoolchildren and expedition members joining the pulling party in operating the drill, sustained with a supply of pancakes and popcorn. Two weeks had been lost due to the flood so it was now a race against time to complete the wells before the end of the expedition. With the temperatures reaching 35°C and humidity at 90% this was exhausting work, but having drilled down to a depth of 200 feet, the job was finally completed.

On 25th August the entire village assembled on the lake shore at Coquinal for the naming of the Elodie Sandford Ambulance Boat by Elodie herself, who, together with her brother, had sponsored the craft. The boat was handed over to the crew we had trained in advance, bringing the expedition to a fitting close. Next day we moved south, stopping to do a couple of days' medical and dental work at the village of San Carlos. The Iruyanez river had by now subsided, so presented little problem on the way back to Santa Ana, where we relaxed for thirty-six hours at the delightful Swiss hotel and held our usual Burns Night supper.

The expedition had been very successful despite the many difficulties and the inclement weather. Most importantly, the project had given real help to people in need in a remote corner of Bolivia and had left us with an admiration for the Moxos people. And it wasn't to be too long before we were back. Dr Ernesto Moses had stressed the need for clean drinking water elsewhere in the region, and so it was that two years later, in April 2011, with the support of Just a Drop, the Simón I. Patiño Foundation and the SES, a further recce was carried out. Working again with the FSH, we put together a plan for sinking more wells along the Rio Beni, while also providing medical aid and checking on the water systems we had previously installed at Coquinal and Ojaki.

Arriving in Santa Cruz, Yoli and I were introduced to a new and valuable supporter. Señora Carolina Hanley, a leading dental surgeon in the city, owner of the local international school and an honorary British consul, made an immediate impression with her boundless energy and enthusiasm. We also met Walter Suarez, a Riberalta businessman and senior Rotarian who would do much to help.

Flying north we picked up tubby Señor Fortunato of FSH at Trinidad and, as fuel prices had escalated, paid US$1,000 for a Cessna to take us across the flooded pampa to Coquinal and Riberalta. Happily, the Coquinal wells were all in good working order. Arriving at Riberalta, we were greeted at the airport by a narcotics detection dog and outside in the city itself by the roar of a thousand motorcycles. This must be the motorcycle capital of the world! Clutching our baggage, we were whisked by motorcycle taxis to the quaint old Hotel Colonial and, with Walter's help, there then followed fourteen frantic and often frustrating days visiting villages in need of potable water. We suffered the usual Bolivian hazards of cancelled air flights, inclement weather, leaking craft, broken-down engines – and a bout of diarrhoea.

A tin boat, hired to navigate the Beni tributaries, was fitted with a seat from a crashed car and a rather tired outboard engine. Preparing to board, we found its bow wedged beneath a giant river barge. Much to the amusement of a pet monkey that was nibbling Brazil nuts on the dock, we heaved and strained in the forty-degree heat to free the craft.

Fortunato did his best to sell the plan for eco-friendly toilets, but the villagers did not appreciate his suggestion of carting away loads of faeces to fertilise their fields. We found several villages where FSH could put in wells, as long as we could raise the money to fund them, and other settlements that were in need of medical and dental help.

Driving through a flooded area, I paused to photograph a charming little girl with a wide-open smile, who was clutching two bedraggled, half-drowned puppies that she had rescued. 'I am pleased she saved them,' grinned her brother, standing nearby. 'They are for tomorrow's supper.'

Back at the Hotel Colonial we bumped into David Dimbleby and a BBC film team. 'Hello,' he greeted me, adding with a grin: 'I can't say I'm surprised to meet you in this jungle!'

Having forged a useful link with Walter, Sonia and their Rotary Club, we flew back to Santa Cruz to hatch an expedition plan with the dynamic Carolina. And in August 2012 a seven-strong team gathered in Santa Cruz. To aid the people, many of whom are indigenous and had suffered badly as a result of flooding, we aimed to provide clean drinking water, medical and dental treatment and educational items for schools. At the same time, reading glasses were provided for those in need as well as some violins for children showing musical talent.

I also wanted to do further research on the strange double-nosed dogs found at Ojaki and to have another look at the Las Piedras Fortress ruins we had found previously. Carolina came along as our dentist and civil engineer Julian Butter, a member of Just a Drop's project team whose broken femur was now repaired, was in charge of investigating potential sites for wells. Michael Elkin, a medical student in the final year of his training, was also an archaeologist and a pianist. Peter Kohler, a long-standing member of the SES, was to act as cartographer and Dave Smith, a retired PT instructor, was the SES quartermaster and a skilled DIY man. So although only a relatively small team, its members were able to offer a wide range of experience.

Yoli had organised stores and supplies and Carolina had arranged for the donation of a large quantity of medicines, some solar lighting sets for villages without electric power and batteries for use with the lighting sets. As the owner of the Santa Cruz International School, she had asked the pupils to collect schoolbooks and usable medicines for distribution to the villages. In total, the quantity of stores thus collected weighed over a ton, so transport had to be hired to get it all to Riberalta, which was to be the rear base camp for the project. Flying up there, we were met by Walter and Sonia Suarez, stalwart supporters throughout.

We had brought two violins from Britain, kindly provided by Claire Ruff, who had been on the Ojaki project in 2007. In Riberalta we presented one to a student at the local university who was showing signs of outstanding talent as a musician, to help her advance her skills. Checking the medicines collected by the Santa Cruz pupils, Mike was surprised to find a stock of Viagra. Later, the children who had been raiding their parents' bathroom cabinets said they just wanted the indigenous people to be happy!

On 28th August we mounted motorcycle taxis to cross the 1,300-foot-wide Rio Beni and the Rio Madre de Dios by ferry. In 2001 we had made a short visit to the Las Piedras Fortress ruins and a group from a Finnish university had later investigated the site. A woman living nearby now led us through the secondary jungle to the ditch surrounding the fortified site. Here, Mike and Peter Kohler made a plan of the settlement that occupies a plateau rising between thirty-three and fifty feet above the surrounding riverbeds. Although damaged by treasure hunters, the 250-acre site shows evidence of significant stonework, with walls and a raised circular mound.

The nearby village had a display of some fine ceramic pots from the fortress that we were able to examine and photograph. The Finnish expedition had believed these to be of Inca origin, dating back to between AD1390 and 1650, an indication that the fortress may have been built by Incan refugees from a 15th-century uprising around the Peruvian city of Cuzco. The suggestion was that they might have descended the Rio Madre de Dios to construct a temporary fortified settlement, with the aim of remaining there for a few years before eventually returning to Peru.

As a thin emerald-green snake slithered through the leaves, we speculated that this might be the lost city of Paititi, built by the Inca hero Inkarri on retreating from the Spanish, but whether or not that was the case it could indicate that the Inca had migrated into the Amazon Basin. However, examination of the photographs by a Mayan-Inca expert in England suggested the ceramics may have been Tiwanaku (AD200–1200), thus predating the Inca empire.

Unfortunately, the leader of the Finnish team had died, and with little interest being shown by the archaeological department in La Paz no further work has been done on this unusual site. It will be an interesting project for future exploration, if it's not completely destroyed by treasure hunters.

The municipality had provided us with a smiling, gap-toothed driver and a six-wheel truck, which was missing two of its four rear wheels and was sagging at the back! Nevertheless, we loaded up our stores and toured the area, examining the water systems already constructed with funds from Just a Drop. Temporary clinics were established in three villages. And at these our dentist and medic treated many patients. To reach one village involved a journey by vehicle to a point where stores and equipment had to be lowered down a cliff before then being reloaded into a boat in which we travelled for several miles along the river.

We arrived at our village destination to find that all the buildings had been destroyed in the flood and the inhabitants moved to a new site well above the high-water mark. Some new houses had been erected, but many people were still living under leaking tarpaulins. Nevertheless, we were greeted by singing schoolchildren who, in spite of the conditions, wore clean, smart uniforms. They were rewarded with textbooks, pens and exercise books, the first they had ever received.

There was no electricity, so Julian, Peter and Dave set up solar lighting systems whilst Yoli handed out reading glasses. Alfredo meanwhile examined the new water system that we had funded and instructed the people on its maintenance. Our hearts were moved when a woman and her young daughter hobbled over to us, both suffering from bleeding leg ulcers three inches in diameter that were eating into their bodies. 'Leishmaniasis!' exclaimed Carolina as she and Mike injected antibiotics around the awful wounds. That was all they could do. Further treatment was clearly needed and it was decided that arrangements must be made to get the woman and her child to hospital as soon as possible.

With two hired 4WDs we then set off westward to Ojaki, where we needed to inspect the water system installed in 2007 that was said to have broken down. After 80 miles the wheel bearings on one car collapsed and a replacement had to be called for on the satellite phone, which meant a four-hour delay before we could proceed. Resuming our journey, we found that the dusty track to the navy base at Puerto Cavinas had not improved and night had already fallen when the leading car reached a swampy stretch. Julian and I went ahead on foot to examine the surface but, alas, an impatient driver decided to move forward without waiting for us to give him the go-ahead. 'Stop!' I bellowed, but it was too late. The 4WD broke through the crust and sank deep into a morass. Fortunately, Dave had a tow rope handy and after we had dug the wheels out of the mud by hand, the second car pulling, plus all hands pushing, we managed to extract the bogged-down vehicle.

To add to our problems, a bushfire was now sweeping towards us and we were lucky to find a turning off the trail that avoided the blaze and led us to a rough hacienda, where friendly cowboys directed us to a diversion that took us around the swamp and the fire. It was 9pm when we reached the Rio Vaqueti, only to find as we looked out across the river that there was no sign of either a bridge of any kind or a ferry. In the darkness, Yoli somehow managed to locate a canoe and, after crossing eighty feet of fast-flowing water to the opposite bank, went off to the nearby village. She returned to announce that if we would set up a clinic for his people, the chief promised to build a bridge for the cars in just three hours the next morning! Neither Julian nor I, as engineers, could believe this was possible. However, swallowing a rather unappetising cold supper and swatting mosquitoes, we wearily pitched our tents.

As Dave cooked pancakes at dawn, we noticed a black pick-up truck parked in the trees. Ominously, there was a bullet hole in the windscreen and the seats were stained with blood. The villagers explained later that ten days earlier the car and its passengers, a local family, had been set on by bandits, who had stolen motorcycles from a nearby ranch and were trying to escape. When the car driver refused to take them they had opened fire, murdering his wife. Somehow the police had been alerted and a gunfight ensued, during which all the bandits were shot dead.

By now, Carolina, Mike and Yoli had crossed the river by canoe and, rolling up their sleeves, were busy setting up a clinic in the village school. Meanwhile a working party of villagers, including women and children, appeared at the riverside to build the bridge. We stood watching in amazement as some of the men swam into the muddy brown stream and started heaving up huge, thick pre-cut planks of hardwood, each around thirty-five feet in length, that had been resting on the riverbed. What emerged was a prefabricated bridge that when not in use simply lay underwater. Whilst the men struggled with the giant timbers, their children dived off the logs and women washed clothes in a scene that resembled a seaside outing. And within three hours, just as the Chief had promised, the bridge, or *callapo*, was in place. It was only held together by its own weight, with neither bolts nor fastenings, but it remained securely in place as our vehicles drove cautiously over it. 'This is the most incredible piece of civil engineering I've ever seen,' commented Julian admiringly.

Having extracted dozens of teeth, including no less than thirteen from one poor woman, Carolina packed up her instruments, Yoli distributed a supply of schoolbooks and spectacles, and the drive to Cavinas continued, only a day behind schedule. Here, to our relief we found a *peke-peke* canoe awaiting us and as dawn broke the expedition headed up the Rio Madidi and on to Ojaki.

Apart from some minor difficulty in navigating through one rapid, our canoe made good progress to Ojaki, where old friends greeted us. The temperature was now 40°C and all of us were glad to be out of the sun's glare.

Local ladies cooked up supper and Yoli opened a bottle of Chilean wine, which went down rather well. Next morning the village children, dressed in traditional costumes, sang and performed dances. As usual, they were rewarded with a supply of schoolbooks, which they seemed to appreciate. I wondered if British children would react in the same way.

The main task at Ojaki was to check the water supply system. It turned out that the generator that drove the pump had broken and a replacement was needed, but the tower and tank were intact and most of the pipework was still in place. However, Julian redesigned the system, which we hoped could be put back into action by a contractor. Spectacles were given to older people and a medical and dental clinic was opened. A man from a nearby village was brought in with a serious machete wound on his arm, caused when he slipped whilst trying to kill a rattlesnake. There were many people with stomach disorders caused by drinking polluted river water and Mike was asked to give a talk on birth control and, later, to explain to a recently married couple how to make a baby!

Dave's sleep was disturbed by a brace of tarantulas scurrying around his bed, but they were speedily dispatched with a blast of insecticide and he arrived at breakfast with one balanced proudly on his forehead. Logjams upriver prevented us from visiting the Nichols family homestead upstream, but, warned of our arrival, Mateo, his three sons and Charlotte, the teacher, managed to reach us by canoe.

As we tucked into our porridge, loud screams suddenly rent the air and women and children could be seen running for their huts as if the devil himself was behind them. And with good reason! Because a large group of around four score of angry white-lipped peccary, among the most feared animals in South America, had appeared at the edge of the village. Seizing guns, spears and bows and arrows, the local men rushed out, one brave fellow charging the beasts on his motorcycle. Squealing peccary ran in every direction, grunting and flashing their tusks. In seconds the football pitch became a battlefield with yelling warriors, flying arrows and the crash of gunfire. Being unarmed, we climbed on to the table or disappeared into our hut, whilst the peccary, with snapping jaws, were hunted down. However, after a few minutes they retreated into the jungle, leaving behind seven dead porkers to provide a feast for Ojaki. Surprisingly, there were no human casualties.

Below Ojaki the rapid had swollen with the rain upriver, so we disembarked whilst calmly ignoring the lurking caiman. Our boatmen and the muscular Mateo, looking like Tarzan, skilfully walked the canoe through. To my relief, our cars awaited us at Puerto Cavinas, largely because Yoli, in her wisdom, had taken the keys away from the drivers. The extraordinary bridge at the Vaqueti was still in place and pressing on we dropped Mateo's party on the main road to get a lift to Rurrenabaque.

At Ojaki we had hoped to see Xingu, the double-nosed dog we had encountered in 2007, but were told that he had been taken to La Paz. However, Carolina located another of these strange dogs in Santa Cruz and before heading north we examined what turned out to be a very old and rather sick animal. Alas, he passed away that very night. And although a vet did a dissection of the nostrils she could not discover any obvious reason why the animal's sense of smell should be enhanced.

Earlier, I'd met Ignacio Espoz Babul in Santiago, Chile, who had a breeding pair of double-nosed dogs and who told me that the police were using them for narcotic and explosives detection. One had even been trained to parachute with his handler! Research indicated that they originated in Morocco or Turkey and Ignacio agreed they may have been brought to South America by the conquistadors. I also discovered that dogs with similar noses have been found all over the world, including at least half a dozen reported in the UK. But they are mostly confined to South America. My research continues.

At Carolina's home in Santa Cruz we were treated to a splendid dinner, with musical entertainment provided by a string quartet of young people playing Baroque music from old Jesuit scores. Guests included the Governor of Santa Cruz, who had just recovered after being shot by robbers. So, one way and another, the evening was a splendid and rather appropriate way to end an expedition to this wild, exotic and largely untamed land.

 ▶ Mission to the Wild Madidi, *Kota Mama 8* Expedition, Bolivia 2012

 ▶ Land of the Moxos, *Kota Mama 7* Expedition, Bolivia 2009

CHAPTER 17

LAND OF MANY WATERS

The battered Russian helicopter landed with a thump, scattering leaves and twigs as it settled into the rainforest clearing. We clambered out and were following blue-uniformed 'Brigadier Joe' towards the thatched huts of the remote Amerindians' jungle village when a sudden commotion broke out among the group of villagers waiting to greet us. Half-naked men, women, children and snorting pigs were scattering in all directions and we soon saw exactly why. Coiled on the path just a few yards ahead of us, hissing with menace, was a deadly pit viper. The serpent's tongue flickered, and its eyes were fixed on Joe, now with his pistol in hand. But even though the villagers urged him to shoot, the brigadier shook his head, saying: 'Even snakes have their place in nature.' And a moment later the reptile slithered away into the bush. This was one of my earliest experiences of working with this thoroughly professional soldier and devoted conservationist.

Operation Raleigh, the four-year global youth expedition that Prince Charles had encouraged me to mount with the SES, was on its home leg in 1988 when the news broke of a massacre of Amazonian people in the very area earmarked for our next project. The Brazilian government had no desire to host a horde of foreign young explorers – or venturers, as we knew them – whilst they were trying to sort out the embarrassing mess, so permission for our planned three-month expedition was withdrawn. However, the venturers were already briefed and equipped for a South American jungle task and, seeking an alternative venue, I turned my eyes to the former British colony of Guyana, the only English-speaking country of that whole vast continent.

Four hundred years earlier, the capture in the Atlantic of Pedro Sarmiento, a Spanish scholar with first-hand knowledge of the Inca people, had provided Sir Walter Raleigh with a mass of useful information. What he learned from the Spaniard was probably responsible for convincing Raleigh of the existence of the legendary great and golden city of El Dorado.

However, Guyana is not quite the same as Brazil. In fact, there is nowhere else in South America that is quite like Guyana, where a muddy, harbourless coastal strip separates the Atlantic from the vast tropical and virtually impenetrable forest that still covers 80% of the entire country. Roads are few and far between and regularly flooded. Even today it can prove a real challenge

to reach the deep interior, where one will be confronted by a host of natural hazards, fearsome creepy-crawlies and disease. The best way to move around, explore and meet the people is by river, as long as you have the skill, experience and courage needed to navigate a canoe over the many rapids. Clearly, it would, in all sorts of different ways, provide a suitably testing environment for our young venturers as they helped to carry out

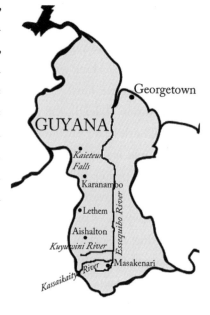

scientific conservation and community aid projects as part of the circumnavigating expedition.

Like many other adventurers in his day, Sir Walter – or 'Water', as Queen Elizabeth I called him – was driven on by a gold fever to seek the legendary, and alas mythical, city of El Dorado. As we were to discover, gold was not the only fever that existed in the humid forests of Guyana. But there certainly is gold there, as our first recce parties found when they met the prospectors – or 'pork knockers', so-called because of their habit of tapping on the shop counter to buy supplies of salt pork.

'It's a fine life,' insisted one, as he riddled silt through an oil drum in a creek, adding: 'Except for the malaria, of course. Everyone gets it. That and the cabouri fly.' However, he failed to mention some of the additional hazards that were to greet our venturers. These included piranhas that can strip the flesh from a drowning bullock in seconds; vampire bats that suck blood and can introduce paralytic rabies; Chagas' disease – a horrible disease that may have killed Darwin, transmitted by a large, beetle-like insect that causes eye swelling and distension of the vital organs including the heart; leishmaniasis that causes skin ulcers and occasionally destruction of the facial cartilage, causing hideous deformities; and onchocerciasis, otherwise known as river blindness, that is caused by worms transmitted by the bite of the tiny blackfly. The worms find their way into one eye and as soon as that habitat becomes crowded, migrate under the skin across the bridge of the nose to the other eye – a disconcerting progression to observe in those afflicted, as we saw in Zaire in 1974.

Notably, the prospector neglected to include the real exotica among the local wildlife, such as furry tarantulas the size of a mop, jaguars, electric eels capable of producing a 600-volt shock, rattlesnakes and aggressive bushmasters, snakes whose fangs can penetrate a leather boot. In particular, he made no reference to the dreaded candiru, the 'toothpick fish', which is said to swim up a careless swimmer's urine stream to enter the urethra. There, I am told, it uses its prickly spines to bury itself firmly: the pain is said to be spectacular. Peeing through a tea strainer is recommended as an effective defence!

The legend of El Dorado is still repeated by the Guyanese, although cocaine has long since replaced the mineral as the main source of wealth in South America. Sir Walter did not know that El Dorado was probably an Inca ruler rather than a place. One can imagine the young king following in his father's footsteps to stand silently as his servants coated his naked body in resin then powdered it with gold dust. Huge torches lit the night and reflected off his muscular thighs and shoulders as he walked to the edge of the lake. Stepping on to a waiting raft manned by ten attendants, the chief was rowed to the centre where he slipped into the dark, calm waters. Gleaming showers of precious dust washed from his body and streaked the dark lake as they slowly sank to the bottom. Along with the dust went treasures: helmets, pendants and jewelled serpents of gold and emeralds.

'El Dorado' – 'the Chief', or 'the Golden One'– was master of untold wealth and purveyor of power beyond imagination. Yet his magic was not sufficient to resist the gunpowder of the Spanish. After Columbus landed on the north-east coast of Guyana in 1498, others sailed in his wake and eventually brought the kingdom of the Incas to its knees. The ruthless conquistadors found enough treasure to fill the holds of a hundred galleons, but never discovered El Dorado's mother lode. Other famous 16th-century explorers turned their ships to the southern continent. They too wanted a share of the fabled booty looted from Peru and Mexico by Francisco Pizarro and Hernán Cortés. Many were convinced that somewhere between the Amazon and the Orinoco lay the lost city and some even now try to find Paititi, a legendary Inca settlement that we too went in search of during previous expeditions, but which has yet to be discovered.

In his quest for El Dorado, Sir Walter led an expedition to the mouth of the Orinoco River in 1595 and penetrated some 400 miles inland. The first of his two expeditions brought him hardship and disease; the second, undertaken in 1616 when he was sixty-four years old, sick and partly paralysed after thirteen years in the Tower, brought him death. On his return to England, empty-handed and accused of breaking the peace with Spain, the brightest courtier of Elizabeth I's court was beheaded by James I.

Guyana had taken almost everything dear to Raleigh, including his health, his life and his son, but that virgin wilderness never robbed him of his courage or his dreams. He wrote: 'I never saw a more beautiful country, nor more lively prospects; hills so raised here and there over the valleys, the river winding into divers branches, the plains adjoining without bush or stubble, all fair green grass, the ground of hard sand to march on, either for horse or foot, the deer crossing in every path, the birds towards the evening singing on every tree with a thousand different tunes, cranes and herons of white, crimson and carnation perching on the river's side, the air afresh with a gentle easterly wind and every stone that we stopped to take up promised either gold or silver by its complexion.'

Until his death in 1618, the old explorer still believed that with just a few more men and a pocket full of gold he would find the kingdom hidden somewhere near the 'Mountains of the Moon'.

These are in the land of the indigenous people of Guyana, but the higher portion of the country's population of around 800,000 are of Indian origin, having first arrived from the Indian subcontinent around 1838 as indentured labourers. There are also large numbers of people of African origin, descended from slaves, as well as Chinese, Portuguese and Caribbean people – an amazing cultural mixture of good-humoured, easy-going people who treat time elastically.

If we were to launch expeditions here we would need sound advice and so I called my old friend the Chief of Staff of the Guyana Defence Force (GDF), Brigadier Joe Singh, whom I had first got to know whilst he was training in England. Joe, a formidable but kindly giant, was known for his love of the wilderness and wildlife. Much respected in Guyana, he was the ideal man to help us launch this expedition at short notice. So almost exactly 400 years after Sir Walter, our 20th-century young exploratory successors returned in his name to Guyana, 'Land of many waters', but not to seek gold.

Charlie Daniel, a lively Royal Marine with whom I had soldiered in the Oman conflict volunteered to lead the Operation Raleigh expedition. Helped by his able wife Jasmina and Nick Horne, my energetic adjutant from earlier in the operation, he set up a project at Kurupukari on the Essequibo River.

El Dorado is but one of the fables of this land. Another is that 'you can never pollute the jungle'. In this respect, the gold miners and prospectors sadly differ from the indigenous people of Guyana, the Amerindians, who use their land and its resources much more carefully.

For these imaginative and handsome people, the jungle is much more than just a source of useful and valuable materials for the outside world. It is their natural home environment in which they have learned how to live in respectful harmony, enjoying its bounty while often remaining more fearful of mythical dangers rather than the deadly threat posed by some of the wildlife. Never mind the snakes, spiders and other sometimes outsized creepy-crawlies, the flesh-eating fish, the caiman and other reptiles – here lurks the one-eyed Bush Dai-Dai, who abducts pretty maidens on sight; the masters of the Jambies arrow, a weapon which shoots tiny pepper seeds into the skin; the elf-like Knoc-o-fo-knoc-o, a creature with straight legs and a large head and belly that will steal your power unless you strike him first, in which case he becomes your slave; and the dreaded Kanaima which can turn into a bird or animal and whistles at night to lure you into the forest. If it catches you, it will push its iguana tail into your bottom, pull out your intestines, tie them in knots and replace them. Understandably, you lose the power of speech, among other things.

Our camp at Kurupukari was once the resting place for cattle on their arduous journey to the capital, Georgetown. Now, as then, the piranhas and caiman have custody of the Essequibo River, while the people of the tiny settlement of Fairview hunt jaguar, distil medicines from plants and shrubs, pound cassava and collect ripe mangoes as they fall from the trees. Purple orchids still grow in profusion and legendary riverboat pilots still brave the cataracts.

For three months in the summer of 1988, Charlie's resourceful deputy, Nick Horne, set up his jungle headquarters on the north bank of this wide brown river and that was where Joe Singh took me to visit them in the battered old Soviet helicopter. It rattled and shook alarmingly as we skimmed over the endless rainforest.

The camp was situated in a place of quite remarkable beauty, populated by kingfishers and toucans, scarlet ibis and laughing falcons. It was also a camp of constant rain and persistent mosquitoes, of chiggers, maggots and blackfly, where piranha and pineapple provided the only fresh food for the team. In keeping with local practice, the loo was a ladder slung across the river and daily body checks by one's 'buddy' for sores and bites in the most intimate of places were essential for health. It did not take long for the message to spread to other Operation Raleigh sites: Kurupakari was not for the faint-hearted.

It was from Kurupakari that the venturers, in the company of Nick and Charlie, canoed across the river to Fairview to build a school for the village children; it was also from here that they departed to repair the bridges deep in the humid rainforest; and from here that they left to cross the swamp and jungle and follow the route of what some call the 'Cattle Trail' but most referred to simply as 'Hell'.

Educated by an Oxford don who had drifted to the faraway town of Bartica, Roy Marshall, a Guyanese man of Arawak and French descent, was determined that the children in the remote hamlet of Fairview should have a school. As a youth he had worked as a gold miner and had also dived for diamonds, plunging sixty-five feet down into the depths of the Mazaruni River, equipped with only a hose, face mask and the hope of escaping the bends that tied men up like pretzels. Now, thirty years old, he grew a subsistence crop of bananas, sweet and bitter cassava, sugarcane and pineapples, and fought the armies of brown Acoushi ants that attacked his crops each year.

Taking the wave of international youngsters in his stride, Roy and the other people of Fairview taught them how to make cassava bread, hunt boar and jaguar and harvest wood for the school, gather wood bark for the roof and sides, black yari yari timber for the frames and level trunks of palm for the floors. Up at dawn, the venturers headed off in canoes, paddling miles upriver to find just the right timber. If their search was successful, the real work then began, felling the trees and bringing them back to the village. Often the sides of the heavily laden canoes barely rose above the water and the efforts of transporting 420 pounds of wood against the current and in equatorial heat built muscles that should last for life.

Heading out from Kurupakari, the bridge-building teams slung their hammocks on buttressed trees, built shelters against the constant rain and sweated off their high-calorie rations. Their work was often illuminated by electric storms that lit the forests for miles around. The venturers cut and dried massive logs of greenheart (*Ocotea rodiaei*) using chains and ropes and strong, young backs. Like Purpleheart (*Peltogyne pubescens*), named after the crimson sap that gushes like blood and turns a violent purple, greenheart is a remarkably tough and beautiful tree. Both are resistant to termites, marine borers, fire and water – qualities not always essential to their other uses as fishing rods, longbows and the decorative butts of billiard cues.

The interlocked grain of greenheart gives the wood its incredible weight of 70 pounds per cubic foot. Dragging their eighty-foot logs to the riverside, our ragged chain gangs bore a distinct resemblance to the Inca slaves of El Dorado. Occasionally, the momentum pitched the huge logs into the river and, heavier than water, they sank without any prospect of salvage. This was the exactly the sort of real character-building experience we had envisaged when launching Operation Raleigh.

The cattle trail was another of the legends of Guyana: hundreds of miles of almost impenetrable track slicing through the country from its Atlantic shoulder southwards to the vast ranches of the Rupununi. Fallen trees and branches vied with creeping vines, mud and swamp in providing regular obstructions. With nothing but jungle in every direction, river crossings provided a welcome but testing distraction, as one tried to remain vertical on slippery logs covered by five feet of dark, fast-flowing water.

The word 'trail' is largely euphemistic. Pioneered in 1922 by courageous ranchers like the legendary Sandy McTurk, it hadn't been used for years, although huge herds of Brahman cattle once braved the jaguars and piranhas to go from the town of Lethem, on the border of Brazil, north to Kurupakari and the capital, a total distance of over 300 miles. On that tortuous journey, each animal lost an average of ninety pounds – if, indeed, it managed to last the distance.

Operation Raleigh had been asked to assess the possibility of recreating an all-weather trail from Kurupakari to Surama and the markets of the north. Everyone, and certainly Roderick, a guide from Fairview, knew that the trek would not be easy, but no-one could foresee the injuries, illness and danger that lay ahead.

Just two days out of Kurupakari the track had deteriorated to the point where only Roderick could read the route, following old machete marks that had scarred the trees. The pace slowed noticeably as expedition members stopped to help companions who had fallen in the thick, slippery mud. It had taken the team three hours of wading through knee-high swamp to cover about as many miles. Neil Hendry, Barry Cochrane and Nigel Symonds wielded their razor-sharp machetes skilfully as they carved the route for the others to follow. At one point, as Neil slashed his way forward, his bush hat was knocked off by a low-hanging branch. When he reached to retrieve it Baz's machete sliced through his hand, cutting the muscles in a long, deep gash.

'Blood poured from my hand as I tried to pull the open wound together,' recalled Neil. A couple of team members quickly bound the cut and laid him on his back, while others built a platform of rucksacks to hoist him above the swamp. At dusk the mosquitoes came in like Stinger missiles and, with no dry wood for a fire, the group spent an uncomfortable night, awakened by the scream of howler monkeys, far louder than any lion or elephant, and by the soft, low growl of a jaguar scenting blood. Fearing infection, Singaporean Farid Hamid sent Neil back to base camp with two others. Jean Lumb, our energetic GP whose hobby was rally driving, met the trio halfway. She first stripped to wash in the murky brown river as a pre-surgery clean-up, then deftly stitched Neil's hand in an operating theatre of razor grass, vines and towering trees.

Only twelve intrepid survivors remained on the cattle trail. Dropping to all fours as they climbed under fallen trees and holding packs aloft as they waded through rivers, it was a very dirty dozen that pushed on, some days covering only five miles as they hacked their way through the belly of Guyana. There was worse to come. The mosquitoes, always bad, became a black wall, leaving a pattern of bites that soon became septic. On the third day, unable to withstand regular baths in bogs and rain, the radio died. Communication with base camp ended.

They continued on, heading south-west to Surama. The fourth and fifth days were spent in the swamps near Iwokrama Mountain, which they were unable to see from under the umbrella of the jungle canopy. The thick, slimy water of the swamp was so deep that the venturers had to swim from tree to tree, hauling themselves along by clinging to trailing vines and traversing deeper stretches with ropes. At night they split palm logs and built a hearth above the swamp, managing to light a fire with splinters of a special wood known only to Roderick. The meagre cheer of a hot brew of coffee and swamp water quickly evaporated. Guyana's cattle trail was testing the young to their limits.

Then a new danger struck. On the same day that Roderick fell ill, young Allison Hollington stood on an electric eel. The pain travelled up her calf to her shoulder, exploding in waves that rocked her body. 'Get out of the water! Get out of the water!' screamed Alli as the serpent-like fish, as thick as a man's leg, circled and turned to attack again. The long fin cut a wake that charted its path like a knife.

Although near hysterics, Alli's instinctive concern was for her companions. Hearing her rising yells, they struggled out of the evil water to the safety of tree branches. In seconds Farid had shrugged off his pack and was by her side, dragging her on to higher ground. He knew that most creatures die if struck by an electric eel; the shock it produces usually paralyses its victims, eventually causing them to drown.

The eel's fearful attack on Alli had come out of the blue and made the small band even more aware of the dangers that surrounded them on all sides. Some they could see, others lurked, invisible, in this dark, sinister, hostile landscape that they were determined to cross. Roderick recovered from his bout of recurring malaria, but long after Allison's spasms of fear subsided, it took great courage to shoulder her pack, put on a smile and step again into the fetid swamp. But, showing tremendous character, she gritted her teeth and forced herself on. After marching, hacking and wading through the claustrophobic and often flooded jungle for over sixty miles, the weary group strode proudly into the little town of Surama, and did not consider that the trail could be recreated. Today there is an abattoir at Lethem and the beef is flown to Georgetown.

The Raleigh venturers were to endure more alarming thrills and spills in this 'Land of many waters' but, encouraged by Joe Singh's enthusiasm for the exploration and protection of the environment, I could not resist mounting further expeditions into the country's lush tropical forests.

CHAPTER 18

OF APES AND ANACONDAS

By 1993 I had retired from both the army and Operation Raleigh and was concentrating instead on organising what were to be somewhat more recreational and yet still extremely challenging Scientific Exploration Society expeditions for groups of adults over the age of twenty-five, irreverently dubbed 'wrinklies' by the younger staff at SES's expedition base. For the first of these ventures, I returned to Guyana.

My old friend Brigadier Joe Singh, Chief of Staff of the GDF, who had looked after us so well on previous visits, knew everyone of consequence in the country and with his generous help we were able to start planning a number of projects aimed primarily at investigating archaeological and zoological mysteries, of which there was no shortage.

One of the first people we went to see was the curator of the local museum in Georgetown, who was very enthusiastic about what we had in mind and whetted our appetites by suggesting a number of zoological curiosities that we might like to look into, including reports of a massive horned anaconda, said to be more than thirty feet in length. 'It must have swallowed a goat and the horns have come through the roof of its mouth,' speculated our herpetologist when we told him about it. There were also tales of an unusual monkey-like primate that walked upright, a bit like the Yeti of the Himalayas. A Swiss geologist had shot a specimen in nearby Venezuela in 1920, but this had since been lost. Another report told of a large, maned cat of a kind unknown to science.

I had also heard that far up the Rupununi River a courageous lady named Diane McTurk, great-granddaughter of the pioneer Sandy McTurk and daughter of amateur naturalist and conservationist Edward 'Tiny' McTurk, was fighting to save the giant otter, a large seven-foot cousin of the British variety, from extinction. Joe felt sure she would appreciate any help we might be able to give her.

Professor Denis Williams, Guyana's leading archaeologist, wanted us to explore some caves said to contain unusual pot burials, and we were also asked to do pollution studies to detect the extent to which rivers were being affected by mining. And an eminent doctor was interested in investigating claims that the villagers of the deep interior were said to gain energy by sucking an aquatic plant known as 'warin moss'. Although the use by the indigenous people of various herbal medicines was well known, further research was needed on some of these substances.

So, plenty of interest for our 'wrinkly' amateur explorers intent on combining some serious ecotourism with the tough demands, challenges and hardships of a true expedition.

To be able to operate for months on end in tropical rainforest, with temperatures in the 30s and humidity around 85%, far removed from all mod cons, all those taking part would need to be the sort of resolute individuals who would not shrink from more than a little discomfort. After interviews, followed by an initiation and acclimatisation weekend spent camping out in the fields and tramping around a wet Wiltshire wood, tackling various team-building exercises and initiative tests, I ended up with a diverse group that included an artist, a couple of marketing executives, a lab technician, a printer, a banker, several computer buffs, a music producer, a solicitor, a trauma doctor, a herpetologist, and a lady who worked for British Rail and kept ferrets. Altogether, our seventeen-strong team was made up of nine men and eight women, including my PA, Carol Turner.

Everyone was assigned a particular responsibility as we set out for Georgetown. Here, even before we ventured into the jungle, there were potential hazards. The rambling metropolis, intersected by canals and tree-lined avenues, is a couple of metres below sea level at high tide, so flooding is a constant threat and all pray that the sea wall will hold, with the effect of global warming adding to concern. Furthermore, the fact that nearly all its buildings are constructed out of wood has meant that Georgetown has been devastated by fire no less than nine times over the last two centuries. In terms of demographics, there is a marked and very noticeable divide between rich and poor, the wealthier cosmopolitan population living in attractive colonial-style houses with flowering gardens, in stark contrast to the poorer people's dilapidated homes, often little more than shacks on stilts.

Joe Singh kindly lent me some well-armed soldiers, a cook and a medical staff sergeant. Trooping into Georgetown's premier hotel, the Pegasus, with cutlasses (machetes) and jungle boots, we caused little concern, but there was no time to admire the sights of the capital, or to experience its notorious muggers.

Our plan was to work at five locations, moving from one to another by air, river or on foot. However, the higher earnings available from mining had attracted most of the local porters so movement onward was usually in Joe's GDF aircraft. The pilots were the best in the country and as a result of their unending search for drug runners and illegal miners they knew every inch of the territory they patrolled. It is not easy to penetrate the country's interior and many educated Guyanese living in the capital have never ventured into it. The all-weather road to Brazil was under construction at the time, but the engineers were having a frightful battle against the rains.

The pontoon bridge across the Demerara had been swept away a few days previously, so our upward journey was mainly by ferry and speedboat. Racing up the wide Essequibo, we docked at Bartica, gateway to the interior, a town of Wild West appearance in which Clint Eastwood, in one of his screen roles as a cheroot-smoking gunslinger, would have felt perfectly at home.

Hauling our stores ashore amongst the long-abandoned dredgers and steamboats, we found the streets and back alleys thronged with miners exchanging hard-won gold for women and liquor, before staggering back, usually broke, into the forest to start all over again. Finding a reasonably clean restaurant and a smiling proprietor, we tucked into a last hearty breakfast, watched by a pack of half-starved dogs.

'How do we get to Kaieteur?' inquired our ferret fancier, eager to be on her way in the steps of Attenborough and Durrell.

'No problem, man.' The dreadlocked Guyanan who had come to meet us grinned. 'We got a Bedford.'

And so he had. Piling into the ex-army four-tonner, recently shipped in from an MOD sale in the UK, we set off on a bone-jarring eighteen-hour drive along a jungle trail. Our liaison officer, Lieutenant Rexford Caesar, was sitting in the front seat, his AK-47 at the ready. 'Bandits?' I wondered aloud, but got no reply. Wedged like sardines into the heaving truck, we endured one of the most uncomfortable journeys I have ever experienced. Spiky branches were swept in and brushed against us, tearing exposed skin and showering us with insects, while at one point Mark O'Shea, our red-haired herpetologist, casually plucked a tree snake from the foliage as we passed, depositing it, wriggling and angry, in his canvas reptile bag.

At noon I hammered on the cab roof and shouted: 'Lunch!' Whereupon Joseph, the dreadlocked driver, pulled up instantly, right in the middle of the track. Carol dug out some squashed avocados and a bottle of Italian dressing that she had thoughtfully bought back in Bartica. We washed the food down with a mug of warm Tang orange-powder drink mix before embarking on another stretch of the mobile torture.

By dusk, having notched up 70 miles, we passed through a shanty village where wide-eyed children gazed at us from darkened doorways, as if confronted by a bunch of aliens. Trying to raise morale among his exhausted passengers, Joseph cried out: 'Only seven more miles to go!' Meanwhile the pot-holes started to multiply. At 0:100 the ruts actually became deeper than the wheels of the truck. Wielding shovels, ropes and using the vehicle winch, we struggled for two hours, slipping and sliding on the glutinous clay, to get through the three-foot-deep slime. Geoff Roy, our rugged photographer and the veteran of several trans-Africa safaris, was suitably impressed.

At 02:30 the dim headlights revealed a gap in the rainforest and the dilapidated tongue-and-groove resthouse at the hamlet of Kangarume. Amazingly, a message sent by Joe Singh had got through so we were expected and the dear old shopkeeper produced hot chicken and rice. Then the rain came, falling in torrents. We found some relatively clean floor space in the house and, not bothering to undress, crawled exhausted under our ponchos.

Daylight creeping through the splintered walls and the irresistible smell of baking bread woke me before 07:00. The shopkeeper produced tuna bu ʹs and coffee. Woodcock Skeet, our GDF signals officer, switched on his radio, gave me the day's messages, and told his HQ exactly where we were.

We eventually reached the Potaro River, where we transferred to a forty-six-foot wooden boat, all of us only too happy to leave the bucking Bedford. The river seemed disappointingly devoid of wildlife, possibly due to pollution by upstream mining, but as we navigated through the towering gorges, the view was both extremely picturesque and at the same time rather forbidding. In just under a couple of hours we heard the roar of a cataract and, rounding a bend, came face to face with the Amatuk Falls, where the water cascaded over a series of steep steps. Here we switched to a couple of smaller craft. It took an hour of heaving and hauling to portage the boats and stores along a well-worn route before we could rejoin the river. The heat and humidity sapped our energy and by now several of the team were pretty shattered.

The following stretch to the Waratuk cataract took barely an hour's motoring beneath even more impressive sandstone cliffs, whose spires rose like those of a Gothic cathedral. The next portage was relatively easy and we actually managed to rope our smaller boat up the falls. A distant murmur grew steadily louder and in the late afternoon we reached a lone hut on the riverbank at Turkeit. Disembarking and climbing up the bank, I found myself looking out over a most spectacular view of the foaming waters of Kaieteur: at almost 820 feet said to be the world's largest single drop waterfall by volume, tumbling into a narrow canyon alive with rainbows. The Potaro River above the drop is about the width of the Thames at Putney and, plunging over the edge of the plateau, it crashes into a natural amphitheatre alive with exotic plants. It is indeed a wonder of the world. As the day died we used our binoculars to watch white-chinned swifts diving through the curtain of spray to reach their nests in the cave behind the falls.

The hut turned out to be a shop, without any stock but inhabited by Benje, a tall fisherman who invited us to sling our hammocks inside. Corporal Warren, our cook, produced a filling meal and we were soon abed. Alas, just before midnight a tremendous storm hit us. Thunder and lightning echoed in the gorge and the rain came in rods. Those who had camped outside were drenched, but somehow retained their humour. And spirits rose as the sun crept into the canyon. Before climbing up to the plateau we tested the river for pollution, using Benje's small punt to get a midstream sample and net some fish specimens. Darren, our deputy herpetologist, caught a brief glimpse of a huge fish. Jane Davis, a keen angler, thought it might have been an arapaima, one of the planet's largest freshwater fish, which is found in South America and can reach over ten feet in length and weigh up to 450 pounds. Jane, a director of a fast-moving consumer goods company, was eager to see one of these monsters, but amid all the excitement of scanning the waters for another sighting we missed the opportunity to photograph a large black cat that John O'Connell, a marketing consultant from Essex, had spotted whilst taking water samples and which he was sure was a jaguar.

The two-and-a-half-mile ascent out of the gorge proved to be a challenge as not all our people were particularly fit or fully acclimatised. Thankfully, Rex had found some local porters to carry the heavier stores, but it was afternoon before we set off and the temperature was 31°C. Only five of the porters returned for the second lift and, even in this remote wilderness, I was reluctant to leave a pile of equipment unguarded.

In the humid heat, our movement was sluggish and lack of sleep, thanks to the spectacular tropical storm the night before, was having its effect. 'It's like climbing an endless staircase in a sauna,' groaned one of the marketing executives as we tackled the 1,000-foot climb. Whilst out doctor, Chris Snailham, and I escorted the slower members up the incline, Geoff, the fittest and strongest member of the team, gallantly returned twice to help.

For the first mile through the rainforest we had only a gentle slope to contend with, but we then reached a forty-five-degree stretch that turned one rather overweight member of the party a worrying shade of red, which then changed even more alarmingly to grey. Chris poured water down his throat and we carried on, moving more slowly and with frequent rests. The sweat gushed out of our pores.

At last we emerged from the jungle and enjoyed an awe-inspiring view of Kaieteur in all its magnificence. Morale rose even higher when, out of the clouds rising above the falls, there appeared a well-built wooden building in which we camped for the night. Next day as the sun was up we could not resist walking down to the edge of the cliff to gaze downward into the tumbling torrents. However, feeling as if we were being drawn into the falling water, we lay flat, peering over the lip to admire the incredible scene.

There followed several days of scientific observations in the surrounding area before we flew on from a local airstrip to the next scheduled location at the village of Paramakatoi. Here, we were greeted by the local MP, a Patamo man named Matterson Williams, along with the village chief. Our main task here was to examine the cave burial site alleged to be in the cliffs nearby. According to a legend that Prof Denis Williams had heard, the cave also contained a large venomous snake that sounded from the description we were given more like a rattler than the giant horned anaconda we sought. Pressing ahead on a recce, Geoff Roy and the MP discovered pottery artefacts along the sides of a small creek. This was an encouraging sign and, joining him with our team, we hacked out some of the dense vegetation and reached the nearby cliff face. The grey lichen-covered rock that faced us was rent by a thirty-inch-wide cleft.

Squeezing in, Geoff, Matterson and I switched on our head torches and advanced cautiously along the narrow passageway, keeping an eye open for snakes while also listening especially for the distinctive sound of a rattler.

Movement in the confined space was further limited by the massive boulders over which we had to scramble and slither. Out of the darkness something fluttered past my head, then another and another. I almost lost my footing and would have fallen into a crevasse had Geoff not grabbed my arm. We'd disturbed a colony of bats. 'Vampires!' muttered Matterson. After another fifty feet or so the tunnel narrowed even further, before then opening into a chamber some twenty feet wide and six and a half feet high. Geoff's lamp picked up something odd. Peering into the shadows at the back of the cavern I spotted a round pottery urn, approximately twenty inches in diameter, standing on a natural ledge. And lying on its lid was a coiled snake! We approached very warily, but there was no darting tongue nor any other sign of life. And as we edged closer I saw why: the reptile was part of the ceramic decoration.

Other small clay pots were grouped around the urn, which Geoff now grasped, carefully emptying out the contents. What lay exposed before us on the ledge was undoubtedly a collection of human bones – but with no skull present. Who was it who had deserved such a burial, I wondered. A chief, maybe? Or, perhaps, judging from the size of the bones, the child of one? Having photographed and mapped the discovery for the archaeological record, we carefully replaced the bones and withdrew.

Negotiating a particularly awkward rocky obstacle in the last few yards of the passageway, I was balancing on a root, using it as a foothold, only for it to snap suddenly under my weight, plunging me into an abyss between the boulders. Luckily, I managed to grab hold of a dangling vine as I fell, which probably saved me from at least a broken leg. Perhaps the tomb was cursed!

'This is like something straight out of an Indiana Jones movie,' commented Sandy Crivello, our American botanist, as we emerged from the cleft in the rock face and told the rest of the group what we'd found.

Helped by Bob Bannister, an ex-RAF first-aider, Doctor Chris Snailham was now running a regular clinic for the locals and, as a result, was gathering quite a lot of useful information. It was the reptile team that benefited most from this, Mark and Darren putting local knowledge to good effect in collecting various lizards, poison dart frogs and two highly poisonous fers de lance, the snake thought to kill more people than any other in South America. A true conservationist, Mark would not even contemplate killing the deadly serpents, but I did have to insist on him releasing them well away from the village. Their most exciting discovery was a little-known peripatus, thought to be the link between worms and insects.

A few days later we emerged from the dark, dank jungle and camped out on a flat plain beneath tall, stately palms. In front of us the Orinduik Falls tumbled over terraces of jasper on the peaty Ireng River that runs along Guyana's western border. Strolling nonchalantly up to us came a fisherman, who reported that he had an anaconda tangled in his net. Our herpetologists were on to this in a flash and went off with the fellows to find the beautiful orange-patterned constrictor firmly wrapped in the mesh. With commendable care they extracted the struggling snake and added it, very much alive, to Mark's collection for future study.

Meanwhile a local lady arrived with a sample of the legendary 'warin moss' for us to test. It grows thickly on the rocks and is hung over fireplaces to dry slowly into a black pulpy mass, she explained. I found it had a distinctly salty tobacco flavour and I wondered if these ingredients had been added, as the plant actually grows in clean fresh water. Those of us who tried it experienced an effect. Rob Matthews, my stalwart deputy, burst into fits of laughter, but I just hiccupped and felt light-headed. Investigation into other traditional medicines took us on long hikes, whilst the snake team managed to save the life of a rare turtle that had swallowed a fish hook.

Our final location was Karanambu, the legendary Diane McTurk's now world-famous ranch. Shaded by cashews and mango trees, this oasis of peace and tranquillity is a wildlife refuge covering 110 square miles that includes five different habitats and is home to a vast array of flora and fauna, including six species of monkey and over 600 species of birds. Owned by the conservation-minded McTurk family for almost a hundred years, it now attracts visitors from all over the world and has been featured in books by David Attenborough and Gerald Durrell, among others.

This whole area of Guyana is one of the world's last frontiers, where cowboys still work cattle in the open range whilst the Macushi and Wapishana tribes trade curare poison and arrow canes for flints with the Wai Wai in the south. All the ranches are measured in square miles and the cowboys are indigenous vaqueros. Battered Land Rovers buck and slide across sunburned grassland broken by scrub and swamp and threaded by creeks, which become torrents at the height of the wet season, large areas becoming flooded, creating the temporary Lake Amuku, where Raleigh believed he would find El Dorado.

Diane was a passionate advocate for the conservation of species and the Rupununi ecosystem, but gave little thought for her own comfort. Her home at the heart of the ranch was simple in the extreme, to the extent that I feared that its wooden structure might be in imminent danger of collapse. Born in this rambling building in 1932, Diane, a charming but formidable lady, had never had the time nor the inclination to turn it into a grand dwelling. Decorated with Macushi weapons and old household tools, it was more like a museum. There was even a dilapidated library that her pet goat had largely devoured. But of her menagerie of exotic pets it was the giant otters that were her real love. Answering her calls, the sleek black beasts would race across the river to feast on the daily diet of fresh fish that her staff caught for them. 'Watch they don't bite your toes,' she warned us.

Bird counts, fishing and reptile studies were made possible by paddling dugouts and using an ancient outboard, but this all added to the experience. Piranha were plentiful but one needed care in handling these aggressive chaps as our medic, Staff Sgt James, found when he lost a large chunk of his thumb whilst disentangling one from a hook.

While her noisy otters entertained us, Diane quenched our thirst with potent rum punches and gallons of homemade lemonade. In return we bent our backs in a tropical downpour to build an artificial holt, or nest, for the otters, located well above the high-water mark. When finished it was stronger than Diane's house!

We had been quartered in chalets around the compound. Even when really tired I'm a light sleeper, and one night in the early hours a slight sound stirred me. Opening my eyes, I became aware that an earlier storm had passed and moonlight was now flooding in through the chinks in the wall. The scratching sound came again and I became instantly wide awake, reaching for my razor-edged cutlass. Could it be a jaguar looking for food? Surely not, as Diane's dogs would undoubtedly have barked a warning. Slipping out from under the mosquito net, I flicked on my head torch to check nothing nasty was on the floor and stepped out of the camp cot. Now the noise came again. Something or someone was on the other side of the door, trying to lift the wooden latch, and at the same time puffing deep breaths.

Deciding that attack would be the best form of defence, I raised my cutlass and wrenched open the door. Facing me was a tubby 500-pound tapir, its long proboscis lifted expectantly, hoping for a snack. Another of Diane's pets, the gentle creature shuffled off disappointedly into the night when it realised there was no food on offer.

Meanwhile, Mark O'Shea was in near paradise with his reptilian friends popping up everywhere. Crossing Diane's airstrip one day with Mark, I was in deep conversation with him when, like a racing rugby wing forward, he suddenly hurled himself in front of us and then picked himself up and turned towards me, grinning triumphantly, with a writhing five-foot rattlesnake firmly in his grasp!

That afternoon Mark gave the local workers a lecture on the need to conserve snakes and even persuaded one or two of the less fearful to touch the rattler. Diane was most impressed as, at the time, she was just in the early stages of planning to set up a wildlife lodge and wilderness reserve for ecotourists. One of our team, Martin Hicks, a solicitor, immediately volunteered to help her draw up the various necessary legal documents. Later, the Karanambu Trust was founded with Joe Singh as chairman and the SES managed to raise a sizeable donation to help make Diane's dream come true, Karanambu Lodge going on to become a celebrated ecotourist destination.

All too soon it was time to move on and we bade farewell to this remarkable woman and her lovely creatures. An open barge took us downriver and Mark was most upset when I refused to have the rattlesnake travel with us.

As we puttered down the chocolate-brown river, majestic storks strutted on the sandbanks and ugly black caiman eyed us from the shallows as we paused to lunch and to release the orange anaconda. Reaching Apoteri village as night fell, we were happy to find a recently renovated guesthouse. Malaria was rife amongst the people, but they gave us a warm welcome and proudly demonstrated the new flushing loo. What a treat! Christianity reached this area long ago, and the next day it was a delight to attend one of the most touching and sincere lamplit evensongs I can remember. Mark had a good day too, thanks to Jane discovering a snake in a loo's cistern!

Homeward bound, we gave all our surplus kit and supplies to these poor but friendly people before boarding Joe Singh's efficient little Air Force plane for a flight back to Georgetown, where we enjoyed a cool beer and a thick, juicy steak at the Pegasus.

Although we had not found any rare apes or maned cats we had sampled 'warin moss' and had carried out our scientific and medical tasks to the full. We had also managed to do something worthwhile for the people of this developing nation who, like many others in poor countries struggling economically and suffering under a heavy burden of debt, were having to exploit their most precious natural assets in order to pull themselves up by their bootstraps.

We got pretty close to the enormous anaconda, albeit without horns: Gideon Williams, an experienced local hunter, told me that only a few days before we arrived a really big one had actually come sliding over the bow of his canoe.

'So what happened?' I asked.

To my horror, he replied: 'We shot it.'

I asked him how long it had been, knowing of the $50,000 reward offered by the Bronx Zoo for any snake over thirty feet in length.

'Exactly thirty-two feet,' said Gideon proudly. 'We measured it with a school ruler. Then we cooked and ate it.'

I groaned and went back to my maps, thinking that perhaps on the next expedition we might have more luck.

CHAPTER 19
TO A JUNGLE EDEN

'Once you've drunk creek water and eaten labba, it is said you will always return to Guyana,' promised Brigadier Joe Singh with a mischievous grin as we sipped our drinks in the mess at the Royal College of Defence Studies. Joe, then deputy commander of the GDF, had dark eyes that seemed to penetrate my very soul – and he can be most persuasive. Unfolding a map, his finger traced the course of the Essequibo River as it ran to what seemed a rather empty corner of his native country. 'This is Gunns Strip, where you will find the Wai Wai, people who really need your help,' he told me.

Having already dined on labba – rather like a giant plump guinea pig – and rodent steaks, washed down with warm, muddy creek water, I would have to say that it is not actually the most appealing feature of expedition life in the rainforest interior of the former British colony. But, even so, I needed little persuasion to accept my old friend's invitation to return once more to see what could be done to assist the indigenous Wai Wai.

Joe told me they were generally happy, quick to find something to laugh about and share a joke, but, as is the way with most Amerindians, they would simply vanish into the forest if upset or offended in any way. Of statuesque build, they love to adorn themselves with beads and feathers, which hang in bunches from their long pigtails and waistbands. But their traditional way of life was disrupted in the 1950s when an American mission was set up near Gunns Strip, a remote locality in the Upper Essequibo area. The missionaries were good farmers and were liked by the Wai Wai, whom they did their best to understand, but, almost inevitably, they were frustrated in their work amongst the people, whose innocent good nature and reluctance to change their ways tried the well-meaning Americans' patience.

The Wai Wai were encouraged to get rid of their shaman – or medicine man – which left them feeling vulnerable. Worse still, attempts were made to persuade them that it was wicked to keep more than one wife, which went against all their natural laws of survival. It would appear that some felt that the 'God man's God' was of no use to them in their jungle habitat, and many of the Wai Wai moved into Brazil, where their skills as hunters and the use of traditional medicines helped them to re-establish their communities.

However, I was told that the 200 or so Wai Wai still living near Gunns Strip had become devout Christians, with Bibles translated into their language, and that a number of them spoke English. At the same time, they still had very little contact and no real trade of any kind with the outside world and although they remained resistant to commercial influences that could upset the balance of their communal way of life, they did appreciate the need for advice on health, education and sustenance.

As a commander of the GDF, Joe was especially keen to do all he could to assist them, for they were the natural guardians of a lengthy stretch of Guyana's border with Brazil. His force lacked the manpower to protect the whole of the frontier, but by posting a signaller with a radio at Gunns Strip, he had managed to establish something of an early warning system, alerting him to any cross-border incursions. As a result, he had already captured a group of 'invaders' from Brazil, and had become a blood brother of the Wai Wai chief.

Meanwhile, increasing numbers of intruders from the outside world had brought in disease and the Wai Wai were being decimated by influenza and colds. Malaria had also come into the area, partly through the activities of the *garampieros* – the illegal gold prospectors and miners who had caused much havoc in the rainforest by poisoning the river waters with mercury. So in 1996, with Joe's enthusiastic backing, I recruited a ten-strong SES team to bring in urgently needed medical aid and carry out ecological and veterinary studies on behalf of this still mostly shy and reclusive rainforest tribe.

Our group included dental and ophthalmic surgeons, two GPs, a hospital porter, a lady vet, an expert on ecotourism and a veteran jungle explorer, Superintendent Vivian Mills of the Sussex constabulary, as my deputy. Dr LeRoy Benons, a Guyanese public-health expert working in Liverpool, was the only one of us who had actually met the Wai Wai.

In the early days of the Dutch and British colonial governments it was said that Amerindians had been used to hunt down escaped African slaves and I had been told a minor degree of distrust still existed between the races. Leroy was of African heritage and I was a little concerned about how he would relate with the Wai Wai.

Two twin-engine Britten-Norman Islanders awaited us at Georgetown's Ogle Airport. After careful weighing of our stores and ourselves on an ancient set of scales, we clambered into the high-wing monoplanes, the cabins superheated by the rising sun. The sweat was streaming from our faces as we took off and the aircraft climbed through billowing clouds to 4,000 feet, only for the cold air at that altitude to then have us shivering. To the west lay the broad brown waters of the Essequibo, which led to Gunns Strip, two and a half hours' flight away. Below us, the 120-foot-high green canopy of the dense forest stretched endlessly to the horizon, broken only by the silver threads of rivers from which Guyana earns its name.

'I doubt if anyone would find us if we came down in that cabbage,' remarked Steve Kershaw, a well-travelled doctor from Manchester. I nodded my agreement, but was more concerned about the possibility of Gunns Strip being flooded, as it often was.

Dark mountain peaks emerged out of the low grey cloud and at that very moment rain began to strike the windscreen. The plane shuddered and droplets dripped from the roof, dampening the map that I was clutching on my knees. As the sky cleared, we saw bright red-leaved trees in the forest canopy and then the jungle opened to reveal the flat grassy plains of the Rupununi savanna, edged by blue-tinged mountains. It was here that Sir Walter Raleigh's chart showed the lost city of El Dorado. Before long, like a theatre curtain falling, the jungle was back and in the distance I could see the Acarai Mountains that run along the border with Brazil. Beneath us the winding Essequibo, barely fifty yards wide at this point, cut through the trees.

My ears told me we were descending, and then I spotted a large clearing with a thin brown scar running down it. 'Gunns Strip,' shouted the pilot, pointing ahead as the ground rose up to meet us. With a slight bump we hit the packed earth. Thankfully, it was not flooded. Our engine roared as we raced past a line of tall palms, pulled up and taxied to make space for the next aircraft.

A blast of oven-hot air struck us as the doors opened, and there, awaiting us, were the Wai Wai. A couple of dozen men, women and children, wearing a mixture of jeans, T-shirts and loincloths, they returned our smiles and stepped forward to unload the cargo.

A warrior with coal-black hair, earrings and streaks of red dye across his cheeks pumped my hand.

'Are you the *Touchau*?' I asked. He shook his head and pointed to a man with curly hair and a thick moustache standing quietly with the crowd. With typical shyness, the *Touchau*, or Chief, stepped forward.

'I am Ekufu Mewsha,' he stated solemnly, shaking hands and then introducing me to the other village elders before pointing towards the jungle, saying: 'Come, there is a guesthouse for you.'

Refusing to let us carry our bags and stores of equipment, he and his people led us along a narrow, swampy footpath. Even the smallest children wanted to carry something, and I gave a near-naked toddler my map case. Hurrying to beat the coming rain, a brisk walk of a mile or so left us with our clothes soaked in perspiration. We reached the welcome shade of the forest just as the first drops fell and a few hundred yards further on we came to a gigantic tree trunk bridging a shallow creek. The youngsters scampered over, making us look rather ungainly as we negotiated the slippery crossing with caution. Beyond this were the thatch-roofed huts of Akotopomo, 'The place of the anaconda', and more people came running out to greet us.

Team quartermaster Karen Friedman, a Herefordshire postwoman, checked our stores into a spacious, freshly cleaned hut, at least a hundred feet long and with a swept earthen floor. We quickly slung our hammocks and mosquito nets between the stout beams and admired the tables and benches set out for us. Ekufu brought us grapefruit juice, which we gulped down, and announced that there would be a meeting with all his people in the circular '*Umana Yana*', the equivalent of a village hall. Truly democratic, the Wai Wai wanted everyone to be party to our plans. Indeed, most of the people and their wide-eyed inquisitive children gathered on the benches lining the huge hut, while others peered in from outside through gaps in the walls as Ekufu described their problems and needs.

George Simon, the Ministry of Amerindian Affairs officer who was accompanying us, gave helpful translations when necessary. Medical and dental treatment was high on the agenda and we outlined the plan to provide inoculations for tuberculosis (TB), mumps, measles and chickenpox, as well as giving polio and anti-tetanus injections. Our vet, Fiona Smith who practised in Crewe, was especially interested in the hunting dogs and the wildlife found in the area. On the question of trading, the elders talked of the cassava graters for which the Wai Wai are famous. They were also keen to trade their handicrafts and blowpipes.

Returning to our guesthouse we found it alive with red cockroaches, scuttling about amongst our gear and enjoying our hammocks, so we decided to name our new home Roach Hall. The children thought our efforts to dislodge the bugs quite hilarious, but offered enthusiastic help in clearing them out.

For the next ten days, in steaming tropical heat, we rarely stopped work. With Janet, the village nurse, and Staff Sgt James of the GDF, we tackled the Wai Wai's various medical problems. Due largely to chewing sugarcane, their dental health was very poor and Dr John McHugh, from the Royal Gwent Hospital, treated seventy patients, extracting over 300 teeth. Doctors Diptish Nandy, the team's surgeon, and Stephen Kershaw ran a general clinic, treating and operating on some fifty patients. We supplied spectacles and also vaccinated 120 villagers, many of them children, against tuberculosis, measles, mumps, polio and tetanus as well as testing for malaria, parasites and the effects of water pollution. Veterinary and zoological studies were undertaken by Fiona and the possibilities of ecotourism were considered alongside plans for a tribal culture centre.

'There doesn't seem to be any crime here,' commented Viv Mills, my second in command. 'Must be because they don't use money.' However, Ekufu reported that someone had been stealing chickens from his farm a little distance beyond the village and that his brother, James, had gone to investigate. Shortly afterwards James returned in a state of some excitement to say that he had arrived at the farm at dusk to be greeted by the sound of a lot of squawking and had been about to go up to the hen coop to find out what was going on when he found himself facing a crouching tawny puma devouring one of the chief's prize hens. With a guttural growl the cat rushed at him, whereupon he had leapt back into his boat and paddled rapidly for home.

'May I borrow your shotgun, Colonel John?' asked Ekufu, on hearing this. I gladly agreed and later that night he went quietly downstream.

He found feathers and chicken entrails littering the pen and, after carefully checking the wind direction, he chose a vantage point, crept into a bush nearby, and sat very still, waiting. At about midnight the moon rose, casting silver beams through the forest canopy and on to the pen. A twig cracked in the forest and a nightbird called, then a rustle of leaves indicated something large was moving nearby. The gun's hammer was already cocked. Ekufu held it very steady, suppressing his breathing and, suddenly, without a sound the predator's head and shoulders appeared in the moonbeam. It sniffed the air. Hoping that the scent of the entrails would cover his own, Ekufu very slowly raised the barrel and, aiming for the animal's shoulder, squeezed the trigger. Fifteen feet away, the killer was catapulted sideways, gave a last mewing groan and died. Having checked that it was definitely dead, the chief left the bloodied carcass and canoed home. Next day we went with him to retrieve it.

'This cat is certainly a lot bigger than the ones I'm used to dealing with back in Crewe,' admitted Fiona as she measured the beast, a full-grown male with pads three inches across. 'Quite a puss,' she added admiringly as she examined the fearsome fangs. The Wai Wai only hunt for food, so it had not occurred to Ekufu to preserve the pelt. But with Fiona's guidance, he took it off to make a rug, in payment for his chickens!

By necessity, the Wai Wai are skilled hunters, famed for their trained terrier-sized dogs. These usually live in the huts with the families, where each dog has its own shelf built into the wall, but the fleas they carry can be a problem. However, the people have found a way to solve this. Every morning before school the children take the dogs to the river and shampoo them with a soap made from a particular root. This treatment effectively deters the fleas, but for a few hours afterwards the village is alive with pink dogs.

Elessa, the village preacher, was also a master hunter and one Sunday after we had attended his service, which went on for several hours, he asked if we would like to accompany him and some of his choir on a hunting and fishing trip. 'Bring your rod and the shotgun,' he said. So, next day we paddled downriver in dugout canoes. At one point we passed some young local boys who were diving, stark naked, from a branch that projected over the water. Seeing us, they placed their hands over their private parts and looked ashamed. 'Don't worry, we are doctors,' called Steve and, satisfied that they had caused no offence, the children smiled and carried on diving.

Piranha must be the easiest fish to catch. One only needs a small piece of meat on the hook and in seconds one is fighting a monster – or so it seems, but it will probably be only a three-pound piranha. Even when they are dead you need to be extremely careful when de-hooking them or you can lose at least part of a finger in their razor-sharp jaws.

We had just ridden a small rapid when Elessa signalled for silence and we clearly heard grunting coming from beneath the hull. '*Basha,*' he murmured and lowering our baited hooks we caught several large, flat silver fish that were swarming under the boat.

As darkness fell, an electric storm was building up and the preacher, his serious face illuminated by flashes of lightning, gripped his longbow in one hand while fending off overhead branches with the other as he directed our paddlers. His torch beam then picked out a pair of eyes glowing bright red in the shallows and, as we inched forward noiselessly, Elessa fitted a long, slender arrow with a barbed harpoon head into his bow. '*Twack!*' sang the bowstring and the water erupted as a four-foot caiman was hit. Moses, one of the paddlers, seized the top of the shaft which floated on the surface, whilst six feet down the detached arrowhead was firmly embedded in the reptile's eye.

There was not a lot of extra room in the canoe to accommodate the reptile as well as ourselves and the hunting dogs, so Fiona squeezed herself into the stern as the writhing beast was pulled alongside and two blows from a sharp cutlass severed its spinal cord. Within an hour our canoe was loaded down with three caiman plus a couple of ten-pound haimara caught on previously laid night lines.

The dogs were now alert and sniffing the cool night air. 'Labba,' whispered Moses and we pulled into the bank. Elessa signalled me to go ahead with the gun and I moved forward, following the terriers, who were hot on the scent. My head torch lit up the path and the undergrowth for twenty yards or so in front of me and we hadn't gone very far when I spotted a striped rodent emerging from the bush. Managing to get off a shot before the dogs closed in, I bagged my first labba. Moses tossed it into the crowded boat where a couple of the caiman were still wriggling in their death throes.

As we drifted back down the creek a fish rose from the depths and touched the surface with its nose. Whilst I watched, it sank down leaving a spreading ring of ripples. It then reappeared, thick, black and about five feet in length, and swam alongside the canoe. I went to prod it with the paddle. 'No!' cried Elessa. 'Electric eel, very dangerous!' In that instant I remembered seeing one in the Boston Museum of Science and being told that it could give off sufficient current to light up a bulb and also recalled the venturer's painful encounter during the Raleigh expedition. We passed more sets of glowing eyes, but Elessa ignored them. We had enough food for the time being and the Wai Wai are always careful not to overhunt.

Next day in the jungle we were taken to their farms where they grew pineapple, banana, cassava, yams and plantain. When an area is to be cleared for the new growth, it takes all the manpower of the village working for a week to cut down the thick, lush vegetation and the Wai Wai are careful to create farms at different levels to overcome the problems of flooding during the wet season. The tribe's use of local resources and traditional medicines gleaned from the forest plants was impressive and we learned that they extracted oil from the nuts of the manicole and turu palms, which they claimed would prevent hair turning grey. We certainly did not see any grey-headed Wai Wai. 'What a priceless commercial asset that would be back home if it could be proved to work,' commented Doctor Steve.

We all wondered what the future held for these gentle people whose quiet, orderly lives centred around their church. The younger members of the tribe were keen to be part of the 20th century, but the very real danger of losing the balance of their lives and the old traditional skills by which they have survived for hundreds of years is ever present. A more informed choice can be made by education, with radio links to the outside world. A proposal by the Ministry of Amerindian Affairs to provide training in business and allied matters is strongly supported by the tribe, as this would allow them to keep control of all their income-generating schemes, such as the sale of produce and handicrafts. They were also well aware that restricting the number of outside visitors to the area would help to preserve their way of life and encourage members of the tribe who have gone outside the area to return.

When we left, we paid our helpers in fish hooks and trade goods. We gave them medicines and a hand-operated Singer sewing machine, as Western clothing is generally worn, although on special occasions the older members of the tribe still adorn themselves traditionally in beads, feathers and hunting trophies. Back in England, we were able to arrange shipment of some illustrated Bibles, kindly provided by a publisher.

Without doubt the Wai Wai had given us a lasting memory of an oasis of peace and happiness, where men, animals and the forest live in harmony. This was indeed a Garden of Eden. 'Will you be coming back?' asked Ekufu as we boarded the plane. I told him that I very much hoped so, and I really meant it.

However, it was to be four years before I did manage to make it back, following a special request from the Wai Wai for my return. Joe Singh, now a Major General in overall command of the GDF, was as keen as ever to support the Wai Wai. But there had been changes. Ekufu and a group had moved north to set up a village with the Wapishana people on the Kuyuwini River.

The Wapishana come from the savanna and are of a very different nature to the forest people. Their appearance is more Spanish than Amerindian and they are, by nature, somewhat sharper-witted and more commercially minded then the Wai Wai. Having had their traditional way of life undermined by the missionaries, the influx of ranchers who drove them off their land, and traders who brought in goods superior to those they could make themselves, they had lost some of their self-confidence and pride in their own achievements and traditional skills and had looked for other ways to survive. While some of them had gone on to become expert balata-rubber bleeders or vaqueros, others had learned to make superb hammocks from hand-spun cotton, and many were employed by the government. At the same time, there had always been a few wheeler-dealers on the edge of the Wai Wai's way of life, trading in the much sought-after cassava graters made by their women, and the prized *Yurua* palms used as the outer casing for blowpipes.

The new *Touchau* at Akotopomo was Paul Chekema, whom I had not met before, and he was facing many problems. Malaria, brought in by Brazilian miners and transmitted by mosquitoes, had recently started to spread and Joe had sent in medicines. At the same time, some of the young were keen to try new foods and wanted to cultivate hill rice, but needed expert advice. Also, animal collectors, operating without permits, had been exploiting the Wai Wai, seeking rare blue frogs and snakes. The Wai Wai were struggling to preserve their intellectual rights and, seeing the power of collective action, were seeking connections with other Amerindian groups.

To sustain themselves, Paul Chekema's people needed to market their handicrafts and create new products. The chief was eager to reaffirm the value of a symbiotic relationship with the forest and show his people how to manage their environment. Joe wanted continuity and had helped by seconding Clarence Rudolph of the GDF, a Wapishana with a Wai Wai wife, to the village. Clarence had lost an eye in a hunting accident, but had an army radio to keep in touch with the GDF headquarters. As I was to discover, he was still a great hunter despite his accident, a skilled boatman and also knew much about the traditional medicine of the jungle. Indeed, Clarence was an intelligent man of many parts and had become, effectively, Paul's deputy.

The SES had no difficulty in recruiting a team with a wide range of experience, including anthropology, entomology, handicrafts, healthcare, public relations and wildlife. We also had a film crew of two hoping to produce a programme to promote the Wai Wai through TV and lectures. Also with us was Yoli, the Colombian economist and now the SES representative in Latin America. Being of Incan descent, it would be interesting to see how she could relate to the Wai Wai. Personally, I took great satisfaction from the fact that three of our team came from my home island of Jersey, which has a proud history of producing expeditioners.

The Honourable Vibert De Souza, Minister for Amerindian Affairs, whose great-great-grandfather actually came from Liverpool, took a close interest in the project and lunched with us in Georgetown. At the time I was helping the Merseyside

Youth Association to raise funds for an innovative youth centre in Liverpool and although I had not met any of the minister's relations, we had six team members from the area. The local *Liverpool Daily Post* newspaper kindly helped us and persuaded their readers to donate hand-operated sewing machines. These were collected by their delivery vans and carried out to Guyana by a friendly airline, but it took two Islander aircraft and a Skyvan freighter to fly the team and all the various donations into Gunns Strip.

Pools of water lay across the airstrip, and we landed in a cloud of spray to disembark in sticky mud. As the heavy plane tried to turn, the wheels sank in and stuck. The pilot clambered out and shook his head. However, Chief Paul and Clarence quickly mustered their people and with much pushing and shoving got the aircraft on to firmer ground. Deolinda, our former cook, gave me a hug and her husband, James, introduced a rather shy Paul, whilst Clarence organised carriers for the cargo.

Looking like an 18th-century African safari, with sewing machines balanced on heads and shoulders, our column set off down the wet track to Roach Hall. The wee beasties scampered for cover as we entered. Nothing had changed.

The villagers listened intently as our Ministry of Amerindian Affairs liaison officer, Vivian Fredericks, explained our plans. They welcomed the medical help and there was much discussion on traditional medicine, although it seemed, sadly, that there were now few old people left who still had expert knowledge. The sewing machines were greatly appreciated and were soon at work in the women's centre. On the question of trading we had to point out that many of their handicrafts were created from seeds and animal parts that we could not export. The colourful headdresses made from macaw tail feathers were a typical example, the sort of souvenir item that I doubted would be allowed through British customs. 'But we do not kill the birds,' protested the Wai Wai. 'We just pull out the feathers and they grow some more.' Anna Nicholas, who had run a mail-order business, also suspected that the feather-bedecked blowpipes with poison tipped darts might be difficult to sell in London! 'How about frogs and snakes?' the people asked, and I guessed they had in mind the recent approaches by illegal collectors.

'Mr Kurt Hertzog from Georgetown offered us two hundred and fifty thousand dollars for an anaconda of thirty feet,' said James. Even if he were talking in Guyana dollars, this was still a lot of money.

'Did you find one?' enquired Harry Raffe, a snake lover from Liverpool.

'Oh, yes,' replied James, 'but it was only fifteen foot so we just asked for half the money.'

'The man would not pay,' added Clarence, 'so we packed him off to Georgetown and reported him to the government.'

They had then released the huge snake, but had apparently kept some other reptiles. 'I'll show you one,' said James eagerly, and a large blue plastic picnic box was dragged out.

'Don't get too close,' warned Clarence, easing the lid open. We gasped at what was then revealed, for coiled inside was a rusty-coloured seven-foot bushmaster, its head poised, ready to strike. 'Bad fellow,' said James as we snapped photos of one of the largest and most venomous snakes in South America.

Harry was admiring a pink-toed tarantula that was crawling up his sleeve when Clarence came in to warn us that a party of foreigners were coming downriver. Lieutenant Courtney Mendoza, our GDF liaison officer, picked up his rifle and ran outside to investigate. Out of curiosity, we followed.

As the canoes touched the bank Courtney and his corporal stood with arms unslung. The newcomers, three white men and a woman with some local guides, looked sheepish. Their leader, a man named Gamill, approached Courtney offering his hand. 'I need to see your passports and permits,' demanded the officer, adding politely but firmly: 'Please come this way.'

In the council chamber Mendoza and Vivian examined the documents. Gamill had no passport, which did not help. We kept clear, this being none of our business, but I couldn't help noticing the mountains of high-quality equipment being carried up to the hut. Mendoza came over and whispered: 'I don't like the look of these people. Please could you inspect their equipment and let me know what you think they are doing.'

By now all their stuff was piled up under the corporal's guard. It included aerial photography, maps, survey gear, folding canoes, an outboard engine and a chainsaw, plus cameras, masses of film and a satellite phone. I found myself in rather an awkward situation, but turning to one of the party I inquired about their activities. 'We're American,' he replied, with a nervous twitch at the corner of his eye. 'We are interested in ecotourism and are looking at streams. Mr Gamill is a zoologist.'

Yoli then spoke to the woman in the group who told her that they worked for a US non-profit organisation. The maps they had were more detailed than any usually available in Georgetown and had pencil markings along water sources. A batea, a gravel-washing pan used to find alluvial gold and diamonds, lay amongst their gear.

Clarence's beady eye had been watching too. 'These guys know all about gold and diamonds,' he muttered as I took Polaroid photos of the equipment for Mendoza, who had now confiscated all the documents, film and the phone.

'Their permit is signed by a secretary in the Department of Amerindian Affairs and not by the Minister – very irregular,' Vivian confided to me once the examination was over.

Using our satellite phone, we called Joe Singh, who congratulated Mendoza and said he would handle it. Two days later a plane arrived to take the visitors to Georgetown and we heard later that they had been deported. Quite what this well-funded group was doing I never discovered, but it made the Wai Wai even more aware of the riches that might be on their land.

There were also some archaeological treasures in the village, Paul producing several fine polished stone axe heads that were later determined to be up to 7,000 years old and had been used to hollow out boats from enormous tree trunks.

Accompanying hunters and their dogs, we saw the effectiveness of their bows and arrows and blowpipes and, using a night-vision device, we were able to observe the nocturnal animals. Our only injuries came from chiggers, little flea-like bugs that burrowed into one's feet to lay eggs, which then had to be dug out with a needle before they hatched. There were few mosquitoes, but the sandflies and ants gave us annoying bites, which needed regular treatment if one were to avoid a tropical ulcer.

Where possible we ate fish, which was abundant, along with hard baked cassava bread and 'farine', rather like All-Bran but made from cassava. Cassava, the staple crop of the Amerindians, starts out as a poisonous root that must be processed before it is safe to eat. One wonders how many people died during the experimental stage before the process was perfected. The plant yields only one crop a year and when the soil is poor, new areas must constantly be found, leading to the 'slash and burn' agriculture commonly seen in South America.

However, the prized cassava graters were the Wai Wai's chief source of wealth and from those sales, reaching as far as the coast, came the acquisition of beads, knives, pots and pans and any other manufactured articles they needed. Some bows and arrows were also sold, although, traditionally, the people did not themselves make the curare poison for the arrow heads. This they usually bought in from other tribes, often the Wapishana. The arrows, about five feet long, are made from curved grass stems that are softened over a fire before being rolled to straighten them. Bird feathers are then attached as flights in a spiral shape, to give the arrows stability. As we saw in the forest, the hunter will carry the poisoned tips in a separate quiver and attach one as required. Years before, I had seen a similar system being used by the pygmies of the Congo.

I enjoyed talking to Clarence whose expert knowledge of the herbs and traditional medicines was admirable. He explained how the poison for the arrowheads is brewed into a thick, sticky jam, often a mixture of toxic substances collected from bark, leaves and vines, whilst the traditional curare is made from the strychnos vine. Poison, he said, is also collected from the venomous and dreaded fer-de-lance snake, but the most virulent comes from the brilliantly coloured black and yellow 'poison arrow frog'.

Every day we were learning more about the lives of these fascinating people. Indeed, they were so self-sufficient that it seemed surprising that they needed any outside help. I was examining a strange fish with an external bone skull and a folding fin that had been caught by David Nicholson, a metalworker and keen fisherman from Liverpool, when our nurse, Cecilia, rushed in.

'Deolinda's son has broken his femur whilst playing football,' she gasped. By now we all loved Deolinda and her adorable little boy Meshak, who had been born without ears and was profoundly deaf. Running over to her hut, I found Christine, our doctor, attending to the child. 'It's a bit more serious than we thought,' she whispered. 'He's bleeding internally and may not survive unless we can get him to hospital ASAP.' Night was falling and there was no hope of calling in an aircraft before the next day. Furthermore, a satellite phone call to Georgetown confirmed my fears. The overstretched health department simply could not afford to send a plane 350 miles for one injured youngster, no matter how serious it was.

Whilst we debated the problem, Ian Stevens, a Jersey brewer and our entomologist, came over and, taking me to one side, said quietly: 'If you can get a plane, I'll pay for it.' So next day a Cessna 206 with a paramedic aboard roared over Akotopomo and Meshak was rushed to Georgetown hospital, where we learned later that he had indeed survived, thanks almost entirely to Ian's generosity.

At a final conference of the Wai Wai elders we gave them advice on crops, ecotourism, education, health and trading. In some ways, the main problem for them is the simple fact that they are so isolated. Without the funds for aircraft, even getting to the regional capital of Lethem involves a journey of several weeks by foot and boat. But in many other ways, I envied them their isolation from the world we live in.

As we prepared to leave there was the traditional exchange of gifts – tools, cutlasses and sewing kits for the Wai Wai; necklaces, bags, bows and blowpipes for us. That night we went to evensong for hymn singing, accompanied by guitars, pipes and drums. As I left, the night sky was full of twinkling stars and I reflected that the scene really was almost biblical.

Elessa, the preacher, shook my hand. 'I expect you will come back,' he smiled. 'And when you do, will you grant me a favour? Will you bring us a grand piano?'

'A grand piano!' I gasped in amazement. 'Have you ever seen one?'

'I've seen a picture of one,' he said. 'As you know, we are musical people and I'm sure we could learn to play it. And if we have something really special like a grand piano it will encourage the young people to stay here and not to go to Georgetown, where without any trade, they will be unable to get jobs and will end up in trouble.'

What could I say? 'No promises, Elessa,' I told him. 'But I'll do my best.'

CHAPTER 20

THE GRAND ADVENTURE

Raising the six-foot blowpipe, I gave a sharp puff and a dart embedded itself in the conservatory's palm tree above the managing director's head. To give him his due, Tony Potter did not even duck but the other guests at the Millennium Copthorne hotel looked a trifle surprised. I was demonstrating the Wai Wai's handicrafts and appealing for support for Paul Chekema and his tribe. I'd decided it would not be wise to illustrate my pitch with any of those more colourful Amerindian cultural items made from what appeared to be endangered species and, having gone on to list some of the things they urgently needed by way of educational and medical aid, I added as my closing line: 'They also want a grand piano.'

'I'll give you a grand piano,' called out Tony.

'And we'll fly it to Guyana,' shouted the British West Indies Airways (BWIA) representative from the back of the room. The media diarists had not missed these remarks and, the next day, the news was out that the SES intended to take a grand piano to a tribe deep in the Guyana jungle. It was just the sort of quirky story the papers enjoy and they had a field day.

'Are you serious?' asked my old Sapper pal, Jim Masters, who had accompanied me on many expeditions. 'How big is it and what does it weigh?'

Within the week Tony called me to say his chairman, Mr Kwek Leng Beng, and his wife were classical music enthusiasts and were delighted by the idea. 'Just say when and where you want the piano.' I faxed my old colleague, Joe Singh, now a retired general and former commander of the GDF, but still our link to the Wai Wai, to see what he, his government and the tribe thought of the proposal. They were enthusiastic, so the only problem now was how to get an 800-pound piano to Akotopomo in working condition.

If BWIA would fly it into Georgetown we could hire a Skyvan freighter to lift it the final 350 miles, and by now our long-time South American representative Yolima Cipagauta was working on a budget. Calling me from her home in Bogotá, she told me: 'I reckon you need to think in terms of ten thousand pounds.' So Anna Nicholas, the dynamic PR lady who had been on the previous visit to the Wai Wai, set to work. Her friends at the *Daily Mail* thought it a great idea and agreed to sponsor us in return for the whole world-exclusive story. Now we needed a small team to carry out the task. Jim Masters recruited Paul Busek, a Royal Engineer Sergeant, and I asked the eminent ethno-biologist, Dr Conrad Gorinsky, if he'd care to join us. Conrad came from Guyana and was an established expert on traditional medicine. We found a musical doctor, Simon Richards, who had been in the army and was now a GP and a choirmaster, and could tune pianos. Yoli, who had established a special relationship with the Wai Wai, would join us from Colombia and the *Daily Mail* appointed Mark Large, an intrepid photographer, to cover the story. Likening it to the film *Fitzcarraldo,* based on the true story of a 19th-century Peruvian rubber baron and his feat of transporting a disassembled steamboat over an isthmus between two rivers, TV production companies were soon on to us. Sarah Jane Lewis, the SES PR, liked the sound of David Goodale, who had spent many months filming the Yanomami people in Venezuela, so we agreed to take him, his sound man, Stephen Foster, and Karen Kelly from the BBC.

However, having seen the news reports, a number of commissioning editors reckoned it was mission impossible and David had a battle to convince the BBC to go ahead with the programme. He only got their backing two days before we departed, when Greg Dyke, Director-General of the BBC at the time, took a personal interest.

Meanwhile the instrument, built by Boyd of London in 1935, was encased in a large packing case, with its legs and lyre removed, and squeezed into the hold of the BWIA transatlantic jet. What hadn't been foreseen was that BWIA used a smaller aircraft for the short trip from Port of Spain in Trinidad to Georgetown and at the last minute we discovered we would have to find another, larger plane for that leg of the journey to Guyana.

After ten days of frantic activity at SES's Dorset base to find a means of lifting the piano, we arranged for a Skyvan cargo plane from Guyana to fly to Port of Spain to collect it. Then BWIA learned that the piano, had to be on the ground at Port of Spain for at least twenty-four hours to clear customs, even though it was in transit. With time now running out, the packers brought their work forward and the piano was rushed to Heathrow with only hours to spare to meet the outgoing BWIA flight. There were further complications when the aircraft then had technical problems in Barbados and was delayed twenty-four hours. By this time the SES expedition manager, Melissa Dice, was beginning to wish she had never heard of the wretched piano! And I sensed that several of my SES colleagues were already concluding that I'd been crazy to undertake this challenge.

However, the BWIA plane eventually came in and, after a dozen transatlantic phone calls, bureaucracy was overcome and the expedition's highly efficient agents, Wilderness Explorers of Guyana, sent their deputy general manager, Teri Ramnarain, with the Skyvan to ensure the precious cargo was collected. She found it sitting all alone on the tarmac! By this time, it had achieved celebrity status in Guyana and was safely landed at Ogle Airport without let or hindrance. But I then discovered there was another problem. Unusually heavy rain had caused the Essequibo River to rise thirty feet and Akotopomo was flooded. 'They're building a new village on a hill called Masakenari – the place of mosquitoes,' Joe told me over the phone, adding: 'It's a few miles to the south.'

Arriving at midnight on 17th October 2000, the team was greeted by a smiling Yoli, who had flown in from Miami two days earlier to purchase rations and camp stores. 'The piano has landed,' she announced with obvious glee. It was with a feeling of enormous relief that I sank into my bed in the aptly named Sir Walter Raleigh Suite at the colonial-style, timber-built Cara Lodge, one of Georgetown's most historic hotels.

Despite the change of climate and the sweltering heat, Jim, as chief engineer, was keen to press on. Although well into his seventies he was still bursting with energy. 'We'll need a trolley or a sledge to move the piano,' he said, sketching a design in Paul's notebook. 'Let's go and find some wood.'

A set of traffic lights had just been installed at the markets and, as our taxi approached, a horse and cart trotted through this innovation, totally ignoring the red light. Two cars skidded to a halt, narrowly avoiding a collision, and a pith-helmeted policemen in a white tunic rushed up to the cart driver shouting: 'You just shot the red, man!'

The wrinkled old driver pulled his horse up in the middle of the road, starting an instant traffic jam. 'How you expect my horse to understand dem things?' he grunted as we moved on in search of a timber yard.

The only wood available seemed to be mahogany, or something similar. 'Wow, you'd pay a fortune for this in the UK!' exclaimed Paul as he tried to drill a bolt hole in the iron-hard plank. The completed sledge eventually weighed 130 pounds.

Yoli arrived with a van piled up with picks, spades, machetes, axes and ropes that she had purchased from shops she had come to know very well since becoming involved with SES expeditions. Lastly came plastic tanks of petrol for the chainsaw and the Wai Wai's outboard motor.

'That makes your load over a third of a ton,' remarked the lovely Teri, who was arranging to fly us to Gunns. Shaking her head, she added with a worried look: 'And as well as all that there are eleven of you, plus two GDF guys, the rations, petrol and that mountain of TV cameras. You'll need two Islander aircraft as well as the Skyvan, and that's going to cost. But as you are a charity, we might get a discount.' Yoli was massaging her calculator to see what our rapidly diminishing budget could manage.

That night we held our final briefing in the Sir Walter Raleigh Suite. Captain Skeete of the GDF brought along two Sapper corporals, and Joe called in to update us on the latest situation at Gunns. The floods had thankfully subsided and there should be a hundred Wai Wai to help carry the load to the village, he promised.

At the ungodly hour of 05:00 on 19th October the expedition assembled at Ogle Airport. It promised to be another boiling hot, humid day as we watched the Skyvan's cargo doors swing open to reveal 'the beast', securely strapped in and ready to be flown where no piano had ever been before.

A fuel problem delayed departure but eventually Yoli and I climbed in alongside the vast crate, decorated with sponsors' logos. The noisy flight through fleecy clouds was smooth enough and then the sinuous, muddy Essequibo appeared below, snaking through the dark green forest.

Throttling back, the aircraft dropped through the low cloud and ahead lay our destination, Gunns Strip. The familiar 600 yards of yellowing grass appeared deserted, but as we circled, figures came running from the treeline. The Wai Wai were there to meet us, but I could only see half a dozen.

The Skyvan bumped down and, with her propellers thundering in reverse, came to a halt beside the Wai Wai. It felt like coming home. Not wishing to close down his motors in this remote spot, the pilot was eager to be off. The people needed no second bidding and had the stores unloaded in a trice. Then, under Paul Busek's stentorian orders, they turned their attention to lifting out the massive crate. 'Rather you than me,' shouted the pilot, wishing us well as he waved farewell.

Within minutes the planes were gone and silence reigned. 'Where is the new village?' I asked and an elder pointed to a distant hill. It seemed very far away. Deolinda had now appeared with Meshak and we hugged. 'Where is everybody?' I asked. 'We were expecting a hundred to be here.'

'Most is working on the new village or their farms.' She smiled. Apparently, Paul Chekema and Clarence were on their way back from the district headquarters at Lethem, but had left instructions for us to base ourselves once again in Roach Hall.

'It's ninety-two degrees,' said Conrad, our scientist, fingering his thermometer as rivulets of sweat ran down our faces.

Clutching a walkie-talkie, Jim strode off with a couple of youngsters to recce the route while the rest of us, along with five Wai Wai, took up the ropes and prepared for a long hard pull.

'We'll need more water,' I told Anna, whose fair skin was already showing the effect of the tropical sun.

'I'll find a stream and fill up the canteens,' she replied and set off with Yoli, clutching our empty bottles.

Paul Busek, in good Sapper style, shouted the order: 'Hands on, pull!' And as we strained and sweated, the mahogany sledge slowly began to slide forward.

'Wonderful!' enthused David Goodale as he stumbled along with his cameras, recording everything for the film.

It was noon, the sun was right overhead and after a hundred paces we were shattered, when, much to our relief, more villagers arrived and, with a cry of 'Wai Wai, strong!' added welcome extra muscle power. Thankfully, Anna got back quickly with the water, but it was jetting out of our pores as fast as we swallowed it. The open savanna that had been a swamp during our last visit was now bone dry. When we hit a pot-hole, a dull '*bong*' came from within the crate. 'Sounds like a cord breaking,' groaned our musical GP, but we carried on. Twice the crate almost tipped over on to a Wai Wai, and I noticed a couple of vultures hovering nearby. By the time we reached the forest every muscle ached.

After an hour Jim was back, reporting that there were some creeks and mud ahead, but no shortage of trees for bridging. The first creek was barely 30 feet wide and in no time the Wai Wai had cut logs on which we could slide the sledge across. Restraining the weighty crate with the pulling ropes, we inched it carefully over the gap. There were several ominous noises from within the crate, and each time my heart missed a beat, but the ground levelled out and, escorted by dancing clouds of iridescent, turquoise morpho butterflies, we moved on, working our way around fallen trees. Excited children ran ahead, eagerly clearing the bush with machetes and laying branches to form a corduroy road over the mud.

It was mid-afternoon when we crossed the last obstacle and what was now the ghost village of Akotopomo came into view. The buildings had been badly damaged by the flood, the *Umana Yana* was a wreck, and many houses had collapsed, but Roach Hall still stood. However, most of the Wai Wai had moved out.

As we settled in at Akotopomo, David Goodale found himself sharing his hammock space with a nest of red-legged tarantulas, whilst the cockroaches scampered happily around our feet. 'They are pleased to see us back,' suggested Yoli.

Jim had examined the jungle that lay between Akopotomo and the new village. 'It will take weeks to get through that and then there's a fifty-yard creek to cross,' he reported. 'I'll have a look at the river in the morning.' We opened up tins of sardines for supper and sipped a mug of Scotch before climbing gratefully into our hammocks.

Next day a Cessna came in with the two GDF Sapper corporals, for whom there had not been room on the earlier flights. They also bought out vital extra supplies of petrol.

The new village of Masakenari was four miles upriver and still only partly built, we were told, but that was where the piano had to go. There were two routes. Going overland would involve making our way through dense forest littered with fallen trees and bisected by numerous streams before reaching the 300-foot-high hill on which the Wai Wai's new home was being built. This would be the safe but very slow option. The faster alternative would be to go by river. The Essequibo, although only flowing at a couple of knots, was dangerously low. Rocks and shoals would make navigation hazardous and there was also a set of rapids which, although no great challenge for a lightly laden canoe, could be disastrous for a boat weighed down with a grand piano.

Joining Jim's recce, the corporals canoed upstream and, due to the falling water level, found the rapids not as difficult as I'd imagined. Jim reckoned that if we could get a big enough canoe we could ferry the piano all the way to the base of the hill, saving ourselves a lot of time and effort. We agreed that he should go off in search of a suitable craft and at that moment Paul Chekema and Clarence arrived with their wives, having travelled by dugout for fifteen hours a day from the Kuyuwini landing. Paul was somewhat tired and subdued and I didn't think he'd really believed we would turn up with a piano, but he nevertheless offered to help us find the sort of canoe we needed.

Sure enough, next day a giant dugout arrived. It was thirty feet long and five feet wide and was fitted with an 8hp motor. 'She'll do,' said Jim, 'but we'll have to take it very steady.' I was not entirely convinced, knowing it would not be easy to force a somewhat top-heavy canoe through the rapid's narrow chute with only a tiny motor. Jim and I sat in Roach Hall discussing options. I felt it could help to fit outriggers in order to stabilise the craft, but my old pal, with whom I'd worked for over forty years, felt confident that the canoe could make it anyway. Still concerned, I bowed to his advice. So the riskier river route would be taken. Needless to say, this delighted the TV team, promising some dramatic footage.

Paul Busek got the pulling party together and with great care the piano was lowered down the riverbank. Using hardwood poles, we gently eased it into the dugout. 'Easily done,' said Paul, with the confident air of an experienced removals man who handled grand pianos every day. Yoli hoisted the SES banner and my lucky Jersey flag over the crate.

'We must be careful not to overload the boat,'I shouted as we pulled away, but within seconds a dozen women and children had swarmed down the bank and clambered aboard. Well, it was their canoe.

'For goodness' sake sit still,' I implored, as we nosed into the current. The rapids came into view as we rounded the first bend and the motorman aimed at the centre of the main tongue of water that streamed down between the black rocks. The river's power doubled, the water surged past, the little engine raced, the dugout rocked, and I thought to myself that if it broached we would be done for, and prayed hard.

But at maximum revs the outboard motor was just strong enough to overcome the force of the water and after a nail-biting few seconds we lurched out at the top of the drop-off and sailed into calmer conditions. 'Thank you, Lord,' muttered Yoli.

In the following canoe the TV team was overjoyed, crying out: 'Can you do that once more?' From their point of view I guess a spectacular capsize would have made even more exciting footage.

Arriving at our destination, we were concerned to see that the route from the riverbank to the hilltop village was narrow and swampy and would be extremely tricky to negotiate. However, one of the elders knew of a shallow creek with closer access to the village. So, landing all the women and children, the great canoe went on upriver to this inlet. The sun was now up and the air thick with insects. Narrow and choked with vines and logs, the creek seemed impossible but flashing axes and cutlasses cleared the way, as stinking gas bubbled up from the depths of the coffee-coloured water. Several times it was necessary to manoeuvre back and forth to get round bends. 'Steady, lads,' cautioned Jim as the hull grounded on a submerged tree, causing the crate to heel over alarmingly. 'We don't want to lose her now.'

The photographers were wading ahead, oblivious of the swamp. 'Great shot!' cried Mark Large.

Thankfully, there was now no shortage of help and soon, with the aid of long poles, the crate was hauled up the steep hill. Grunts and groans punctuated the baking-hot air as the summit came in sight, with the Guyana flag flying proudly above the half-built school. For the last leg the faithful sledge was used again. Women, children and braves were now fighting for a place on the drag ropes. Jim broke in with a chorus of 'Hurrah for the CRE' (Chief Royal Engineer), the Royal Engineers' regimental song, and the vast box was carried triumphantly into the shade of the thatched roof.

'I can't wait to see if it's still in tune,' said Conrad Gorinsky, whose ethno-biological work had taken second place to piano pulling. The GDF corporals Karl and Gmawale shouldered their AK-47s and helped Paul to unscrew the crate.

Everyone peered at the gleaming polished wood and brass fittings reflecting the afternoon sun. As the elegant instrument emerged the Wai Wai stood in awe, as if it were something that had come from outer space. Now came Simon Richards's big moment and he carefully removed the padding around the keys and hammers. We all then held our breath as he placed his fingers gingerly on the ivory keyboard and played a few notes. To everyone's great relief it sounded absolutely fine and Simon struck up 'God Save the Queen'. It was an emotional moment.

Beaming smiles broke out on sweat-stained faces. 'We've done it!' cried Anna. 'And, what's more, it's still perfectly in tune.'

Quietly, two of the young Wai Wai musicians who had been watching Simon at the keyboard came forward and, despite being guitarists and having never before had the opportunity to play a piano, they sat down and, to everyone's astonishment, performed a passable duet, improvising as they went along.

'They really have a natural ear!' exclaimed Simon.

'Excellent, excellent,' enthused our TV producer, before adding: 'However, I'd like to get some more shots of it being brought up to the village through the jungle. Perhaps you could just take the empty crate downhill and carry it for a few hundred yards.'

I restrained my language in front of the children!

In the days that followed, Jim, Paul, Karl and Gmawale worked on completing the school building and also designed a water-pumping system for the village. Simon handed over the medical supplies we had bought for the clinic and treated several patients, and a set of ENT inspection instruments, donated by a retired Dorset GP, were presented to Janet, the village nurse. Dennis, the headmaster of the school, was unwell so he was very glad of the help Anna and Yoli gave him in teaching the children, whose smart, clean uniforms would have shamed some British primary schools.

Conrad discussed herbal cures with Clarence and the villagers and recommended natural sources of malaria prophylactics. Simon also used his tuning forks to test the hearing of Meshak and some children who had been born without ears. We felt it would be wonderful if something could be done to improve their hearing. Several times I had noticed that Meshak appeared to be able to hear me if I shouted very loudly near him, so perhaps there was some hope.

My good fortune was to have the chance to see a new stretch of the Essequibo. A party of older Wai Wai had gone to visit friends in neighbouring Suriname and, as the river was falling, it was felt they might have difficulty in making the 100-mile journey back upstream in a small canoe. So, leaving Jim and a party working at the village, I went with Conrad, Mark, Karen and Yoli and two teenage hunters, Aaron and Elijah, to meet up with them, taking extra supplies of food and petrol to help get them home. This journey took us through completely uninhabited territory, with breathtaking scenery, and because the water level was so low we came across exposed rocks in the riverbed decorated with ancient petroglyphs representing animals and other strange symbols. One especially fine design depicted a jaguar attacking an anaconda. I photographed and made sketches of these mysterious signs for further research by the Walter Roth Museum in Georgetown.

Aaron and Elijah were incredible marksmen with their powerful bows and took every opportunity along the way to go hunting for food to take back the village. I had to admire their skills as Aaron brought down a high-flying turkey-like powis with a snap shot, while Elijah picked a green iguana out of a tree with his bow. A two-toed sloth hung by its curved claws from a branch and blinked its long eyelashes at us as we passed. 'He very lazy,' commented Elijah.

To the east, a lone blue mountain of the Amuku range rose above the emerald jungle as we wound our way in between outcrops of grey rock. Whilst there was still light we found an idyllic campsite at the Kassikaityu junction and ate pasta and some delicious slices of pacu, very like Scotch salmon, while sitting on rocks still warm from the sun.

We managed a few hours' sleep before the hunters called us and at 02:00 hours, pulling on my wet jungle boots and trying to thread the laces in the blackness, I made a mental note to have some zips fitted to them when I got back home. Having stowed our kit, we set off in pitch darkness and paddled quietly downstream. Yoli checked our route using the GPS, while, nearby, nightbirds called and the frogs croaked a chorus. A troop of giant otters could be heard splashing and howling in the flooded forest and as we got nearer their cries sent a shiver up my spine, although I knew they were no danger to us. 'They hunting fish,' whispered Aaron. I could well understand why the Spanish explorers called them 'river wolves'.

Karen had fallen asleep by the time we turned into a small jungle creek, where, in the dim torchlight, Elijah was watching something in the water and then, in a flash, plunged in his hands and hauled out a wriggling baby caiman. This caused a shoal of small silver fish to burst upwards out of the water. Karen woke with a yell as some of them came showering down into the canoe, sliding all over her. 'Shhh!' cautioned Aaron and we paddled into the bank. The dogs seemed to anticipate something and hopped ashore with Aaron, who was now clutching an old shotgun having left the caiman in the boat. We sat in silence, waiting. After a few minutes, there came a shot, followed by the sound of the dogs yapping. Then silence fell again, until, moments later, Aaron's shining body appeared from the bushes. He proudly held up two powis birds, killed with a single shot!

It was daylight when we reached the campsite that the boys called Monkey Jump, from where Moses and Mapiri, whose fathers were in the party that had turned east towards Suriname, and where we had been hoping to rendezvous with them as they made their way back. But there was no sign of them, so we made bashers with our hammocks, nets and tarps strung beneath an old hut frame.

Roast powis and mashed potato with garlic and ranch sauce filled our stomachs and I picked up the BBC World Service on my little radio. News of assassins being arrested in Paraguay and of the pound being worth €82 seemed very distant, but I got through to Teri on our satellite phone to check on the flights out. I hated the idea of leaving this demi-paradise. The minor discomforts and hazards were a small price to pay for the peace of mind one enjoyed being alone and self-sufficient in a wilderness. At dawn, there being still no sign of the boys' fathers, we left bags of food and a note tied high in a tree, climbed back into the dugout and motored home.

The Yukanopito Falls had a six-foot drop down which we had glided fairly easily with the current on the way out, but it was a different matter getting the canoe back up the lengthy cataract. Whilst Aaron stayed on the motor the rest of us leapt in and, with feet sliding and slipping, struggled to push the craft up through the foaming water. 'Stay aboard and guard the cameras,' I shouted to Karen above the roar of the water. This she did and shot some dramatic film. We made little progress for quite a while, and I was seriously concerned that the force of the river would capsize the boat, thinking to myself: *How damn stupid. We come to help a party of elders and get stuck ourselves!* By the time we got up the rapids we were pretty exhausted. Even Elijah looked weary, so we made camp and lit a fire to dry our sodden clothing. The labba we had for supper warmed us up and I was soon in my hammock, pulling my sleeping bag over me and falling sound asleep.

At midnight something woke me and automatically I reached for my cutlass, but quickly realised that the two shadowy figures

I could see moving towards the campfire were Elijah and Aaron, coming back from a night hunt. 'Any luck?' I asked Aaron, who, in reply, held up a live caiman.

'And I got a bush cow too,' he added in hushed tones.

'A bush cow?' I queried. 'Do you mean a tapir?'

The boy nodded. 'Too big to move.' He smiled. 'We get him tomorrow.'

At daybreak we found his 500-pound victim, killed with a single shot from close range. I would never have believed that a round of 12-bore BB shot could bring down the largest mammal in South America. Indeed, the carcass was too large for us to carry, so Elijah butchered it into three pieces.

I did my best with a fishing rod and was soon pulling out a piranha every minute. When I got nine, Aaron touched my arm. 'Enough,' he said. 'We must not take too many or there will be none left for the years ahead.' I was impressed that a fifteen-year-old Wai Wai should think like that.

A great welcome awaited us at Masakenari. Food was not plentiful at this time of year and the tapir fed the entire village. Because they do not overhunt there is no shortage of game and fish, whilst their small farms produce yams, cassava, bananas, and other fruit and vegetables.

Using the satellite phone, I had been able to order a pump and pipes for a new water system, plus additional medical supplies and spares for the chainsaw, all of which Teri purchased in Georgetown. Thanks to the efforts of Anna and Simon, making use of his skill as a choirmaster, a concert was arranged and on Friday 27th October the Wai Wai children gathered outside their new school. Their parents came too and on this green hill surrounded by rainforest, a hundred voices sang 'Swing Low, Sweet Chariot', 'Humpty Dumpty', 'Steal Away' and many Guyanese songs. Simon and the local musicians played the 'Prelude in C Major' by J. S. Bach, Beethoven's 'Moonlight Sonata' and Chopin's 'Nocturne'. It brought tears to several eyes. A feast of curried tapir, farine and smoked fish followed before the expedition made its way back to Roach Hall. Next day Paul Busek organised a football match, which we all enjoyed, despite it being played in an energy-sapping temperature of 34°C.

Out of respect to Karen Kelly, a Scot, we had our traditional Burns Night supper, with haggis, tatties and neeps kindly provided by Stahly's Quality Foods. Karen read the famous 'Address to a Haggis' at this final dinner. The Wai Wai had seen us celebrate the legendary poet in the past and were not surprised. In fact, they quite enjoyed a piece of haggis. One warrior asked if it came from a beast we hunted in Britain.

When the Skyvan returned it brought in the items for the water supply as well as the medical supplies and chainsaw parts. We gave our small Honda generator to the village along with many other items needed to re-establish the community in their new home. The grand piano had proved to be the catalyst that attracted all this valuable support. I felt our mission had been accomplished. As the preacher had said – God sometimes moves in mysterious ways.

 The Grand Adventure

CHAPTER 21

PIANO TUNER'S EXPEDITION

By 2002 the young Wai Wai musicians had mastered the piano and the BBC film *The Mission: A Grand Adventure* had been shown worldwide, publicising the tribe and their needs. The piano had become an icon but, not surprisingly, it needed extensive repairs and retuning. At the same time, the tribe felt that they would benefit by creating an Ecotourist and Research Centre (ERC) at Akotopomo, hoping that the income from up to 150 visitors and scientific researchers per year would provide the means for further education for their children and would also allow them to purchase much-needed medical supplies.

Joe Singh was now executive director of the US charity Conservation International in Guyana and the SES agreed to organise another expedition to help with the setting up of the centre while also repairing and retuning the grand piano. Meanwhile, the Guyana government was working with Conservation International to set up a protected area that would cover the Wai Wai territory.

For the new expedition we recruited a group of twenty-four people, including agriculturalists, builders, craft advisers, an economist, engineers, a doctor, dentist, nurses, a naturalist and, thanks to the BBC, no less than three adventurous piano tuners. Eleven of the group came from Jersey, sponsored by the States of Jersey Overseas Aid Commission. Yoli, our South American representative, would be there again and also with us this time was Brenda Wynn, the secretary of SES, whose wit and humour could always be relied upon to liven up any party.

We were divided into two teams, whose time in the field during the month-long expedition overlapped, with a small HQ consisting of myself, Yoli and a detachment of GDF soldiers as security. While the main group concentrated on mapping routes by boat and on foot for use by tourists and others who might wish to go into the jungle to watch wildlife and visit the site of the fascinating petroglyphs we had found, our doctor and an RAF dentist gave treatment to those in need and one of our nurses, Sarah Royal, a veteran of many SES expeditions, carried out an anthropological study.

However, the village musicians were especially interested in the retuning of the grand piano. Tania Staite, an energetic and talented London-based tuner, was also a skilled piano builder and, assisted by the other tuners, Graham Harris and Andrew Brown, she inspected the instrument. After stripping out piles of moths, cockroach eggs and droppings, she pronounced it to be in pretty good shape, all things considered. 'It's up to pitch in the base section, only a couple of cents flat in the middle octaves, but the quarter-tone is flat in the top two and a half octaves,' she reported. I nodded, trying to look as though I understood exactly what she was talking about. As the temperature reached 32°C, Tania proceeded to take the instrument apart and then rebuild it. 'Considering it's around seventy years old and of mediocre construction, its condition is not as bad as I'd imagined,' said this impressively forceful lady. 'In spite of the heat and humidity there is no evidence that it has significantly deteriorated since you delivered it. But if it were to be put under a heat-conducting tin roof instead of the present palm thatch, it certainly wouldn't last long.'

Meanwhile, Andrew and Graham were installing an electric keyboard that my friend Elodie Sandford, who was also part of the team, had generously donated for the church, along with a small generator. As the first notes rang out the children rushed in, wild-eyed, and started to clap. The impact of music was clearly making a real difference to the Wai Wai, but I sensed one of the church elders was worried about something. Had we, perhaps, upset them in some way?

'Is there a problem?' I asked.

The church elder smiled and looked a little embarrassed. 'Yes, I'm afraid there is,' he said. 'A few days ago a hunter found an abandoned jaguar cub and bought it to the village. He made a cage for it with a good door and kept it under his house, but last night the mother came, broke into the cage and took back her cub. She may come back looking for revenge and I worry about our children.'

This was a timely reminder that, despite pianos and keyboards, we were living in wild and dangerous forests. As if to emphasise the point, a thin green tree snake swung down from the makeshift cookhouse roof as Yoli and Deolinda prepared bakes for lunch. And, next morning, I found a pink-toed tarantula in my boot, which luckily, as a habit, I had shaken out before putting on.

A little later a cry rang out from the direction of the river. A fishing net had entangled a five-foot anaconda. 'It's a young one,' I shouted to one of our Jersey team, who was about to strike it. 'Just try to hold it still and we'll get it out.' To give him his due, he gripped the writhing reptile, while I, with the aid of my Swiss army penknife's scissors, managed to cut it free.

'I hope its parents aren't out there,' commented Brenda, a regular swimmer who loved to take her morning dips in the Essequibo.

Indeed, the river served as our normal bathroom, always used enthusiastically by the GDF Sappers. Both were fine figures and

Orin, at six-foot-five, weighed 220 pounds. Furthermore, they were intensely religious. I thought that they might be Seventh-day Adventists, since they read the Bible assiduously every day. 'Cleanliness is next to godliness,' said Orin when I met the pair of them on their way to have their discreet dip one morning at dawn. Hardly had they entered the water when there was a 'Whoop' and one of our lady members, who it transpired was something of a naturist, ran stark naked through the village and plunged in. The effect on the two soldiers was such that they spent all day reading the Bible.

James, Deolinda's husband, had returned from his management training in Georgetown and was eager to start work on getting the research centre set up. In fact, a group of enthusiastic American birdwatchers had already arrived and Joe had sent in a solar power expert to organise electricity for the village.

Leaving the piano tuners and the builders at work, I started mapping the ecotourist nature trails. With a small team of animal lovers, I set out by canoe to the lesser-known reaches of the Essequibo and its tributaries. Chief Paul and Elessa – the vicar, as I called him – came along, and Yacuare, son of Mawasha, a famous Wai Wai leader, took the helm. Pushed on by a 10hp outboard, the leaky dugout covered many miles. Pairs of vivid blue and gold macaws flapped out of the towering canopy, shrieking like alarmed crows, their powerful wings waving steadily as they turned about to inspect us before proceeding upriver. Along the banks glistening kingfishers swooped and dived. Parakeets, the occasional harpy eagle and stately herons eyed us, whilst hummingbirds hovered in the bushes. It was a birdwatcher's paradise.

On the water, packs of bold giant otters challenged us with raucous, eerie cries and bared fangs, swimming like dolphins alongside and diving just ahead of the bow. Monkeys scrambled through the branches and, interestingly, one large one with a pale brown woolly coat and a black dorsal stripe could not be identified. The non-stop croaking of thousands of frogs started as darkness fell, rising and falling as if orchestrated by a hidden conductor, but we had no problem sleeping.

Daybreak was heralded by the roars of the howler monkeys and, close to one of our camps, the sound of grunting coming from the forest nearby signalled the presence of shaggy, feral black bush pigs. Larger than the peccary, they were prized food, but bolted before we had the chance to get a shot.

Approaching its watershed in the Acarai Mountains, the river was fed by a score of small streams and tributaries. Using our machetes, we hacked our way through several logjams, but were eventually brought to a halt by the tangles of fallen trees on both the Sipu and the Watuwau rivers. The forest floor was dotted with recent tracks of labba, deer, capybara and ocelot as well as the paw prints of a fair-sized jaguar. 'They will still be here when we return to hunt another day,' remarked Yacuare, with a shrug. A little disappointed that our exploration had been cut short, I decided to go north instead to explore the mysterious Kassikaityu, or 'River of Death'.

It was said that this river had a large population of enormous anaconda. Joe Singh had seen a twenty-five-footer here and there were stories of even larger specimens. The explorer Schomburgk had been here in 1837 and had written: 'We saw a large, *comoti* snake [probably an anaconda], which, gorged with its prey, lay inactive in a swamp, emitting a very offensive smell. I wounded it with a ball, whereupon it made a rush towards us, and obliged us to retreat. It appeared to be about eight yards long and was the largest I ever saw.'

In the 1950s Nicholas Guppy, one of the first scientists to explore the untouched rainforests of the Guyana–Brazil border, had shot a colossal anaconda believed to be between eight and ten inches in diameter and around thirty feet in length. Wounded, it had, alas, disappeared into deep water.

The low level of the water caused us to ground on shoals as we bumped our way through the rapids beyond Akotopomo, but we then turned west into the silent, slow-flowing Kassikaityu, where we were hoping to find the nest of a monster constrictor Yacuare had seen recently.

'Is somewhere around here,' he hissed, pointing with his paddle at the dense foliage. Orin gripped his rifle as we pulled in. The Wai Wai indicated a narrow track of crushed grass leading into the bush and we followed as quietly as possible, although if there were an anaconda coiled in its nest, I guessed it would pick up the vibrations of our approach. After treading nervously for a few yards we came into a small clearing – or, at least, that's what it appeared to be. But on closer examination one could see something very heavy had flattened the undergrowth for an area of several hundred square feet.

Some broken animal bones lay scattered around, possibly vomited up by the giant snake after digesting its catch. 'It must be huge,' muttered Yoli, but Yacuare pointed back towards the river.

'He's gone fishing,' he said, and we returned to the boat.

Records in Brazil say anaconda can reach sixty feet in length and the legendary Colonel Percy Fawcett claimed to have wounded one in excess of that. But our naturalist, Tim Liddiard, maintained that a serpent of that size would not be able to move far on land and thus would probably be largely aquatic.

After about ten miles we came to the Guana Rapids. A long black caiman was poised, waiting for a meal in the still water. It lay unmoving in the shallows, its unblinking yellow eyes watching us closely. The rapids were gentle, and we ascended them easily, marking the location with my GPS and noting numerous petroglyphs carved on the smooth rocks.

I like to make camp well before dark but, being keen to get as far up the river as possible in the time available, it was 17:00 before we pulled on to a rocky shelf and erected our bashers and hammocks. Paul Chekema immediately went fishing for supper and took my shotgun to look for labba. Darkness fell rapidly as Brenda and Yoli produced a tasty meal of 'Smash' and sardines, with an enjoyable slug of Brenda's 'medicinal use only' Bénédictine to wash it down! The Amerindians dined well too, on farine and a fat pink-fleshed haimara that Paul had hauled splashing from the shallows.

As the moon rose above the treeline we lay on the warm rocks and listened to Paul's tales of this awesome river, once the home of the Taruma tribe, said to have died out from smallpox caught from early European visitors. By 1952, there were just four known survivors still living among the Wai Wai, and they had since died, but there were rumours that some still survived deep in the forest.

I coaxed Paul and his men into telling us more of the Taruma. Legend had it that their ancestress was the daughter of an anaconda and thus no anaconda was ever harmed by them. Indeed, the snakes were regarded as members of the tribe and were treated with great respect – and caution. 'Tomorrow we reach Anaconda Rock,' said Paul. 'It was there that an old man doing his washing was swallowed by a big snake, but the warriors made a large hook to catch and kill him.' Such legends were strong enough to deter the Wai Wai from swimming in the dark waters. Orin looked rather sceptical, but kept his rifle close by.

For breakfast I made omelettes from powdered egg and the Wai Wai asked for seconds. We were on the river early and above the roars of the howlers heard the rumble of rushing water. Around the bend appeared a jumble of eroded rocks through which tumbled foaming streams. 'Crab Falls,' called Paul. 'We have to get out and push.' So it was over the side and ropes were carried out on to the slabs. Water cascaded over us as we pulled and pushed with all our might. Where possible the helmsman dropped the propeller in to give some added help, but it took fifteen minutes to haul and guide the heavy dugout up through the tossing waves of the cataract before we could rest in the blistering hot sun.

Around us petroglyphs, shaped like Maltese crosses, and depictions of men and animals had been carved into the rock. A few seemed fairly recent, but most appeared truly ancient, with designs unlike the modern Wai Wai art. What was their purpose, I wondered. Anthropologists usually suggest that such engravings might have served as territorial boundary markers or as records of battles or successful hunts. Or they may have had some ritual or spiritual significance. We took time to photograph and sketch the designs in this natural art gallery.

'They often seem to be found at waterfalls,' commented Brenda as she sketched one in her notebook. 'Maybe they are simply carved at meeting places.'

Paul knew nothing of their history and, judging by his expression, I reckoned Elessa thought they might be evil. As if to emphasise this, the sky blackened and the clouds opened to deliver a short, sharp shower as we made our way to Anaconda Rock. By the time we reached the massive, forbidding boulder the weather had cleared and steam was drifting off the river. Hundreds of multicoloured butterflies danced and drank on the rocks and bird calls echoed along the bank.

'Look,' whispered Yoli. Ahead of us a large black head of some creature was cruising through the shallows.

'Anaconda?' I queried hopefully.

'No, that just a big male otter.' Paul grinned as it turned to flash its fangs at us before sliding beneath the water.

Whilst Paul and Elessa fished, we took a snack on the beach before turning for home. 'I must come back to this strange place,' I scribbled in my log.

'There is a man's grave near here,' said Paul as we made our return journey.

'Who was he?' I asked, my curiosity aroused. Paul only knew he was a government official from Georgetown. However, he offered to show us the place. Looking into the dense jungle and considering the time, I asked how far it was.

'It's right here,' said the chief, pointing into the greenery.

Scrambling up the muddy bank the Wai Wai's cutlasses opened the path and, to my astonishment, there it was. A rectangular stone mounted on an eight-foot cement slab. We could just make out an inscription that read: 'Augustus Josef Cheong FRGS, FSI, born in 1898 and died of beriberi in 1933.'

I was later to discover that Cheong was a surveyor and deputy leader of a group commissioned to survey and mark the border between British Guiana and Brazil. Knowing beriberi to be a disease caused by a lack of vitamin B, I wondered if, being of Chinese ancestry, he had tried to live on rice alone. The river is teeming with fish and the rainforest is full of powis and labba, so it seems strange that he could not survive in this natural pantry. However, it was clear that he must have been greatly respected for his colleagues to have gone to the immense trouble of carrying a weighty tombstone and cement all the way to this remote spot, 350 miles south of Georgetown, to mark his grave. The roots of a tumbling tree had tipped up the slab, but there was no sign of a skeleton. We photographed it for the Royal Geographical Society, as a record of the last resting place of one of their illustrious fellows, who had been claimed by the 'River of Death'.

Rejoining the Essequibo, Paul stopped to see a campsite recently used by the first visiting ecotourists. We were horrified to find empty rum bottles and garbage. Such thoughtless vandalism very understandably displeased the Wai Wai and was not at all what they wanted in their Garden of Eden.

Work was slightly behind schedule at Akotopomo, despite Jersey builders Bob Randel, Dennis Troy and the rest of the team having worked non-stop to complete the accommodation block. Two smart long-drop loos had been built, the museum walls were up and the solar lighting installed, but we needed loads of palm fronds to thatch the roofs. We only had a day left to complete the job and so I asked Paul to spur the villagers on to a final extra effort in order to help us out. Paul gave me his usual slow smile and, sure enough, early next morning canoes weighed down with manicole palm products appeared. Almost the entire village turned up and by sundown the ERC was complete. God, and indeed the Wai Wai, does move in mysterious ways.

Unforgettable was the moment when, after two weeks' work, our musicians got the piano and the keyboard playing to their satisfaction, and on a cloudless November morning, we marched the three miles from Akotopomo to the new village and found Elessa proudly awaiting us at the door of his thatch-roofed church, now packed with Wai Wai in their Sunday best.

Excitement filled the air. This was one of the greatest events the people had experienced – a full-blown concert to be broadcast, in part by satellite phone, to the BBC and tape-recorded for the future. The children had been practising for many days and the old hunter, Mariwanaru, had donned traditional tribal costume specially for the occasion, his jet-black hair filled with white turkey feathers and a blowpipe in his hand.

All we foreigners were welcomed with a song and led forward individually by our smiling hosts. Tania, her jungle boots hammering the pedals, accompanied the choir, starting off with 'Morning Has Broken', followed by 'Shalom' and 'Jesus Loves Everyone'. Andrew and a young Wai Wai followed with J.S. Bach's 'Prelude' played on Elodie's keyboard and then Tania came back with 'Venetian Gondola', whilst the Wai Wai played their guitars and pipes. 'Away in a Manger' and 'Steal Away' almost bought tears to my eyes before Elessa hesitantly played a solo piano piece.

Tania gave a great rendering from *West Side Story* and the children ended the show with The Beatles's 'With a Little Help from My Friends' and 'Good Night With a Lullaby'. As the notes died away tumultuous applause broke out and I grinned, thinking how this had all begun with a throwaway line in a speech in a London hotel.

Outside, a feast had been prepared with the grilled piranha, bush hog, farine and cassava bread, washed down with a sorrel-flavoured fruit drink chilled in the clinic's new solar-powered fridge.

Deolinda, our splendid cook, came with me as I walked to the airstrip at the end of the expedition. Skipping along beside us was her little deaf son Meshak, his leg now fully mended. She gave me her lovely self-conscious smile, but tears were welling up in her big brown eyes. 'Can you do anything for him?' she asked, quietly touching her ear.

We must seem able to perform miracles, I thought and, shaking her hand, promised that I would try. This sounded very inadequate, but I didn't want to build up false hopes.

As our plane taxied out, she was standing by the airstrip, wiping her eyes. A lump rose in my throat, and I vowed to return one day to this green hill far away.

However, it was not until ten years later, in 2010, that we returned, to survey a tractor trail through the jungle to shorten the journey that the Wai Wai children would have to take to and from the secondary boarding school at Lethem.

On this occasion the party, led by civil engineer Julian Butter and surveyor Tim Harrison, covered the fifty-four miles from Masakenari to Parabara on the Kuyuwini River. Another surveyor, Duncan Strong, along with agronomist Simon House, joined Clarence Rudolph, his wife and son in a canoe with a small outboard to bring in fuel and supplies from the vehicle roadhead at Aishalton village to join me on the remote Kassikaityu River. In covering 250 miles, they were rewarded along the way with some fine sightings of wildlife, including a jaguar perched on a branch over the water, a large troop of giant otter and an anaconda, which nipped Simon while he was trying to measure it.

Back in Masakenari we gave dental and medical aid and attended the village sports day where Meshak, the earless boy, won the high and long jumps as well as the 3,000-metre race through the forest. It was an amazing feat. And, having examined him, Steve Kershaw, our doctor, felt surgery might give him at least some hearing. Later, with the help of our friend Joe Singh, Meshak did have a successful operation, so, happily, my promise to Deolinda had been fulfilled.

A potable water supply for the village was designed by Julian and builder John Arathoon, but sadly, as predicted, the grand piano had only survived for a few years in the tropical climate. Surprisingly, the keyboard Elodie Sandford had provided still played well.

However, the BBC film of the delivery of the piano continues to be shown worldwide and the publicity helps to attract support for 'the children of the forest', as the Wai Wai are known. Thanks to Joe Singh's efforts, the US charity Conservation International and the German KfW Development Bank contributed $8.5 million to a Protected Areas Trust fund. This led to the preservation of the Wai Wai territory and the establishment of park ranger stations, with the Wai Wai themselves becoming rangers. And solar-powered communications and a new clinic have been set up in Masakenari. All in all it was a very satisfactory end to the work of so many people who, in the course of several expeditions spread over seventeen years, had done such a lot to help the kindly Wai Wai to live more happily and healthily in their jungle Eden.

CHAPTER 22

IN REMOTE COLOMBIA

Rising 18,700 feet above Colombia's Caribbean coastline, the towering peaks of the rugged Sierra Nevada are home to a wide variety of wildlife, including the world's greatest number of endemic species of birds as well as numerous mammals. The largest of South America's big cats, such as puma, ocelot and jaguar, still prowl the forested slopes, along with spectacled bears. Overhead, the great condors circle the snowy summits and there are few flowers and plants that will not grow somewhere in the rocky landscape, with its varied microclimates and diverse habitats.

Over 30,000 indigenous people justifiably guard this sacred territory, but in the past fifty years they have suffered gravely at the hands of both terrorists and paramilitaries.

The Arhuaco, Kogi, Kankuamo and Wiwa tribes are descendants of the ancient Tairona civilisation that flourished here, working their farms and building elaborate cities, until the conquistadors arrived in 1529. The ruthless Spanish enslaved all those they could capture and forced

the survivors to flee into the snow-tipped peaks and valleys of this little-known wilderness. Whilst the invaders conquered and destroyed the ancient civilisations to the south, the Tairona managed to live on amongst their remote temples, supported by their unique style of farming. Those still living in the south-east of this spectacular region are the Wiwa.

Our attention was drawn to the Sierra by SES member, HSH Prince Leopold d'Arenberg, who had made a private visit to the legendary Ciudad Perdida ('Lost City') of the Kogis on the eastern side of the mountains. If one could only get permission, it was clearly a place begging for exploration. However, the descendants of the Tairona were not known to welcome visitors and it would therefore be essential to gain their confidence by offering help in return for the privilege of entering their world. So, with the help of a Kankuamo liaison officer working in Bogotá, Yoli set up a recce and in 2014 we met the leaders of the Wiwa people in the old colonial town of Valledupar.

Hours were spent talking with and listening to the white-robed '*Mamos*', the tribal elders and spiritual leaders, outlining our intentions and convincing them of our integrity. Throughout these long discussions they chewed wads of coca leaf. To aid digestion, they sucked lime, made from seashells, out of phallic-shaped gourds named 'poporos'. It was like watching a hamster enjoying lunch, but although coca is the source of cocaine, it takes six pounds of leaf to produce an ounce of the drug. We know that in a less concentrated form, coca dulls sensation, limits fatigue, reduces hunger and it has been chewed in South America for a thousand years. Fortunately, masticating the small green leaves does not have the same effect as ingesting powdered cocaine.

Eventually, the Wiwa gave permission for an initial expedition that would provide aid in a number of ways. They were in need of schools, medical help and simple engineering advice. At the same time, they were keen to spread their philosophy that 'the younger brothers', as outsiders are known, are in danger of destroying the world.

We learned that the Wiwa remain true to their ancient laws, believing in a spirit world, the '*Aluna*', in which every tree, stone or river has a place. Contact with this unseen entity is maintained by divination, a mental process of composing questions and interpreting answers emitted from a primordial sort of earth mother.

The *Mamos* are in effect priests, magistrates, healers and counsellors who have undergone many years of training in the art of divination. Even so, they are not regarded as infallible by their people, who have the right to question and criticise them. The *Mamos* teach that, through ignorance or arrogance, the rest of us are bent on global destruction and that, linked to us, they too will be dragged down to destruction, that if we do not mend our ways, the world will die. Furthermore, they are convinced that through their work and communication with the *Aluna*, they alone can maintain the ecological balance of the planet, fearing that if they fail mankind will create an ecological catastrophe. In this respect, at least, it seems now that they were way ahead of the rest of us, with a claim to be the world's earliest eco-warriors!

In February 2016 our eighteen-strong team was warmly welcomed by Yoli's family in Bogotá and later by the Wiwa in Valledupar. The El Niño effect had caused a drought, with temperatures of 40°C in the shade, which was quite a change for those who had flown into Bogotá from more temperate climates. As a consequence of the drought and failed crops, some Wiwa children were dying from starvation and undernourishment.

Our party included, as ever, two British doctors, two dentists, a nurse, engineers, a surveyor, aid workers, a biologist and an anthropologist, along with interpreters. Language was always to be a problem throughout the expedition, as none of the Wiwa spoke English and only a few of us spoke good Spanish. At Valledupar our medics were joined by a local Colombian health team, including a doctor, dentist and nurses, who were to work with us throughout the project. The local Health Department was most supportive and kindly provided extra medicines and water sterilisation tablets for our use.

Four-wheel-drive vehicles had been hired from the Wiwa, but they were fairly ancient and several defects had to be corrected. Frustratingly, a one-ton cargo truck that had been ordered in advance was found to be stranded an hour's drive away in another town and, being of Venezuelan origin, was not permitted to enter Valledupar for some obscure reason. We did not enquire too deeply about this, but still urgently needed a truck to carry all our rations and stores, including many boxes bulging with medicines and schoolbooks. After numerous phone calls, the somewhat embarrassed Wiwa produced a dilapidated replacement vehicle, for hire at an exorbitant rate. Yoli, who carried our treasury lashed to her body, was actually quite relieved to be free of a few million of the local pesos!

Our convoy eventually set off along a fine tarmac road for San Juan del Cesar, the gateway to Wiwa territory, located on the fringe of the Sierra, where more greetings and a welcome lunch in a local café awaited us.

Thankfully, some of the cars had air conditioning, as the heat was pretty intense when we drove up into the foothills to the village of

Achintukua and set up our first base camp. Before we even entered the settlement there first had to be a ceremony conducted by the local *Mamos* at a sacred place, with a ritual that involved clutching leaves and passing them to the elder, impregnated with our inner thoughts. This all took time when we were anxious to get on with erecting our tents. In the thatched village hall there were more welcoming speeches, including, to our surprise, one by a lieutenant colonel, who had arrived with a hundred well-armed soldiers in full combat gear.

'My job is to keep you safe,' he said, wearing a grim expression. This was our first indication that the area might not be quite as peaceful as it had appeared during our recce. We knew, of course, that there had been sporadic ongoing conflict between the government and the Fuerzas Armadas Revolucionarias de Colombia (FARC) rebels for over fifty years, but the presence of the colonel's troops, clutching multiple grenade launchers, machine guns and festooned with belts of ammunition, plus a friendly Labrador sniffer dog to detect explosives, made us aware that there was a heightened security problem.

'We have orders to check every area in which you intend to work before you go there,' explained our escort. It transpired that Colombian government negotiations with the FARC terrorist groups aimed at securing a final agreement on a lasting peace had suddenly been announced. As a result, up to 400 armed FARC fighters had assembled less than twenty miles from our base camp, including some supporters who had flown in by helicopter from neighbouring Venezuela. Most of these FARC fighters later returned to their jungle bases, but the rival National Liberation Army (Ejército de Liberación Nacional, ELN) rebel group, which was not involved in the negotiations, had not signified their intention to cease operations. Furthermore, they were moving into territory that FARC had vacated, and although there was no known threat to us, the authorities were concerned that they might target us to achieve publicity. I phoned the British ambassador, whose advice was to carry on, but to obey the army's instructions.

Being on high alert, the Colombian army, who provided protection for us throughout the expedition, had to limit our deployment. All this understandably caused much concern to some of our members, several of whom clearly feared for their safety. And while those of us with military experience were not unduly worried, others needed reassurance that we were all in good hands. It was a testing situation. Some of our planned projects had to be dropped, but we continued with our programme of medical and dental aid. Reading glasses and schoolbooks were distributed, whilst limited botanical and wildlife studies were undertaken.

One of our major jobs was the building of a primary school for forty pupils at the remote village of Limoncito, which sits on a mountain some five hours' uphill march from the nearest vehicle road. Funds for this had kindly been provided by the Newport Uskmouth Rotary Club and although all the necessary materials had to be carried up by men and mules, work was already well under way before we arrived. Colin Boag, a former senior Royal Engineer officer, led a group to inspect the site and found that the main building had been erected, but still needed plastering. The bathrooms, housed in a separate building, also had to be completed. The plastic water tank chosen by the Wiwa was clearly unsuitable, given the high temperatures, so more cement had to be hauled up the hill to build a concrete version. After the usual welcome ceremony conducted by the

Mamos, our doctors and dentist treated the people and schoolbooks were presented. All this was much appreciated and a Rotary plaque was duly fitted to the school wall.

Communications were never easy and for this phase we depended on our satellite phones and our well-tried Motorola walkie-talkie radios. Although the Wiwa often had mobile phones, coverage was very limited. Amazingly, it was possible to use mobile phones if they could be attached to certain wooden pillars or trees in some villages. The *Mamos* seemed to have blessed this system!

At the villages of La Peña de Los Indios, El Machín and Marocaso, our engineers studied the need for bridges, health clinics, road improvements and water supply systems, going on to produce detailed designs. Schoolbooks were also given out and our doctors and dentists worked nonstop, treating over 250 patients. For those in need, we also distributed more than 160 pairs of reading glasses.

Due to the security restrictions, we were unable to look for the double-headed snakes reported in a particular area, but heard that one had recently been seen with heads at both ends of the body. Strange as it may seem, this is not an unknown phenomenon. The Wiwa are great conservationists, but our wildlife studies were limited by the security situation, although we did see foxes, rabbits and squirrels. Happily, there was no evidence of either overhunting or deforestation.

Restrictions on our movements also prevented us from visiting archaeological sites, of which several were said to exist in the forested mountains. However, we were able to study some fascinating giant carved boulders near Achintukua, believed to be a sacred map of the Sierra, but more likely to be a natural geological feature.

At Marocaso the army reported ELN terrorists in a village only a couple of miles away. 'They know everything about you,' confided a sergeant, 'but as they are communists and you are helping the poor, it is unlikely they will cause problems.'

In order to enjoy thirty-six hours' rest and recuperation we drove north to a so-called 'People's Recreation Centre' on the Caribbean coast. Getting there involved driving around the eastern side of the Sierra, along roads that lead to Venezuela. Military and police checkpoints, supported by armoured vehicles, were stationed along the route but did not delay us. Petrol smuggled in from Venezuela was on offer for sale at the roadside by vendors raising money to buy food to take back across the border, where there is a severe shortage of everything except petrol. Even loo paper was much in demand in Caracas!

Somewhat frustrated, we swam and, as usual, toasted Robbie Burns with a dram or two, despite the temperature.

Back at Valledupar, in blistering heat, we held a conference to present the results of our medical and dental work and the engineering projects to the Wiwa government. As a result the Mayor of San Juan del Cesar agreed to fund some of the projects. It was indeed a very positive ending and hopefully the Wiwa will receive more financial support and healthcare in the future. Despite constraints imposed on our deployment, we had accomplished the majority of our tasks to aid these unusual people and been privileged to go where few foreigners had been before. The Wiwa thanked us profusely and seemed to have appreciated our efforts.

Thanks to the support of Nikon UK, Daniella Parkinson and Yoli shot a video film of the whole project and hopefully the Wiwa will be able to use this in future as a record of their culture. Although somewhat frustrating, our time with this indigenous tribe had been like a visit to a different world, and was well worth the effort.

Meanwhile, the tireless Yoli had received another request, to help a tribe on the southern border of her country, and in May 2017 we ventured once again into the steaming Amazon jungle.

In my dream I was back in the Congo jungle with the thunder of tribal drums reverberating through the heavy night air. However, waking slowly, I realised the drumming was real – indeed, the floor of the hut on which I lay was positively shaking! The electronic beat and the excited cries of the dancers made sleep impossible, so pushing aside the mosquito net, I flicked a three-inch cockroach off my leg and staggered out to protest. Driven on by a flashing electronic keyboard and bellies full of homebrewed 'chicha', a popular fermented beverage made from maize, Ticuna villagers were gyrating in a wild frenzy around their football pitch.

'What on earth is going on?' I yelled at the '*Curaca*', the headman.

'We celebrating Mother's Day,' he roared back.

'So, where are the mothers?' I asked.

'Gone home to bed,' he retorted, gulping down more chicha.

The frenzied dancing, with its ear-splitting accompaniment, continued until dawn broke at around five o'clock. There was no way to escape the audio torture and no-one slept that night. We were 1,000 miles south of Bogotá, in a remote area where there were no roads or airstrips. Around us the dense Amazon rainforest, crowding in on the riverbanks, seemed to amplify and reflect the sound on to us. 'If you want our doctors and dentists to help you and if you want books for your schools and reading glasses for your older folk, we have to sleep,' I explained to our semi-inebriated hosts.

Our team of seventeen volunteers had come together to aid the Ticuna and carry out a range of scientific studies along the winding Rio Loreto Yacu, which branches off the mighty Amazon, close to Colombia's southern borders with Brazil and Peru. This was in response to a request by Rusbel Torres, the president of Aticoya (the Association of Indigenous Authorities). Most of the indigenous people in the Colombian Amazonas region are Ticuna, renowned for painting and basketmaking, and some 8,000 of them live here, with many more found in Brazil and Peru. The province was created in 1934, when the League of Nations interceded in a long-running border dispute between Colombia and Peru. Surrounded by almost impenetrable jungle, its capital, Leticia, has a population of 48,000 and is only linked to the outside world by an airport and the Amazon River.

As we were to discover, the Ticuna villages enjoyed some government support, but lacked many basic essentials, such as clean drinking water and medical aid. To advise and assist these people living along the remote river, our expedition included doctors, dentists, an economist, a professor of environmental management, an agriculturalist and others with special experience and skills.

Flying into Leticia one gets a good perspective on the scale of the Amazon, the endless rainforest and the many tributaries running into the world's second-longest river. Indeed, this vast forest, pumping oxygen into the atmosphere, is of fundamental importance to life on our planet. Yoli and naturalist Sergio Leon of the Ecodestinos company had spent a year working with Rusbel Torres to organise the expedition, greatly assisted by Medical Mission International (MMI), a Canadian-based medical charity that provides spiritual and compassionate healthcare worldwide. Waiting for us at Leticia on 14th May 2017 was a twenty-six-foot ambulance boat we had built with funds generously provided by Clinique La Prairie, the famous clinic at Montreux, Switzerland, well known to my friend

Anna Nicholas. Fitted with a 40hp outboard, the blue and white aluminium craft was to accompany us throughout the project. We had also chartered a hundred-foot riverboat with a 70hp outboard to carry the team and equipment. This was to be our flagship and proved invaluable to the venture. Rusbel also helped out by providing a thirty-three-foot stores boat for medical equipment and we had a couple of collapsible dental chairs loaned by MMI.

After a comfortable night in the Zuruma Hotel and a good steak with a very passable bottle of Cabernet, we embarked at the bustling port. At the chaotic dockside, we carried our cargo over swaying planks on to a wobbling pontoon and lowered it into our boats. By noon all was aboard and we set sail for Puerto Nariño, the second town of Amazonas. Sailors on the grey Colombian Navy gunboat guarding the port gave a friendly wave as we headed upriver on the two-hour voyage under a blistering sun. Canoes and *peke-peke* boats, carrying Ticuna ladies sheltered by colourful umbrellas, passed by on their way to market. At Puerto Nariño grey dolphins swam out to greet the flotilla and Rusbel welcomed us at a simple reception, with dancers giving a lively performance.

Following rest in a local hostel and a filling breakfast, we re-embarked and turned off the Amazon on to the Rio Loreto Yacu, setting off for our first base at the village of San Francisco. Here a smart lady *Curaca* showed us buildings in which we could sling hammocks, and then took us to the local clinic. As often happens, the person with the padlock key was away, so the lock was hammered off and our medical and dental teams set themselves up in the overheated rooms. The temperature outside was 29°C and very humid, but patients began to gather for treatment, miracle cures or just out of curiosity. Cathy Lawrence, a professional comedienne from Toronto, entertained them with a giant set of teeth and a huge toothbrush, whilst somewhat perplexed mothers breastfed their babies.

Eager to test the camera traps, Professor Alastair Driver of the University of Exeter led a team to a position deep in the forest. Down on the river, Canadian Dr Adriaan Van Der Wart filmed dolphins with his tiny drone. The Ticuna gazed in amazement, but a nest of black vultures took absolutely no notice as the drone hovered nearby. The village children joined in and Alastair was presented with a couple of water snakes. 'Mildly venomous,' he muttered as they were measured and photographed. Back at the camp, Esther Vela Miranda, a jolly, smiling cook we had recruited in Puerto Nariño, was already busy preparing tasty meals. However, it was not long before most of us were in our hammocks.

Scrubbing my teeth at dawn next day, I noticed to my horror that the ambulance boat had disappeared. However, it turned up a little later, driven by its hung-over helmsman. He had just taken it back to Puerto Nariño – 'for safe keeping,' he mumbled – and was fired on the spot. Hector, our young Colombian mate on the flagship, then proudly took over the helm.

Thanks again to the Newport Uskmouth Rotary Club and friends of expedition members, Yoli had purchased a vast number of books for the village schools and there were soon lines of pupils queuing eagerly for these. Meanwhile, Anna Nicholas and our youngest member, Hugh Fagan, who, usefully, had been Captain of Fishing at Winchester, gave out reading glasses. Spanish-speaking Peter Manns soon found the resident shaman and interviewed him as part of his cultural studies. To everyone's joy, both grey and strawberry-pink dolphins rose up beside the ambulance boat. Alastair's camera traps captured video of paca, rather like large guinea pigs, and a strange nocturnal bird named the conamo. Swatting mosquitoes and sandflies, we viewed these images after supper.

Beneath a blue sky we sailed upriver between the jungle-clad banks and, after two hours, reached San Pedro. Standing on higher ground, the hutted village of around 200 inhabitants lay close to the Peruvian frontier. Spaces for our hammocks were found in various buildings and Esther produced a fine supper of roast paca, fried banana, yucca and fruit salad.

Although we had Motorola walkie-talkies and a satellite phone for emergency communication, we once again noticed that many Ticuna possessed mobile phones and simply by placing them against a particular pole in the village could make calls worldwide! I guessed the post must have marked a high spot just within range of the distant masts, or perhaps it was just magic! How different this was to those days on the Congo when we used the talking drums, I reflected. But as night fell, dark clouds swept over the village bringing torrential rain, thunder and vivid lightning. Yoli's tent, which had survived a dozen expeditions, flooded and we all got a little damp. However, there were clear skies the next morning, and we redeployed our camera traps. In fact, if one wanted to see wildlife, it was only necessary to look around the village, where many of the children had pets. In one hut a turtle and a tortoise crawled around amongst the chickens, a little girl clutched her protesting squirrel monkey and a boy fed his sloth fresh banana. Out on the river a blue macaw landed on the ambulance boat roof and strutted along to peer in at the occupants. Ever trusting, Hugh put out his hand to the bird and promptly got pecked! John Arathoon, our builder and engineer, tried to help the Ticuna with their machinery and was presented with a dozen *peke-peke* engines that needed attention. It was clear the owners knew little about maintenance. However, John and Peter Manns managed to get three of them working.

In all the villages we saw mobile phones, TV sets and even digital projectors in the schools, but the people lacked clean drinking water, well-equipped clinics and simple school textbooks. It was said that before elections, politicians were generous with such luxury goods, but the people still needed the basics. We noted that the Ticuna struggled to make a living, though hunting, fishing and the growing of some fruit and yucca in the forests helped. Joel talked to us about the need for ecotourism and markets for their handicrafts, but we wondered what would attract visitors to these remote settlements. To ensure all was well, Rusbel called to see us and explained the role of the ambulance boat to the elders, who seemed very appreciative.

At night we conducted surveys for caiman along the waterways, but with the river levels so high, most were hiding in the flooded forest. However, in the darkened jungle Adriaan was able to photograph plants as part of his study of bio-semiotics, a new interdisciplinary field that explores meaningful relationships and communication throughout the world. Back at the village, we found extraordinarily beautiful scented plants that only bloomed at night. At dawn on 19th May a fisherman brought in a weighty catch, including a large pacu that Esther speedily butchered for supper. To Alastair's joy, the camera traps recorded a video of a rarely seen tayra, rather like a giant stoat, along with her pups. And one evening a hunter came to tell us all he knew about what he claimed to be a legendary water tiger, one of the animals of the Chinese zodiac. We had been led to believe it was probably a black jaguar, but from his description it seemed more like a large giant otter. Sadly, he had killed it and used it to make traditional medicines.

The clinics soon filled with patients and Varinder Bassi, our British Army dentist, reported a record number of extractions. I doubted that the Ticuna had ever met a striking bearded, turbaned dentist previously! Meanwhile, Hilary Napier, one of our doctors, dealt with a baby with a raging temperature, whom we evacuated to the hospital at Puerto Nariño – the first patient to benefit from our ambulance boat.

Alas, the happy mood of our stay was somewhat blighted by robbers slashing through the mosquito nets of John Arathoon and Simon House's hammocks and stealing their belongings. Joel, the young chief, tolled the school bell to call a village meeting, and the shaman summoned to investigate the theft claimed to have identified the thieves. However, no items were returned.

Moving downriver we ran another clinic at the village of '12th October', named after the day Colombus 'discovered' America in 1492, and dispatched a camera trap party to camp deep in the forest overnight. Although bird diversity increased as it distanced itself from the village, no mammals were spotted. However, invertebrate life was prolific, including pink-toed tarantulas, giant bush crickets, dragonflies and a five-foot Brazilian rainbow boa. John Mackenzie-Grieve, our ornithologist, was in demi-paradise with his counts, and working with the sharp-eyed Sergio Leon identified no less than 150 species, including five previously unseen in the region. The sighting of a horned screamer and four hoatzin high in the forest canopy was a special treat. Unfortunately, our visit to '12th October' had to be terminated by the deafening noise of yet another Mother's Day celebration, which seemed to follow us downriver. At San Juan del Soco, however, the villagers were prepared to postpone the party. To our surprise we found the weather-beaten remains of an old eco-hotel that the people hoped could attract visitors once again. These Ticuna were keen to improve their standard of living and wanted our advice, guidance, clinics, schoolbooks, glasses and, indeed, anything else we could do to help them.

The young *Curaca*, Gilbertson, offered us a large *Maloka* (meeting house) with a thatched roof that could accommodate forty hammocks, and the eco-hotel's huts still had ceramic loos and showers that worked… most of the time!

Furthermore, Alvaro, the local pastor of the Evangelist Church, turned out to be the leading hunter and offered to guide teams in the forest to set up the camera traps.

Our dentists, Varinder and Jackie Ansic, were soon busy extracting teeth and advising on dental hygiene, and our doctors and surgeon, Yasmin Jauhari, coped with a great many patients, many of whom suffered from worm infestations. The younger patients were comforted with a gift of an animal puppet or a teddy bear to encourage them to protect wildlife.

As the children queued to receive schoolbooks, pencils, rubbers and rulers, our engineers studied the water problems. Surprisingly, a contractor had built a thirty-foot tower with a water tank and had even put in pipes connected to all the houses, but had not installed a pump to bring the water up from the river! I promised to see if we could help with that at a later date. Elsewhere, Morton Risberg, a Norwegian Army officer, was totally absorbed in the rainforest, and agriculturalist Simon was fascinated by the dolphins and fishing.

The deputy *Curaca*, Dago, was keen to tell us about his people's history and he set to work to create a wall painting showing the origins of the Ticuna. Adriaan and Maya Boyd, our quartermaster, were fascinated by this remarkably talented man and filmed him at work, while on the ground beside him a small constrictor was busy trying to swallow a mouse! Ignoring this, Dago explained that Yo'i, the mythical hero of the Ticuna, was depicted fishing in a lake in Brazil, their original home. The fish in the lake, he told us, eat the black seeds of the huito plant and turn into black people. The fish that eat the plankton become yellow people, or Asians, and those who eat the white fruit of the yucca grow into white people, whereas those who eat the caiman become brown-skinned Ticuna. At the base was an anaconda, lord of the underworld.

The Ticuna, he added, believe there are three worlds. The sky is the spirit world, the lake is the terrestrial world and finally there is the underworld. Looking down, I noticed the snake at our feet had been killed by the mouse biting its way out of the serpent's stomach! A strange world.

One evening Gilbertson brought along a fourteen-year-old girl, already a trained shaman, to talk to us. She had attended a shaman's school and, for one so young, addressed us with great confidence. I noticed she wore a crucifix and questioned her. 'There are bad shaman and good shaman,' she replied, touching her crucifix. 'I am a good one and cast good spells… and sometimes I can cure illness.' Indeed, at another village we came upon a herbal medicine training centre.

Our usual Burns Supper was held beneath the stars twinkling in a cloudless sky, totally free from light pollution. Stahly's haggis was served together with an unexpected local dish. Alvaro the pastor had asked if he could bring something for the dinner and turned up with a six-foot caiman he had caught that morning. It had a fishy flavour and, had we not been told what it was, few would have guessed. The Ticuna tucked into this, and also loved the haggis!

A dram or two and some Chilean Merlot helped to wash it all down. However, the hot, humid night did not encourage reeling, so we were happy just to sit back and watch Ticuna dancing in traditional dress, and listen to songs by the children.

Feeling a little sad, we said goodbye to our new friends as they helped us load the flagship. The moment was lightened by Simon, who fell into the river whilst carrying a box of rations. However, to make up for his unsuccessful fishing he emerged from the depths clutching a tin of sardines! The Ticuna brought us simple handicraft gifts and adorned some of our team with jet-black tattoos. In return we handed over food, tools and medical supplies. Alvaro said a prayer and blessed us, but Gilbertson and Dago could not bear to leave us and insisted on coming all the way to Leticia.

Pausing to bid farewell and hand over the ambulance boat to Rusbel at Puerto Nariño, there was just time for Alastair and a few stalwarts to buy a captive six-and-a-half-foot anaconda and, placing it on a giant Victoria lily, release it into the wild. Back in Britain we organised an event in London that raised the funds to complete the water supply system at San Juan. At that point I felt that the mission was well and truly complete.

 You **Tube** **Colombian Amazonas Expedition 2017**

CHAPTER 23

WITH THE AMERINDIANS

OF ECUADOR

THE COFÁN

In 2006 the Ecuadorian Ecotourism Association asked the SES if we could undertake an expedition to aid the indigenous Amerindian communities of Cofán and Kichwa people in north-east Ecuador. Yoli, our representative in South America, reported that the Cofán nation remains one of the oldest intact cultures in the Americas, with a recorded history going back over 500 years, and that a community of 130 people at Zábalo, on the Rio Aguarico, were said to be the last surviving members of the tribe in Ecuador. They badly needed a supply of clean water, hygienic latrines and materials for their school. And at Zancudo, another riverside settlement, a 106-strong Kichwa

community also lacked clean drinking water and required materials for their small school. Both villages needed medical and dental aid and some basic first aid training.

Something extraordinary and very intriguing then emerged. A white man, we were told, had recently become the Cofán's tribal chief, and had been leading them in a determined campaign to defend their ancestral tribal lands from intrusions by oil companies. Under his leadership, the Cofán had attacked drilling platforms and had taken workers prisoner, forcing the government to negotiate. It was, as we soon discovered for ourselves, a fascinating story featuring an extremely colourful character.

The son of American missionaries, Randall Borman had been raised with the Cofán. As a youngster he had wrestled with caiman and anaconda, had become a crack shot with a blowpipe and had learned how to use the jungle plants and fruits. Having then gone to university in America, he returned to live with the tribe, married a Cofán girl and founded the village of Zabalo. Fluent in English, Spanish and Cofán, he was a tricultural hybrid, holding American and Ecuadorean passports. And having had an American university education, he was able to cultivate supporters in the USA and to take on the oil companies in court. Furthermore, in a country where many consider tribal people inferior, his white skin had opened doors usually closed for indigenous chiefs fighting for their land rights. With his political skills, Randy had been able to influence Ecuadorian politicians and media, while also winning public support for the Cofán. Now he was seeking to provide the tribe with income by introducing ecotourism.

At our first meeting he explained how he hoped that his people would be able to act as scientific Sherpas, taking visitors on jungle safaris to give them what he described as 'a deep inside understanding of Amazon ecosystems and culture'. Not surprisingly, he came to be regarded as something of a latter-day Tarzan! He more than justified the sort of tourist development he had in mind by pointing out that it would not involve the need for the Cofán to sell themselves with fake tribal dances. 'Instead', he said, 'they can preserve their culture by using their encyclopaedic knowledge of traditional medicinal plants and the love of the forest.'

The villagers of Zancudo and Zabalo were keen conservationists, more than happy to promote ecotourism in a largely unexplored environment, home to over 800 species of bird, 150 species of mammal and several thousand species of plant, many of which are used for herbal remedies by the local shaman. They were also eager to promote the sale of their handicrafts, a range of practical, decorative and artistic items made from materials found in the forest. In addition, he said, there were archaeological sites, believed to have been part of the Omagua culture, yet to be properly investigated.

The Colombian FARC terrorists were known to have bases inside Ecuador and I was concerned about encountering them. However, Randy felt they would not wish to draw attention to themselves and would leave us alone. So, with this remarkable man's approval and the endorsement of the Ecuadorian Ministry of Environment, our twenty-strong expedition arrived at Quito. We were the usual mixture of scientists, engineers, doctors, dentists and photographers, many of whom had been with me on other ventures. Driving past the statue of conquistador Francisco de Orellana, I was reminded of his epic voyage in 1541 when, foraging for food for Gonzalo Pizarro's ill-fated exploration party, he had set out in boats down the Rio Napo and then, being unable to return against the current, had discovered the Amazon. Now we were to sail down the Rio Aguarico, another tributary of the great river.

Dropping down from the cool air in Quito – at 9,350 feet, the second-highest capital city in the world after La Paz – we were soon sweltering at 35°C in the Amazon Basin. A major task was to install a clean water system at Zabalo, provided by Agroconsultores of Quito and funded by Just a Drop.

At the riverside town of Lago Agrio we boarded four sixteen-foot fibreglass Eco canoes. Randy had encouraged the people to establish a workshop to produce these slim, fast craft to replace dugout canoes and avoid the indiscriminate felling and unsustainable use of forest trees. Speeding down the jungle-flanked Rio Aguarico, we were greeted by smiling Cofán at Zabalo where four ecotourist huts and a large dining room store had already been built. Julian Butter, Phil Sargent and the Agroconsultores engineer set to work on the water system with the equipment we brought in. The plug that drained the storage tank, mounted on the fifty-foot steel tower, had jammed, but farmer Simon Brown found some spare metal and manufactured an improvised spanner to free it.

At the same time, doctors Roy D'Silva, Birgit Hartberger and Nathan Buckley set up a clinic, dentist Graham Catchpole extracted numerous rotting teeth and opthalmologist Joel Somerville tested eyes and dished out reading glasses, whilst anthropologist Rachel Jepson studied the lifestyles of the Cofán. The people were happy to show the medicinal plants to Leoni Chandler and display some fascinating pottery dating back 600 years to Mel Bell and Carol Eid. Maps of the villages were produced by engineer Bethan Lewis whilst Lucy Thompson and Mel painted the new toilet block, built as part of the facilities for ecotourists. Elodie Sandford and Jonathan Hood compiled a photographic record of everything that was going on and Yoli shot a video film. It was pleasing to see the Cofán's enthusiastic wildlife conservation efforts and in particular a programme to breed yellow spotted turtles. John Mackenzie-Grieve, who did our zoological studies, noted that the Cofán claimed to have already released no less than 50,000. Commendably, the Cofán did not even attempt to kill the long black snake that emerged from Elodie's tent and wriggled between my feet!

As we were completing our work, a runner rushed in from the downstream Kichwa village of Zancudo with the news that two men had fallen from a height of sixty-five feet when a metal tower they were working on had collapsed. Roy, Yoli, Lucy and Leoni sped off in a canoe and found one poor chap with a broken rib and dislocated hip and knee. After being given some first aid, the most seriously injured casualty was sent by the fastest boat to hospital at Lago Agrio. Grateful for our help, the Kichwa were eager to show us a little-known lake named Imuya on the Peruvian border, which they claimed was alive with wildlife.

On a warm, humid August morning we loaded our canoes and set off downriver. Luis, the Zabalo President, and his son joined us in tribal dress, along with a Kichwa guide. Reaching the Ecuador–Peru border we dispensed reading glasses to the Ecuadorian soldiers and gave five gallons of petrol to the Peruvian border guards, so they could run their generator and watch football on TV.

Turning east, we cruised into a string of lakes, alive with waterbirds and giant otters, but soon our passage was blocked by floating islands of emerald-green weed three feet high. Even at high revs the outboard on the leading canoe could not push us through and we sat gripped in the dense green weed, like an icebreaker caught in a frozen polar sea. Rocking the boat as the motor roared did no good, but grasping the stems of the plants and all pulling together we inched forward. Luis stood up at the bow peering ahead, trying to identify a clear way and eventually saw a route. Breaking out of the claustrophobic grip of the weed beds we entered the elusive lake where, to our joy, pink dolphin were surfacing as they pursued their fish suppers.

Tucked away in a patch of forest stood a dilapidated fishing lodge with some chalets – not four-star accommodation by any means, but the roofs of the chalets were partly intact and as long as one trod carefully on the rotten decking the elevated buildings were habitable. We pitched our tents inside and cooked supper. There being no breeze, the heat was suffocating and I wondered how we could extract ourselves from this eerie waterworld.

Using a spotlight and a night-vision device, a wildlife team sallied forth on a caiman hunt while the rest of us cleared our sleeping area of the pink-toed tarantulas that descended from the rafters. At 01:00 I awoke, conscious of movement beside my tent. Clutching my machete, I eased out of my sleeping bag, flicked on the head torch and found myself face to face with the biggest rat I've ever seen. As I struck out, the evil-looking rodent dodged this way and that before racing up my arm and diving off into the night.

Fishing, dolphin spotting and swimming in the cold, dark waters of the lake, thankfully free of piranha, completed our visit. To escape the weed islands on the return trip we cut poles with forked ends to help us push our way through and battled back to the border posts and home to Zabalo.

The Cofán enjoyed the haggis at our Burns Night supper and a few drams of J&B encouraged them to dance and perform traditional plays. The night ended with reeling in the moonlight, before the Cofán, well-filled with home-brewed chicha, tottered off to their huts.

Returning over the Andes to Quito, we passed through a snowstorm at 13,000 feet, but after our team had departed Yoli and I drove back to the warmer Cofán village of Sinangué, along with Byron Leon of Agroconsultores, to inspect the water supply that Just a Drop had funded. Freddie Espinosa, from Randy's office, accompanied us and again there was a friendly greeting from the Cofán, now clad in their traditional dress. They had also brought along a large pet monkey. The chief cut a fine figure with his necklace of jaguar teeth and I asked if I might photograph him. Whipping out his mobile phone he replied: 'Let me ask my shaman if that's OK.'

We came away satisfied that everybody involved had gained something worthwhile from the expedition. The Cofán had their clean water and a few less rotten teeth, and we had learned much more about this brave little tribe, who were managing to maintain their traditional way of life while at the same time making good use of some of the benefits that the modern outside world had to offer.

THE ACHUAR

Despite living in the headwaters of the world's second-longest river, the indigenous people of Ecuador's Amazon region desperately needed potable water – fresh water that is uncontaminated and safe to drink. There were more tasks to do for the Cofán but in Quito we were introduced to a wily pastor from a religious foundation who was seeking aid for a tribe of Achuar people living in a remote village named Chikianetza. The only access was by air, using a strip the people had built themselves, hoping to attract aircraft. Having secured some government help and a promise of military air flights, the pastor persuaded us to invest funds from Just a Drop to set up a water supply system at the village. And so it was that Yoli and

I, together with the pastor and four helpers and a collection of schoolbooks for the village children, set off from Quito at 01:00 hours on Friday 10th December 2009 in an unheated minibus, driving over the mountains at the start of a hectic visit to the allegedly quite savage Achuar.

At the Fort Militar Amazonas, in the oil town of Shell Mera, originally established as a Shell Oil Company base, soldiers in camouflage gear and a pair of Armstrong guns (circa 1918) guarded the gate. Juan Fernandez and two colleagues from Agroconsultores were already there with trucks of water-supply equipment. The pastor's party was five-strong and we were five but to erect the tower and set up the system would be a challenge!

The smartly uniformed commanding officer of the Air Unit spoke good English and explained that the promised helicopter was being repaired in Quito and would not be available until Monday. Rather than hang around in the dusty town reeking of oil, I took the water engineers to complete a task at Sinangué. Arriving in the area at dusk, we decided to delay crossing the fast-flowing river that lay between us and the village and pitched our tents on the bank, before dining on ravioli washed down with Chilean Merlot.

A storm broke in the early hours of the morning, flooding our tents, and then, some hours later, a Cofán canoe appeared to take us across what was now a raging torrent. Our engineers struggled to repair the water pump, but got it going in time for us to snap photos for Just a Drop and enjoy a Cofán feast of soup, tasty capybara, peccary, rice and plantains. I noticed that the old lady sitting beside me was nursing what appeared at first glance to be a baby but which, on closer inspection, turned out to be a young woolly monkey that then proceeded to pee all over her. Eager to get on to the next village, we could not leave until the Cofán had performed a dance routine for us. It was nightfall by the time we got to Lago Agrio, where we found rooms at our old haunt, the Hotel Arazá, and, having dried out our sodden tents, downed a bottle of Cabernet Sauvignon and fell asleep in seconds.

At dawn Cofán canoes took us to Dureno, their 'capital', where a government water system, allegedly costing $250,000, had been incorrectly connected. As so often in such places, the problem was that the local engineers were not trained to maintain complex systems. Whilst our engineers produced a costing for me to submit to Just a Drop, a shaman blew tobacco smoke over a sick young girl to extract a devil from her and once it had departed we returned to Shell Mera, where the CO assured us that the helicopter was on its way. At 15:45 a giant Russian-made Mil Mi-17 thundered into the base.

Chikianetza was not shown on any of the maps we had and the pastor had flown ahead in a light plane, so we were not sure exactly where it was. However, the helicopter pilot had a rough idea of its location. So, crammed with water pipes, pumps, schoolbooks, footballs and cement, plus our team, the chopper took off. Peering out through the broken windows, we watched the dense jungle race by a hundred feet below the shuddering fuselage. Daylight was ebbing as we touched down. The pastor was waiting there to welcome us, looking benign, and while the huge propellers continued to swirl overhead the Achuar tribesmen rushed to unload, urged on by the pilot anxious to get home in daylight. With an ear-splitting roar, the great beast then disappeared over the trees, it's downdraught sweeping away the roofs of a couple of huts. As it grew dark, chicha beer, whose ingredients are chewed in the mouths of the older women, was served as a welcome drink, followed by monkey soup and a hearty supper. I did not relish either the beer or the soup, but refusal is taken as a grave insult. Pedro, the Achuar chief, explained their polygamist society, stating that if a warrior had five wives he must maintain them all and must take breakfast with each one every day. Discussion on the building of a twenty-foot water tower was prolonged by Pedro's considerable consumption of chicha making him garrulous, and I grew increasingly impatient to retire to my sleeping bag.

At 03:00, bellowing and screams rent the air, but it was only a massive white bull having its throat cut in preparation for a ritual feast that the Achuar had planned for the next day. As the sun rose, the bugs attacked, but Pedro had already marshalled his warriors and within a couple of hours had made a good start on erecting the water tower, using lengthy tree trunks, while also burying the pipe from the pump to the tower.

The thousand-gallon water tank was still at the Fort Militar Amazonas, and a satellite phone call then revealed that the helicopter had broken its tail on landing after bringing us out and that the delivery of the tank would therefore be delayed. The friendly commanding officer of the Air Unit promised to send a Cessna to collect us when available. Meanwhile our engineers decided that the tower was too low and in the wrong place anyway! I could see that we might be stranded for some time. The sky blackened after lunch and another violent tropical storm erupted, with thunder and vivid lightning, forcing a postponement of Pedro's cultural event.

On 17th December the sun shone, work on the tower continued and the Achuar entertained us with dancing, music and a storytelling session. Yoli distributed schoolbooks and rucksacks to the children and we gave the chief a Swiss army all-purpose tool. The youngsters garlanded us with necklaces and Pedro at first wanted me to accept a bleeding leg from the bull as a gift, before eventually presenting me with two cuddly guinea pigs, which I discreetly passed to a small boy, who I suspect will have eaten them.

Anxious to return to his flock in Quito, the pastor chartered an expensive twin-engined plane and departed with his people, leaving my group to be extracted by the promised Cessna. Meanwhile we discovered that the school only had thirty-five pupils, not the 123 the pastor had asked us to supply with books. Furthermore, the cement brought for the tower had been purloined for the church. However, our prayers were answered and a couple of military Cessna 207s eventually arrived to whisk us back to the fort. Later, one of those in which we flew suffered engine failure and crashed, killing all on board. So, neither the happiest nor most satisfactory of expeditions – but in the end the Achuar did at least get their water supply.

THE WAORANI

Our reputation for providing clean drinking water for remote communities was growing and in 2011 the Ecuadorian Ministry of Environment asked if we could provide assistance of a similar sort for another tribe, the Waorani. Like the Achuar, the Waorani had a fearsome reputation. Adrian Warren, an SES member and a skilled photographer, had encountered them before and he told me how, in 1956, they had made world news headlines when they speared to death five American missionaries who had landed their light plane on a riverside sandbank, with well-meaning plans to set up a mission there. Outsiders may have been shocked by the manner of the missionaries' demise, but to the Waorani it was nothing out of the ordinary, said Adrian, explaining that spearing apparently accounted for 40% of all deaths among the tribesmen, usually as a result of interfamilial vendettas. A further 20% came from attacks by outsiders, a fact that may have influenced their way of greeting the unfortunate missionaries. Snakebite and other accidents were to blame for most other deaths, with only 1% being from natural causes.

The Ministry of Environment's Lorena Tapia provided further information. 'To Ecuador's predominant indigenous group, the Kichwa, they are known as *aucas* – "savages",' she told us. 'And there is, indeed, much about their lifestyle that might invite the label. They have no writing, no reason to count higher than ten and no history other than a tribal recollection that their ancestors came from "downriver long ago". They roam naked in the jungle, hunting monkeys and birds with wooden blowguns and curare-tipped darts; to kill wild pigs they use spears. In the past they are said to have speared the incapable elderly, whilst unwanted babies were strangled with vines, burnt, buried alive or just abandoned in the forest. By and large their contacts with any outsiders have not been notably peaceable. However, it is the Waorani themselves who have suffered in recent times, especially from the intrusion of international oil companies into their land. Originally, there were believed to be six villages in Ecuadorian Amazonas, but through fragmentation these have grown into an estimated forty-four settlements with populations of varied sizes up to around one hundred and sixty. Deeper in the interior are another group of Waorani, the "untouchables", who have chosen to live traditionally and completely apart. They threaten to kill anyone entering their territory. The Ecuadorian government respects their independence, but no-one knows exactly how many of these "untouchables" there are, although it is thought there may be up to four separate groups.'

Today the Waorani are increasingly threatened by Western ways and diseases. In many areas their water systems have been polluted by crude oil and chemicals, and by heavy metals, as a result of irresponsible practices in oil drilling and mining. Roads cut into their hunting grounds have been populated by *colonistas* and people of other tribes eagerly seeking land. The Waorani complain: 'The government want our land, the oil companies want our oil and the missionaries seek our souls.' They are very much aware that they are at the top of a slippery slope that will lead to the loss of their culture and the destruction of the abundant sources of food and natural medicines on which they depend. At the same time, they have come to accept the need for medical treatment, schoolbooks and, above all, potable water.

On a recce in 2011 Yoli and I, along with Byron Leon from Agroconsultores, had visited the Waorani villages of Tobeta, Yawapade, Miwawono and Ñoneno to plan the aid programme. We saw the impact of the oil companies first-hand and noted the pollution of streams and the widespread litter. Oil pipelines and roads had cut through pristine forest. Chinese workers were living in temporary camps and rangers told us of the decline in wildlife. The Shiripuno River, running past Ñoneno village, was polluted with chemicals from the oil wells and totally undrinkable. Many Waorani suffered from hepatitis B and gastric problems, and I myself developed a nasty tummy upset.

Arriving at Tobeta, we found the wizened Chief Davo Enomenga and his wife holding the frightened drivers of two oil company trucks at spear point. Demanding a toll to drive through the village, Davo refused to budge until the drivers had contacted their boss by mobile phone and suitable payment was agreed. We kept out of the dispute and simply got on with distributing schoolbooks and spectacles to the villagers.

Camping nearby in a ranger station surrounded by a high fence, Octavio Cabiya, a Waorani ranger, told us more about the local situation. Only two years before a group of 'untouchables' had killed a family of *colonistas* that had strayed into their territory. Back in the 1980s, he said, missionaries had arrived and had persuaded a boy and girl from Ñoneno to come out of the forest and learn Spanish. The girl, Dayumi, then aged thirteen, was taken to the USA to learn English, but the boy sadly died. The missionaries later used a helicopter with loudspeaker to persuade the Waorani to come out and live at a missionary camp. Octavia and many others had agreed to do this and they had then met up with Dayumi, who had returned from America. She was by then fifteen and pregnant, claiming to have been seduced at the missionary base.

In return for working at the camp, the Waorani were rewarded with clothing and Coca-Cola, but according to Octavia, when the missionaries then vaccinated them, up to thirty died. At that point the Waorani then rebelled and speared seven of the missionaries to death, before fleeing back into the forest. The army arrived but were reluctant to follow the killers into the dense jungle, so no-one was punished. Octavia's people returned to Ñoneno, which was where we met them.

Just a Drop had agreed to fund the work and in September 2012 I returned with an expedition to join with Agroconsultores engineers in installing the water system and providing aid. Our twelve-strong group included an architect, two doctors, an RAF dentist, two retired Royal Engineers, a barrister, a surveyor, a property manager and an economist. The British Embassy in Quito kindly donated a supply of books for the schools and the SES provided a grant to purchase more books and medical supplies.

Having been briefed by the Ministry of Environment, we drove past puffing volcanoes and down into the Amazon Basin, spending our first night at the popular El Auca hotel in the booming oil town of Coca. This gave us an introduction to local wildlife, the hotel garden being home to agouti rodents, cheeky squirrel monkeys, colourful macaws and large tortoise.

Yoli had already purchased rations, stores and tools for the project. Next day we set out on the Via Auca, a tarmac road flanked by a major oil pipeline that led south through the jungle, past *colonistas'* homesteads and on to a track into the Yasuni National Park. Despite its status as a World Heritage Site, this too had been infiltrated by the oil companies. Pitching our tents at the Waorani rangers' station, we were joined by two Ministry of Environment officers, Paola and Luis, and set off to make an initial visit to the Tobeta community, whom I had met on the previous year's recce. We arrived to be greeted by the sight of Davo, the chief, waving an axe and a machete menacingly as he engaged in yet another fierce argument with an oil company truck driver. Unwilling to break off from haranguing the unfortunate driver, he left it to the female president of the village to agree the arrangements for our programme.

Very calmly, Myriam Nagomene, the village president, set up the thatch-roofed community's 'cultural centre', as she called it, to be used as a clinic by Steve Kershaw and Roger Schofield, our doctors. Meanwhile, Agroconsultores's engineer, Ruben Pantoja, was hard at work completing the new drinking-water system that involved water being pumped up from an unpolluted creek to storage tanks on a ridge above the village and then connected through a filter system to the scattered houses and the school.

At Miwawono, a hilltop village community of 150 people, we set up our clinics in an open-sided agricultural shed. As the temperature reached 37°C, our RAF dentist Karina Fletcher, helped by Katherine Gillmore, was soon busy pulling out rotten teeth, a supply of teddy bears made by ladies in Bournemouth handed out to ease the pain for children needing extractions, whilst Issy Gallagher issued reading glasses. Alas, the expensive water-supply system set up by the municipality needed reconstruction and could not be repaired in the time available, so our engineers pressed on to Yawepade, a village of one hundred people, where the energetic chief quickly marshalled his people to complete the configuration of a ten-foot-high water tower. With the help of a bulldozer that happened to be conveniently on hand, we heaved a 1,000-gallon plastic water tank on to the tower. Ruben then pumped water from a creek 1,300 feet away and by the end of the day we had naked toddlers and warriors leaping about under a cascade of water. The village women, who previously had to endure barefoot treks at night along a snake-infested path to the creek to fetch water, many of them bitten along the way, were especially delighted. 'I think of this every time I turn on a tap at home,' commented Mark Entwistle.

The Waorani looked anything but hostile, although a lady from the Ministry of Justice, escorted by several armed police, arrived to make sure we were safe.

Moving on to a Ministry of Environment centre on the Rio Shiripuno, we appreciated comfortable beds and welcome showers.

In the armed police's operation room was a grim video of a *colonista* woman's body that had fairly recently been recovered, pierced by numerous spears. '*Aucas*,' we were told, the officers pointing to a series of coloured pins on a wall map.

Canoeing on down the Shiripuno, the river snaking through dense vegetation, we passed a couple of anaconda curled up in a tree and, after a couple of hours, reached Ñoneno, where the indefatigable Ruben was soon hard at work getting the water system operational. Leaving him to carry on with the help of the villagers, we continued on downstream. Before long the sky blackened, thunder echoed through the forest and vivid lighting illuminated the dark water. The rain pounded down and navigation became a challenge for Tim Harrison, our surveyor and also, fortunately, a master mariner, who was crouched in the bow keeping a sharp lookout for logs. Several submerged bits of timber crashed against the hull, threatening to split the seams, while the unblinking red eyes of caiman watched us from the banks. After three hours our thoroughly bedraggled team reached Shiripuno Lodge to be welcomed by owner Jarol Vaca and his Waorani staff, who produced a tasty, well-presented meal. Jarol, an ecologist, had built the lodge deep in pristine rainforest as a way of training Waorani to organise and support responsible ecotourism as a means of sustaining their way of life.

The western Amazon Basin is one of the last great wilderness areas and it is possible to walk from here to southern Venezuela, a distance of 1,200 miles, without crossing a single road. It was indeed a privilege to be at the heart of the Yasuni Biosphere and Waorani Ethnic Reserve. Based in wooden huts, with comfortable beds and even bathrooms, we were to have the opportunity to explore the jungle with Jarol and his colleague Fernando, two self-taught English-speaking biologists. Wearing gumboots for protection against the deep mud and snakes, we spent four days tramping the trails, instructed by these skilled guides. Jarol strode through the forest, clutching a telescope and tripod and recording animal calls to be replayed later through a small loudspeaker as a means of attracting replying calls and enabling us to catch a glimpse of rare species that were snapped by Justin Snell, our architect and photographer.

High in the canopy monkeys played, whilst at ground level the guides' sharp eyes spotted frogs, crickets, praying mantis and a wide variety of spiders and other insects. There were fascinating trees and shrubs as well as banks of fungi flowering on fallen trunks. On the river we saw tubby capybara and caught fish for supper. At night, spectacled caiman lay on the banks, their eyes reflecting the torchlight. Altogether, the experience provided a fascinating and informative lesson in biology and botany.

Returning upriver we paused to inspect Ruben's work at Ñoneno, where the new installation delivered clean, treated and filtered water 2,600 feet to the village. A deadly coral snake squirming in the reservoir did not disturb the engineers and after we had inaugurated the system the village children danced in the water sprayed from the outlets and gifts were exchanged.

Back at Coca, we celebrated with a Burns Night supper, Tom Gallagher reciting the 'Address' in broad Geordie. In Quito the Vice-Minister of the Ministry of Environment, Señora Mercy Borbor-Cordova expressed her sincere thanks to SES and Just a Drop for all the help provided for the indigenous peoples of Ecuador. Yoli dispatched a message to Expedition Base in Dorset simply announcing: 'Mission accomplished – no-one speared!'

▶ **Waorani Expedition, Ecuador 2012**

 ▶ **Cofán Expedition, Zabalo, Ecuador 2008**

CHAPTER 24

HISTORIC FOOTSTEPS

IN THE WAKE OF DRAKE

At the time of Operation Drake, the first of the two major circumnavigations organised for young people by the Scientific Exploration Society, my friend Keith Hamilton Jones was Britain's ambassador in Costa Rica. 'You must come to Costa Rica,' he insisted when we got into conversation at a party in Devon. 'In 1979 it will be the four hundredth anniversary of Sir Francis Drake's landing and I intend to erect a memorial commemorating the event.'

In 1579, having rounded Cape Horn and captured the treasure-laden Spanish galleon *Cagafuego* off the coast of Ecuador, Drake had sailed on to Costa Rica and the Isla del Caño, where he found a safe haven in which to carry out urgent maintenance work on his flagship, *Golden Hind*. But then, with the hold of his ship already overflowing with gold, silver and jewels from the *Cagafuego*, another Spanish vessel fell into his clutches.

From a hiding place in the lee of the island, his men had sailed forth in a pinnace – 'blowing trumpets and firing arquebuses in the air', according to a contemporary report – and boarded the passing cargo ship without a fight. A small barque, it had no treasure aboard, just a cargo of maize, honey and

sarsaparilla, but it yielded a very different and even more valuable prize in the form of two Chinese pilots, fully equipped with charts mapping the so-called 'China Run' that the Spanish had established across the Pacific between Mexico and the Philippines.

Such an unexpected windfall caused Drake, who had been preparing to head back home to Plymouth, to change his plans completely. He may well have been worried anyway about the dangers of retracing his route around the Cape, since his escapades on the way out had left hornets' nests of angry Spaniards, who would no doubt be waiting to intercept him on the return journey. Now he had been presented with an exciting alternative that combined the convenience of a safer escape route with the pioneering challenge of finding a new way home. Being the kind of man he was, Drake did not hesitate to go for the main chance. Pausing only to lay a false trail by continuing northwards up the coast of America to the site of modern-day San Francisco – where he claimed what is now California for the Queen, naming it New Albion on account of the white cliffs that reminded him of Dover – he turned westwards and set sail into the unknown. It was at this point that he started thinking seriously in terms of completing a round-the-world voyage.

During the twelve days that he remained in the area around the Isla del Caño, careening *Golden Hind* and searching for fresh water and other supplies, he also spent some time in a secluded bay situated on the Osa Peninsula, which juts out from the south-western corner of Costa Rica. This picturesque inlet is known to this day as Drake Bay and one of our main purposes in going to Costa Rica was to take part in the ceremonial unveiling of two special plaques commemorating the historically significant visit of the first Englishman to circumnavigate the globe.

Undaunted by a torrential rainstorm, some sixty Costa Rican and British guests reached the remote site to unveil what is an impressive memorial. Afterwards we entertained the party on board Operation Drake's flagship, the brigantine *Eye of the Wind*, lying at anchor at almost exactly the same spot occupied by *Golden Hind* 400 years earlier.

Along the coast lay the 14,500-acre Corcovado National Park, already well known for its wildlife and environmental preservation. Although the Costa Rican National Parks conservation system was only begun in 1970, nine years later it already encompassed 3.5% of the country's total land mass. This was a greater proportion than found in any other Latin American country and, indeed, there are very few nations anywhere in the world that can boast such impressive concern for their natural resources.

Regrettably, I did not have time to visit Corcovado but, being fascinated by the Costa Rican attitude to conservation, I vowed to return. Perhaps Drake had heard of the gold-filled rivers flowing into the Pacific and may even have seen the sophisticated gold artefacts made by the pre-Colombian indigenous people. In fact, it was not until 1937, when two Italian scientists came in search of artefacts, that gold was rediscovered. Collecting pails of sand they were astounded to find nuggets large enough to be picked out by hand. Word spread and a gold rush ensued. For many decades miners sought their fortunes in the boulder-strewn creeks that bisect the emerald-green forests of the Península de Osa.

The area became known as the 'Wild West' and a similar code of conduct was established. For years, it was a simple way of life for a special breed of men. Honour and respect were the keys to survival and it is said that one could leave one's gold in one's shack and be gone for days without worrying that someone would steal it, but you could be killed in an instant by the slash of a machete if you showed disrespect at the *pulperia* – the local grocery-store-cum-bar. An article published in *Argosy* magazine in 1965 stated that 'life is rugged, food is scarce, and women are almost non-existent... but the place does have one thing to recommend it – gold, lots of it'.

Unfortunately, by the late 1960s miners were not the only ones interested in this mountainous region. The rivers that tumbled from the hills were home to some 20,000 people. Traders, merchants, middlemen, drug peddlers, bootleggers, poachers, hired guns, prostitutes and bar owners came to seek their fortunes – or to find a place to hide – and the old timers no longer left their stash unguarded.

A major logging consortium then moved in, intent on exploiting the commercial potential of the immense forest of trees, only to run up against impassioned opposition from an international conservation foundation determined to protect the last unspoiled tropical rainforest left in Central America. Economics, politics and natural history clashed and the Osa became a battleground. Thankfully, the environmental interests won and in 1975 the whole area was declared a legally protected reserve, Corcovado National Park going on to become recognised today as one of the most biodiverse places left on the planet.

However, although most of the gold miners were forced to leave the designated park area along with the loggers, a few still remain on the banks of the Carate River, named after the carat, or karat – the measurement used to define the purity of gold. Sheets of black plastic provide shelter, rice and beans provide sustenance for this shrinking band of prospectors and their precious Costa Rican coffee, and the throaty calls of the howler monkeys wake them up at dawn.

As in the days of old, even a meagre strike can provide liquor for a celebration.

On the northern side of the park, a totally different community exists. Living there is an indigenous group of 300 or so calling themselves Guaymi that came over the border from neighbouring Panama in the 1960s and settled in an area from which the Costa Rican government had ousted a logging company who were in conflict with local *campesinos*. In 1985 the Guaymi received 2,700 hectares as a tribal reserve, where they now struggle to make a living in the humid forest.

It was quite out of the blue in 2014 that I received an email from Lana Wedmore, an American ex-Operation Raleigh venturer who had been with us in Australia and had gone on to achieve her lifelong dream of setting up an eco-friendly lodge in the jungle. Passionate about saving the environment, she was seeking to protect the Osa Peninsula rainforest and invited Yoli and me to visit her at her famous Luna Lodge. From what she told us it was clear that there was something worthwhile to be done and so, with SES backing, we formed a twelve-strong team.

Our main priority, as ever, was to aid the Guaymi with medical and dental treatment and reading glasses for those in need. Chief Mariano Marquinez Montezuma kindly allowed us to use his spacious lodge as a base and even provided a unique hardwood dental chair carved from a local tree. Making full use of this, RAF dentist Ian McGarty carried out extractions, whilst our medical officer, Dr Jane Orr, treated patients in a storeroom. Shirley Critchley distributed glasses and schoolbooks and Yoli lectured the local children on conservation, using woollen puppets of turtles, peccary and jaguar, all made by members of the 'Knitwits' knitting group from Bournemouth.

Mark Entwistle, a chartered surveyor, mapped a number of eco-trails in the dense forest, set up for visitors by Chief Mariano, and Laurence Villard prepared a short history of the Guaymi people. Wildlife studies were carried out by reptile enthusiast Chris Kershaw and tracking expert Perry McGee, although relatively few animals were spotted in the area, possibly because of hunting. Deep in the forest we came across an extraordinary carving of a face with a feathered head dress, fifteen square feet, on a cliff face. Who had fashioned this and when? Mariano did not admit it, but because it was cut in heavy clay rather than rock, we suspected it was modern. While we were examining this fine piece of art, Chris casually pointed out that I was standing on a young venomous fer de lance hiding in the vegetation! We moved on gently. Meanwhile, Tom Gallagher and Richard Brown, both retired Royal Engineers, examined a damaged bridge and planned a new footbridge to be built on the main access trail to Corcovado Park.

Violent thunderstorms then struck the area, almost causing a serious accident when a tree weakened by termites crashed down between some of our tents. On 8th July we moved our base to Carate on the coast. Welcomed by a flock of raucous scarlet macaws, we met Lana and Costa Rican naturalist Gary Gomez, who had gathered a team of local people to set up shelters in a grove of tall palms beside the community church. In spite of numerous snakes and scorpions, this was a splendid campsite. The church was used as a clinic and a shelter during the worst tropical storms and a local woman became our hard-working cook, often aided by Yoli. Troops of monkeys raced around in the treetops and at 05:00 hours every day the roars of the howlers sounded reveille. In Corcovado Park, wildlife was much more common. Squirrels, spiders, white-throated capuchin monkeys and tamandua anteaters were spotted by the team, while Baird's tapir, ocelot, puma and even jaguar were reported by the guides.

British biologist Phoebe Edge of the Sea Turtle Conservation Committee of Corcovado, based in Costa Rica, briefed us on the programme to protect these endangered creatures nesting along the beaches. Our task was to assist in the refurbishment of the hatchery and at Carate a baby hawksbill sea turtle was discovered and guided safely to the ocean. This was the first sighting of the species in this area.

Our major job was the construction of a footbridge on the trail leading into the park. Engineers Tom and Richard tackled this, assisted by most of the team and with some extra help from some of the local gold panners. Gary Gomez, a man of many skills and impressive strength, played a leading role in the project. The original plan was to build a seventy-five-foot suspension bridge and a professional design was produced in the UK, but the park could not afford it. However, the energetic park director Etilma Morales came up with an alternative plan, using stocks of illegally cut timber that had been confiscated by her staff. The hardwood decking, bank seats and metal fittings arrived, but a problem arose over the two forty-foot main beams. A landowner had agreed to allow Gary to cut up a fallen tree on his property, but under Costa Rican law a special permit was required even though the tree was dead. Etilma produced the necessary permit, but the owner claimed he needed another. Three days of negotiation and lengthy phone calls to San José eventually produced the additional permit, but the landowner still prevaricated. At that point, with patience and time finally exhausted, Lana and Etilma instead managed to acquire two costly alloy girders in nearby Puerto Jiménez. These were rushed to Carate and, using welding kit borrowed from a friendly villager, were cut to size, with bolt holes burned through them.

The girders were then loaded aboard a massive ex American Army six-wheeled truck and hauled to the start of the trail. Regulations do not permit vehicles to travel on the beach, so a horse and cart were found. The girders then had to be placed sideways over the axle of the cart and a detached set of wheels fitted to each end. At low tide, this Heath Robinson transport set off for a slow two-mile progress up the beach. Amazingly, the skinny horse made good headway and the girders were soon in position, with Gary, the engineers and the rest of the team all working flat out in the 30°C heat to complete the job before our scheduled departure.

Meanwhile a steady flow of patients came to our clinic, where Melissa, a local dentist, also helped out. Shirley distributed reading glasses and taught children to play badminton with rackets brought from Britain. Perry, who runs the National Tracking School in Britain, instructed groups of young volunteers who were assisting the turtle project, whilst Yoli distributed hula hoops.

Our hosts, the Corcovado Social Development Association, wanted to create a sustainable community centre, so Mark surveyed a site on which it was planned to include a primary school, a health post, a small store and a meeting hall alongside the existing church. To allow for rising sea levels predicted as a result of global warming, the buildings were to be on stilts.

Chris was delighted by the diversity of wildlife he managed to find in the forest, including a large number of snakes. Deer and a tapir ventured right into our camp. American Villa Peche made long lists of the colourful birds spotted, including a huge white harpy eagle that hunted spider monkeys. Meanwhile, Shirley and a group spent time with the gold panners on Carate River and even found a gram themselves!

On Friday 17th July the bridge was completed. As Lana arrived to perform the opening ceremony, wearing a summer dress and straw hat and bearing bottles of champagne with which to celebrate the occasion, a waterspout corkscrewed in from the ocean, bringing with it a torrential downpour. Standing defiantly in the deluge, Lana cut the tape with a Swiss army knife and we downed the 'champers'. Sheltered by a huge banana leaf, Shirley snapped some photos and we trudged back to camp while the storm continued to rage around us. At our usual Burns supper, the Carate people relished the Stahly's tinned haggis and listened attentively to the odes.

On our last day we helped to clear the litter from a twelve-mile stretch of beach, a regular biannual operation aimed at preserving the beauty of the area and helping to protect the turtles. Most of the flotsam and jetsam brought in by the tide was plastic, some clearly from Japan, tons of which was taken to Puerto Jiménez for recycling. On the coast road back to San José we crossed the bridge over the Rio Tárcoles, where giant American crocodiles congregated, warming their ugly bodies in the sun, reminding one of Africa rather than South America.

WATER AND ELUSIVE BEARS

In 2012 the SES, in conjunction once again with the water charity Just a Drop, were approached for assistance in an ambitious scheme to supply potable water to village communities in an area around Cuzco in Peru by tunnelling into a mountain and Yoli and I were invited to visit the site by Condor Travel, who were helping to fund it.

Being hosted by this well-known travel company, we enjoyed a rather more upmarket reception than we had previously grown used to in South America. Accommodated in the luxurious Hotel Monasterio in Cuzco was quite an experience. The hotel stands on the site of a monastery built in 1595 on the ruins of the palace of Inca Amaru Qhala. A 300-year-old cedar tree stands in the central courtyard surrounded by attractive gardens and stone cloisters. It was a memorable introduction to historic Peru.

The village of Misminay, high in the Andes at 12,660 feet, was in desperate need of potable water due to the presence of gypsum in their existing wells. It was proposed to drive a 12,000-foot tunnel into a nearby mountain and collect water that filtered through the volcanic rock and clay above. This could then be piped down to a reservoir and supplied to village standpipes. The cost was estimated at US$100,000 and, as we puffed our way up the slope, I used my dowsing rods to locate subterranean streams and examined the rock. I was assured by the Peruvian engineer accompanying us on the recce that similar water projects had been successfully established along the Andes and after examining his plans and costings I gave my approval. We then retired to a celebratory lunch of local dishes, at which we were entertained with singing and dancing by villagers dressed in traditional costume. Unfortunately, both Yoli and I went down with a tummy bug, possibly resulting from the lunch, that dogged us for the rest of the visit. Heavily dosed with Imodium, we nevertheless managed to give a PowerPoint presentation on the work of Just a Drop in the imposing chapel at the Monasterio. I declined most of the spectacular dinner that Sammy Niego of Condor had kindly provided, but did manage a small plate of roast guinea pig while we discussed plans for a future expedition.

The flight home from Lima was far from smooth. Looking out from the departure lounge, I noticed fuel pouring out of one of the engines of our plane parked outside. As anticipated, this was followed by an unintelligible announcement informing everybody that American Airlines had filed for bankruptcy and that their pilots were flying 'by the book'. This meant a day's delay before, following several bureaucratic hold-ups and, due to more leaking fuel, the flight was cancelled. By this time one woman was in hysterics and the Peruvian passengers were preparing to riot. The members of the overworked ground staff were doing their best to help and, by good fortune, I got talking to a charming girl on the desk named Michelle, who quietly switched me on to a LAN-Chile flight via Madrid. I recorded in my log that she must have felt sorry for this poor old boy!

Once aboard I found myself seated next to the loo, which was frequently visited by a group of seemingly incontinent nuns. A rubbery omelette sustained me until we reached Madrid, where, thankfully, I was able to get a connection, only to find that the Iberia flight did not offer any onboard services whatsoever, no food nor water. I arrived at Heathrow hungry and parched, and immediately downed gallons to restore my body fluid level. So ended an epic a visit to a water project!

It was to be several years before the Misminay project was finally completed, owing to complications encountered in drilling the tunnel or gallery. In the meantime, we launched another expedition to Peru in 2014, thanks again to help from Condor Travel. At the request of the Desarrollo Rural Sustainable organisation we aimed to support the somewhat isolated Yanachaga–Chemillén

National Park in western Peru, where efforts were being made to preserve the fauna and flora, especially the spectacled bear. The area is composed largely of cloudforest, rising to over 9,000 feet and surrounded by a buffer zone with many poor villages. As well as Condor, donations were received from a number of individual sponsors, including Stephen Fry, who is passionate about spectacled bears. The nineteen-strong expedition included doctors, an army dentist, nurses, a paramedic and engineers, an agricultural expert, a botanist, zoologist, a video cameraman and a wildlife photographer. My friend Julian Butter came as deputy leader and Yoli was again responsible for organising everything.

Enjoying fine weather, the work started in the area to the west of the park, where the biological group under Julian worked at the Huampel research centre and Ben Clayton was able to film the fascinating courtship dance of Andean cock-of-the-rock birds. Meanwhile the medical and community aid teams worked among the village people. Moving to the eastern side of the park, the biological team used a large canoe to ascend the rapids of the Iscozacin River up to the Paujil research station. There, in the dense rainforest, they encountered kinkajous, porcupines and woolly monkeys. And although the spectacled bears proved frustratingly elusive, snakes, birdlife and insects were prolific. The porcupines were very tame and became regular visitors to their camp, one actually trying to get into Dr Katherine Welland's tent! Paujil proved to be extremely well run by a group of dedicated and enthusiastic wardens and the expedition zoologist, Dr Amy Hall of Jersey Zoo, was enthralled by what she described as a uniquely isolated and diverse environment.

In the villages the medical teams worked long hours to treat around 400 patients, while the dentist dealt with over 150. At the clinic we were shown the effect of snakebite serum being used on a writhing patient who had had a close encounter with a rattlesnake. Not a pleasant sight.

Medical supplies, schoolbooks and reading glasses were distributed in the villages and giving spectacled-bear teddies to children was recognised as a popular and effective way to encourage the conservation of wildlife.

Dave Smith, our enterprising quartermaster, and retired police inspector Mike Grady repaired numerous items of machinery, while Steve Clarkson from New Zealand gave useful agricultural advice, with a special interest in local fish and edible snail farming.

As so often seems to happen, it was only on the last day of the expedition that one of our drivers revealed that his father grew avocados and was plagued by spectacled bears that raided his trees. To distract them he placed barrowloads of rotting avocados in the forest. Amy and photographer Gregory Guida immediately rushed off to the site, where they found tracks of five bears but, alas, didn't actually see any. However, they left a camera trap on site in the hope that it would take photos of these elusive creatures, which apparently it did. When the bear hunters returned, we had our final debriefing in the sunlit garden of a small hotel we used as a rear base.

For me, the expedition seemed to have come to a satisfactory end, until I became aware of small blobs of white light crossing the vision of my right eye. 'I think you'd better see a retinologist,' advised our doctor and, as soon as we reached Lima, Yoli rushed me into an eye clinic.

'I have a friend who may be able to help,' confided the ophthalmologist, sending me off to see a senior doctor of the Peruvian Air Force. 'A fine eye surgeon,' he assured me.

So, after a hurried meeting with the Wildlife Department to pass on our report we met the major at his home. 'You have two small tears in your retina,' he stated as if it were nothing much, but by this time I was seriously concerned. 'Come with me,' he said, leading me out to his nearly new hybrid car, of which he was very proud.

Weaving his way through the rush-hour traffic, he drove me to the eye hospital, which was packed with patients, most of whom I judged to be poor people from the surrounding countryside. Sitting me down on an optical examining chair alongside another patient, he explained how he could repair the tears with a laser. The major's confidence was reassuring and after administering eye drops he started work on me and the other patient simultaneously. Various green lights flashed on and off and more patients trooped into the room, but in an hour the treatment was finished. At the reception desk I parted with a very modest sum for an excellent and painless job of work by a highly skilled surgeon. Later examinations back in the UK proved just how successful the treatment had been, but it was a strange way to end an expedition, which,

most gratifyingly, won high praise from the park authorities and the Peruvian Ministry of Health.

THE SEARCH FOR HMS *WAGER*

When directing the global youth expedition Operation Raleigh in Chile in 1986, the local chairman, Admiral Charles Le May, suggested that I should send divers to locate the wreck of the legendary British warship HMS *Wager*. Although time did not permit us to do the task, I did study accounts of the loss of the ship and twenty years later SES agreed to support an expedition.

The wreck of HMS *Wager* in May 1741, and the survival of a number of her officers and crew is one of the great sagas of the sea. Part of a British squadron of warships under the overall command of Commodore Anson, the twenty-eight-gun square-rigged sailing ship struck rocks close to a remote island in Chilean Patagonia, later to be named Isla Wager. The captain, David Cheap, and many of the crew managed to reach the island safely and as the ship was the store vessel for the squadron, they were able to salvage sufficient food to exist on the island for many months. However, once ashore a dispute arose regarding the captain's powers of command over the soldiers who had been aboard and the sailors, who, once the ship was wrecked, were no longer entitled to be paid by the navy. To some eyes, what now happened amounted to mutiny and after the captain had shot dead a midshipman, the survivors split into two groups. The captain and a party of officers and men, about twenty in number, eventually sailed northwards in open boats hoping to reach civilisation, while eighty-one crew members and soldiers went south in an extended longboat, through the Straits of Magellan to Brazil but only thirty survived this perilous voyage. Some died of starvation, others drowned and several were murdered by 'savages' when they went ashore along the way. However, as a record of a journey in an open boat amongst the cruel rocks and currents of the Magellanic region, this story is without parallel.

Meanwhile, Captain Cheap's party, which included Midshipman Byron, later Vice-Admiral Byron, grandfather of the famous poet, suffered unimaginable privations before being helped by friendly Chono people who took the last remaining four survivors in canoes to the island of Chiloé. There, thanks partly to the civilised and kind manner in which Commodore Anson had treated Spanish prisoners and also to the natural friendliness of the local people, the four officers, including Byron, were cared for extremely well. A local beauty begged the handsome Byron to marry her, and her uncle, a rich priest, offered him a treasure if he would. Byron, a staunch naval officer, believed it his duty to return to England and declined. It is known that the Spaniards recovered some cannons and a blacksmith's anvil from the wreck and after many months in Chiloé the survivors were sent to Santiago where again they were treated with much kindness. Even the Spanish Admiral sent to defeat Anson took a liking to them.

Considering that Britain was at war with Spain this was remarkable. Furthermore, Midshipman Byron was a great favourite with the women of the city! As the war ended, the four reached England, by which time Anson had returned in triumph and was now an Admiral. A further thirty-two members of the *Wager's* crew had also come home by various means. A court martial absolved Captain Cheap of blame for the loss of HMS *Wager* and no action was taken against those members of the crew who had disobeyed his orders. However, to avoid such a situation recurring, Admiral Anson introduced an Act of Parliament in 1748 extending naval discipline to crews wrecked, lost or captured. This was one of the reasons that led to the formation of His Majesty's Marine Forces, now the Royal Marines, in 1755.

Byron later returned to the area, leading a voyage of exploration during which he also searched for survivors of HMS *Wager* who had stayed behind and become part of the indigenous community, but found only blue-eyed, fair-haired children! However, he never forgot the enormous kindness and hospitality of the people of Chile, one of the earliest examples of Anglo-Chilean friendship, well remembered in naval circles and certainly known to Rear Admiral Lord Cochrane, an ex Royal Navy officer who later founded and commanded the Chilean Navy against the Spanish.

As well as trying to locate the wreckage of HMS *Wager*, our multitask venture in 2006 involved a twelve-strong land-based team under Colonel Mike Bowles, a stalwart former British Defence Attaché in Brazil, that was to work with Chilean scientists to study the botany, entomology and the Steffen and Jorge Montt glaciers, and perform community aid tasks in the remote township of Tortel.

Operation Raleigh had operated here and the town folk remembered HRH Prince William, our future king, working on the communal toilets. As a result, HRH had been made 'an illustrious son of Tortel'. However, we learned that Tortel's sewage system had since fallen into disrepair and was no longer in good order. Apparently, it discharged into the fjord beside the town and went out with the ebb, only to return on the incoming tide, causing gastrointestinal problems for the people. Just a Drop agreed to fund work on this, while the Rivers Foundation, which had often supported the SES community projects, kindly provided a large quantity of material for the local school and clinic.

To lead the diving team in search of HMS *Wager* I appointed the charismatic Major Chris Holt, a former Royal Engineers bomb disposal officer who then recruited a team of experienced divers. They had the challenging task of locating the wreck on the storm-bound coast of Patagonia. To support the work of the two groups, Yoli and I planned to set up a base in Tortel from where we could communicate by satellite phone and radio. Both parties would make videos. Len Vanderborn would film the land group and Lynwen Griffiths would cover the divers. We were also fortunate to have the logistic support of Graham and Carmen Gloria Hornsey and Adrian Turner, who had remained in Chile after Op Raleigh.

On 5th November our expedition assembled at the small town of Coyhaique, gateway to Chilean Patagonia, aided by CONAF, the Chilean National Forest Corporation. Two days later, breathtaking scenery raised the sense of remoteness as the team drove south through mountains with their towering snow-covered peaks. The terrain changed regularly from lush mountain pasture to deep deciduous woodland and scattered lakes of crystal-clear blue water, teeming with trout.

Tortel, built on the side of a hill alongside a deep fjord, had no streets, only wooden walkways, and was still inaccessible by road. All stores therefore had to be moved by local boats from the end of the vehicle track to huts made available to us by the mayor, or *Alcalde*.

I was very aware that this was an ambitious venture, made no easier by the unpredictable weather, which brought frequent storms racing in from the Pacific. The state of some of the local boats was also of concern, and the promise of the Chilean Navy's 130-foot petrol boat *Puerto Natales* was especially welcome. Chris Holt was less impressed by the good ship *Buzetta*, which our friends in Tortel had assured us was a seafaring vessel, easily able to carry his team to Wager Island, although admitting that the toilet was not quite ready. In his log Chris recorded a conversation with the skipper:

'Louis appeared more like a horseman than a sailor. His wide brimmed gaucho hat combined with his height (short), forearms (Popeye like) and moustache (Adolfian) meant that he looked interesting. Sadly, the initial descriptions of just the toilet not being quite ready were stretching the truth a little:

"Louis, this cabin is not ready – is it the toilet?"

"No – galley."

"What about the bridge, Louis?"

"No ready."

"The hold?"

"No ready."

"What about the engines Louis?"

"Eeeees a no ready."

It became immediately clear that we would not be leaving Tortel in a local boat for at least four days, if not a week, and that we would need to rely on the Chilean Navy if we were to get any useful time on Wager Island.'

Thankfully, the well-equipped patrol boat *Puerto Natales* appeared with a willing and able crew. Two experienced Chilean Navy divers were aboard and, as Chris discovered, Lieutenant Martin Goajardo was a useful communicator and the muscular chief diver, Jaime Soto, possessed impressive strength that he would put to good use whenever needed.

As they set sail, the sun beat down and dolphins raced along in the bow wave. However, in the weeks ahead both the land and diving parties were to experience ferocious weather, burning sun alternating with torrential rain and violent hailstorms. Keeping a record I noted that the highest temperature varied between 9°C to 18°C as squalls swept into the fjord.

Mike Bowles's group was to carry out flora and fauna surveys and examined the potential for ecotourism in the area, in addition to providing aid to the people. CONAF had sent along Piero Caviglia and Claudio Bravo, geographers studying glaciers. These two energetic young men became highly popular with the land party and their enthusiasm for their country and the environment was infectious. My friends Shirley Critchley and Sarah Royal had brought in a mass of equipment for the school and soon had the children organised into producing a play. Meanwhile, engineers Bethan Lewis and Stuart Jackman worked with the local authority to sort out the sewage problem. At the clinic, dentist John Holmes set up a mobile dental surgery that had been donated to the town.

Whilst Yoli and I monitored the weather and negotiated for suitable boats to keep him resupplied, Mike deployed to the Steffen glacier north of Tortel. This slow-moving, frozen mass is the most southerly of the Northern Patagonian Ice Field and was believed to be gradually reducing in size due to global warming.

The Patagonia ice fields are among the most important ice bodies in the world from a glaciological point of view and CONAF believed analysis of the behaviour of the glaciers was important in relation to the climatic changes. Thus Piero and Claudio's work was of great value. Moving as far as possible by boat, the team eventually had to roll up (or remove!) their trousers and wade into the icy rivers emerging from the glaciers in order to set up camp. The sudden appearance of a helicopter was found to be part of a search for a Swiss climber who had fallen into a deep crevasse on the glaciers, leaving an accompanying novice stranded on the ice. Happily, he was rescued, but the climber had died, a sad reminder of the hazards of working in this challenging terrain.

Undaunted, Mike's team continued working with our entomologist, Dr Nicholas Gold, and were pleasantly surprised to find both butterflies and moths present in spite of the inclement weather. His greatest discovery was *Bombus dahlbomii*, a golden-yellow bumblebee of thumbnail size. Describing this, Nicholas said: 'When William Congreve opined that Hell hath no fury like a woman scorned, he had clearly never had to put a large, angry bumblebee into a jam jar.'

The botanical studies fell to Dr Donald Mclintock, who was delighted with the collection he made for the Royal Botanic Garden in Edinburgh. As one of our medics, he was also interested in the mysterious tragedy that had taken place on Isla de los Muertos, a small island four miles north-west of Tortel, where 59 loggers had met mysterious deaths in 1906. Local people thought the cause was starvation, but some believed them to have been poisoned by their employers to avoid having to pay their wages. However, scurvy seemed a more likely answer. Whatever the truth, around thirty tombs with crosses remained and the island has been declared a Historic Monument.

Meanwhile, out in the stormy waters of the Golfo de Penas, the 'Bay of Sorrows', Chris Holt and his divers were camped on Wager Island. Using the information recorded by the Vice-Admiral Byron and other survivors of the wreck, they diligently searched the rocky shoreline. Bracing washes in the stream that ran past their tents and the experience of squatting on a log that served as the communal loo demanded a healthy sense of humour.

Their meals consisted largely of rice, pulses and Beanfeast, a meat-substitute product used on Operation Raleigh, supplies of which Yoli had obtained from Graham Hornsey. On the 11th November, Armistice Day, Chris conducted a service to remember HMS *Wager*'s men who had lost their lives so far from home. Captain Crawford and the crew of *Puerto Natales* joined them and a British Legion wreath was laid on a rock. Underwater, the drivers probed the beds of twisting kelp, searching the silty seabed for artefacts, but not even a discarded wine bottle could be found. On shore they struggled through dense, unforgiving vegetation seeking signs of the *Wager* survivors' camps, until drenching rain and violent gusts of wind forced them back to their tents. Back at Tortel we strode up and down the wooden walkways, seeking advice from the mayor, port captain and townspeople to pass on to Chris and Mike. Advancing fronts showed up on my barometer and one moment I worked in shorts, but within an hour had to don every garment I had.

On 16th November the barometer was rising and Mike had problems recharging his satellite phone, so Yoli and I loaded supplies and a spare battery on to the fishing boat *Tamara*. Due to her narrow beam she listed dangerously in the swell, but the sea calmed and we reached Estero Steffen to be greeted by pairs of gaggling Magellan geese. Transferring to a leaking rowing boat, we reached the camp to be welcomed with a mess tin full of hot Beanfeast, whilst Mike briefed us on his plan to move on to the Lucia Glacier. In biting cold wind we sailed back to Tortel to learn that *Puerto Natales* had to be repaired and would be replaced by her sister patrol boat *Puerto*

Arenas to bring the divers home. We also learned of a Chilean university archaeological team arriving to seek the *Wager* and that they had hired *Tamara*. I suspected a little professional jealousy of the sort that archaeologists sometimes display.

On 20th November everything started to happen at once. Yoli and I climbed the 260 slippery steps to attend the official opening of the mayor's clinic, on which we had worked, only to find that the mayor had forgotten all about it! Back at the base hut, gazing at the alpine scene of the greeny-grey fjord and the snow-capped peaks, I called Chris on Wager Island. Having found nothing, he wanted to move his camp westward and after juggling our available resources we arranged to dispatch a large fishing boat named *Santa Fe*.

By this time, however, a storm was raging at the divers' base and *Santa Fe*'s skipper was not prepared to risk crossing the turbulent channel that separated Wager Island from the mainland. She did eventually reach them, but then developed engine trouble and when Chris went to investigate he found smoke rising from the cramped engine room and a crewman working in the rising water level. Two large truck batteries were afloat and arcing against the metal fuel tank as the engineer tried to relight his sodden cigarette. Preparing for the worst, Chris donned his life jacket, but a few minutes later the engineer emerged clutching a handful of rusty parts that he tossed overboard before going below again and restarting the engine.

The move to the new location proved to have been inspired. Andy Torbet, the rugged and endlessly optimistic archaeologist, had made his way inland to some high ground that he believed to be the 'Mount Misery' described in the *Wager* survivors' logs. On return he confidently announced that the wreck must be just off the shore. Moving an inflatable along the shallow creek that ran a few metres from their tents, diver Chris Hunter swore as he stubbed his toe on something hard. Seeking to remove the obstacle, he cleared the sand and gasped at what he uncovered. Lying across the bed of the stream was what appeared to be a large section of a ship's hull. Could this be the lost wreck?

Back in the fjord, the land team sailed to the homestead of a local named Rafael to survey the retreating Jorge Montt Glacier, from which massive blocks of ancient ice were caving. Joining them a few days later, we were greeted by a large sea lion as we edged slowly between the mini icebergs. Sarah Royal, who had been running the base whilst the stalwart Chileans, Claudio and Piero, ascended the glacier, briefed us. Our stay was prolonged due to bad weather and we found a bed in Rafael's farm, which he hoped to turn into a B & B once the long-awaited road reached Tortel. That night a fatted lamb was roasted over an open fire and washed down with Chilean Merlot as we hoped for news from the divers on their storm-swept island, praying that the Chilean navy would be able to bring them out. As it turned out, they had just one day's food left when *Puerto Arenas* came butting through a choppy sea.

Later Chris reported that the wreckage was remarkably well preserved and lying under only twenty inches of water and four inches of sand. They had found four frames of a hull section with at least eight pieces of hull planking attached. Constructed completely of timber, the joints were made with trenails, wooden fixing pins that could be clearly seen. This would be consistent with *Wager's* construction and, more importantly, the size and shape of the timbers were of a type he had expected to find.

There were a number of interesting features – three rectangular cut blocks that could either be repairs of a split timber or evidence of her conversion from an East Indiaman to a warship; some ceramics applied to one of the timber ends, perhaps as a waterproofing putty used when she was repaired earlier in her voyage; and, finally, evidence of rough cutting and burning at the edges of some of the timber planks. Sadly, there was only one artefact, a musket ball discovered wedged between two of the frames.

Andy and the Chilean archaeologists were pretty certain this was indeed the remains of HMS *Wager*, but how on earth had she ended up in the creek, in less than two feet of water? The massive earthquake in 1960 (9.5 on the Richter scale) that had raised the surrounding ground area by up to twenty-three feet and had changed the outline of the island seemed a likely explanation.

In Tortel there was much rejoicing. The *Alcalde*, hoping for an influx of tourists, hosted a feast and thanked us for the sewage works. CONAF were delighted with the glacier surveys and scientific studies.

Back in Santiago I received a cautionary message from the First Lord of the Admiralty, reminding us that HMS *Wager* was still British property and stressing that we must not publish photos of any skeletons discovered! Two years later we were told Tortel was designated a World Heritage Site.

 The Quest for HMS *Wager*, Chile 2006

 The Osa Peninsula Expedition, Costa Rica 2015

The Search for the Spectacled Bear

ASIA AND PACIFIC

CHAPTER 25
THE ABODE OF GOD

Operation Raleigh had an enthusiastic committee in Hong Kong that selected many fine young people to join our expeditions. They would often be sponsored by Eric Hotung, a wealthy Anglophile and leading member of the Hong Kong community, and meetings with this extremely generous gentleman were always memorable.

Seeking his help for a long-cherished expedition to Tibet, I sat on his patio gazing out over the twinkling lights of the great city, sipping his favourite brandy. Having kindly agreed to back a mountaineering and scientific research project on Mount Xixabangma, in the Himalayas near the border with Nepal, Eric noticed it was 2am. 'I'd better run you home,' he said, and we climbed into one of his highly polished Rolls-Royces, with his chauffeur at the wheel.

Along with David King, a co-director of Operation Raleigh, I was staying in an apartment belonging to one of David's friends, who happened to be abroad at the time. David had gone back to the apartment soon after dinner, leaving me to enjoy a nightcap with Eric and assuming that I would be following on very shortly. However, arriving a good deal later in the Rolls, Eric and I found the door locked, with no sign of the security guard, who had long departed by then.

'Never mind,' smiled Eric, by then in his sixties. 'I'll get you in.' And with that he got the chauffeur to park the Roller close to a convenient drainpipe, handed him his jacket, hopped on to the bonnet and shinned up the pipe. How would I explain this to the police if he fell, I wondered. But on reaching the roof, my incredibly agile friend felt his way around the wall to another drainpipe and descended into the garden. Then, taking a small fruit knife from his pocket, he picked the lock on the garden gate, prised open a full-length window, entered the house and let me in through the front door. In the morning David, who held a position in Interpol, was amazed to see me, having remained asleep throughout the break-in. I learned later that Eric was something of an experienced cat burglar, having broken into the Japanese Army HQ in Shanghai during World War II to steal information for the allies. This extraordinary man now made possible our 'Jade Venture' expedition to climb Mount Xixabangma, the 14th-highest peak in the world at over 26,000 feet, while also making a study of the fauna and flora.

In September 1987 our science and mountaineering teams set out from Kathmandu by bus. I led the science team, which included my American friends Pam Stephany and nurse Paula Urschel, some young scientists and my pal Dr John Davis. Nearing the frontier, the

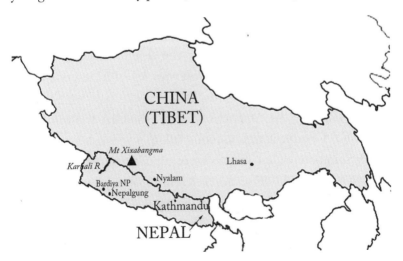

road was blocked by rockfalls, which meant we were at least able to acclimatise well to the altitude by having to march northward over the mountains. British climber Julian Freeman-Atwood, together with Army Lance Corporals John House and Jim Kimber, goaded on the 178 porters carrying our four tons of stores up the narrow paths. Each man bore a large box labelled 'Jade Venture' and an ICI logo.

Filing up a narrow mountain path, we came upon some American tourists, who watched the procession with interest. 'Tell me, sir,' inquired one elderly gentleman, 'what's ICKY?'

I looked puzzled for a moment until I realised that he was referring to the ICI logo. I quickly explained that ICI were our sponsors and manufactured, amongst other things, fertilisers and explosives.

'Looks as if you have enough to fertilise the whole of China, then blow it up,' retorted the American.

At this point John House happened to walk past carrying a steam lance to be used to drill holes in glaciers for the purpose of making scientific measurements. The evil-looking lance bore a strong resemblance to a weapon from *Star Wars* and displayed the words 'Made by British Aerospace', who also manufacture missiles. To contribute to the confusion, John wore a T-shirt inscribed 'Jade Venture – The Empire Strikes Back'.

'Oh, I get it,' the American winked. 'The CIA has companies like ICKY. Good luck to you, young fellow.'

Perspiration poured off us as we continued to climb up the high, steep slopes, picking off tenacious leeches that dropped from every bush. It was a fit, lean group that finally reached the border with Tibet and met our Chinese liaison officers, sent to keep an eye on us. As we threaded our way across a rockfall a distant rumble heralded another landslide. 'Hurry! Hurry!' cried our Chinese interpreter as we slipped and slithered on the loose scree covering the mostly obliterated trail. We had just completed the traverse when house-sized boulders came crashing down the mountains behind us. It was a close call and I was pleased to find a sturdy old Chinese army lorry awaiting us at the end of the trail. Ignoring the drizzle, we clambered aboard to wind our way through the precipitous gorges once known to caravan traders as 'The Gates of Hell'.

Far below us the rapids of the River Po, or Bhote Koshi, roared a greeting as the cold, white water tumbled from the great glaciers of the Himalayas to the plains of India. At the little town of Nyalam, old stone buildings and tin sheds provided a backdrop at the junction of two rivers. Now at 12,000 feet, we puffed and panted as we set up camp in the icy wind.

Leaving our mountaineers under my Sapper pal Henry Day to head straight for the base of the peak, I took the scientific team around to the north of the mountain in the Chinese lorry to study the archaeology, fauna and flora and made a base camp beside the still blue waters of Lake Paiku. Climbing into the snowfields, our chief scientist, Dr Henry Osmaston, an incredibly fit sixty-five-year-old, discovered a field of extraordinary gigantic ice pinnacles, over 130 feet high, at the edge of a glacier. Some 20,000 feet above sea level, they stood in rows like dragons' teeth. Such formations are only found on the north side of the Himalayas. Henry was most excited but returning to our camp he made an even stranger discovery. Leading across a snow-covered ridge lay a line of large, perfectly formed footprints, made since he had marched up the slope earlier. What animal could exist at this altitude, the scientist wondered as he carefully photographed the prints. They seemed to be made by a primate. Was this a clue to the legendary Yeti? On reflection, I reckoned it was a bear. Later, however, I photographed what appeared to be an upright figure some 800 yards away. Another shot of the same spot taken a little later showed nothing!

My twenty-three-year-old daughter, Emma, one of our nurses, made a contribution to the biological collection by catching a small fish at 19,000 feet on the northern slopes of Xixabangma. Herds of yaks bearing large red flags advanced, looking like troops of tanks, but actually part of a religious event. Our tents attracted the locals, who, unfortunately, took a liking to our boots and stole those left under the flysheets.

We could not continue without boots and the nearest place to buy replacements was Kathmandu, but if any of us Europeans left Tibet our visas would not permit us to return. However, the restrictions did not apply to our Hong Kong-based member, Ivan Hui, and he generously offered to go all the way back to Nepal to get replacements, which saved the day.

For the next part of the expedition, we drove back to the south-eastern side of Xixabangma. To reach the base of the mountain we needed yaks. Overnight, their price doubled! Although yaks appear large, clumsy creatures, they move with surprising grace, trotting quickly up the narrow trails on their dainty hooves, their flowing hair waving in the breeze. Said to be the most efficient, all-purpose animal in the world, they provide their owners with butter, meat and milk, as well as wool, clothes and even tentage. Their dung dries quickly in the sun and is used as fuel and building material, but they can be ill-tempered and obstinate. I noted the caution with which their handlers approached their sharply pointed horns and, as the beasts often suffer from violent diarrhoea, the herdsmen were also wary about getting too close to the other end! In our train were also several dzo, a cross between the yak and domestic cattle that, although smaller, carries the same load as its big brother.

Plodding up a gently sloping valley, it was a pleasant, easy walk, giving us time to enjoy the magnificent scenery and observe our surroundings. The whistles of the yak herders became for us the strange music of the mountains.

In the early afternoon we reached a major obstacle. A huge moraine rose 1,400 feet above a fast-flowing river. At an altitude of over 14,000 feet and in thin air, it took us an hour of puffing up an ill-defined path to reach a cairn, bedecked with prayer flags. Beyond the crest lay our intermediate base and we camped amongst piles of ration boxes, the emergency stores. Next day, after a steady climb through boulder fields, we reached Henry Day's main base, with its yellow tents nestling among the rocks in the shadow of the mountain. At 16,500 feet and only some five miles from the summit, this was to be our home too.

Our lead climbers, Luke Hughes and Stephen Venables, were already part way up the virgin east face of Xixabangma that rose at a sixty-five-degree angle from the glacier below. Meanwhile, John Davies and I used the lightweight Avon inflatable to begin a hydrographic survey of the clear, cold lake at 16,952 feet above sea level. 'You'll be dead in a couple of minutes if you fall in,' said John cheerfully as we launched the craft. Later we discovered that we had unwittingly established the world altitude record for rowing a boat!

All was going well until the BBC World Service brought news of a hurricane in Britain, the stock market crashing and storms sweeping up into the Himalayas! Unsurprisingly, on 17th October ominous dark clouds swept up from Nepal and as dusk fell the temperature registered below zero and the first flakes of snow began to swirl around the tents. Later that night the storm struck and raged for the next thirty-six hours. It was bitterly cold and pitch-black inside our little tent. Emma's breathing was laboured and rapid. I was having difficulty too. *Is it the altitude?*, I wondered. And yet we had been above 16,000 feet for several weeks and were fully acclimatised. Reluctantly pulling my arm from the warm sleeping bag, I rolled down my glove and glanced at the faint luminous dial of my wristwatch. It was 03:00. *Funny*, I thought, *it's very quiet outside, with no sound of wind.* My shoulder touched the tent wall: it was solid. Not just frozen stiff as usual, but as solid as concrete. I remembered that it had been snowing lightly as we turned in. Now we were virtually entombed and starting to suffocate.

'We've got to get out. Get dressed quickly!' I shouted.

'Father, why must you always do things at three o'clock in the morning?' came my daughter's sleepy reply.

There was no time to be lost. Pulling on thick socks, overtrousers, boots, balaclava and outer gloves, I turned to the entrance. The tent door was frozen solid too, and it took several strong pulls to open the zip. A wall of snow cascaded inwards. Now we heard the wind and, digging through the snow with our mess tins, cleared a way to gasp fresh air. My torch beam reflected off the flakes driven horizontally by the fury of the storm. Nearby I heard cries of laughter, but in the blizzard I could see nothing. Suddenly a brilliant blue flash of lightning showed the girls' tent had collapsed. With amazing good humour they staggered to the more robust army mess shelter. In base camp everyone dug to save tents and stores, whilst on the slopes of the mountain the climbers kept a wary vigil for the ever-present threat of an avalanche.

Camp two was totally buried, three precious video cameras and much of our best film lost. At 20,600 feet, four mountaineers were marooned for three days. Our advanced science camp was cut off on a distant glacier. The deep snow, shortage of fuel and the fact that no yaks could possibly reach us soon changed the expedition into a battle for survival. The mountaineers evacuated most of their camps and Henry Osmaston's party had an epic escape from their glacier in what was, by now, a full-scale blizzard. They were lucky to reach base camp with only mild frostbite.

To make matters worse, a petrol stove exploded in our mess tent and Annabelle Huxley, a member of the science group, and I were only saved from serious burns by the rapid action of Paula and Emma, who hurled us, flaming, into a snow drift. Our demi-paradise had become a freezing hell. Eventually, the storm passed and, as the sun broke through, temperatures rose again. However, we now had to contend with a six-foot blanket of soft snow. We'd have given much for a pair of skis in our retreat! As the sun swung past, we trudged along a high ridge in knee-deep snow. Exhausted, we camped beside a massive boulder, the women in the one tent we carried and the men sleeping in their bivvy bags in the snow. A French climber coming up from Nyalam warned us that another storm was predicted. We radioed this news to Henry Day and wondered how on earth the climbers would get out in the event of further heavy snowfall.

Finding shelter in a herdsman's stone hut, we met Polish climbers Wojtek Kurtyka and Halina Sickaj, who generously shared their 93%-proof 'mountain tea', a greatly appreciated brew. Supper was rich fruit cake, retrieved from an emergency-stores dump we had left on the way in. Fortunately, it was packed with calories! Stepping outside to scan the moonlit mountain face I saw something move.

It looked like a couple of foxes, but at dawn Wojtek showed me fresh wolf tracks. Next day two shaggy wolves followed a couple of hundred yards behind us as we plodded downhill.

Finally reaching Nyalam, we learned of a number of tragedies caused by the blizzard. People had frozen to death in buses trapped in the high passes on the Lhasa road, villagers had died of hypothermia, and several expeditions had lost men in avalanches. A group of Tibetans watching us hobble in shook their heads in amazement that we had survived our stay on Gosainthān, the Sanskrit name for Xixabangma, meaning the 'Abode of God'.

Now all we had to do was to reach Kathmandu. The road along which we had driven forty days before was blocked in a hundred places by landslides, and the twenty-five-mile walk through the 'Gates of Hell' was littered with mud, rocks, fallen trees and tangled telephone wires. Pausing only to go in unsuccessful pursuit of a Tibetan mouse for the zoological collection, we pressed on. It was dark when we stumbled into a hut on the outskirts of Zhangmu, our frost-nipped feet hurting like hell, and begged a welcome dish of noodles. Refreshed, we traversed the worst landslide of all, guided by a drunken Tibetan and a fading pencil torch. 'If we could see where we were going, I don't think we'd do this,' remarked John as we scrambled over the loose rubble and around cascading waterfalls.

After a night in a flea-ridden dormitory at the local hotel, we crossed the frontier into Nepal. Disappointed tourists waited in vain for permission to enter Tibet, for foreigners were banned once more following riots in Lhasa. Chinese hostility seemed to be emphasised by the roar of a nearby explosion that sent rocks flying around us. Our newly acquired Nepali porters dropped the baggage and fled for their lives, whilst we sheltered beneath our packs and prayed that the Chinese army engineers would cease blasting.

Finally, we reached Kathmandu, where good friends Jim and Belinda Edwards took us in and provided a wonderful feast. I needed it. I had lost twenty-six pounds and the nails of both my big toes had been detached by frostnip. On the mountain, Steven and Luke came tantalisingly close to the summit, but were turned back at 23,950 feet by strong winds. The team had spent the night in a snow cave with the temperature at −35°C, but although denied the peak of Xixabangma they did reach the summit of nearby Pungpa Ri at 24,426 feet. We had lost all our equipment on the mountain, but did bring out the scientific specimens and no-one died. I shall certainly never forget my visit to the 'Abode of God'.

CHAPTER 26

MAMMOTHS AND TIGERS

On my way to Tibet in 1987 I had paused for lunch in Kathmandu, as one does. Filling my glass with ice-cold beer, my chum John Edwards told me: 'I've got a mystery for you to solve in west Nepal.'

'Tell me more,' I replied, instantly intrigued.

'There's a huge creature destroying the locals' crops and scaring the pants off them,' he said. 'They say it's a mammoth.'

I chuckled sceptically. 'Get a few facts and I might look for your giant one day,' I replied, never imagining that this would turn out to be the start of a quest that would lead to an astounding discovery.

Three years later a bubbly young woman named Sarah Bamfylde, veteran of an Operation Drake expedition to Papua New Guinea, burst into my London office and thrust a photograph into my hands. 'I took this from a canoe on the Karnali in Nepal,' she said excitedly. 'What do you think it is?' The snap showed what appeared to be a massive, very strange-looking elephant with a great bump on its head, huge tusks and a heavy tail. Could this be Edward's mammoth? Zoologists I consulted were as curious as I was, mainly because of the very unusual shape of the head, which they could not explain. Some thought it might be a tumour resulting from a bullet wound, but they all urged me to go and find it. So began the quest.

It was to be an incredible pursuit – comic at times, occasionally back-breaking, and made all the more extraordinary not just by the nature of our quarry, but by the make-up of the team of amateur explorers that set out on its trail. The members included senior professionals from the worlds of big business, banking, insurance, accountancy and the law, mostly middle-aged people looking for an exciting new challenge. The first time I had led such a diverse and inexperienced group on an expedition was when, just a few months before Sarah Bamfylde came up with her photograph, I had gone in search of some amazing archaeological ruins in the Kalahari, a highly successful enterprise that had proved an excellent and enjoyably effective means of reviving creative thinking and remotivating mature people.

So now, in February 1992, with the support of Jim Edwards (John's older brother and owner of the famous Tiger Tops Lodge), our group set out over the mountains, accompanied by forty porters. Our aim was to explore the Karnali River gorges with inflatables *en route* to the remote forest of Bardiya in the Terai region of southern Nepal. Breathing hard on the slope for three days got us all much fitter. However, we were nervously apprehensive as we approached the river. It had never been navigated at low water and the rapids were likely to be obstructed by huge boulders.

'It may be technically more difficult, but the current should be down,' confided Megh Ali, our muscular chief boatman, as we enjoyed a preprandial mug of rum by the campfire.

We hit big water on the first morning: 'Paddle together,' screamed Megh as the inflatable slid down a cascade into the wall of towering waves. Freezing glacier water washed over us as we bounced through foaming torrents, hitting rapid after rapid.

One especially dangerous obstacle forced us to lower our craft, unmanned, on lines, but in eight days we navigated no less than sixty-eight cataracts, charted the river, caught fish for science and the pot, and counted birds, crocodiles and mammals, although still no sign of giant elephants. Reaching the Bardiya reserve, we found an undisturbed wilderness, with the thick, riverine forest, grasslands, dry hills and the Sal woods being home to a density of wildlife and birds.

On 7th March a huge fish-eating crocodile watched us cruise out of the last great gorge into the jungle-covered valley and as the sun set we found five lovely female elephants and their *phanits* (mahouts) awaiting us on the bank. Honey Blossom and her sister, Luksmi, had come with three younger elephants to carry us on the next phase of the quest. With raised trunks they trumpeted a welcome. In the days ahead we would come to love these lumbering jumbos as they transported us through the dark forest.

Having erected our tents, we clutched steaming mugs of tea as we listened to the news from the trackers, who had been working ahead. 'Only last night a *tulu hatti* [big elephant] destroyed a banana plantation two hours from here,' reported Pradeep Rana, the naturalist who was to direct the hunt.

'How big?' I asked.

'The footprints are very large, you must go see for yourself,' replied Pradeep.

'I'll go,' volunteered John Hunt, an enthusiastic manager of the Marks & Spencer store in Belfast. Being a marathon runner and skilled at estimating the requisite waist size of ladies' knickers at a glance, I reckoned he was suited to the task!

Clutching his tape measure, John left at dawn and, moving through the dripping grass, soon picked up fresh tiger spoor and the track of a large rhino. Then his Nepali tracker pointed out a vast circular print in the mud. '*Tulu hatti!*' he hissed. The print was fresh and water oozed into the impression as they measured the diameter. 'Twenty-one inches, multiplied by six for the shoulder height – wow, that's ten foot six!' whispered John, calculating the size of the beast by a tested formula. 'A very big elephant!'

It was still dark when, very early next morning, festooned with binoculars and cameras, we hauled ourselves up the elephants' tails and into the stout wooden howdahs. I chose to ride Honey Blossom, the matriarch, and quickly made friends with this four-ton pachyderm by passing her a banana. At the river the elephants pushed down the bank and then, tucking in their hind legs, slid gracefully down on their bottoms. Like five fat cruisers in line ahead, they entered the swirling water, leaning into the current, feeling their way forward. On the other side, we picked up the previous day's tracks and headed into the forest.

The elephants knew their way through the almost impenetrable jungle. Without breaking their stride, they would extend their trunks to tear off any succulent-looking vegetation within reach, stowing it neatly into their cavernous mouths. If one's hat blew off or one dropped anything, at the *phanit*'s quiet order the highly intelligent creature would pick it up daintily with the tip of its trunk and hand it back over its head. Branches or creepers high enough for the elephants to pass beneath, but likely to strike the passengers, would be broken off or pushed aside by the trunk.

Our sharp-eyed naturalist saw it first. 'Look!' he called out quietly, pointing. I saw nothing at first, but then the grey background I had assumed was a patch of sky beyond the trees began to move. It seemed that an enormous pile of rocks was sliding silently through the forest; then a huge creature emerged. Its great domed head, heavy tusks and bulbous body gave it the appearance of a fat old gentleman with spare tyres and double chin. A thick, serpent-like trunk sought our scent. 'My God!' gasped someone. A second grey mountain was moving into view, even more massive than the first, his enormous tusks curved upwards and his huge head crowned with an even higher dome. Flapping their ears to cool themselves, the ghostly apparitions came on, moving effortlessly towards us, pausing only to pluck some choice branch or seize a trunk full of grass. The giants were fifty yards away and our mounts were shaking with fear. They too had never seen anything quite like this before, but their *phanits* spoke gently, coaxing them to retreat slowly across a riverbed.

Measurements of the footprints showed Raja Gaj (king elephant), as our trackers named the big fellow, to be eleven foot three inches at the shoulder, while Kancha (younger one) was around ten foot six inches. I knew they must be among the largest Asian elephants ever seen, but could not explain their unusual shape, nor why they apparently existed only in this particular remote valley. But I doubted they were mammoths.

For ten days we followed them at a discreet distance, sometimes catching up with them in dense jungle and at other times in the tall grass along the river. We stalked each other in a slow-moving game of cat and mouse. They seemed to regard us with amused indifference, although when they were together and we got a bit too close Kancha would act as an escort and see us off. At other times the two of them would show off to our girls, as we called our female elephants, dusting themselves with clouds of dirt or bending stout trees. We had heard report of wild females, but didn't actually see any.

The BBC World Service news had just ended and I had closed my eyes when Pradeep called out: 'Come quickly, Raja Gaj is here.'

'What, in camp?' I exclaimed, putting on a sarong and grabbing a torch.

On the moonlit path to the elephant lines I found the *phanits* agitated and frightened. 'Big elephant has taken Honey Blossom,' wailed one of them.

Sure enough, her tethering chains were broken and she could not do that herself. Just inside the forest we saw a black mass and I shone my torch. It turned and I faced two enormous tusks. Thirty feet away stood Raja Gaj. His eyes reflected the light then, ears forward, he came shambling at me in a deliberate charge. But as I flicked off the torch, he stopped. Elephants have poor sight and the wind was coming from him. Quietly, someone thrust our image intensifier into my shaking hands. Now able to see in the dark, we stood silently watching him in the green electronic light as he tried to locate us. His long thick trunk sniffed the air while just beyond him I could see Honey Blossom.

'Get everyone among the boulders by the river for safety,' I ordered as the *phanits* advanced with torches of burning grass. For a moment the raider stood and I thought he would charge again, but then with a snort he wheeled and, pushing down a two-foot-thick tree as if it were a matchstick, disappeared into the darkness. Before Honey Blossom could follow, her *phanit* climbed up her tail and on to her shoulders, driving her back to camp. A disappointed lady and a brave man! I returned to the campfire, looking ridiculous in sarong and flip-flops, and poured myself a stiff Scotch.

When news of our discovery reached the outside world, there was immediate interest. Some zoologists suggested the massive size and strange shape meant they were survivors of a herd that had existed in isolation for many years and could be mutants, the result of inbreeding.

To investigate the mystery further I led ten more expeditions over the next thirty years to study these extraordinary creatures. Professor

Adrian Lister, now of the Natural History Museum, joined us and handled the scientific research. Sue Hilliard, a fingerprint officer of the Merseyside Police, developed a way of footprinting the wild elephants using Polaroid cameras and computers. Herpetologist Mark O'Shea came along to study the reptiles.

We soon discovered four large bulls, but it was not until 1997 that two wild cows and a calf appeared in front of us one dawn. Eventually, we established that Raja Gaj had a thriving herd of over fifty tucked away in the Sal forest. With the advent of DNA testing we sought to get a sample from Raja Gaj. There were no volunteers to pluck a hair from his great body, but Adrian eventually obtained a sample from his dung. Compared with the DNA of Siberian mammoths and many domestic elephants it clearly indicated that our giants were Asian elephants. However, there was an interesting comparison with the skull of an ancient elephant, *Elephas hysudricus*, that Adrian tracked down in a Kathmandu museum.

The study continued and, realising they had a unique tourist attraction, the Nepali government sent in a battalion of soldiers to keep out poachers. A postage stamp showing Raja Gaj was issued and we took in a team from Cicada Films to shoot a TV film that went out worldwide. The well-known actress and conservationist Rula Lenska joined us for two expeditions and helped us to publicise the Bardiya park. And together, she and I published a book, *Mammoth Hunt: In Search of the Giant Elephants of Nepal.*

Throughout our expeditions we became aware of the damage caused by wild elephants to villages around the reserve. One village in particular suffered badly, and as a result was putting out poison to kill Raja Gaj and his herd. To win the hearts and minds of the villagers we always took them gifts, including a first computer for their school and reading glasses. Our doctors and dentists treated patients and, to show the children that not all elephants were wicked, we got them to ride our domestic jumbos and play football. We also set up a fund to pay for the schooling of the three children of a farmer killed by a wild elephant while trying to protect the family's stock of grain. We learned much about the local culture and met their shamans, one of whom even claimed to have brought people back from the dead.

Various other beasts apart from the elephants were sighted and there were one or two close encounters of an alarming kind. Seizing the tail of a serpent disappearing into the bush, herpetologist Mark O'Shea unexpectedly found himself struggling with a sixteen-foot Burmese python, which then nearly got the better of him. However, once coiled inside a sleeping bag it calmed down and we discovered a deep bite in its back, possibly from a tiger. Dr John Davies, our Medical Officer, stitched it up and the reptile made a complete recovery. Later, John removed a bamboo spike from one of our domestic elephant's feet. Quietly, she stood up, lifted her foot and stroked John's back!

In no time Mark had an impressive snake collection that included a lively black Indian cobra and a highly venomous Russell's viper that Honey Blossom had spotted by her foot. There was also an unidentified water snake caught in the river. The collection was kept in plastic tubs in the science tent. Alas, one night a sudden violent storm collapsed the tent and the snakes escaped. We had an interesting time collecting them in the pitch dark. Sadly, the water snake, a much-prized rarity, got clean away.

A joy to behold was a young 'blue bull' antelope, or nilgai, that had been tamed by soldiers guarding the park and trained to sniff out poachers. There were also numerous man-eating mugger crocodiles as well as the huge but relatively harmless gharial fish-eating crocs. Sloth bears were reckoned to be more dangerous than tigers and were always avoided, but one of our Nepali guides, named India, had an extraordinary way of handling aggressive animals. Sitting safely on Honey Blossom, I watched fascinated but concerned as he stood unflinching in front of an angry, advancing Kancha, and when the menacing beast was only thirty feet away waved his arms and shouted, 'Go back,' whereupon the tusker stopped in his tracks, lowered his trunk and strolled into the forest. I had previously come across a white hunter in Kenya who seemed to have the same rapport with even the most fearsome and distrustful wild creatures.

Without doubt it was the big cats that provided us with the greatest thrills. The alarm calls by the langur monkeys and the spotted deer (or chital) frequently warned us of the presence of the splendid Royal Bengal tiger which was multiplying in the area at the time.

In 2012 I took my three grandchildren, aged nine to fourteen, plus six other youngsters on a family expedition, which they loved, especially when it came to helping the *phanits* bathe their elephants in the river at the end of the day. We had several exciting encounters, and when an angry tigress charged the elephant on which we were riding, my grandson Jack grabbed my arm saying: 'I don't want to be eaten, Grandpa.' Indeed, there is nothing more terrifying than the blood-curdling roar of a charging tiger.

One of my most memorable experiences involving big cats came on an earlier expedition when we found ourselves in an area where there was a most unusual concentration of tigers. Dinner had just finished when a series of deep roars reverberated through the forest.

Above: Dave Smith cooks pancakes at Rio Vaqueti, Bolivia, 2012 (page 266)

Below: The remarkable submersible bridge, or *callapo*, we used on the Rio Vaqueti, 2012 (page 267)

Below: Kaieteur Falls, Guyana (page 289)

Above: Geoff Roy with an anaconda, Orinduik Falls, Guyana, 1993 (page 294)

Above: Wai Wai elder, Masakenari, southern Guyana, 2000

Below: Umana Yana (community meeting place), Masakenari (page 303)

Above: Masakenari village, southern Guyana (page 326)

Below: Lessons on the grand piano we brought from England to Masakenari, 2000 (page 319)

Above left: Major General Joe Singh, visiting us at Masakenari, 2002 (page 323)

Above right: Dave Smith with a giant cane toad, Masakenari, 2010

Below: With the Wiwa, displaying the 'lucky' Jersey flag I always carry, Sierra Nevada, northern Colombia, 2016 (page 349)

Above: The Clinique La Prairie ambulance boat on the Amazon near Leticia, Colombia, 2017 (page 358)

Below: Erecting the water tank at Yawapade, Ecuador, 2012 (page 382)

Above: Shirley Critchley fitting glasses for the Guaymi, Osa Peninsula, Costa Rica, 2015 (page 390)

Below: We use woollen puppets on all our expeditions to encourage children to protect wildlife. Pictured: Yoli with spectacled bear puppets, Peru, 2014

Below: Chris Kershaw measuring a Guaymi carving, 2015 (page 391)

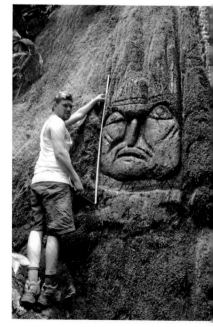

Above: The HMS *Wager* diving team at Tortel, southern Chile, 2006 (page 403)

Below: Chilean scientists Piero Caviglia and Claudio Bravo at the Lucia Glacier, 2006 (page 405)

Above: My daughter Emma sharing my tent on the slopes of Mount Xixabangma, Tibet, 1987 (page 420)

Below: Stephen Venables (*left*) and Luke Hughes (*right*) on Mount Xixabangma, 1987 (page 419)

Stephen Venables on Mount Xixabangma, 1987 (page 419)

© LUKE HUGHES

Above: An early meeting with the 'king elephant', Raja Gaj, in the Bardiya forest, western Nepal (page 428)

Above: Our outstanding photographer Deepak Rajbanshi and his faithful Nikon on the 2019 Bardiya expedition

Below: Royal Bengal tiger wading the Karnali River in Bardiya

Above: Crossing the Karnali River, Bardiya, 1995 (page 427)

Below: Capsizing is a common accident on the rapids. Pictured here: A capsize on the Trishuli River, Nepal, 1992

Above: Judith Heath, the expedition botanist of the Explorers Club and SES, crossing the Brahmaputra in Arunachal Pradesh, India, 1993

Above: Apatani woman (page 439)

Below: American Bob Atwater of the Explorers Club with Parbati Barua, 'Queen of the Elephants', at Manas National Park, Assam, 2015 (page 454)

Above: With Pam Stephany and our guide, flying the Explorers Club flag in the Tavan Bogd mountains, Mongolia, 1991 (page 473)

Below: Przewalski horse, Khustain Nuruu National Park, Mongolia (page 483)

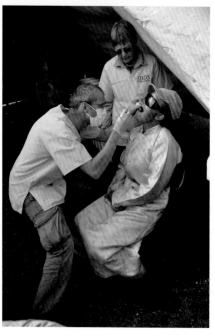

Above: British Army dentist Major Riaz Usmani (Royal Army Dental Corps) at work in Mongolia's Khovd region (page 491)

Above: SES Council Member Peter Felix wearing his head net to protect against mosquitos on the 2016 expedition in Mongolia

Below: A feast in a nomad's *ger*, western Mongolia, 2005

Above: Aircraft fitter and Colonel J. W. Harris (United States Air Force) (*right*) beside the newly painted logo on his P-47, April 1944, Nadzab air base, Papua New Guinea (page 509)

Below: Captain Mike Gambier, Royal Marines (*2nd from right*) and his patrol on the wreck of Colonel Harris's P-47 in the Finisterre mountains, Papua New Guinea, 1979 (page 509)

Above: A baby artrellia (Salvadori's monitor) – the much-feared lizard, Papua New Guinea, 1979 (page 512)

Above: A tribesman of Papua New Guinea, pictured here at the national festival of PNG tribes at Mount Hagen, 1979

Below: Leg-rowing fisherman on Inle Lake, Myanmar (page 519)

Clearly, two tigers were fighting, or perhaps mating – tigers make similar noises at the height of passion! However, next day we had a group going out on foot to view birds, so I decided to take the precaution of sweeping the area of twelve-foot-high elephant grass in the surrounding area, which, as it turned out, was just as well.

Mounted on five of our jumbos, we entered the towering grass. Nothing was visible among the tall stems, there was no discernible movement of any kind, and not even a bird called. Then, with no warning, the largest tiger I'd ever seen rose up right in front of my elephant, Laxmi Kali. Roaring its head off, with teeth bared, the tiger reared up on its hind legs. I saw the huge paws striking out, the claws like a handful of carving knives. Laxmi Kali shrieked, lashing out with her trunk, and the snarling cat rolled to one side and disappeared.

Moments later, Nick Turner came on the walkie-talkie. 'There's a bloody great tiger beside us,' he yelled.

'Take a photo of it and let's get clear,' I retorted.

Nick did just that. But better still, Londoner Sheila Sulley, riding with Nick, captured the encounter on video film, complete with roars! Then to our astonishment the tiger, whom our Nepali naturalists named Snow White because of the pronounced white markings on the face, sat down in an open patch as if nothing had happened. 'He must have a kill near here,' said guide Ram Din. So, leaving three elephants to keep an eye on Snow White, we backtracked to the site of the initial confrontation. Taking quite a risk Shakali, another guide, climbed down from Laxmi Kali and, along with Ram Din, searched the ground. They made an extraordinary discovery. In an area of flattened grass splattered with blood and fur, lay the paws and head of a tigress. Snow White appeared to have torn the female apart and eaten her. No-one I knew had ever come across such a case of a tiger killing and devouring another full-grown adult.

Carrying the grisly remains back to camp, we took them to the tent of Andrew Mitchell, our zoologist, who was enjoying a lie-in. His wife Laura woke him, holding the skull up to the bed whilst we made a low roar. Andrew opened his eyes, focused and yelled. Only the previous day he had almost fallen off his elephant and into the jaws of a tiger while making a recording for the BBC. Later, Snow White killed a local woman and was said to have then been captured by the wildlife department and taken to the zoo in Kathmandu; a rather sad end.

Amazingly, I was the only casualty on our elephant quests, although my injury was no fault of our elephants. As a cameraman, I was sitting directly behind the *phanit* which necessitated holding on to the corner posts of the howdah as it swayed from side to side. At times the movement is pretty violent and one has to grip hard. By the end of one expedition I had lost the feeling in the end of a finger on my right hand and could hardly feel the camera button. John Davis diagnosed carpal tunnel syndrome. 'Bricklayers get it and if it doesn't get better you'll need to have an operation to free the trapped nerve,' he explained. Back in Britain, a surgeon in our local hospital set to work.

'How did you do this?' he enquired as I submitted myself to his knife.

'Riding a galloping elephant,' I replied. He looked mildly surprised as he sliced open my palm. With my arm in a sling, it made a great story at dinner parties.

I returned to Bardiya in 2019 for an expedition organised by local conservationist Rajan Chaudhary, during which we noted a huge increase in the tiger population, sadly resulting in several fatal attacks on the people. This, coupled with the pandemic, is having a detrimental effect on this last piece of the Terai wilderness and those who live there. We sent out some much-needed funds and, Covid permitting, hope to return once more to this enchanting refuge of giant elephants and the magnificent Bengal tiger.

 You Tube Bardiya, Nepal 2019

 You Tube Operation Raleigh, Return to Nepal 1992

 You Tube The Giant Elephant Quest in Bardiya, Nepal 2012

 You Tube The Beast of Bardiya

CHAPTER 27
KIPLING COUNTRY

Ever since 1873, when the British Raj sealed off a remote mountainous region in the north-east corner of India to save it from cultural destruction by missionaries, what is now the state of Arunachal Pradesh has remained one of the most isolated and hidden places on earth. Sandwiched between Bhutan, Tibet and Myanmar, it is a land of mountains, turbulent rivers and extremely dense jungle. Almost every scrap of open ground is cultivated, with village houses built of bamboo standing on stilts on steep hillsides. In 1993, the population of 800,000 was mostly Mongol and made up of around twenty-six different tribes, mostly animists worshipping the sun and the moon, although there are also scattered Buddhist and Christian communities.

After independence in 1947, the Indian government maintained the Raj's policy of separation, naming the region the North-East Frontier Agency and effectively creating a country-within-a-country, to which even Indians from elsewhere in the subcontinent could only gain entry if they had a special permit. It became almost totally closed in 1963 following an incursion by China, who claimed it to be part of Tibet. Renamed Arunachal Pradesh in 1972, it had no major airport and its borders were manned by the tough but polite soldiers of the Assam Rifles, many being Gurkhas from Nepal. It had remained largely cut off, with very few of the people living there ever having contact with any foreigners, certainly not Europeans.

I had long hankered after an opportunity to explore this forbidden and little-known province. Nearly all those to whom

I mentioned my interest in the place, including many Indians, responded by looking blank and asking: 'Arunachal Pradesh? Where is that exactly?' They had never heard of it. Then in 1993 my chum John Edwards got in touch to say he'd met the Arunachal Commissioner for Home Affairs, who had expressed interest in the possibility of inviting a small party of scientific explorers to visit the state. It would not be cheap: US$200 per person per day, but for this the local government would provide accommodation, meals, guides and transport, including boats, vehicles and elephants.

This was an offer I could not refuse and through the Scientific Exploration Society and the Explorers Club I set about recruiting a team. We soon had botanists, doctors and students of traditional medicine, a zoologist and John Hunt, now an experienced elephant handler, who was to make a video of the expedition. Eight in all, we came from Britain, India, Singapore and USA. Once word of our impending expedition got out, the phone began to ring off the hook with calls from orchidologists and other specialists eager to join us.

But transport was severely limited and accommodation would barely be sufficient for our eight members, so we had to turn them down.

The monsoon hits north-east India in June, but the rains usually start in April, so we had to move fast if we were to go there before the deluge that makes this the wettest place on earth, with an annual rainfall that can reach 500 inches. Within just a few weeks we were on our way. Equipped with jungle boots, lightweight waterproof Gore-Tex clothing, Swiss army knives and mosquito nets, plus supplies of Colman's Mustard, spices and Quaker Oats to supplement our rations, we flew first to Delhi and then on to Assam.

Arriving in Assam we moved on by bus to the border with Arunachal Pradesh, proudly producing our prized permit at the many police and military checkpoints. 'Tell me what it's like in there – if you come back!' said a Gurkha sergeant.

Political unrest in Assam in recent years had led to tight security, but on reaching Itanagar, the capital of Arunachal Pradesh, we were quite overwhelmed by the warmth of the hospitality with which we were received. Our arrival coincided with the Mopin Festival, equivalent to an extended harvest festival, and white-robed women dashed up to smear rice-flour paste on our faces and insisted on dancing with us. The charismatic chief minister, Gegong Apang, gave us an enthusiastic welcome and made a point of displaying our $21,000 fee for all to see. With no industry or taxation there was very little community income of any kind and our cheque must have made a sizeable contribution to his budget.

We soon discovered that apart from some locally brewed rice beer, or *apong*, the state was dry, which perhaps helped to account for the almost total absence of crime. Furthermore, there was no evidence of drugs, begging or dishonesty of any sort. Indeed, the people seemed to have high moral standards and a strong belief in family values, especially noticeable in the way that they respected and cared for their old folk.

Venturing outside the capital, we drove on narrow roads and over Bailey bridges through the jungle-covered hills in ancient Indian-made Ambassador cars, reminiscent of the old Morris Cowley. In the villages we stopped at along the way, we were invariably greeted with smiles by the villagers who, being mostly small in stature, were curious about our height and were eager to see everything we carried and simply to touch and feel our clothes. A Polaroid camera and an image intensifier, which enables one to see in the dark, astounded them. Our American navigator Eric Niemi's GPS, which was only the size of a large pocket calculator and used satellites to give our position, was completely beyond their grasp, but they loved to look through binoculars. The place was caught in a time warp.

For us, however, the tribesmen's deadly poisoned arrows, razor-sharp swords and bamboo armour were, in their way, equally impressive. The bearskin-clad warriors performed fearsome war dances, while the young women, with their high cheekbones and flashing eyes, enchanted us. The elders told tales of great tribal battles of the past and the chiefs, or 'Jurors' as they were called, were proudly dressed in red jackets copied from the uniforms worn by the British political officers who encountered these hill-country people in the last century.

Everything seemed to be made of local materials. The neat villages of bamboo houses were decked with pagan symbols and, in the case of the Apatani tribe, with high masts on which the men performed ritual aerial acrobatics during festivals. The Apatani women were considered to be the most beautiful in the area and had often been kidnapped by the neighbouring Nyishi tribesmen. So, to disguise their beauty, the ladies had facial tattoos and ugly wooden nose plugs inserted in their upper nostrils. However, we noticed that this brutal disfigurement was largely confined to the older women; the younger ones remained naturally stunning!

Walking along a track one day, we were suddenly confronted by a massive buffalo-like creature. Its great black head and sharp horns showed just above the vegetation as it glared at us with a malevolent gaze. We had met a mithan. These strange creatures are a cross between a gaur (*Bos frontalis*), an Indian bison, and the domestic cattle that roam freely in these hills. But we were assured that, despite appearances, they were really quite gentle. 'You can catch them with salt,' said the Apatani.

Next day we set out prepared and, sure enough, soon found a snorting bull in our path. John Hunt approached with outstretched hand and to our astonishment the huge black beast ambled forward to lick the salt. Apparently, the people caught them in this way, to be sacrificed at a crop-planting festival. It seems the mithan must be slow learners!

Most nights we slept at Circuit Houses, simple accommodation for visiting officials, with hot water carried in by servants, but few other luxuries. There was little evidence of the Raj having penetrated these remote jungle fastnesses. Indeed, British policy had been to leave the tribes well alone, especially in the wilder border areas, sensibly calculating that they would be happier and less of a threat if left to their own devices.

In central Arunachal Pradesh we encountered the Adi people, living in beautifully built traditional houses, many roofed with heavy palmyra-leaf thatch. Their granaries were mounted on mushroom stones to protect the crops from rodents. Some of the older men wore green and purple embroidered waistcoats and ornate necklaces and also sported basket-weave hats, whereas the women wrapped themselves in shawls and woven sarongs. They were indeed a most colourfully attired and friendly people. However, due to a tragic misunderstanding, Noel Williamson, a British political officer, and his escort had been massacred by the Adi. Although this led to violent retribution by a punitive force, today's descendants of those who suffered as a result bore no grudge and led us on a gruelling fifteen-mile march to see the memorial set up by the British to honour Williamson and his men. Standing in the village where the administrator was hacked to death, a brass plate set in stone reads: 'On this spot was murdered Noel Williamson, Assistant Political Officer, Sadiya, 31st March 1911.' The villagers still tend it as a mark of respect.

Sadly, guns had now reached the tribesmen, who were rapidly destroying the wildlife. The government was aware of this and was preaching conservation, but it would take a long time to convert these traditional hunters. Thankfully, logging had not so far made a serious impact on the 80,000 square miles of virgin forest.

In the east, the Namdapha reserve was home to many animal species. The area is a true wilderness, a vast stretch of lush green vegetation, rising from 600 feet above sea level at its lowest point to nearly 15,000 feet at the summit of Dapha Bum mountain. The immense diversity of plant and animal life is staggering. The whole tract represents an assortment of forest biomass: tropical wet evergreen jungle in the lower reaches, mixed deciduous forests in the middle, and temperate alpine growth in the heights, where great herds of noble takin (*Budorcas taxicolor*), a cross between a cow and a gnu, and, very occasionally, the elusive snow leopard are to be found.

The forest at the lower level is multi-storey, with impressive trees like hollock, makai and the towering hollong, which can exceed 150 feet in height. The flora is so thick with undergrowth, canes, bamboo and spiralling interwoven climbers of every sort that it is virtually impenetrable. Slipping and sliding up and down muddy forest tracks, we found signs of elephant, tiger, leopard, gaur, bear and deer, but in the dense vegetation one was lucky to catch a glimpse of anything except the ubiquitous leeches that attached themselves to us at every step. Overhead a few brightly coloured birds flitted by, whilst the raucous cry of the hoolock gibbons gave warning of our approach. The trail was illuminated by a dull green light that at times gave an almost translucent appearance to this eerie world. The occasional serpent slithered away amongst the leaves and vivid butterflies floated ahead of our muddy steps. Huge trees rose up like pillars, reaching for the sun, which beat down on the canopy high above. Lianas and vines hung in a tangled mass to trip the unwary.

Off the track, visibility was rarely more than ten yards and all the time the jungle resounded to the drip, drip, drip of the condensed humidity, interspersed with the occasional crash of some giant tree falling at the end of its life. When the rain comes it falls in torrents, instantly turning tracks into quagmires. The thick brown mud, ravines, gullies, dense jungle and fast-flowing rivers make this one of the most challenging pieces of terrain I have ever encountered.

There were other surprises in the mysterious forest. Enjoying a tiffin of hard-boiled eggs, oranges and potato eaten off a banana leaf, we sat beside a bubbling spring of chalky water. It was not especially remarkable until one of our guides tossed in a lit match. With a 'whoosh' the surface burst into flames as some odourless invisible gas ignited. 'Magic.' Our Indian zoologist grinned.

'Methane,' retorted Dr John Davis as the fire danced on the water.

Scaling the steep slopes was like climbing a never-ending ladder in a Turkish bath. Sweat poured from us and John Hunt gashed his elbow in a fall.

Passing one village, we met a young man in jeans and a T-shirt who explained that he was a student from the University of Calcutta. 'My parents live nearby,' he explained. 'They've never met white people. Would you have tea with them?' How could one refuse? So we shook hands with a dozen curious villagers and sipped tea.

Noticing John's injured elbow, a lady produced a bowl of sticky black paste and offered to apply it to the wound. 'Go ahead,' agreed our doctor. 'Let's see if this traditional remedy works.' As it was coated on the gash John winced, but in moments it set like dried molasses and the next day when it was peeled off the wound had almost completely healed.

In the dense Namdapha jungle, Judith Heath, our intrepid botanist, demanded transport to carry her above the reach of the ubiquitous leeches, so we went in search of an elephant. A female with a four-year-old calf was duly produced. 'She will not go without her baby,' explained the owner. 'So you must pay for one and a half elephants.' Then he went on to say that Auntie must also come to help look after the calf, so the bill was actually for two and a half elephants. I protested, to no avail, fearing that the calf would delay our journey, which indeed it did, frequently getting lost, and generally behaving like a precocious child, screaming whenever smacked by Mother.

A deep torrent barred our way at one point and we feared the little one would not cross, but she simply seized her mother's tail and was towed across. The mahouts were amazed when John Hunt, who had trained with our elephants in Nepal, climbed on to the mother and rode her with great confidence.

Only a third of the 77 square miles that made up the reserve had been explored. Overall, it is a botanical wonderland, with fantastic air plants and orchids adorning the towering trees. Dr Keith Shawe of the Natural Resources Institute and Judith were in heaven. Meanwhile, we also had an important entomological task – seeking *Propholangopsis obscura*, a giant grasshopper two inches long, first discovered by General Sir John Bennett Hearsey, Divisional Commander of the Bengal Presidency during the Indian Mutiny of 1857, who dropped his pith helmet on it. An enthusiastic naturalist, the General is remembered, among other things, for having dismounted to pursue a rare butterfly whilst his regiment were fording a river under fire. With scant regard for his own safety, he chased it with his net and later pinned it to his topi. Inspired by General Hearsey's gallant action, the expedition collected a host of grasshoppers on behalf of the Natural History Museum.

Our veteran expedition doctor John Davies and his medical colleague Dr Tan Chi Chui made an extensive study of the fascinating traditional medicine used by the tribes. Python fat is prescribed for wounds, bears' bile for dysentery and over thirty medicinal plants for treating malaria, headaches and other ailments. In only fifteen days we had explored a botanical demi-paradise, as yet unspoiled by outside influence. We appreciated the wisdom of the government in restricting visitors to serious scientific groups and foreigners able to be of assistance. We felt especially privileged to have been the first scientific expedition to explore the region for almost fifty years, and prayed that its unique culture would continue to be maintained and protected from overexposure to the outside world.

It was to be a while before I was able to return to this fascinating area, but in November 2001 I organised an SES expedition to assess the possibilities for future expeditions in Assam, Meghalaya and Nagaland.

Flying into the uninspiring Assam town of Dimapur, we drove in 4WDs up the winding road to Kohima, capital of Nagaland and scene of some of the bloodiest fighting of the entire Burma campaign when, in April 1944, a small British Commonwealth force battled to hold back the Japanese invasion. Some of the fiercest hand-to-hand fighting took place around what was then a tennis court in the garden of the Deputy Commissioner's residence on Garrison Hill, a ridge overlooking the little town that is now the site of the Kohima Commonwealth War Cemetery.

Breathing in the clean, cool mountain air, we walked silently amongst the impeccably maintained graves, laid out as if they were a regiment on parade, and gazed at the bronze plaques bearing moving epitaphs from loved ones, such poignant reminders of the courage of the gallant men who died there. The 2nd Division Memorial summed it all up with the words: 'When you go home, tell them of us and say for your tomorrow we gave our today.'

Elsewhere, in villages around Kohima, further memorials again reminded us of the supreme sacrifice made by so many British Commonwealth and Gurkha soldiers, who gave their lives while driving the Imperial Japanese Army back to final defeat in Burma.

Many tribes had gathered at the great Hornbill Festival in December, providing a unique insight into the culture and traditions of the Nagas. Being a restricted area, Nagaland had few foreign visitors and we found ourselves the centre of much friendly and curious attention. Pulling out our cameras, we photographed muscular warriors carrying spears and swords and demure maidens in traditional dress. Then, rather to our surprise, they produced their own cameras and asked if they could take pictures of us!

The village of Khonoma stands on a high ridge north of Kohima and it was here, in 1879, that the Angami killed the British Political Agent, Guybon Henry Damant, and then besieged the small garrison at Kohima. His body was never recovered, but after the siege was lifted his decapitated head was buried with full military honours.

In 1944 the Nagas, now on the side of the British, used their headhunting skills to good effect against the invading Japanese. Indeed, they provided valuable assistance and intelligence for the British. One of their leaders was a remarkable English lady named Ursula Graham Bower who, at the age of twenty-three, had come to India in 1937 to study the anthropology of the Naga. Given the rank of Captain, she was the only British woman to hold a combat command position in this campaign. Several of the older Nagas still remembered her. We found the village peaceful and friendly with fascinating stone-built gateways, heavy monoliths and solidly constructed houses. Many Naga lived to a great age and there was a tombstone of a man who reached 122.

By contrast, Tuophema had more bamboo houses and a recently constructed visitor centre, where we stayed in traditional huts furnished with comfortable beds and bathrooms. Even the somewhat erratic electricity supply worked most of the time. A high standard of catering provided traditional dishes prepared by the local staff and a small, well-presented museum gave a useful introduction to the village.

Hiking through the jungle-covered hills, we noted sadly that local hunters had decimated the wildlife. From a historical point of view, we were interested to find wartime Japanese trenches. At some of the villages we discussed water supply problems with a view to carrying out improvements on a future expedition. And listening to the elders we became aware of disputes with the Indian government. There are still many Nagas who pray for independence from India. The Kohima Museum held displays illustrating the history, art and culture of the fourteen major tribes of Nagaland, as well as military equipment from the epic Kohima battle. On the slope of Garrison Hill a complete Lee Grant tank still stood defiantly.

Descending into the plains, we paused to attend a gathering of the Zeliangrong people, one of the largest Naga tribes. Photojournalist Nikki Dunnington-Jefferson and I were presented with beautiful shawls and *shadors* – long, loose cloaks – especially welcome during the chilly nights at 5,000 feet. Unable to resist a quick visit to the famous wildlife park of Kaziranga, we rode on elephants and in jeeps to view several rhino and wild jumbos. Over eighty tigers were reported, but proved difficult to find, as usual. Unfortunately, hordes of local tourists with noisy children and the unexpected cold weather did not enhance game viewings.

Our drivers kept trying to overtake traffic on blind bends but, miraculously, we survived on the twisting road leading to the sprawling former hill station of Shillong, old capital of Meghalaya. Somewhat relieved, we booked into the iconic Pinewood Hotel, a tea planters' retreat with spacious rooms, coal fires and piping hot showers. Recuperating in the bar, we met several knowledgeable expats and planned the next phase of our recce. I'd hoped to get to Riangmaw, little known home of the Khasi people, known for its abundant wildlife, but also said to be in need of a water supply system. However, insurgent activity forced us to cancel this visit. Whilst alternatives were arranged we attended the regular 'Siat Khnam' archery event. This involves elderly Khasi men loosing off numerous arrows from small bows at a circular straw bale. Bets are placed on the archer who puts the most arrows into the target.

At Cherrapunji, then the wettest place on earth with an astonishing annual rainfall of over 400 inches, we viewed one of the world's tallest waterfalls, albeit a little short of water at the time, but nevertheless impressive. The massive escarpment provided an awe-inspiring view of Bangladesh. The land here is rich in coal and limestone and a cement factory belching pollution into the otherwise clear mountain air was evidence of this. Women and children scrape a meagre living digging coal from short, unventilated tunnels that often flood. It was a scene reminiscent of the Welsh valleys in the 19th century. The early Baptist missionaries who came here from Wales must have felt at home! Indeed, one of the noticeable features of both Nagaland and Meghalaya was the high proportion of Christians. Having been supplied with an overgenerous picnic, we gave most of it to the miners, who were overjoyed.

Moving westward, the expedition was glad to find Tura at 1,145 feet somewhat warmer, and at a Garo village a great welcome awaited us. The people here are animists and the beams of the chief's house were decorated with the symbols of the sun, moon and stars. A cockerel was slaughtered and its entrails examined for predictions of the success of our visit. Fortunately, the bird's innards were in good order and there followed a feast that was almost literally washed down with copious quantities of rice beer swigged from a long-necked gourd held several inches from one's mouth. It required skill and practice to drink this successfully and without too much spillage. The Garo then celebrated for several hours with colourful dances accompanied by drumming, horn blowing and symbol clashing, all performed around a central pole at the foot of which burned a bowl of incense. Clearly enjoying the party, old ladies stood by smoking strong maize-leaf cigarettes and applauding. We were encouraged to join in and our doctor, James Mehta, led the way. A local police officer eventually signalled the end by firing his rifle into the air, whereupon everybody retired to their bamboo huts.

As we drove away from the area we came across a tall, bearded, hairy man, stark naked. The girls chuckled, but our guide assured us that this was not a Yeti but a hermit who lived in the forest. The expedition ended in Guwahati, where we discussed plans for a future visit with the celebrated former hunter, Dinah Choudbury, and conservationist Mike Nampiu, a rugged character whose grandfather was Scottish. As a result, a full-scale expedition to Meghalaya was scheduled for 2003.

The village of Riangmaw was home to some 200 Khasi, originally a nomadic tribe, who had been brought to the area by the government in 1975. The climate here is dominated by the south-east monsoon, which brings eight months of rain, and few outsiders enter this isolated area, largely cut off from the rest of Meghalaya by steep-sided jungle-covered hills. Mike Nampiu reckoned there were elephant, tiger, leopard, boar and black bear here. The huge Indian bison was also present and there were rumours of another giant unidentified bovine of some kind.

Flying into Guwahati on 18th November 2003, our fourteen-strong team drove up to our old haunt at the Pinewood Hotel. After meetings with local officials I fell into bed beside the flickering flames of a coal fire, reminding me somewhat of my youth in a Herefordshire vicarage.

Driving on to the police post at Shallang, we were briefed on the current counter-insurgency campaign. Apparently, the paramilitary forces had recently killed three insurgents and captured five others who had been smuggling in guns from Bangladesh for rebels in Bhutan. 'You must leave your passports with us,' ordered the police commissioner, adding by way of explanation: 'In case you are taken prisoner by the insurgents hiding in the forest.' A good start to an expedition!

From Shallang, a sixteen-mile track had been cleared specially for us by Riangmaw villagers. Using this, our convoy of battered Indian jeeps and a couple of old lorries carrying a solar-powered water supply system to be installed by our engineers battled its way up and down the one-in-four slopes. Ploughing through a river, one truck, happily bearing the name *Gift of God*, became well and truly bogged and we were forced to make a temporary camp for the night.

At dawn Mike Nampiu and our Indian drivers fashioned a tow rope from twisted vines with which to haul out the stranded vehicle. Meanwhile, John Edwards's cooks produced delicious porridge and scrambled eggs, whilst we beat off an invasion of bloodsucking leeches. On the last of the hills we disembarked and, slipping and sliding in the mud, heaved the underpowered jeeps up the slope. Shortly after that an accountant, a conservationist, a doctor, two dentists, a nurse, four engineers, two community aid workers, a farmer and a podiatrist, accompanied by John Edwards and a cook, reached Riangmaw. A party of beautiful girls in their best dresses greeted the mud-splattered expedition at a welcoming archway decorated with flowers. Their leader, Martina, a student on leave from her college in Shillong, spoke good English and became our liaison officer. Once she had explained to the rest of the villagers what we planned to do to help them, we set up camp beside the football pitch and started work.

Helped by nurse Sarah Royal and podiatrist Marie Murphy, Dr John Davis made a nutritional survey, whilst dentists Peter Fletcher-Jones and William Murphy dealt with a queue of patients and Sue Craxton and Shirley Critchley handed out reading glasses as well as clothes and schoolbooks for the children. Suffolk farmer Sir Charles Blois sought information about local agriculture and heard how crops were being ravaged by wild pigs and elephants. And a tiger had just eaten the village's last cow!

I was keen to find evidence of a legendary giant bovine that the Khasi people called 'Si Prot', and on 24th November our wildlife survey team, led by Mike and a Riangmaw hunter named Bin, set out on for a 3,000-foot-high ridge that lay south the village. Following a narrow game trail, we marched over some challenging terrain and across bubbling streams. The density of the vegetation meant that we didn't see much wildlife, although elephants could be heard trumpeting around us and we glimpsed a sambar deer. At the top of the ridge we found an abundance of pitcher plants, which trap insects with sticky slime, and Bin caught a young monkey who was clearly lost. Much photographed, it was duly released and almost as a reward we spotted a huge bovine footprint five inches across and six inches long. Whatever had made this was certainly pretty big, but I suspected it was likely to be a large gaur bull that I would not have fancied meeting face to face on such a narrow jungle track. Nearby a tiger roared and Bin became concerned. In recent weeks a village hunter had shot and wounded a tiger that had taken his cow.

Following up, they came on the injured beast, which had charged, knocking the gun from the hunter's grasp before mauling him. A colleague, armed only with a spear, had climbed a tree, but then bravely descended, grabbed the gun and shot the tiger in the heart at point-blank range, killing it. Sadly, the wounded man did not survive.

Elephants had also killed villagers and one herd had remained around the body of a woman they had trampled to death for several days. As we had discovered in Nepal, elephants detest any manmade objects in their area. A government-financed pipeline, connecting Riangmaw to a spring a few miles away, had been destroyed by elephants within days. The water system we installed, with the aid of funds from Just a Drop, was therefore designed to draw water from an eighty-foot-deep ravine close to the village. Our civil engineer John Thackray, together with Les Vandenborn, worked with the locals to place a solar-powered thirty-volt electric pump in the stream and another in a tank about forty feet higher up to propel the water to a 1,100-gallon tank at village level. Extra parts had to be brought from Shillong, but on 30th November we held a simple ceremony and, as I turned on the tap and the water flowed, I just hoped that the villagers would make the effort to maintain it.

Wildlife surveys led by Mike Nampiu continued, and we had a lucky escape when a black bear came scrambling down a tree with claws outstretched and charged Bin, who was at the head of the column. He fell back into a farmer carrying a shotgun who managed to raise the gun and shoot the roaring beast. Bears have poor eyesight and Mike reckoned it was asleep and simply surprised by our approach, but it was a sad occasion that we all regretted.

Although we did not find the Si Prot we did see evidence of unusual dwarf elephants. And, hopefully, we had helped to make life a little easier for the people. To celebrate, the grateful Khasis danced and sang and we did the hokey-cokey in return. The villagers apologised, quite unnecessarily, for having nothing much to give us, but pressed oranges, rice wine and bamboo handicrafts on us as we headed back to Shillong.

My next visit to north-east India was in 2015. In northern Assam, overlooked by the towering mountains of Bhutan, lies Manas National Park. Some 1,000 square miles of jungle and uninhabited stretches of grassland form a pristine wildlife habitat. This is the haunt of herds of wild elephants, buffalo, massive Indian rhino and the Royal Bengal tiger. Rare animals such as the pygmy hog, the hispid hare and the golden langur monkey have also been discovered here and it is an ornithologist's paradise with a wide variety of birds, including the famous Bengal florican, a type of bustard.

Due to past political upheavals, the wildlife has suffered from poaching, illegal logging and human encroachment. However, following a ceasefire, former insurgents, poachers and other young people formed a new force with the Forest Service to protect this special place. Known as the Manas Maozigendri Ecotourism Society (MMES), this unique community-based organisation was the first such body to be established in India to promote conservation and ecotourism. This is truly a case of poachers becoming gamekeepers.

At the time, relatively few visitors had made the three-hour drive out from Guwahati. But in April 2015 I was invited by the Bodoland Territorial Council to lead an expedition to this remote area. Our task was to study the wild elephant population and catalogue other creatures, while encouraging the local people to help in preserving the fauna and flora. For this, a twenty-one-strong international team was recruited, including a doctor, a dentist, engineers, scientists and a fish farmer, many of whom were members of SES and had joined me on previous expeditions. Sarah Lawton, who had developed a passion for elephants in Bardiya, made all the arrangements for the venture and Tessa Donovan-Beerman, another Bardiya veteran, directed our zoological observations.

Sarah invited the famous Parbati Barua to talk to us about all aspects of elephant handling and the situation regarding the thousand or so wild ones in the park. This remarkable lady was the daughter of Prince Prakritish Chandra Barua of Gauripur, a legend amongst the fraternity of elephant lovers and handlers and said to be the world's leading expert on Asian elephants. He had caused some surprise by nominating Parbati to inherit his mantle when she was still quite young, but she had gone on to devote her life to elephants and their handlers in north-eastern India.

On our arrival at Manas, Parbati came to dinner immaculately and elegantly dressed for the occasion, putting our team in expedition clothing slightly to shame. Hailed as 'Queen of the Elephants' in Mark Shand's bestselling book and TV film of the same name, Parbati was already well known globally. Speaking quietly, but with authority and in a commanding voice, this petite lady enthralled us. Later, joining us at the park's elephant training camp, she introduced us to the domestic herd and their endearing babies.

The park staff provided twelve domestic elephants for the expedition, along with a newly designed howdah for us to test. It would only carry two passengers but was believed to be kinder on the elephants than the square box-like version. As dawn broke each day, we would come yawning from our tents to sip hot, sweet Assam tea before mounting the trusty pachyderms and setting off through the swaying stalks of emerald green grass, often twelve feet high.

The game was clearly not worried by our presence, and we were able to catalogue the numerous wild elephant, water buffalo, deer and other small mammals. Our birdwatchers were also rewarded with sightings of the rare Bengal florican. One could get within a few yards of snorting rhinos and scampering wild boar, which seemed to regard us as being part of the elephants we were riding on. My own mount was followed everywhere by her year-old baby, Naughty. I couldn't resist giving the five-hundred-pound youngster a banana each morning, but thereafter she would not leave me alone, almost knocking me off my feet on several occasions in her eagerness for another treat.

In the patches of dense jungle along the riverbanks were troops of agile monkeys, including the beautiful golden langur, and scores of colourful birds flitted between branches. We kept a careful watch for snakes, as several extremely dangerous ones inhabit Assam. A large python managed to eat one of our cook's chickens before the wardens captured the thief and moved it away from camp. Earlier I had an unforgettable encounter whilst crossing a dry stream bed in a jeep. On the baked mud there appeared to be a black water pipe. 'What's that?' I asked, thinking it was part of a water system. The car stopped and as I dismounted, to my amazement the pipe began to slither towards me.

'Stand still,' hissed Rustom, our ranger. 'King cobra!'

Although no-one could be persuaded to measure it, I reckoned it to have been about fourteen feet long. Slowly, it advanced with its flicking forked tongue seeking moisture in the cracked stream bed. Absolutely fascinated, we stood stock-still watching the world's largest venomous snake, known to be aggressive and its poison said to be strong enough to kill an elephant. A mid-body bulge indicated it had just eaten, probably another snake, and it was in no hurry, which allowed us time to film. Tapping the ground with my stick caused it to raise its menacing hood before it slid into the bush.

Apart from some violent thunderstorms that cooled things down, we sweated gently on our elephants at 30°C and at the day's end it was a delight to bathe with our jumbos in the clear, cool river, scrubbing them with stones or split coconuts, which they enjoyed as much as we did.

We met the extraordinary MMES group of former insurgents, ex-poachers and young people turned conservationists that were mentioned earlier. A pretty tough bunch, they now hunt those who would kill the wildlife.

With future aid in mind, our engineers examined a proposal to sink a 260-foot borehole to provide clean drinking water for one community. Medical and dental help was much appreciated by the Bodo people, who rarely receive dental treatment, and our dentist, Susan Evans, extracted over sixty teeth! As usual, children who had a tooth removed were comforted with a teddy bear or animal puppet. Reading glasses were also given to those in need. Many who have witnessed intolerance at surgeries in Britain would be impressed by the way these patient people waited hours in the boiling heat for treatment.

Thanks to the help of the Newport Uskmouth Rotary Club, we also provided the local school with their first computer and set up a link to children in England. Welcoming villagers showed us the silkworms that keep them supplied with beautiful fabrics and handed out local rice wine whilst we watched delightful displays of dancing. Fortunately, our contact with the wildlife was free of accidents, although my wife Judith did have one anxious moment.

Driving in a small open jeep she spotted a tigress with her cub cooling off in a puddle. A rare sight indeed, but then a herd of elephants and their calves emerged from the bush and an angry matriarch took exception to the tiger and the jeep. Tucking in its trunk it charged, trumpeting in rage. It was only twenty feet away when the game warden behind Judith fired his rifle into the air. In a cloud of dust, the beast halted and then backed off into the scrub. As Parbati had warned us: 'Female elephants are unpredictable when protecting calves.'

 ▶ Beyond the Brahmaputra 1993

 ▶ The Meghalaya Riangmaw Expedition, India 2003

CHAPTER 28

IN GENGHIS KHAN'S
FOOTSTEPS

As a schoolboy, the country that most excited me was Mongolia, or Outer Mongolia as my geography teacher referred to it, the main reason for my boyish fascination being the fearsome reputation of its all-conquering emperor, the legendary Genghis Khan. Apart from that, what stuck in my mind from those classroom lessons was the wild and rugged remoteness of the high plains on this roof of the world, its nomadic people and the extreme climate. My heart therefore leapt when, whilst I was directing Operation Raleigh in 1988, a friend at the Foreign Office phoned me with an invitation to lead an expedition there. 'Now that the Russians are moving out, the country is set to become fully independent again and a delegation from the Mongolian government has requested young people from Britain to go and carry out some aid projects there,' he explained. 'Would you be interested?' Later he admitted that we were the government's least costly option!

Two years later, as perestroika spread, I flew out to investigate the possibilities. Aeroflot had kindly upgraded me to a first-class seat and I felt like a member of the presidium as we winged our way over the endless forest and steppe. Sensing that a meal was about to be served, I lowered my tray table from the back of the seat in front, only for it to flop down on a broken hinge, refusing to stay upright. Pressure on the call button produced the stewardess, looking as if she might be one of Russia's leading female weightlifters, who glowered at the offending table and then, with a flash of inspiration, grunted the single word 'Moment', and headed for the galley. *Ah! Gone to fetch her toolbox*, I thought. A few minutes later she reappeared, wrenched the table back into its foldaway position, placed a bottle of warm champagne on the seat beside me and commanded: 'Drink.' Perhaps that was the answer to all problems in Russia! Finally, our meal arrived – two thick doorstep slices of bread separated by a thin smear of fish paste, wrapped in cling film.

My unsmiling neighbour, who appeared to be an important official, KGB maybe, inspected his sandwich with the care of a connoisseur, then called for the weightlifter, to whom he indicated that something was amiss. Seizing the plate, she stamped off towards the economy section. I watched, fascinated, as she plucked a plate from the tray of a red-faced peasant woman, peeled the sandwich apart, nodded in satisfaction, exchanged it for the official's meal and marched back. All seemed happy with that, although the peasant did look a little sad. I had discovered one of the differences between first-class and economy travel on the Russian state airline at the time: in first class you had butter in sandwiches; in economy you did not.

At Irkutsk a jovial party of Russian military personnel joined the flight, along with a Belgian leather merchant, *en route* to

Ulaanbaatar. Well prepared with a bottle of Black Label Scotch whisky, the Belgian generously offered me a glass. However, when the scent reached our fellow passengers, a cocktail party erupted around us. Clearly, I was the first British officer the Russian soldiers had met and they were determined to get as much vodka as possible down my throat. Finding myself talking to someone wearing a blue uniform and who spoke some English, I asked if he was in the air force. 'No, no.' He smiled. 'I am the pilot.'

At Ulaanbaatar I politely declined an invitation to join the merry band to continue the party at the Russian Embassy and, finding myself alone in the arrivals hall, was perplexed by the immigration form, written entirely in Mongolian.

'Welcome to Mongolia, Colonel,' said the almond-eyed beauty in a leather miniskirt as she brushed aside a lock of long black hair that hung over one eye. 'I am here to look after you. My name is Minjin which means beaver.' She smiled. 'And my sister is called Khulan, which means wild ass.'

My God! I thought. *This must be a KGB honey trap.* But there was no opportunity to flee as my damnably attractive escort led me out of the airport to the waiting Volga. Sitting in the back were the rest of the welcoming committee, including Sean Hinton, a young British musicologist who spoke fluent Mongolian and became my most valued advisor.

Travelling into Ulaanbaatar, Minjin briefed me in perfect, but somewhat Victorian, English.

'Where did you study my language?' I asked.

'In Moscow, I do hope it is correct.'

I assured her it was, perhaps just a little quaint.

'Oh, the tapes were very old,' she replied.

By two that afternoon I had explained Operation Raleigh to a dozen Mongols, before going through it all again for the benefit of the Minister of Education. After almost seventy years of Soviet domination, Mongolia, landlocked and sandwiched between Russia and China, was about to become truly independent. However, the departure of 400,000 Soviet troops along with the probable withdrawal of Russian aid was going to cause immense problems in a land roughly the size of Western Europe with a population of around 2 million and few natural resources. The Mongolians needed new friends.

Slightly to my surprise, the minister appreciated the value of hordes of Raleigh venturers invading his country and suggested that we fly to the most remote *aimag*, or province, to see if it would be possible to set up a series of community aid and conservation tasks there. The following day Minjin, Sean and I found ourselves jostling to get aboard a well-used Mongolian Airlines (MIAT) Antonov An-24 airliner. The seats were utility and not designed for fourteen-stone colonels, but as I did my best to make myself comfortable we were soon winging westward above the vast rolling sands of the Gobi before passing over frozen lakes and snow-capped mountains, as we neared our destination. The other passengers stared at us with mild curiosity throughout the flight. Sitting next to me, a small lad picked his nose thoughtfully and watched everything I did.

Bright sun and a bitter wind greeted our arrival at Khovd. On the tarmac a short, smiling gentleman advanced and introduced himself as Mr Terbish, rector of the local Pedagogical Institute. He was to be our host and later to represent Operation Raleigh in the region. Here the arid Gobi Desert meets the Altai Mountains and in the far north-west the Tavan Bogd range extends across the borders with China and Russia. The highest point, Khüiten Peak, at 14,291 feet dominates an area of alpine magnificence. The sharp ridges of the mountains and the eternal snowscapes are the birthplace of glittering glaciers leading down to sparkling emerald lakes. Khovd city, home to 20,000 Mongols, Kazakhs and other racial groups, is the capital of the *aimag*. Apart from the government building and a colourful theatre the place was drab and dilapidated.

In our hotel, warmed by a bowl of boiled mutton and some soggy rice, we began a long round of briefings. We explained Raleigh, and local officials outlined their own needs, which included medical help, the construction of refuge huts for travellers, bridges, biological studies and, above all, English teachers.

Within a few hours I was ready to see something of the countryside and we bounced over the desert in an old Russian jeep, with a singing driver. I realised that few, if any, Westerners had ever visited this area. There were unclimbed peaks, rivers that had never been navigated and tales of primitive nomadic tribes existing out in the wilds. By 11am the next day I'd seen enough to know that this was an ideal place for an expedition, but that it would be no picnic. The only transport would be the short, sturdy Mongolian horse and the heavily built Bactrian camel, a double-humped, ill-tempered beast whose disposition is not improved by the wooden nose peg inserted through its nostrils to which strings are attached for the purpose of steering. The horse saddles would also be a problem. Made of wood and designed to accommodate a dwarf, they would cause grave discomfort and perhaps serious injury to the average European male. We decided that we would have to seek venturers with small bottoms who could ride well. A few jeeps and trucks might be available and the ancient biplane at Khovd Airport was said to be airworthy, despite appearances!

The Altai rise from the desert to over 14,000 feet, many summits towering high above the source of a number of major rivers, including the Khovd, one of Mongolia's longest. The mountain lakes offer a quiet retreat for numerous varieties of birds, including swans, geese and other waterfowl, whilst golden eagles, buzzards and kites glide above. Although it was cold and dry at the time of our recce, Terbish explained that when the rains came in the summer, the desert would turn green, providing lush pasture for the cattle, goats, horses, sheep and yak herded by the nomadic people. Being a biologist, he was eager to tell me all about the wildlife, which included the vigorous mountain sheep or argali, wild goats and even the rare snow leopard. Wolves, he told us, were known to attack domestic animals and there were also bears and deer in the region. Being so far from the moderating influence of the oceans, surrounded by mountains and situated at a relatively high altitude, Mongolia's climate can produce unpredictable weather, as we were to discover. I guessed bland meals of fat mutton, yak meat, rice and rock-hard cheese washed down with salted, milky tea or *kumiss* (fermented mare's milk) would not be to the taste of all our young people.

Back in Ulaanbaatar, the minister gave his approval for a full-scale expedition but, meanwhile, the country was in turmoil and early one morning great crowds gathered in Sükhbaatar Square demanding democracy. It was an eerie experience, standing amongst the demonstrators, facing the lines of unarmed soldiers guarding the parliament and wondering if tanks were waiting in the side streets. The orderly nature of the mass demonstration was most impressive. A crowd of some 12,000 sat quietly in the square with banners displayed, while a big bass drum beat a remorseless thump, thump, thump, like some giant clock ticking away metronomically. Hour after hour, day after day, the crowd came to sit and stare at the parliament. Was this what broke down the walls of Jericho? It certainly worked, because the authorities bowed to the will of the people and Mongolia did indeed become democratic.

The Russians in our hotel were worried and one day, as I waited on the steps outside for our battered Volga, a medalled Soviet General appeared, impatiently looking for his vehicle. Our car was approaching when the Russian moved forward, and I feared he was about to take it. 'I think that's our car, General,' I said.

The great man spun round. 'Ah, English, how do you know I'm a General?'

'Because I'm a British Army Colonel,' I retorted.

'At the Embassy, I suppose?' he suggested.

'No, actually I'm with the Ministry of Defence in London.'

'So what are you doing in Mongolia?'

'Planning an operation, General,' I replied. Before he had time to respond to that his car then arrived, but as his aide swept him away he gave me a long, penetrating look. Heaven knows what he told the KGB!

Flying home I paused at Irkutsk to meet some much friendlier Russians, keen to host a Raleigh expedition. On a whistle-stop tour of the region, I was entertained at numerous dinners where local dignitaries made lengthy speeches in Russian, interpreted for me by an army lieutenant, who, as a result, hardly had time to swallow a mouthful of his meal. However, everyone seemed to be very much in favour of a Raleigh expedition.

One evening my hosts left me to my own devices and, following their directions, I joined a dinner party in a beer cellar. The diners were holidaying Eastern European teachers. No-one spoke English, but with the help of a dictionary we managed to communicate. The menu included a dish from each country represented at the dinner, but because they only learned I was coming at the last moment, it had not been possible to include an English course. However, pointing to the waitresses at the far side of the restaurant, they explained they had found some T-shirts bearing English children's songs. I assumed they meant nursery rhymes, but as the waitresses approached I saw to my astonishment that they had a cartoon emblazoned across their ample bosoms accompanied by a caption that read: 'AIDS kills, so don't be silly, get that condom on your willie.' Apparently, a free issue from the World Health Organisation!

Back in London, I set about fundraising for the expedition and SES member Sir Richard Branson kindly set up a scheme on Virgin Airways to collect passengers' loose change at the end of flights, and with this we were able to finance a TB vaccination programme.

The following year American banker Pamela Stephany, Sean and I did a complete recce of the northern part of the region, whilst Ann Tweedy, another Explorers Club member, led a team to examine the southern area. Meanwhile, recruiting was going well, with lots of would-be venturers with small bottoms, mostly girls, applying.

It was in the spring of 1992 that, ably assisted by my efficient PA Sally Cox and Sean, I launched the first major Western expedition to Mongolia for over fifty years. British Rail kindly offered help with transport, but the collapse of the USSR prevented us from travelling on the famous Trans-Siberian Railway, so the personnel were flown in under my second in command, RAF Squadron Leader George

Baker. Meanwhile, Corporal Tony Martin, a stalwart Commando Sapper, supervised the transport of containers of freight by sea to China, by rail from there to Ulaanbaatar and then by trucks for the final 1,000 miles to Khovd. Keeping the local drivers away from the women and vodka proved quite a challenge!

By May, a tented base camp had been set up beside the shallow Buyant river. It was still cool and sandstorms played havoc with my sturdy 'ger', a circular, canvas tent-like dwelling similar to a yurt. The Mongolian economy was deteriorating at an alarming rate. Food and fuel were rationed, and construction materials were like gold. However, Mick Ponting, our energetic vet, had procured a string of horses and several camels. We borrowed a battered old GAZ jeep and also arranged to hire an Antonov biplane. Amazingly, the locals produced a radio phone to link us with the outside world and we also had Plessey radios for internal communications.

Back in Ulaanbaatar I collected the venturers – sixty-six of them from abroad along with twenty Mongolians. I also met the Anglican archdeacon for the area, who needed no persuasion to accompany us and hold a Whitsuntide service in the field. This must certainly have been the first Anglican service ever held in that remote region.

While in the capital I had tried to buy some frying pans and trailed from one understocked shop to another. An assistant claimed she had one, but then strangely produced a trumpet. She looked so disappointed when I tried to explain that it was not what I was after that I bought it anyway for the equivalent of ten pence and thereafter roused the camp every morning with badly played reveilles.

The flight to Khovd was quite an eye-opener. We thought we had chartered the plane exclusively, but when the gate opened crowds of other would-be passengers, claiming to be related to the pilot, stampeded towards plane, where a well-built air hostess beat them back with a stick before allowing us to board. The standby passengers then crowded into the luggage bay, while small children were passed around to sit on our knees and finally a few strap-hangers came aboard to stand in the aisle for the whole journey. The loo was out of commission, so after two hours we landed at a settlement, aptly named Mörön, where everyone tumbled out to relieve themselves on the grass – women on the left, men on the right – before flying on!

George's camp was composed of a few circular *gers* for the senior members and two-man tents for the young. To supplement the food, we brought vegetable seeds from Britain and, using the abundant manure from our horses, I prepared a small plot outside my *ger*, labelling it 'The Garden of Eden'. As a local lady of doubtful virtue who helped around the camp had also assisted with the digging, some joker had added 'Dug by the Whores of Babylon'.

Beneath the deep blue sky and in radiant sunshine we deployed the army of young explorers to a host of tasks. Astride the frisky pony-sized horses, and with camels carrying the rations, the mounted teams carried out botanical and mapping tasks on the snow-capped mountains. Lessons in white-water rafting were given on a convenient 2,000-foot stretch of impressive rapids emerging from the Khovd River gorge, whilst some of the venturers built a fine stone classroom to serve as a school. The local nomads were especially grateful to our vet, who stitched up a mare, severely bitten whilst defending her foal from a wolf.

Fourteen miles east of Khovd, the reed-fringed Har-Us Nuur – which translates as 'black-aqua lake' – covers an area of 609 square miles and is an ornithological paradise. Unfortunately, it also has a formidable mosquito population, though thankfully not of the malaria-carrying variety. Our birdwatchers nevertheless spent most of the day under protective nets.

Another group used ex-Russian army stores to build a 246-foot suspension bridge. Named the Jeremy Irons Bridge in recognition of a generous donation from the actor, it looked very fine when I arrived at the site with the local commissioner for the official opening. Speeches were delivered and ubiquitous vodka bottles produced. Then our photographer, Ian Robinson, arranged the entire team across the span to record the occasion for posterity, including Mick Ponting and his horse Caesar. As our guest of honour was now a little unsteady on his feet, I kept him at one end, which was just as well. Suddenly, there was a sharp crack as a locally made clamp gave way, releasing one of the main supporting cables and causing the decking to tilt over. Venturers grabbed the handrail, while Caesar performed a graceful leap off the bridge on to the bank as if he did it every day. Poor Ian, festooned with cameras, did a backwards somersault into the river. The commissioner made another speech saying it was no-one's fault and that such things often happened in Mongolia. As Ian poured the water from his cameras, Mandy Grey, the young British Rail engineer who had directed the building, bit her lip but remained admirably unfazed. 'OK, let's get it repaired,' she sighed, and before long the structure was secure once again.

Our medical team organised a TB vaccination programme. Once the flask was open, all the vaccine had to be used, so our group, led by a blind Japanese girl, galloped from *ger* to *ger* inoculating the nomads. Since 1985 Raleigh had assisted SEE International, a non-profit organisation based in California, whose volunteer surgeons and nurses carry out cataract and other sight-restoring operations in the developing world. Under the eminent American surgeon,

Dr Harry Brown, a team flew into Khovd, where we established a clinic. Patients were then brought in by venturers and, working with Mongolian surgeons, SEE restored sight to sixty-three people, one of whom was the mother of the regional premier, which was to prove very fortuitous.

A message I always dread on an expedition came crackling over the radio early one morning. 'There's been an accident,' reported mountain leader Julian Freeman-Atwood, his tense voice underlining the severity of the incident as he told us what had happened. Lindsay Griffin, one of Britain's finest climbers, had been moving through a boulder field when, without warning, a huge granite rock had toppled over, pinning him to the ground and mangling his left leg.

Julian and American mountaineer Ed Webster had gone on well ahead and had already set up camp when it happened, so Lindsay was alone and unconscious. When he came to, the top of the trapped leg had turned purple and gone numb. To restore the flow of blood, he somehow managed to drag a rope from his rucksack and make a sort of pulley system with which he raised the rock a fraction. As the pressure reduced, blood flowed back into the shattered limb, but with it came excruciating pain. By this time it was 6.30pm, and the accident had happened at around three o'clock. Puzzled by Lindsay's long absence, Julian and Ed had retraced their route and, hearing faint cries, eventually found him. It took three laborious hours of work with elaborate pulley systems to shift the boulder and haul the stricken man out. His leg was pulped, with multiple compound fractures. For the next fifteen hours they struggled to descend 1,000 feet to a flat area where a helicopter might land. Here they put him in a tent by a stream with rations and painkillers and set off to get help.

It had then taken all next day, struggling over snow-covered crevasses without sleep and little food, to reach their base and the vital radio. 'Can you get a helicopter to us as quickly as possible?' Julian pleaded.

'Leave it to us. Get some sleep and I'll call you in three hours,' I told him, wondering where on earth I'd find a chopper that could reach Lindsay before his wound, the wolves or the cold killed him. Sean Hinton and I examined the maps, whereupon I suddenly realised to my horror that Julian and Ed had carried him down into China!

The ancient Soviet biplane was on the airstrip. I knew it could land at Bayan- Ölgii, some seventy-five miles east of Khüiten Peak, and from there a truck could carry a rescue team to the base of the mountain. But even then, with luck on their side, it would still take at least a two-day march over difficult terrain to reach Lindsay. There was fuel for the old plane and although it was a forlorn hope we dispatched some eager young climbers with doctors Chris Snailham and Jan Kennis, a Belgian surgeon. Meanwhile we tried frantically to find a helicopter by telephone. Suddenly Sean cried out: 'MIAT have a chopper and they reckon they can get fuel – but it's going to cost twenty-six thousand dollars!'

'The insurance will cover it,' I grunted, just praying it would get there in time.

It was the next day before the huge Mil Mi-8 transport helicopter reached Khovd only to find that there was no fuel available there. So, together with the pilot, Captain Nyamaagiin, I dashed off to see the premier, whose mother had been successfully treated earlier by SEE, and he generously agreed to release a ton of precious aviation fuel from the emergency reserve. But it was 4pm by the time this was trucked to the airport and the helicopter was airborne. Meanwhile, my assistant Sally Cox was arranging an air ambulance to jet the 1,800 miles from Hong Kong, but it needed government permission to land in Mongolia. Happily, the ever-helpful British ambassador, Tony Morey, sorted this.

Every hour's delay increased the risk of infection and the loss of Lindsay's leg. Lying alone in his tent, he sipped water from the stream and swallowed painkillers. He never really expected to see a helicopter. When the Mil Mi-8 thundered over Julian's base camp, the biplane party, which had marched non-stop, was just about to start up the awful Potanin Glacier. 'Here comes the school bus,' yelled Ed Webster, as the bulky machine, quite unsuited for mountain rescue work, lumbered into sight and, leaping aboard, he guided it to Lindsay's tent, located some ten miles distant at an altitude of 12,800 feet. In the thin air this altitude was at the extreme limit for the groaning, juddering chopper, but somehow Nyamaagiin coaxed it upward, the whirling rotors carrying them over the col until they spotted the blue tent on a ledge. Too heavy to hover at such an altitude, the gallant captain made five attempts to roll land on to the ledge, but each time the boulders defeated him. Eventually, he had to drop the rescuers two miles away. As they set out to get to Lindsay, the aircraft whirled away. *Wonder where he's going*, thought Ed as he and the rescue team raced for the tent. Inside, Lindsay lay wracked with pain but he managed a weak smile.

It was 6.30pm and night was falling as the team dragged him back to the clear patch of land where Captain Nyamaagiin had dropped them on the way in and waited. There was no sign of the helicopter. At the base camp Julian was almost frantic with worry. What could have happened? Had they crashed? The consequences were too awful to contemplate.

At 9.30pm, to their intense relief, the stranded team heard the heavy throb of the aircraft returning. To reduce weight, Nyamaagiin had flown to a lower altitude, landed and shut down, allowing time for the casualty to be moved. Then restarting, he had offloaded the heavy batteries and returned. With Lindsay safely aboard, he stopped off to retrieve his batteries before flying on to Khovd. It was an incredible act, balancing weight, fuel, altitude and the advancing darkness to snatch the injured man from what we now knew must be Chinese territory, and in July 1993 the brave and brilliant captain deservedly received the Queen's Commendation for Valuable Service in the Air from the Princess Royal in Ulaanbaatar.

As the 'school bus' landed at the Bayan-Ölgii airstrip to refuel, the engines cut out – the tank was dry! And, once again, there were no fresh supplies available at the strip. There was now no time to waste and Lindsay needed urgent emergency treatment. Commandeering a van, the medics rushed him to the small local medical clinic, where the director's desk had to serve as a makeshift operating table. Using Swiss army penknives, our doctors cut away tattered clothing and rotting flesh to find that bone was sticking through the skin. 'Splints?' asked Chris. There were none, so Sean hacked up a filing cabinet with an ice axe. Back at the strip they found the chopper syphoning fuel from an Aeroflot airliner that was collecting emigrating Kazahks. The ever-resourceful Captain Nyamaagiin had somehow managed to swap five bottles of vodka for eighty-eight gallons of fuel.

A great grin spread across Lindsay's[4] face as I stepped aboard. 'Sorry about all this,' he muttered before adding: 'But John, I have

---

4. Lindsay Griffin recovered, became President of the Alpine Club. He still climbs.

something very important to tell you.' Next day, as we waited for the Learjet to arrive from Hong Kong, he told me of sighting a large auburn-coloured creature that seemed to walk upright in the mountains, not far from where Julian Freeman-Atwood had spotted some strange tracks, quite unlike snow leopard or bear, that appeared to have been made by a biped.

Tavan Bogd has extraordinary alpine scenery, quite different to anywhere else I had been in Mongolia. Few outsiders had seen these incredible mountains before our expedition and later, when riding through the swirling mist on our shaggy ponies, I found it difficult to imagine anything large living in this land of snow, ice and swamps. However, there were tantalising tales of 'almas', or Yeti. Many local people seemed to consider them unremarkable and talked as if they were simply primitive people. In general, the descriptions were similar. The males were said to be six to nine feet tall and the females five to six feet. Their heads were somewhat pointed and the bodies covered in reddish-grey hair. We were told that the creatures walked upright and had powerful back legs allowing them to leap up to three feet vertically in the air from a standing start. The footprint, similar to a man's, was often larger and wider. The body shape is that of a heavily built human and the females are said to have pendant breasts, which they toss over their shoulders when they run! It seems they are afraid of water but not fire. There are stories of almas warming themselves by abandoned fires. There are also tales of females raping male hunters. However, they were generally reported to be very shy, usually fleeing from humans. Their only sound is said to be a shrill cry. Reports of almas are more numerous here than in most areas of the world and there are many who will readily admit to having seen them. Although it may be a myth, the almas are part of Mongolian folklore and a number of eminent local scientists have spent much time and effort researching the mystery.

My driver, Gansukh, a dour, taciturn man and a hunter of some repute, showed me where he had watched a nine-foot-tall creature covered in reddish hair walking upright for 550 yards. We managed to get copies of photographs of the footprints taken by a Khovd journalist. They looked human, but at least size 16!

Having endured temperatures varying from -9 to 35°C, the expedition ended in August just as Mongolia started to run out of aviation fuel completely, meaning that we had to hire a fleet of open ten-ton trucks to carry us back to Ulaanbaatar. The six-day journey was largely uneventful until we reached Karakorum, site of a city built by the great Khans. Later, after it had been ravaged by invading Chinese armies, a monastery was erected on the site.

As we paused to visit the white stupa-topped walls, temples and shrines, the sky grew black and a howling wind brought clouds of swirling sand, closely followed by torrential rain, thunder and lightning. Sheltering in a gateway I heard a different sound, '*rump, rump, rump*', followed a few seconds later by a '*crump, crump, crump*' overhead.

'What on earth's that?' I asked one of our Mongolian army captains.

'Thunder,' he replied.

As the rain fell in rods it came again. Being very familiar with the sound of gunfire, I protested: 'That was definitely artillery.'

'No, just thunder,' he insisted.

Back at the camp the noises came again even louder and hot shrapnel fell in the trees. 'Under the trucks,' I cried, everyone thinking I was mad until Tony Martin drove in shouting: 'There's a load of civvies firing bloody great ack-ack guns skyward at the edge of a wheat field. Are we under attack?'

Back in Ulaanbaatar I asked a Mongolian colonel if they had artillery at Karakorum.

'Oh no, those are weather guns that shoot chemicals at clouds to prevent hail forming and destroying the crops,' he explained.

The farewell party at the British Embassy, generously hosted by the ambassador, revealed the affection many of our young had for their Mongolian opposite numbers, and as the train to Beijing pulled out of the station next day there were copious tears. I became more aware than ever of the effect operations Drake and Raleigh were having on international friendships and understanding. But I too had fallen in love with this 'land of eternal blue sky' and in July 1994, along with my adventurous son-in-law, Julian Matthews, I led a new expedition to the Khovd region.

It started badly. Our Air China aircraft broke down at Heathrow, causing a frustrating delay of two days. However, we eventually reached Khovd, where Sean Hinton's tour company had arranged for us to carry out archaeological, botanical and zoological studies, as well as seeking evidence of bubonic plague carried by fleas on marmots – rodents that look rather like large squirrels.

Flying into Khovd on the chaotic local airline, our twenty-strong team was joined by several Mongolian members of the 1992 Raleigh expedition, including Mr Terbish, now a professor at the university. Driving north in a battered Russian jeep and a well-used troop-carrying vehicle, we paused to survey some Bronze Age tombs before camping in a gorge that I knew of old. Here, Marigold Verity, an accomplished musician, soothed the buzzing of the mosquitoes with her Welsh harp, whilst melancholy calls of wolves echoed from the cliffs.

Beneath the gleaming peaks of Tsambagarav, known locally as the 'Sacred White Mountain', was a pleasant grassy valley 8,000 feet above sea level that we had earlier named Shangri-La, and here we met up with my swarthy old friend Horjer, whose family livestock now grazed on the rich summer pastures. Sean, who had hired horses, together with three camels to carry our stores, passed me the reins of a handsome black gelding I named Nero. Meanwhile, our vet, Francis Wolverton, wormed the mounts and treated two foals savaged by a wolf. Riding over treacherous rocky slopes on a botanical survey, we gazed out over the rolling landscape. Nero collapsed under me three times, perhaps due to the worming, the altitude – or possibly my weight! Even so, he proved extremely sure-footed, although I did have to lead him on slowly for much of the way up to the snowline at 11,700 feet.

Faced with a myriad of wild flowers and plants as we continued to climb, botanist Barry Phillips was in paradise! Back at camp we donned warm clothes and dined around a dung-fuelled stove as Marigold played 'Greensleeves' and our grooms sipped vodka and sang melodiously. Concerned by the presence in the area of wolves, Horjer persuaded a few of us to accompany him to lay an ambush. At sunset we rode to a nearby valley and, putting the horses to graze 330 feet or so away, hid behind some boulders. Horjer, clutching his rifle, took the first watch, but at 01:00 hours when my American pal, Eric Niemi, and I relieved him, he was sound asleep! At 05:00 the sky lightened sufficiently for our binoculars to reveal our horses scattered throughout the valley while, silhouetted on a distant ridge, were four shadowy figures. An alpha wolf sitting upright and three others were watching our horses intently, but were too far away for a shot. In spite of our effort to remain undetected, they eventually sensed us and slunk away, leaving us to round up the horses.

Moving on through the windswept mountains, we passed many glaciers and, when the sun broke through the low cloud, collected more plants. Snow showers and hailstones the size of large marbles showed just how desolate this landscape could be, but riding on we kept the horses well clear of the ill-tempered camels. Having erected our traditional *gers*, which were carried by the camels along with the rest of our stores and equipment, we were usually snug and warm at night, with Marigold providing musical entertainment round the campfire each evening after supper.

Riding ahead one morning I spotted four well-clad horsemen, stationary on a ridge. As I got closer I saw that they each had a golden eagle perched on their heavily gloved right wrists, feathers ruffling in the breeze. The hunters smiled and muttered a greeting as they continued to scan the valley for prey. 'We need marmots,' I explained via Toggo, our interpreter, who told them about our bubonic plague study. A little later the older man shouted, pulling off the bird's hood and, with her six-and-a-half-foot wings beating, she raced towards an unsuspecting rodent. At the very last moment, she swooped down, her yellow talons reaching out in front of her, and after a quick struggle we had our marmot. The problem was to retrieve it from the predator's grasp! A hands-on lesson on eagle falconry followed, but my bird preferred to land on my pith helmet rather than my gloved arm. And a fourteen-pound eagle comes in with quite a bump!

Using an antiquated Russian .22 rifle and traps, we collected further marmot specimens. We then donned protective clothing and swallowed prophylactic penicillin before combing out and bottling the fleas that could carry the virus. Marigold, meanwhile, had been studying the local social and religious culture and was delighted to come across two elderly lamas who had emerged from hiding when Buddhism was restored. Most of their colleagues had been murdered in the 1930s, but now these old gentlemen had donned their saffron robes once again and were striving to re-educate Mongolians in their faith.

On 31st July we changed our horses. I said a sad farewell to Nero, the shaggy black gelding who had carried me so surely over the mountains, and exchanged him for one that I named Basil on account of him having a mane like a fox's brush. With a gentle but strong temperament, I reckoned it was a fair swap as we re-entered the mosquito-ridden lowlands. Plotting Bronze Age archaeological tombs and petroglyphs, we turned east, passing the remains of Jeremy Irons's bridge. As predicted, the winter ice flows crashing down the Buyant River had swept away all but a few upright metal joists.

As we neared the old campsite, a woman came galloping on her horse across the steppe towards us, amazingly clutching a baby. '*Sain baina uu,*' ('Hello') she cried, holding out the bonny blue-eyed eighteen-month-old, and I recognised the 'lady of easy virtue' who had tended my garden during the 1992 visit. Gratefully accepting a few small gifts and some cash, she smiled and said, 'Tank you, English,' before riding back to her *ger*.

We were joined aboard the typically crowded flight to Ulaanbaatar by a party of gruff Austrian hunters in Tyrolean hunting gear, clutching rifles between their knees and thus having little room on their laps for the several babies that the standing passengers passed around. On arrival, Sean invited me to meet a colonel and inspect a hundred obsolete wheel-mounted Russian machine guns that the army wished to sell. I promised to mention them to a friend in Britain who bought vintage weapons, but could make no promises. The colonel looked disappointed.

The Ministry of Health expressed gratitude for our bubonic flea collection and provided permits allowing us to take them home for examination. Alas, our plane once again broke down in Beijing and the baggage was offloaded, but fortunately the customs did not ask what was in the sealed metal boxes! Somewhat to my relief, the tests in Britain proved negative.

CHAPTER 29
BENEATH THE ETERNAL
BLUE SKY

Inspired by the expeditions carried out by palaeontologist Dr Roy Chapman Andrews in the 1920s, I had always longed to visit the Gobi Desert. Said to be the model for Steven Spielberg's Indiana Jones, the discoveries made by this accomplished American explorer included the first known fossilised dinosaur eggs and the skeletons of numerous prehistoric reptiles. My opportunity came in 2011 when the SES was approached about the possibility of undertaking an expedition to provide a much-needed fresh water supply for a remote community living near the 110-mile-long Khongor sand dunes, which rise 2,500 feet above the surrounding arid landscape. The charity Just A Drop offered to help fund a well and, at the same time, my old friend Professor Terbish was seeking help with botanical and zoological studies.

Accompanied by three female Mongolian scientists – palaeontologist Dr Delgermaa, palaeogeologist Ms Enkhtuya, and Dr Dagdan Suran, head of the Department of Botany at the National University of Mongolia – our expedition flew into the desert airport at Dalanzadgad, capital of the Gobi. That afternoon we were quite surprised to be greeted by five minutes of torrential rain as we presented books to a school, before then driving out to see Chapman Andrews's celebrated flaming cliffs, so named because of the spectacular way in which the red and orange colours of the rock are highlighted in the rays of the setting sun.

Next day, Terbish introduced us to our expedition transport – a couple of dozen sturdy camels. Bawling, groaning and defecating, these double-humped 'ships of the desert' regarded us with an arrogant, supercilious expression. Having shed their heavy winter coats, they stood proudly in their soft, summer tan-coloured wear. The weather-beaten bow-legged owners, clad in loose calf-length tunics knows as *deels* and woollen hats, eyed us dubiously, as if to say: 'I wonder how long this lot will last in the saddle.'

Their doubts were justified. Next morning, we climbed on to the embroidered saddles gripping the forward hump, which, lacking fat and liquid, provided little to hold on to. Then, protesting loudly, the tall beasts rose up in a series of jerks as if intent on shedding this unwelcome burden. A thin, plaited rein led to the cruel wooden nose peg thrust through the nostrils. Turning his head, my camel watched me from beneath his feathery eyebrows. I had precious little control, but on the touch of my heels we ambled off across the stony plain. Within a hundred yards the effect of riding on a moving backbone became apparent and at the first stop I added another blanket beneath my bruised buttocks.

Dr Suran had shown us photos of the plants in which she was especially interested. The sun was high and my pith helmet growing warm when I spotted one of the very blooms she was looking for. Seizing my camera, I set about persuading my obstinate camel to let me dismount, but before I could alight he had extended his long neck and gobbled up the plant! By the end of the day, many of us preferred to walk than ride.

A drilling rig at the Gobiin Anar well site had drilled to a depth of 230 feet before the bit became immovably stuck in the bore. Mongolia had run out of diesel anyway, so work stopped.

Nevertheless, our help was appreciated, and we started building a stone-walled pump house. Gathering rocks from the nearby hills, Flight Lieutenant Jack Holt RAF filled the kitchen truck and an antiquated trailer so that Steve Clarkson, a New Zealand builder, could fashion a neat three-walled hut. Meanwhile, Sapper colonels Mike Law and Tom Gallagher urged the local labourers to give a hand. Victoria, a young, long-limbed blonde in our team, worked best in hot pants and a skimpy T-shirt, but this proved too much of a distraction for one of the Mongolian drilling team, who failed to look where he was going and walked straight into a brick wall!

Terbish had found us accommodation in some comfortable, if overheated, *gers* at a local tourist lodge. Other guests were slightly disconcerted by our presence. At one point Mike Law had to extract a Frenchman who was taking undue time in the only shower. 'But I'm a three-star General,' he complained indignantly, to which Mike responded: 'Well I'm a British Colonel – time's up!'

The zoological team was busy preparing to scour the area for specimens, but did not have to look far, Mike immediately collecting a viper from the steps of the ladies' loo while, as a desert wind blew up, a hedgehog sought shelter beneath one of the *gers*. By dawn we were enveloped in a howling sandstorm, similar to the one I remembered from North Africa. Driven by clouds of stinging grit, we sought cover and thanked God we were not on the camels. Thankfully, the wind had dropped by mid-afternoon and we held a little ceremony to declare the pump house officially open.

Back at the lodge, a tasty dinner was served, and a lithesome young waitress entertained us with some impressive tabletop contortions. Calmer weather prevailed for our next task and, moving north with our palaeontologists Degy and Toygel, we soon spotted the white bones of a 73-million-year-old fossil. A swell of excitement swept through me as the skull of a vegetarian horned protoceratops emerged from the loose sand. Tom made a drawing to show what it would have looked like, coming up with something similar to a rhinoceros. He also sketched a 73-million-year-old carnivorous velociraptor, the remains of which Degy had unearthed. Pleasingly, Richard Weeks, a kitchen fitter from Yeovil, found the skull of a 70-million-year-old rat.

Pleased with our discoveries, we paused to watch the traditional Naadam Festival at Bayangol. This annual three-day countrywide sporting event, dating back to Genghis Khan, features horse racing, wrestling and archery, and whilst the major show is in Ulaanbaatar, the smaller local events like the one we saw are rather like a country fair. Although it celebrates the 'three manly sports', women take part in both the archery and the riding. Generally, Naadam is an excuse for people to dress up and enjoy themselves and is becoming increasingly popular in modern-day Mongolia.

Alex Redshaw, who planned to join the army, and young solicitor Richard Gerrard bravely entered the all-comers wrestling match. They lasted barely a minute, but the crowd applauded generously. On my radio the BBC reported the creation of South Sudan and the arrival of Rupert Murdoch in London following the demise of his *News of the World*; and unconnected, there was dancing in Bayangol.

The expedition ended with a memorable visit to Khustain Nuruu National Park. In 1878 Colonel Nikolai Przewalski discovered the stocky, erect-maned horses, believed to be the last true wild variety. Alas, by 1968 hunting and zoo collecting made them extinct in Mongolia. However, they were reintroduced from zoos in 1992 and throughout our expeditions we studied these unique, proud creatures at the reserves, sixty miles west of Ulaanbaatar.

Our next expedition to Mongolia took us to meet the Tsaatan, the most southerly dwelling reindeer herders, who originated from Siberia. In a remote area of mountain and forest to the west of Lake Khövsgöl, the Tsaatan live in tepees, known as *urts* rather than *gers*. These are better suited for the local environment and easier to transport as the nomadic people move around with their reindeer herds. Our Mongolian agents, Urana and Terbish, had learned that a particular group were in need of reading glasses, medical and dental treatment and schoolbooks.

So, on 7th July 2013, our twenty-one-strong group, including a number of old friends, assembled in Ulaanbaatar. There was the usual collection of skills, with a doctor and a dentist, equestrians, builders, engineers and amateur zoologists. Four Mongolian scientists joined us, this being a welcome opportunity for them to study some fascinating people living far from the beaten track and to do useful research for the National University. Flying into Mörön, we drove north. At one point, during a lengthy hold-up while our stores truck was being extracted from a muddy morass, our zoologists made good use of the delay by collecting narrow-headed voles in sunken metal cone traps, and bats in mist nets. On 12th July we made camp on a grassy field by the clear, rippling Khogliin River, where sixty-five horses awaited to carry us, and our stores, to the summer camps.

Annabelle Burroughs, our highly competent 'horse mistress', liaised with the heavily built Batarmunck, leader of our horsemen, and together they matched riders and packs to the various mounts. A powerful black fourteen-hand beast I named Cromwell showed that he could easily carry me, and like a squadron of cavalry we set off, wading through the deep river, the water up to the horses' bellies. A scenic ride took us uphill through meadows alive with wild flowers and into the larch forest. Rivers still coated with thick winter ice and boggy patches of black mud had to be negotiated with care as we climbed higher. At dawn, our tents were stiff with frost. The horses performed pretty well, although Barry West's mount kept sitting down beneath him and Peter Manns got kicked whilst dismounting. To my dismay, Cromwell felt he should be the lead horse and would break into a gallop whenever I released the reins. The cooks did an amazing job unloading the pack animals each night, erecting a mess tent and serving a tasty four-course dinner.

At an altitude of over 7,000 feet and with the thermometer reading 25°C we entered a wide, treeless valley in which we came upon a collection of white *urts*, home to a small Tsaatan community. As we approached, a flurry of ptarmigan startled Cromwell and when several smiling Tsaatan children, mounted on heavily antlered reindeer, came to greet us our horses took exception. However, the Tsaatan seemed delighted to see us and pleased to have buyers for their handmade horn and stone artefacts.

Peter, conducting a study of these unique reindeer people, noted that the *urts* were very similar to the tepees that were associated with Native Americans. Conical in shape, they were constructed from up to thirty wooden poles cut from trees, with a hole at the apex. The frames would once have been covered in reindeer hides, but now rectangular sections of canvas were more commonly used. The doorway faced east towards the rising sun and was covered by a canvas flap. In winter, snow was packed around the outside to prevent wind blowing under the canvas walls. Each *urt* had a stove in the centre with the flue extending upwards to the hole in the apex. They all appeared to be equipped with solar panels, which powered short-wave radios, used to communicate with other settlements, as well as small TV sets capable of receiving Mongolian and some Russian channels.

Each *urt* accommodated a single family of parents and children and we learned that villages usually consisted of anything from three to nine such dwellings, occupied by interrelated family units. Marriages were mostly between individuals from different valleys or areas, and were for love, not arranged. Once married, a girl would normally move to her husband's settlement, where the couple would build their own *urt*, with the help of other family members.

At the settlement we visited we watched the children going off on reindeer to a school that had been set up in a designated camp in the same valley, where they were educated all year round. The adults told us that the level of education received was good. Peter noted that the people spoke Tuvan, although Mongolian was taught, as was writing in the more modern Cyrillic script. All settlements had their commonly owned herds of domesticated reindeer and some also kept sheep and goats and, to a lesser extent, cattle and horses. The reindeer were tethered to short stakes overnight and fierce guard dogs were used as a defence against wolves, a common threat. The night before our arrival in one village, a guard dog had been badly mauled.

Reindeer are central to Tsaatan culture. As well as serving as beasts of burden, they also provide food in the form of milk, cheese and yoghurt, but are never slaughtered for meat. And thanks to the allowances paid to them by the government, few people any longer trade in reindeer antlers, used as an ingredient in Chinese medicines. As a result, many of the beasts we saw had very large, well-developed antlers. Being nomadic, the Tsaatan move camp four or five times a year in pursuit of fresh grazing, particularly the white lichen on which their animals feed. They use rifles to hunt red deer, wild boar and foxes and, given the chance, they'll also shoot the predatory wolves, whose ankle bones sell well as good luck charms.

The decline in population caused by migration to the towns seemed to have been halted, again thanks to the monthly government allowances, and more young people were adopting the traditional nomadic culture. On moving camp, the log frameworks of the *urts* were left in situ for future use, whilst the canvas and all other belongings were packed up and loaded on to the reindeer.

After arriving at the settlement, Peter and I were invited to enter one of the *urts* and, as elsewhere in Mongolia, squatted on the left side, whilst the family sat on the right with the father seated opposite the door. Tea and reindeer milk were served from the ever-burning wood stove and I noticed that the tea came in large compacted blocks, unlike the leaves we use at home. Our hosts also handed out chunks of cheese cut from slabs hanging from the roof to dry.

Our horses had been left loosely tethered outside and the ritual tea party was suddenly disturbed by whinnying and the thunder of hooves as our mounts bolted away from an inquisitive reindeer. It took several hours for our herdsmen to bring them back, giving Peter plenty of time to question the people and me to enjoy a snooze in the sun.

Becoming conscious of something snuffling nearby, I raised my pith helmet to find myself in the path of several hundred reindeer, who were gently stepping over me! Meanwhile, Peter had learned that some twenty-three families totalling 140 people lived in the valley, herding around 1,400 reindeer. He was especially excited to be introduced to a forty-three-year-old shaman named Altzang. This spiritual and ceremonial leader was happy to discuss his skills and his work with the people, who are predominantly shamanist rather than Buddhist. Rather like old English monks, he cared for their spiritual needs and treated the sick with herbal medicine. Often called upon to arbitrate in disputes, he helped to resolve domestic problems, forecast the weather, and foretold the future.

Altzang also described how he spoke to the dead – 'As easily and clearly as others speak on the telephone,' he insisted – and how he frequently sought advice from ancestors and, in particular, previous shamans. He believed that ancestors sent messages to help and guide us, and to protect us in our daily lives. These messages were delivered by birds, he explained, recommending that everyone should listen to their song. He claimed to have travelled with the spirits to visit many foreign countries, and that he could transport people to different locations. Able to control the forces of nature, he could cause rain to fall over the area of a fire. Nature does not like to be manipulated, he said, but will accept this if it is at the request of a shaman.

Deeply concerned about changes in nature in recent years, Altzang had noticed that river levels were lower, that grazing was declining and that there was less rain and snow than previously. Also aware that temperature changes were now more extreme, he believed that the sun and the moon were changing their patterns, and the positions of the planets had altered. He feared that this was caused by advances in modern technology and said that the spirits had told him that man is ruining nature. 'There is too much mining and too much gas is being released from the earth,' he stated, adding that the spirits of nature were very angry and upset and had shown him the future, which he refused to reveal, but which sounded ominous. His predictions were similar to those of Western environmentalists and the Colombian Wiwa, especially when he went on to praise tree planting.

Sensing our interest, he invited Peter and four of our team to attend a shamanic ceremony that night, on condition that no photographs were taken. At dusk the group rode out to his *urt*, where he asked everyone for particular questions they would like the spirits to answer during the ceremony. With the temperature dropping to 2°C at midnight, our group, plus many villagers, were gathered in the *urt*. By now the shaman was cloaked in strips of coloured cloth and wearing a tall headdress, festooned with strips of material and with a thick fringe obscuring his face, the purpose which, he explained, was to conceal him from evil spirits.

Breathing very heavily, to the point of hyperventilation, he began to dance, waving his head vigorously from side to side, and chanting a monotonous dirge. Banging a large drum, he continued to gyrate wildly, while two assistants kept him clear of the stove, also rolling him numerous suspiciously scented cigarettes and keeping him supplied with tea and reindeer milk.

After an hour of dancing, he threw his drumstick to spectators and received appropriate responses. Various manoeuvres followed before, near to collapse, the shaman sat with his head in his hands, breathing heavily. Revived with more tea and milk, he gave each individual the spirits' answers to their initial questions. Most were fairly generic, with something along the lines of 'don't worry, it will sort itself out' being a stock reply. While some comments were wide of the mark, others were pretty accurate, rather like you might get from a village-fair fortune teller.

'What did you think of it?' I asked Peter.

'Wherever I go, I will certainly make time to listen to the birdsong,' he replied.

Next day Royal Navy dentist Angie Critchlow extracted thirty-four teeth, Izzy Gallagher distributed schoolbooks, Sue Bromhead counted ptarmigan, and Cynthia Hardyman and Mongolian botanist Dr Oyumaa collected flowers. After many hours scouring the hillside, fish farmer Janet Wood and Professor Terbish were overjoyed to find a toad, a rare lizard and seven salamanders.

On 17th July we rode back twenty miles to the Khogliin River, hammered by a short heavy hailstorm and with Barry West and Bob Atwater's horses collapsing under them in a swamp. Unhurt but filthy, they remounted and we made camp by 4pm, landing four grayling and a five-and-a-half-pound salmon-like lenok from the river. The long drive to Mörön was enlivened by one Russian minibus shedding its exhaust pipe and a wheel falling off the stores truck. 'We'll be able fix it in an hour,' said Professor Terbish, but as I had doubts about that I insisted on the team pressing on to Mörön in the other vehicle. Here, an underused tourist *ger* camp, delighted to have guests, produced a hot meal and beer. And the next morning at dawn, somewhat to my amazement, the stores truck drove in on all four wheels. Mongolian mechanics, it seemed, were masters of improvisation. A visit to Khustain allowed Janet Wood to do a quick survey, finding fifty Przewalski horses with several foals, whilst the botanist had a real field day. After a lively Burns Night supper we returned to Ulaanbaatar to celebrate the birth of Prince George back in Britain.

My fascination with Mongolia continued and I launched two more expeditions to carry out scientific tasks and to aid the people. With the support of the SES there was no shortage of volunteers.

Returning to the spectacular Altai range in July 2016, we rode up into the snow-capped mountains north of Khovd, which I had first seen during the Operation Raleigh expeditions twenty-four years earlier. This wild region with its diverse terrain and rustic infrastructure was beginning to attract tourists, but there were still rare plants to seek, archaeological sites to record and zoological studies to be made. Once again Professor Terbish and our agents, Great Genghis Tours and Expeditions, organised the programme and logistics.

This time our international team numbered twenty-three, including Ruth Le Cocq, a skilled 'horse whisperer' from Jersey, and Dr John Leach, an experienced dowser with an interest in the legends of the almas. Together with doctors, a dentist, a biologist and engineers we joined Mongolian specialists on a variety of tasks. Mounted on spirited horses and accompanied by two sturdy camels carrying emergency supplies, we were supported by well-used Russian minibuses. An overloaded former Soviet Army kitchen truck, which frequently broke down, was only kept going by the ingenuity of its driver.

Several horses arrived unbroken and provided an interesting start to our ride up to the higher altitude. Camping near a gentle stream at 9,500 feet, we enjoyed memorable views across a wide valley dotted with *gers* and livestock, but several suffered minor altitude sickness. Meanwhile, our army dentist, Riaz Usmari, did a roaring trade and quartermaster Dave Smith took determined botanists and zoologists up to the snowline at 12,000 feet. Returning to camp, they reported seven ibex and numerous spiders and ladybirds while the botanists had found the greatly endangered *Saussurea involucrata Matsum. & Koidz.*, known as the cabbage plant. This upright leafy green plant is much in demand as the main ingredient in traditional cure-all medicines used to promote blood circulation, diminish inflammation and to treat rheumatoid arthritis, among other things. Our Mongolian botanist, Byambagerel Suvan, whose father had been with me in 1992, was overjoyed by the discovery.

Directed as before by archaeologist Dr Munkhbayar of Khovd University, we located numerous burial sites and previously unknown petroglyphs dating back 3,500 years. Alas, the good doctor's English was limited to an occasional excited muttering of 'Bronze Age!' but, with his dowsing rods extended, John Leach located subterranean burials. Later, back in Khovd, John and I dowsed the ruins of the Manchu fort, built in the late 1700s. The temples, graveyards and homes of the ruling Chinese families were destroyed after a siege in 1912, but a dowser in England had done a remote dowsing exercise and had produced a map marking where he believed hidden weapons might be located. John and I checked the site with our rods. The ground was littered with ancient shards of pottery and we sought evidence of buried artefacts between the broken down thirteen-foot-thick walls. In a couple of hours, we had four strong responses and, checking these against a model of the fort in the local museum, found that they corresponded with the site of the former Manchu ambassador's residence. An exciting excavation project for a future expedition!

Struck by sudden changes of weather, we endured several violent storms and were crossing a wide steppe when the sky blackened once again as we made for our rendezvous with the distant kitchen truck. As the breeze freshened, puffs of sand rose from the ground and a herdsman galloped over, pointing anxiously at the metal trekking pole protruding from my daypack and shouting a warning that I didn't quite understand at first. Almost at once a vivid fork of lightning plunged into the steppe 500 yards away followed instantly by a crash of thunder. 'Lightning conductor!' yelled Dave by way of explanation as, unbidden, our horses turned their tails into the rising wind. I tucked the pole safely away as a howling gale struck us, bringing a deluge of hailstones the size of marbles rattling like machine gunfire on our riding helmets. For ten minutes we hunched up in our saddles, buffeted by violent gusts, but our horses stood firm, heads bowed, unperturbed by the storm. When the squall swept away across the plain we cantered towards the kitchen truck, now embedded in deep mud, and helped the team to erect the marquee.

The rest of our group had found themselves near a *ger* and, seeking shelter, were welcomed in with bowls of hot tea and mare's milk. Imagine that happening in Dorset! Ending the expedition amongst the Przewalski herd at Khustain we had more scientific success, finding a venomous Halys viper amongst the rocks and spotting wolves lurking at the forest edge.

It was very satisfying to have done so much useful work for Mongolia over several years and, to our surprise, the Minister for the Environment decorated me as an 'Honoured Worker – First Class', a tribute that I accepted on behalf of the whole team.

We were back in Mongolia two years later in 2018. Having found a drone so useful in Colombia, we decided they would enhance our work in Mongolia, so when Matthew Whittingham, a computer expert working in Singapore, offered to bring one along I accepted it gladly. My grandson, Jack Matthews, eighteen years old by this time and well over six foot tall, borrowed another from the SES film producer Alan Campbell. These two drones played a significant part in filming the expedition and enabled us to get revealing aerial shots of the archaeological sites. Paul Lodge, another retired Sapper Colonel, became the deputy leader and many other pals joined the team.

Also equipped with camera traps and a night-vision device, our twenty-four-strong party made the now familiar flight to Khovd, where a spectacular Naadam was in progress. How Khovd had changed since my first visit in 1990! Smart 4WDs now queued on a tarmac road to enter the festival stadium car park and brightly coloured buildings flanked the wide streets once edged by grey Soviet-style concrete blocks. The only unchanged aspects were the bright blue sky and the proud people, who now jostled to enter the showground.

The colourful traditional uniforms, the oompah-pah bands, the muscled wrestlers and *deel*-dressed archers were a photographer's delight. However, the real highlight was always the horse races, where the juvenile jockeys hung on for dear life as their stocky mounts demonstrated their stamina in races over courses up to twenty miles long.

Driving east the next day, we put up our tents near the Khoit Tsenkher caves to photograph and sketch Palaeolithic wall paintings dating back to 15000bc. Clambering through the rocky caverns, we sent up clouds of fine choking dust, but managed to sketch the remarkable Stone Age paintings of wildlife, including elephants and something that looked remarkably like a kangaroo. Archaeologist Dr Munkhbayar was delighted and we put our drones to good use over burial sites. Appropriately, the BBC World Service reported an incredible rescue of a group of children stranded in a cave in Thailand, with the help of some British cave-rescue experts.

After a journey southward, frustrated by the wretched kitchen truck's frequent breakdowns, we reached a sunlit Baatar Khairkhan mountain valley. Our washing in a bubbling stream provided amusement for friendly nomad children, who arrived to gape at us. A bright young girl spoke good English, learned in Ulaanbaatar, and, eager to practise her linguistic skills, she confided that her parents' *ger* housed a solar-powered TV. That night, Jack and other football fans, armed with some beer, set off to watch the World Cup final on Russian TV!

Riding out in search of burial sites, botanical specimens and creatures great and small, we found our horses friskier than usual. Dr Darikhand, the Mongolian dentist, was not as experienced a rider as most of her countrymen and, spooked by a horsefly, her mount suddenly bucked violently, hurling her off and kicking her. Peter Manns and John Leach also had bruising falls. However, John was able to continue dowsing and went on with his study of the local customs and culture. Jack, whose long legs almost touched the ground when he was in the saddle, confided: 'Grandpa, I think I'd rather walk.'

The highlight of the zoological programme was the search for the critically endangered saiga antelope. Standing around three feet high at the shoulder, this weird-looking steppe dweller was noted for its large head and bulbous nose. Its downward-pointing nostrils filtered out dust whilst feeding and warmed the frigid air it breathed during the severe winter months. Males displayed horns with pronounced rings, growing to a length of up to twelve inches, which like rhino horns were unfortunately much in demand for Chinese medicine. The saiga was superbly adapted to the harsh semi-desert conditions, but in 2015 some 200,000 had died in Kazakhstan from an infectious lung disease and now great efforts were being made to protect them.

The herds migrate for up to 600 miles between their winter and summer feeding grounds and Terbish believed there might be some to be found south-east of Khovd. So, bidding farewell to our horses, we drove in the Russian minibuses past a huge open-cast coal mine, indicating that the area had been covered in dense jungle in prehistoric times. Entering a wide, treeless valley dotted with groups of browsing, untended camels, we battled in strong wind to erect our tents, watched by several pairs of stately demoiselle cranes.

Fanning out, we combed the valley in our vehicles, walkie-talkies and binoculars at hand as the light was fading. Suddenly, a Mongolian zoologist pointed into the distance and we caught a glimpse of several sandy-coloured antelope around 800 yards away. Over the next couple of days we tracked these strange, shy animals and, using long lenses, eventually shot photographs and video film of a herd of over a hundred, our eyes watering with the almost overpowering smell of wild garlic.

The Khovd black market did well, with many of our team buying the traditional *deels*. At the airport the Antonov An-2 biplane we used in 1992 was now a memorial and I was glad not to be in it as we flew to Ulaanbaatar in a violent thunderstorm. Static electricity flickered along the wings as our plane was hurled around like a feather in the storm; several of us sent up a silent prayer.

At Khustain around 80 Przewalskis appeared, allowing us to approach within 100 yards, much to the delight of our equestrians. We looked back with satisfaction on the dental and medical aid, distribution of reading glasses and the completion of a wide range of scientific tasks. Back home, Alan Campbell used Matt and Jack's film to produce a fine visual record of a successful expedition that had whetted our appetites for yet another return to this enchanting wilderness and its eternal blue skies.

 Altai Mountain Expedition, Mongolia 2016

Mongolian Baatar Expedition 2018

 Khövsgöl, Mongolia 2013

 Gobi Desert, Mongolia 2011

CHAPTER 30
THE MYSTERIOUS ISLAND

There was a time when no sailing ship was welcome in Papua New Guinea (PNG). The approach of any such vessel to the reef-bound shores of the island was regarded with deep suspicion and hatred by the coastal villagers, and landing parties could expect to be greeted by a hail of spears and arrows. This was hardly surprising, because for many years European visitors had only one use for the wild, remote and exotic lands named by the first Portuguese explorers *Ilhas dos Papuas* – Islands of the Fuzzy-Haired – and that was as a source of strong young slaves to be carried off and sold on the world's lucrative labour market.

Happily, attitudes have changed since then and *Eye of the Wind*, flagship for Operation Drake, sailed into Lae in August 1979 to a fantastic reception. However, although the people were friendly, the environment remained as hostile as ever.

The island, second largest in the world after Greenland, is shaped like a giant turtle swimming in the south Pacific seas just above the northern tip of Queensland, Australia, and divided neatly down the middle by a straight north-south border between the Indonesian territory of Western New Guinea in the west and PNG in the east.

It is an untamed tropical wilderness in which soaring mountain peaks rise out of stinking mangrove swamps, mighty rushing rivers gush through plunging rocky gorges, and baking arid scrubland gives way to wide delta quagmires. And overall, it is shrouded in dense, impenetrable jungle, which is why it was still one of the least-explored areas on earth. The inaccessibility of the interior meant that nothing at all was known about it until the first aircraft flew over it in the 1920s, and existing maps compiled from aerial photographs still contained blank spaces marked 'Cloud – Relief Data Incomplete'. That is the modern equivalent of the mythical creatures, the Gogs and Magogs, with which the old cartographers used to fill the unknown areas that nobody had been able to reach and chart.

It is not just the terrain that makes PNG so inhospitable. The climate and the creepy-crawlies – which seem to be bigger, nastier and more plentiful than anywhere else in the world – add further dimensions of discomfort and danger to life outside the few air-conditioned townships. The feverish steam-heat humidity of the lowlands soon leaves one limp with exhaustion, and the catalogue of lethal wildlife includes the world's largest crocodiles, enormous pythons that can break every bone in a full-grown pig's body before swallowing it whole, and small snakes just a few inches long with a bite so venomous that they can cause death within a matter of

minutes. There are outsize lizards, scorpions and spiders the size of your fist. Mosquitoes, which I personally regard as the greatest threat of all, are also particularly virulent there.

One way and another, it is a real battle against the elements to survive in PNG. Everything stings or bites or causes rashes and infections, and the best that 20th-century technology could provide in the form of salves, lotions and repellents sometimes seemed powerless to protect one's skin against continual attack. Clothes rot and the most rugged jungle boots crack up in half the time it would take anywhere else. Even my pith helmet, which for eleven years had kept me cool, dry and safe from falling coconuts in some of the most godforsaken corners of the world, finally surrendered to the atmospheric extremes of PNG and sprouted a terrible green mould. Fortunately, the *Daily Mail* kindly persuaded Moss Bros., who had presented me with the original in 1968, to make me a new one. What all these horrors added up to was, without doubt, the finest Adventurous Training area in the world! This was why I had brought the Young Explorers (YE) of Operation Drake here.

However, the local language was challenging. Known as pidgin English, it appeared to be a controversial mixture of many tongues including English, German and the local Muto. On arrival, John Girling, the British Consul at Lae, passed me a dictionary, adding: 'This may come in useful'.

Struggling to learn a few phrases, I found a piano was *'Bocus you kickim he shout out'*; a helicopter was *'Mix master, hem blong Jesus Christ'*; and our Patron, Prince Charles, was *'Number one picinini blong missy queenie'*. If someone left PNG for good, the expression was *'Him gone, buggered up, all gone finis'*.

There were some pitfalls and I noted '*pusim*' meant 'to copulate with' and not 'to push' ('*siubim*' is the correct word for 'to push'). Thus if one needed a shove for a vehicle one should not invite a local person to '*pusim mi*'.

The Operation had its headquarters in a collection of wooden houses that formed the Lae Lodge Hotel. Tents and radio masts were scattered about in the hotel grounds around which people in jungle-green uniforms scurried back and forth, carrying stores, mending engines, planning movements, shouting orders, and making occasional detours to the swimming pool. On a typical day the operation room would resemble the stock exchange attempting to cope with a collapse of the Western financial system. Eleven different people would be competing for the use of just two telephones in their simultaneous efforts to discover why ten YEs had not arrived on the flight that morning, where to obtain paint for the ship's hull, spare parts for a vehicle stranded in the mountains, alcohol in which to preserve botanical specimens and a boat to transport three scientists to one of the outlying camps – the local village chief, who had promised the loan of his own canoe, having been arrested and thrown in prison on charges of drunkenness. On the other end of the lines, the ten YEs would be trying to contact us to explain why they had missed their flight, and journalists would be attempting to call, wanting to know if any romances had blossomed on the ship's Pacific crossing. But no-one could get through because the lines were permanently engaged. Around the walls impressive flow charts showed who was supposed to be where and what they were responsible for, intermingled with press cuttings and photographs depicting the expedition's progress. The Operations Officer, in this case Captain Mike Knox, was visibly going grey as he attempted to match the ever-growing requirements of the expedition's projects at different locations around the island with the limited transport available.

On an earlier recce I had sought to gather information about the unknown upper Strickland River. The local Defence Force Commander told me: 'That's a really mysterious area. Few have been there, and we'd love to know more about it – what the river is like, what the people who live there are up to, what sort of wildlife exists in the area and whether there are any minerals.'

The Defence Force library had no aerial photographs. 'Haven't got that far yet,' said the Australian captain. 'It's a hell of a place to fly into.' So clearly, if we were to tackle this region, we would have to get our own photos.

The river falls 1,000 feet over 75 miles and for much of this distance it is enclosed in a deep chasm, known as 'the Devil's Race'. Low cloud obscures the area for much of the year so that even an air recce was unlikely to reveal what secrets lay beneath the swirling mists and the dark green rainforest canopy. But I felt there must have been a series of falls, or perhaps just one big drop somewhere along the river. If we were to explore the region, we would need to use that river. An experienced bush pilot we spoke to in the capital, Port Moresby, was not encouraging. 'If you get clear weather it's because of high wind funnelling up the gorge and even the army planes won't be able to cope with that,' he told us. 'You'll need a real power bird to get you through; and if you hit that turbulence, you'll smash right into the rock.' Even if one survived a crash, the chances of being found didn't sound good, and the reaction to any intrusion of the tribes of headhunters, still thought to exist in the more remote regions of the interior, was unpredictable and quite likely to be hostile. And then there were the crocodiles! It didn't sound particularly inviting.

Helpfully, Barbara Martinelli, an elegant and courageous American seconded to us by Pan Am, referred to as 'Missy White Straw' by the locals on account of her flowing blonde hair, managed to borrow a powerful light aircraft from the Gestetner Corporation, along with an experienced Australian pilot, Noel Frewster. Arriving at Wewak on the north coast, we found the weather to be favourable and decided to go ahead with the recce of the high-altitude valley. Barbara had the still cameras and took the rear seat, whilst I held the Canon 8mm Cine in the front and flicked it on to the slow-motion setting. The twin-engine Cessna 310 was an ideal aircraft for the job and we were soon climbing south into the towering peaks.

At 12,000 feet, we crossed a rocky ridge and winged our way through the crags of this mysterious land. Suddenly, Noel pointed. 'Look, it's clearing,' he shouted. Sure enough, the clouds ahead of us were rolling back to reveal an emerald-green valley surrounded by towering cliffs and dark mountains. Noel took the Cessna through the valley at 1,000 feet and we saw the river winding its way fairly gently at first and then tumbling over rocky ledges in foaming fury before plunging into the narrow, vertically sided gorge. As the aircraft banked sharply, I looked out to see a wall of rocks racing past – very close. Blasts of wind shook the Cessna as it twisted and turned through the mountain pass. Noel gripped the controls, his face a study of concentration, beads of sweat running down his cheeks. 'Hold on,' he hissed through the intercom as the nose lifted over a jungle-covered ridge. Our bodies flattened against the back of our seats as the surge of power took us up, clearing the trees by no more than fifty feet. The tumbling brown river had almost disappeared in the dark green foliage that now covered the entire valley bottom and seemed to close over the top of the canyon. Eventually, we emerged from the mountains and saw the endless flat swampland of the lower Strickland ahead.

'That's fine, Noel,' I yelled. 'Can you take us back at low level?' The Australian pulled a funny face, and we reloaded our cameras. The return journey was the most exhilarating flight of my life. Manoeuvring his aircraft like a fighter plane, Noel hurtled through the great cleft in that dark green wilderness. Barbara and I concentrated on filming, but the gravitational forces on some of the turns were such that my arms felt like lead, and I could hardly lift the camera. Cliffs and jungle shot past the wingtips. We saw underground rivers emerging, huge caves, strange trees and then a single rope bridge strung across the river. *So, someone does live down there*, I thought. Even so, there was no other obvious sign of any human habitation.

Our aerial recce provided sufficient information for Major Roger Chapman and Captain Jim Masters, two of my most experienced officers, both ex-Blue Nilers, to take in a ground recce party. The going was horrendous, as harsh and inhospitable as you are likely to find anywhere in the world. When not scrambling and hacking up and down almost sheer-sided ridges covered in dense undergrowth, you are likely to find yourself picking a careful path across limestone rock so sharp-edged that the soles of the toughest boots will be shredded after a few miles. Even seemingly open areas, which might appear from the air to be smooth carpets of green turf, usually turn out to be covered in kunai grass fifteen feet high, which is so difficult to cut through that a fit man can be reduced to sweat-soaked exhaustion within a matter of yards.

We had also learned that the interior tribesmen were often extremely primitive and their reactions to outsiders unpredictable. The early patrols had adopted a policy of sending ahead shouters – native guides who would go forward and bellow out advance warning of the party's arrival in the area and call in any tribes in the locality for a meeting. Salt and tobacco would then be handed over as a gesture of friendship and, once the ice had been broken, impressive shooting displays with rifles would be laid on to discourage any hostile notions. Although we were never attacked, we carried weapons on the advice of the Defence Force, but more for protection against 'salties', the giant estuarine crocodiles.

I talked to all our outstations daily by radio. One evening Roger came on loud and clear and in great excitement. After telling me that they had been forced to make a hair-raising 3,000 foot climb up the side of Strickland Gorge, he added: 'We've found some people.' Unusually bad conditions cut him out, but words like 'primitive', 'stone axes' and 'no white men' came through and I knew they had achieved the ultimate goal in many armchair explorers' minds. Quite simply, he'd bumped into a lost or unknown tribe.

Next morning, communications improved and I learned it had taken them nearly ten hours to claw their way to the top. They had to move with the utmost caution, hauling themselves up on vines and roots, feeling for tenuous handholds in the crumbling rock. By the time they eventually made it, they barely had the strength to rig their hammocks and swallow a hurriedly prepared meal of dehydrated food before flaking out. Then, striking inland in search of a suitable clearing in which to land the planned resupply helicopter, they picked up an old hunting track and smelt woodsmoke. Creeping further along the path, they glimpsed through the trees a small clearing in which stood two low, rectangular huts, with wisps of blue smoke filtering through the thatched roofs. Then figures were seen moving about, and the sounds of children playing and pigs squealing flitted across the forest. No settlements were thought to exist here.

Roger at once sent ahead two of his native Duna bearers – Harirega and Ayape – and when he saw that they received a friendly welcome he led the rest of the patrol forward into the clearing. As he did so, Ayape pointed towards the man with whom he had been conversing in a strange dialect and when Roger extended his hand, the small bearded fellow grasped it firmly and held on determinedly, clearly not wanting to let go. Meanwhile, some of the men had seized the pigs and run off, whilst women and children lay down and moaned. There then followed a bizarre four-way conversation, English being translated in pidgin – the nearest thing to an official language in PNG – so that Harirega could then rephrase the message in Duna for the benefit of Ayape, who was the only one familiar with the dialect spoken by the tribesmen.

In this tortuous way it was established that the village they'd discovered was called Tigaro and that the inhabitants were nomadic Pogaia. There were five families in the group, which numbered fifteen altogether. The man hanging on to Roger's hand so affectionately was called Kiwanga. The chief, who was away working in the village 'gardens' but, due back at sunset, was named Kemba. When he eventually made an appearance, he confirmed that his small tribe had never seen a white man before, a fact that seemed to be rather amusingly borne out by the way in which Roger's white team members were subjected to close scrutiny and the occasional curious prod.

The fascination was mutual. Kemba and his people were clearly untouched by modern civilisation. Their most sophisticated and prized possessions were two steel axe heads that they had traded with other tribes in the Bulago Valley, where they had been introduced originally by one of the later colonial Kiap (District Officer) patrols. Otherwise, they had only stone tools and implements and their other possessions were made from natural materials. Barbed or notched arrows of razor-sharp split bamboo were used with six-foot-long hardwood bows for the daily wallaby hunt. Some arrows had three or four prongs for catching birds or fish.

The women appeared in the evening, carrying taro and sweet potatoes (or '*kaukau*') in '*bilums*', net baskets hung from their heads. They wore only grass skirts, while the men covered themselves with a loincloth in the front and, over their backsides, a hanging bunch of '*tanket*' leaves known evocatively in pidgin as '*arsegrass*'. Most wore thin armbands made of bark. Kemba sported a necklace of large cowrie shells and a kina shell shaped like a half-moon on his dark chest. They existed on a diet of root crops grown in their forest 'gardens', augmented with whatever they could hunt down. Their precious domestic pigs were only slaughtered on very special occasions and otherwise treated with loving care. The women walked around clutching piglets as if they were their own children, even suckling them in emergencies. Men guarded pigs more jealously than their wives and children, one tribesman explaining: 'Women and children very easy to make – pigs more difficult!'

Friendship was further cemented with small gifts, including a mirror, and it was agreed that our party would spend the night in the village before clearing a landing site for the helicopter next morning. The villagers watched spellbound as my voice came through on the radio from base 350 miles away. Eventually, they grew bolder and fingered everything of metal, glass or plastic with childlike glee. Cigarette lighters and binoculars were considered quite amazing.

My arrival next day in a giant RAAF Chinook brought the Stone Age face to face with the 20th century in the most spectacular fashion. The idea of a simple supply drop was changed because we decided that the patrol might as well take advantage of this situation and hitch a lift back to the banks of the Strickland. Alas, the stone axes had not cleared the last few feet of tree stumps and landing proved impossible, so we remained in the hover as our people struggled aboard. It was one of the most worrying ten minutes of my life, as the huge machine bucked and swayed in the jungle clearing. The 'lost tribe' looked on in amazement at our monster, which, for them, must have been the equivalent of a spacecraft landing in a city-dweller's backyard. Some wept and others were immobile with fear. When they saw Roger's bearers, Harirega and Ayape, being pulled in through the open ramp, perhaps they thought the great bird was devouring them.

As the Chinook lifted off and rose above the tiny jungle clearing with a deafening roar, the 100mph downdraught from its twin rotors created a mini-hurricane that raised a swirling cloud of dust and whipped the surrounding foliage into a frenzy of dancing branches and wildly fluttering leaves. Fifteen near-naked brown bodies prostrated themselves on the ground, their hands clamped over their ears, their foreheads pressed to the earth, not daring to look up. As the scene receded, I peered down anxiously at the prone forms and wondered what must be going through their minds. Fifty years previously, when aircraft first arrived in PNG, similar encounters had given rise to the cargo cults among the isolated tribespeople, who understandably concluded that the strange white men who descended from the skies in the birdlike machines packed with wonderful goods must surely be gods. They had frequently left gifts of fruit and vegetables in front of parked aircraft to encourage the gods to return with more 'cargo'. It was fascinating to speculate about the legends that might grow up around our meeting with Chief Kemba's people.

Meanwhile other parties were scouring the jungle for scientific specimens and historical remains of World War II. The stalwart Royal Marine, Mike Gambier, keen to join in again after his experience on the Congo, led a patrol deep into the Finisterre Range to locate a crashed wartime USAF bomber, reported by the local people. Climbing to over 10,500 feet through undergrowth so dense that they often had to crawl, their guide did indeed lead them to a wreck, but not the one they were looking for. It turned out to be a P-47 fighter, with its cockpit still intact. Painted on the fuselage were the words 'Pilot: J. W. Harris', but there were no human remains. However, on reporting the discovery to the USAF, we learned that Colonel J. W. Harris had not been piloting that day and now lived in Dallas, Texas, where I later met him and exchanged photos of the plane he referred to as 'Dear old Betty', then and now.

Back on the coast, in primary forest, my friend Captain Anthony Evans set up a scientific research camp, complete with a walkway in the forest canopy like the one we had used in Panama. Here botanists, entomologists and zoologists had the time of their lives studying the fauna and flora at close quarters, one hundred feet above the ground. Ben Gaskell, an eccentric chiropterologist, trapped bats to his heart's delight. Despite being in the middle of the jungle Ben insisted on dressing for dinner in full tropical evening dress, including a white tuxedo and white shoes, leaving most of the rest of us looking like badly dressed scarecrows. And he kept everybody amused with his conjuring tricks and his pranks.

Fortunately, several snakebites did not prove to be venomous, but the mosquitoes and sandflies caused more than a little irritation. Supplying the camp by boat, my army driver, Ray Thomas, did a splendid job and also provided transport for our inspirational chairman, General Sir John Mogg, when he flew out from the UK to visit the team and to see for himself what we were doing. The sight of a four-star British General in uniform certainly amazed everyone.

Cruising the coast, marine biologists aboard *Eye of the Wind* were overjoyed to come upon a school of some forty sperm whales, many leaping awesomely clear of the water. Deciding to get closer in order to film them, we used an inflatable and approached to within thirty yards and, not wanting to disturb them, cut the engine. We got excellent photos and were heading back to the ship when three whales appeared nearby, and we decided to get one last close-up. Army Air Corps pilot Frank Esson was handling the engine. He now shut it off and we paddled gently towards the leviathans. Filming with my 8mm Cine I saw a gigantic tail rise out of the leaden sea, then fall and disappear with a great splash. Then, as I adjusted the zoom, a dorsal fin appeared, coming straight at us. 'Shall I start the engine?' asked Frank calmly. But I was concentrating on filming and, looking through the viewfinder, was strangely detached. The dorsal fin came on. 'Shouldn't I start the engine?' shouted Frank, and without waiting for an answer, he did. It was just as well because by now the bull whale's massive head was rising beneath us, while the 'dorsal fin' was still fifty feet away. What we had seen was actually the fluke of its tail! Luckily, the motor fired first time and we motored away to safety, just in time, pursued for a short distance by the huge creature, its cavernous jaws and rows of molars rising in a ghastly scissor-like movement behind us. A second more and we would have been lifted out of the water and probably smashed to death by his tail. Aboard *Eye of the Wind*, the crew had enjoyed a grandstand view of the drama and thought it extremely funny.

Another marine task was to survey Japanese wrecks lying in the clear coastal waters around Rabaul. Royal Engineer and RAF diving teams trained our young divers and I accompanied them on a visit to the huge freighter *Manko Maru*, sunk by the RAAF in 1943. It was some 150 feet to the deck and I recall climbing down the sunken ship's mast to view the holds full of tanks and trucks whilst, in the cabins, skulls and bones lay undisturbed. Diving at that depth needed a long, slow return in order to allow for decompression and avoid the bends. We knew all about a local souvenir hunter who had descended with a barrel, which he then inflated on the seabed and used it to lift up his finds. Tragically, he became fatally entangled with the barrel and, out of control, shot to the surface. His body was retrieved, with his eyes having popped out. A timely warning!

Keen to lay to rest the rumour that a twenty-foot fire-breathing, man-eating dragon existed in south-west PNG, the government provided us with a weather-worn coaster to carry a team to the western province. Accompanied by our government liaison officer Miss Somare Jogo, a holder of the Duke of Edinburgh Gold Award, and zoologist Ian Redmond, we sailed into the Coral Sea. Alas, our boat's Buddha-like skipper had not thought to bring a compass and was not familiar with the area, so after running aground several times in shallow water we sent our photographer, Chris Sainsbury, wading ahead of us in the crocodile-infested shallows with a prismatic compass to take bearings on distant islands.

Having eventually reached Daru Island, the provincial capital, we went to see the Premier, Tatty Olewale OBE, who happened to be Somare's uncle. Seated at lunch and reading from a gigantic leather-bound Bible whilst his pet parakeet hopped about on his shoulder, he rose to greet us with the words: 'Colonel, it is the Lord who has brought you to us.' After the adventures of the previous days, I was inclined to agree. As soon as we told him about the 'dragon' we were seeking, he immediately summoned his brother, the head postman, who was able to tell us a great deal about the creature known to them as Artrellia.

Now that she was at home, Somare adopted local dress and went off, topless, to seek information on Artrellia. The hospital confirmed that a man had been killed by one some time ago, and, on the mainland, villagers told of sightings of a huge lizard with fearsome claws, that walked upright and could breathe fire. Several weeks of diligent searching only revealed a swamp, alive with thick black eel-like snakes, said to be blind, that only women were permitted to catch for some reason. Cathryn (Margot) Barker, my intrepid PA, leapt into the morass in bra and pants. Eventually she felt something rather large squirming past her legs and seized it, dragging out a heavy, black, eyeless snake almost six feet in length. Moments later she then felt another serpent wriggling around her feet, one that felt thinner and much livelier. Thrusting her hand back into the mire she grabbed hold of it – or rather, it grabbed her – and as she pulled it out she was bitten four times by a rather unpleasant diamond-headed snake about three feet long. Fortunately for her, it wasn't venomous.

The Sunday before Christmas, I went to matins in the little village church. Singing 'Hark! The Herald Angels Sing' in pidgin did sound strange, but the sincerity of these indigenous people was most impressive. Strolling out into the bright sunlight, I paused to talk to the vicar. 'Do you really believe in the stories about Artrellia?' I asked. He'd been educated in Australia, and I reckoned him to be a sensible, level-headed man.

'I know he exists,' replied the pastor. 'And sometimes I wish he didn't, because my people think he's a devil, like an evil spirit. But he's just an animal, sometimes a bad animal.'

'Well, if we caught one, would it convince your flock that it was no evil spirit?' I ventured.

'Sure,' he replied, nodding his head.

'Then how on earth can we do that?'

'Oh, you fellows won't catch him – you make too much noise tramping around in the bush. You need good hunters,' he stated firmly, adding as an afterthought: 'Our choirboys are good hunters.'

'How much to hire the choir?' I inquired.

The little priest smiled. 'Well, we do need a new church roof,' he said, looking wistfully at the tattered thatch.

'How much will that cost?' I asked.

'Ten dollars,' came the instant reply. He then suggested that I should offer the reward at the village council that evening, saying that in that way I'd get all the hunters helping, ten dollars being about the equivalent of a month's wages in local currency.

'But don't tell them about the reward till seven o'clock,' he cautioned, 'because I want to leave at five. And, by the way, can you let me have some shotgun shells?'

Sure enough, the mere mention of money resulted in a mass exodus into the jungle of every able-bodied man in the village, armed with everything from bows and arrows to an antique blunderbuss.

From Daru, our little boat penetrated up a jungle-fringed river, supposedly unmapped. We were therefore astonished upon rounding a bend to see a sleek, well-kept motor cruiser moored to the bank, with a UN Development Programme flag fluttering at its masthead, a striking young blonde woman in a bikini stretched out on the foredeck and loud rock music blasting from the sound system. We couldn't believe our eyes! She propped herself up on one elbow and called out: 'G'day, mates' in a broad Australian accent.

I doffed my pith helmet and inquired if she was on her own.

'No, Bruce is down below, trying to fix the freezer,' she replied.

At that point her colleague emerged. 'Strike a bloody light,' he drawled. If we had been amazed to come across him in such a back-of-beyond tropical backwater, it was clear that he was equally surprised to be confronted by a boatload of explorers that included Viscount Gough, one of the expedition's sponsors who had joined us on our quest, a pith-helmeted British Army Colonel and a motley crew of others.

'What are you doing here?' we inquired politely, as Bruce handed out ice-cold cans of Foster's lager.

'We're carrying out a crayfish survey,' he told us.

'But there aren't any crayfish in these waters,' insisted our zoologist, Ian Redmond.

'I know, mate, but don't tell the UNDP,' countered Bruce, with a broad grin and a wink. We learned that he had recruited his 'assistant', as the blonde was officially designated, by placing an advert in a Sydney paper that read: 'Good looking Sheila required to accompany adventurous male on scientific survey in PNG.' He had then spent several weeks interviewing volunteers before deciding which one he fancied would be best able to help him on what sounded like a less than onerous assignment. *Nice work, if you can get it*, we thought!

Next morning, we heard that the pastor himself had managed to shoot a big lizard somewhere deep in the forest and was on his way back with it. We returned at full speed and, by the time we arrived, a large crowd had already gathered around a strange-looking creature roped to a bamboo pole. Accepting his $10 the vicar assured me that this was Artrellia.

The fearsome-looking reptile's dark green skin was flecked with yellow spots and its square head housed a set of needle-like teeth. The eyes twitched malevolently as it tried to squeeze itself out of the vines binding it to the pole, but the most impressive part of its anatomy were its claws – enormous black scimitars that were quite out of proportion to its short, thick legs and the rest of its body. The tail was long and thin and twice the length of the body. I noticed the village dogs kept well away from the dying beast with its fearsome talons. The mouth and tongue together produced a red and yellow effect. 'You see – fire!' insisted the Pastor, and, indeed, I saw at once how the tongue, darting in and out in the sunlight, could have helped to start the legend of a fire-breathing dragon, especially when spotted clinging vertically to a tree trunk.

What Ian Redmond immediately identified as a monitor lizard, known as Salvadori's monitor and the crocodile monitor as well as Artrellia, was badly injured and so Ian humanely put it out of its misery. As soon as it was safe to handle, measurements were taken. It was no dragon but, even so, it was still a pretty impressive fearsome specimen at just over six feet from head to tail. Once Ian had performed his post-mortem, he was able to confirm that it was only a youngster, which left plenty of room for speculation about what size a full-grown adult might reach. Meanwhile, one of our patrols that had been keeping vigil beside a remote water hole reported that they had seen several sizeable specimens coming to drink at night, including one monster estimated at twelve feet, with a head similar in size to that of a horse. Alas, it was too dark for photography. But who knows what size these creatures could grow to in the deepest interior of what still remains a mysterious and largely unexplored area of Papua New Guinea?

 Operation Drake to St Lucia, Panama and Papua New Guinea 1978–79

CHAPTER 31

THE GREAT BURMESE

VOLE QUEST

Ever since I'd studied the World War II campaigns in Burma, I'd been fascinated by this land of contrasting terrain and people. From the northern icy mountains, where Hkakabo Razi rises to just under 20,000 feet, through to the jungle-clad hill ranges and fertile plains, the Irrawaddy River winds its way south to the tropical swampland in its delta region.

Thanks to John Hinchcliffe, a friend from my time with Operation Raleigh, I was able to carry out several wildlife expeditions in Myanmar, as it now prefers to be known. And in 2005, much encouraged by the discoveries of a new species of deer by the eminent American naturalist Alan Rabinowiktz, I returned.

Rabinowitz admitted there might well be other unknown animals living in the vast, thinly populated jungle, where distant snow-capped peaks rise majestically above the emerald treeline. Furthermore, there were rumours of colonies of rare voles in this remote region. As President of the Vole Club, I was drawn to one of these rodents, in particular.

Père David's vole (*Eothenomys melanogaster*) is described as a soft, shaggy, sooty-brown mouse-like beast with a blunt nose, short legs and a small tail covered by short hairs that obscure the rings of scales. The soles of the feet are said to be hairy behind the pads, the young are blackish, and the females have four teats. Sightings of the little fellow had been made near Imaw Bum (13,000 feet), where a specimen brought in by a cat measured 141 millimetres from head to tail tip. Before being consumed by the hungry people who regard it as a delicacy, it was weighed at 27 grams. There had also been reports of other voles invading northern Myanmar, including the Chinese vole (*Pitymys Pinetum*) and the Korean meadow vole (*Microtus montebelli*), but these usually live at lower altitudes.

However, my real interest was Père David's and with two vole-unteers from the Vole Club, I launched an expedition to the valleys leading down from Myanmar's icy mountains. Lady Pamela Coleridge, who had played a leading role in seeking the dwarf chimpanzee on the Zaire River Expedition, and my wife Judith, who studies voles in Dorset, accompanied me. Equipped with measuring tapes and cameras with close-up lenses, we set out clutching drawings

of our target. It seemed there were no photographs of this elusive mammal – indeed, I sometimes wondered whether it was actually a myth. Did Père David's vole really exist?

In Yangon we were met by our friendly and helpful German agent Carsten Schmidt who, excited by the quest, cried out '*Ja-vole!*' and led us to the comfort of the old colonial Savoy Hotel. Here our plans were laid and wildlife experts consulted while we built up our strength before flying north to

our first objective, Inle Lake. Some fourteen miles by seven miles and almost 3,000 feet above sea level, this vast shallow waterway is dotted with patches of floating vegetation and canoes propelled by boatmen standing on one leg, with the other wrapped around a paddle, a strange technique that enables them to row while at the same time looking out for fish from a height – and, occasionally, spotting voles. This is where we expected to make a first sighting of our quarry.

Speeding along in a swift long-tailed boat, we passed through villages where the fishermen live in attractive houses that rise on stilts from the still waters. We noted the great array of flowers and vegetables cultivated in floating gardens, creating a useful feeding area for voles. Talking to kite-flying children, potters, weavers and silversmiths, we sought information on the wee beasties, but although we saw burrows in the banks of streams and canals and heard of rodents attacking the tomato plantations, there was no sign of Père David's, Chinese nor Korean voles. The presence of hordes of cats, trained by monks to keep fit by leaping through hoops at the Nga Phe Kyaung Monastery, may have accounted for the voles' decline. We discovered another reason for their decreasing numbers at our hotel, where it was said the French chef served Fricassee de Vole on special occasions.

Disappointed but undeterred, we drove to Heho (no connection with the seven dwarfs!) and embarked on a Yangon Airways flight that, despite the fact that its logo depicts a flying elephant, happily became airborne without any difficulty. At Mandalay no flights were available to the far north, so our intrepid trio braved the express train. Booking a sleeping compartment in 'Upper Class' and escorted by a string of porters bearing our baggage, we waited patiently for the station to open.

Pam and Judith had stocked up with rations, some vintage Myanmar Merlot (actually quite drinkable), water, loo paper, insect repellent, air freshener and blankets. With military precision the gate swung wide at 15:45 hours and regiments of travellers made a dash for the carriages. Second class, first class and lastly Upper Class were soon filled with families and smiling children. Monks prayed on the platform before boarding and food vendors sold their wares through open windows. Our compartment had four leathery cots and bolts on the door. The window, once opened, would not shut but at 30°C that was no problem.

At 16:15 hours, with several loud blasts on its hooter and with children still climbing in through the windows, the big yellow diesel-electric began hauling us north up the 300-mile narrow-gauge track to Myitkyina in Kachin State. Seated near the dining car, we were soon visited by a jolly waiter who offered us tea, coffee, beer and whisky, urging us to take plenty of refreshment as the arrival time at our destination could not be predicted. The smell of spicy cooking drew us to inspect the dining car. Greeted by staff, somewhat surprised to encounter foreigners, we were shown the kitchen where two sweaty cooks slaved over a glowing open fire. The smoke from burning logs added an aromatic air to the carriage. Other diners offered us a taste of their noodles and Judith gallantly ordered a dish. The steward was delighted and offered a free whisky!

By now most passengers had got stuck into the betel nut, said to kill worms in the digestive tract, produce mild stimulation and promote a sense of well-being. And there could be no denying that, in spite of their blood-red teeth, our fellow travellers were certainly very friendly. Even the solemn-faced guard, armed with not one but two old Lee-Enfield rifles, was amiable. I enquired if he thought it likely he would have to use them, pointing out that the barrel ends were blocked with wads of blanket. He replied by working the well-oiled bolt with enthusiasm. The novice beside him bent his head in prayer. Stepping over piles of sleeping babies, I regained the compartment to find that Pam had used her Swiss army knife to open the wine.

As usual in the tropics, darkness fell rapidly and as the train clackety-clacked through the jungle, branches swept into the open windows, depositing beetles that Judith dispatched with a well-aimed squirt of potent bug killer. Unperturbed, we chewed roast chicken legs and opened the second bottle.

Earlier I had managed to squeeze past some incontinent nuns to visit the loo and a kindly child had held the door shut whilst I was within, but now the corridors were packed with sleeping monks and soldiers lying on rented mats. Clearly, we were cut off from the vital facility. Luckily, the ladies were innovative travellers and Pam's knife was used to remove the tops of plastic bottles in order to create serviceable bedpans. Equally fortunate was the fact that there was no-one in the bush country alongside the track in any danger from the disposal of the refilled bottles!

Stops were made at lamplit stations, where cheroot-smoking women bearing trays of hors d'oeuvre, illuminated by burning candles on their heads, offered a wide variety of dishes to our windows, while small boys proffered local liquors for the hard-headed, and then with a '*woo-woo*' we were off again. Under our blankets, helped by the Myanmar Merlot, we enjoyed an uneasy sleep, being rocked from side to side, rather like riding an elephant. In the corridor it was dead quiet. I wondered if anybody ever went to the loo. The dawn came up like thunder, as Kipling wrote, but it was another eight hours before we chugged through the rice fields into the World War II battle site of Myitkyina. It was mid-afternoon and after twenty-two hours cooped up on the train we were not sorry to step down into the glaring sunlight of the old colonial town.

Later, sipping Tiger beer beside the moonlit Irrawaddy, we planned our move north. Fortunately, there was a plane going to Putao (where Fort Hertz once stood) and next morning the snow-packed summits at the eastern end of the Himalayas greeted us. Northern Myanmar has a history of political conflict and security at airports was strict. Examining the fifteen copies of our special permit, the immigration officer asked: 'Why you come Putao?'

'To study voles,' I replied.

'Ah, so.' He nodded, clearly appreciating the importance of our mission.

Making a base at the Putao Trekking House, standing at an altitude of 1,342 feet, we got our first indication of the voles. The people, studying our drawings, nodded their heads in recognition and told us: 'Poo!'

'No, no,' I replied. 'It's a vole.'

'Poo', they insisted.

Perhaps my sketch has given the wrong impression, I thought.

A lady who spoke some English came forward. 'Here we call that a *poo*, or a *pwe*,' she explained. 'They are found in the fields.'

So the search started in earnest. Over the next few days we tramped many miles, asking the Kachins to show us a *poo* or even a *pwe*. We examined mouse holes, rat runs and likely stream-bank habitats, with no sign of a vole, but then intelligence revealed that they might be found on the Mali Hka River. Pam organised a long-tailed boat and a gastronomic feast with wine, a cook with a guitar, three curious schoolteachers and a Nepali white-water guide. Having issued life jackets, our helmsman navigated the turbulent rapids in fine style. After each he cried out, '*Pwe!*' – or perhaps it was 'Phew!', an expression of relief.

Half-naked gold panners watched us speed past as we entered a gorge with towering sides that led to an extraordinary island. Fairy Isle, named because of a local myth, was littered with what looked from a distance like Henry Moore sculptures, but which, on closer inspection, were found to be eroded pillars of rock. One had clearly been carved into the image of a vole, but there was still no sign of the living animal! As Judith and I were celebrating our Golden Wedding Anniversary, Pam had arranged a beautifully iced and decorated cake and we opened the wine, enjoyed delicious grilled river fish and sang to the cook's guitar.

Back at base, our guide – the rather aptly named Stanley – announced that the *poo* were at the Mula River. He then went on to say: 'Too far to march, no cars. Can you ride bicycles?' I had not cycled in fifty years, but a fleet of multi-geared, brakeless bikes was provided and we peddled north, wobbling uncertainly as we endeavoured to avoid bullock carts, much to the amusement of the local children who cheered us on. After four bottom-slicing miles on a narrow saddle designed to castrate, we reached the river. An old Tibetan knew of the *pwe* and, with Stanley translating, told us: 'They spend most of their time mating in their underground burrows in the mossy ground of the rhododendron forests below Hkakabo Razi.'

Even with my reborn cycling skill, I doubted we would reach it by bike, so it was back to base. This was downhill all the way. With very little help from the brakes, it became a hair-raising ride, holding on for dear life, dodging Chinese three-wheelers, ox carts and dogs.

As dusk descended a small sooty-brown creature scuttled under my wheel but there was no way I could stop. Stanley joined me at the bottom of the slope, where a grassy verge had brought me to a halt.

'Why didn't you stop?' he exclaimed. 'You ran over a *poo*!'

Despair was slightly reduced by a passable bottle of claret that, by a miracle, Pam found in the bar.

After arduous expeditions, it is important to relax and write one's report, so we flew south for a magnificent dinner in Yangon with an old Burmese friend from Sandhurst and a few days at the beautiful Ngapali Beach, where we dined on sumptuous seafood as the sun set over the Bay of Bengal. When Covid is overcome and peace returns to Myanmar we certainly hope to return to seek the elusive Burmese vole and to continue exploring worldwide.

ENVOI

When speaking to young men and women I point out that although they might not yet have much money in the bank, they are probably blessed with health, vigour and energy, prize assets that they may no longer be able to call upon quite so readily by the time they are old enough to have achieved financial security. I therefore strongly urge them to make the most of their youthful vitality by taking the opportunity, while they can, to go out and see the world, meet new people and experience different cultures, while at the same time maybe doing something, however small, to make the world a better place. Joining an expedition could be one great way of ticking all those boxes.

Not that expeditionary exploration is only for the young. People today are living longer and staying fitter through middle age and even into retirement. And many will have gained the sort of lifetime experience and wisdom that could benefit developing nations, help to protect the environment, conserve wildlife and fight disease. Older folk may not have the all-round physical strength and stamina to take part in Outward Bound training or the Duke of Edinburgh's Award Scheme, or to join organisations such as the British Exploring Society. However, many find that participating in a worthwhile and reasonably challenging project can be both enjoyable and rewarding.

You do not need to be a muscle-bound Superman or Wonder Woman; as long as you are medically fit and maybe able, at a pinch, to run for a bus, there is scope to join an expedition team and make a real difference for people in need in some faraway places with strange-sounding names, while also helping to overcome some of the existential problems that our planet faces in the 21st century.

I trust I may be forgiven for looking back with considerable pride on the successes of the many outstanding people of all ages, and from many very different walks of life, who have been involved over the years with the Scientific Exploration Society in UK and Jersey, and on operations Drake and Raleigh International and Operation New World. Their achievements stand as an inspiration to future generations of adventurous men and women eager to broaden their own horizons while doing something practical and hands-on to help others.

FURTHER INFORMATION

Details of the Royal Scottish Geographical Society, the Scientific Exploration Society, Just A Drop, the British Exploring Society and the Explorers Club may be found on their websites.

Lectures and forthcoming expeditions led by John Blashford-Snell are listed on his website: ⌀ johnblashfordsnell.org.uk.

ABBREVIATIONS

BWIA: British West Indies Airways
CONAF: Chilean National Forest Corporation
CRE: Chief Royal Engineer
ERC: Ecotourist and Research Centre
ETO: Ethiopian Tourist Organisation
FARC: Fuerzas Armadas Revolucionarias de Colombia
FSH: Fundación Sumaj Huasi
GDF: Guyana Defence Force
JBS: John Blashford-Snell
MAF: Mission Aviation Fellowship
MIAT : Mongolian Airlines
MMES: Manas Maozigendri Ecotourism Society
MMI: Medical Mission International
PNG: Papua New Guinea
QM: Quartermaster (or Logistics Officer)
RGS: Royal Geographical Society
RSG: Reconnaissance and Support Group
SAS: Special Air Service
SBS: Special Boat Service
SES: Scientific Exploration Society
YE: Young Explorers

ACKNOWLEDGEMENTS

It was largely thanks to the encouragement and inspiration provided by the late General Sir John Mogg that adventurous exploration became part of my life. All our expeditions, most of which I have been privileged to lead, have been group efforts and I must emphasise that any success we have achieved has, without exception, been very much down to great teamwork. I do wish I could mention all those who played a part, many of them in very significant ways, but the list would run into thousands. However, I owe every one of them my most sincere thanks.

Sir Chris Bonington, Dr Will Cave, Rajan Chaudhary, Shirley Critchley, Alasdair Crosby, Alasdair Goulden, Anthony Haden-Guest, Stuart Heydinger, Major Chris Holt, Rear Admiral Kit Layman, Ken Mason, Julian Matthews, Andrew Mitchell, Dalannast Munkhnast, Anna Nicholas, Eric Niemi, Malcolm Peach, Ian Robinson, Deepak Rajbanshi, Geoff Roy, Chris Sainsbury, Richard Snailham, Matt Whittingham and Anthony Willoughby have kindly allowed me to use their diaries, reports and photographs.

I am also especially grateful for the generous support of Robert Glen, Chairman of E. P. Barrus Ltd, and the late Harbourne Stephen, formerly Managing Director of the *Daily Telegraph*, Jessamy Calkin at the *Daily Telegraph Magazine*, Great Genghis Expeditions, the Just a Drop water charity, Jaguar Land Rover, the *Daily Mail* and Nikon UK.

The Scientific Exploration Society has helpfully provided access to its expedition reports and produced the majority of the photographs from its archives. They have been located thanks to much hard work by Dave Smith and Ros Wardall.

Miraculously, my able assistant, Jenny Rose, has cheerfully managed to turn my almost illegible scribbles into text and sketch maps. The considerable help of Alan Campbell in producing our expedition film footage is much appreciated. Yolima Cipagauta, who played a leading part in many of the expeditions in Latin America, has skilfully checked the appropriate chapters. Mike Cable interrupted his golf to do a most helpful edit, greatly improving my work.

Sarah Jane Lewis's PR expertise has been of the utmost assistance over many years and I am deeply grateful to Charlie Morison for her help with the promotion in the field and at home. The most welcome aid of Arnie Wilson and Francine Fletcher is also much appreciated, as is the considerable assistance of Val Smith and Gail Lloyd at our Expedition Base at Motcombe.

Throughout, my adventurous daughters, Emma Cave and Victoria Matthews, their husbands Will and Julian and my ever-supportive wife, Judith, have given me enormous encouragement. As indeed have many friends in my 'ancestral home' on Jersey and in delightful Dorset.

I am most grateful for all the help and encouragement of the Bradt team, especially Adrian Phillips who had faith in an old explorer, as well as Claire Strange, Susannah Lord, Anna Moores, Ian Spick, Hugh Brune and Ross Dickinson.

If I have unintentionally failed to mention anyone who played an important part in these ventures, I beg for their forgiveness. I have resisted describing the characters of those who took part, although many were outstanding personalities, and their achievements speak for themselves. If anyone was at fault on our expeditions, it was me. Furthermore, although I kept a log throughout my travels, I accept responsibility for any factual errors.

INDEX

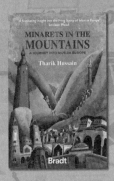

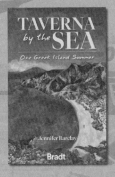

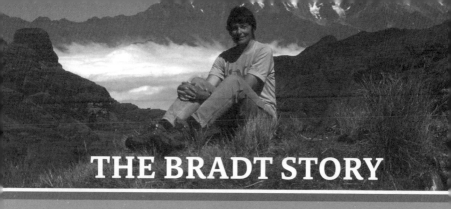

THE BRADT STORY

In the beginning

It all began in 1974 on an Amazon river barge. During an 18-month trip through South America, two adventurous young backpackers – Hilary Bradt and her then husband, George – decided to write about the hiking trails they had discovered through the Andes. *Backpacking Along Ancient Ways in Peru and Bolivia* included the very first descriptions of the Inca Trail. It was the start of a colourful journey to becoming one of the best-loved travel publishers in the world; you can read the full story on our website (bradtguides.com/ourstory).

Getting there first

Hilary quickly gained a reputation for being a true travel pioneer, and in the 1980s she started to focus on guides to places overlooked by other publishers. The Bradt Guides list became a roll call of guidebook 'firsts'. We published the first guide to Madagascar, followed by Mauritius, Czechoslovakia and Vietnam. The 1990s saw the beginning of our extensive coverage of Africa: Tanzania, Uganda, South Africa, and Eritrea. Later, post-conflict guides became a feature: Rwanda, Mozambique, Angola, and Sierra Leone, as well as the first standalone guides to the Baltic States following the fall of the Iron Curtain, and the first post-war guides to Bosnia, Kosovo and Albania.

Comprehensive – and with a conscience

Today, we are the world's largest independently owned travel publisher, with more than 200 titles. However, our ethos remains unchanged. Hilary is still keenly involved, and **we still get there first**: two-thirds of Bradt guides have no direct competition.

But we don't just get there first. Our guides are also known for being **more comprehensive** than any other series. We avoid templates and tick-lists. Each guide is a one-of-a-kind expression of an expert author's interests, knowledge and enthusiasm for telling it how it really is.

And a commitment to wildlife, conservation and respect for local communities has always been at the heart of our books. Bradt Guides was **championing sustainable travel** before any other guidebook publisher. We even have a series dedicated to Slow Travel in the UK, award-winning books that explore the country with a passion and depth you'll find nowhere else.

Thank you!

We can only do what we do because of the support of readers like you – people who value less-obvious experiences, less-visited places and a more thoughtful approach to travel. Those who, like us, take travel seriously.

Bradt GUIDES
TRAVEL TAKEN SERIOUSLY